The Birth of Mass Political Parties

Michigan, 1827–1861

The Birth of

MASS POLITICAL PARTIES

Michigan, 1827-1861

RONALD P. FORMISANO

Princeton University Press
Princeton, New Jersey   1971

Publication of this book
has been aided by a grant from the
Whitney Darrow Publication Reserve Fund of
Princeton University Press

This book has been set in Linotype Times Roman

Printed in the United States of America
by Princeton University Press

TO EVA AND VICTOR

Contents

Tables

Acknowledgments

One who believes in the full, free exchange of information and ideas among scholars, no matter how much he gives, always takes much more from others. I feel now a sense of being enmeshed in a seamless web of intellectual and personal debts. What this book owes to Lee Benson anyone familiar with his ideas and work will know. For heroic attempts to clarify my thoughts and trim my prose, I thank John J. Waters, Jr., Paul Kleppner, Janice A. O'Hare, Herbert Gutman, William G. Shade, and Lynn Parsons. When some of this manuscript was a dissertation, Robert A. Skotheim and Raymond C. Miller helped it (and me) survive the vicissitudes of graduate student life. Men like William J. Bossenbrook and John Weiss should be part of everyone's education. In 1967-1968 I taught at the University of Pittsburgh and profited from the stimulating concern of the history faculty with the work of other staff members. Jerome V. Jacobsen gave me encouragement at a crucial point.

Summer fellowships from the University of Rochester and the American Philosophical Society helped me to finish writing this book, and the University provided the competent typing of Claire Sundeen. Any researcher is fortunate to have the aid of such persons as Bernice Sprenger, Alice Dalligan, and Irene Dudley of the Burton Historical Collection, Detroit Public Library; of Dennis R. Bodem and Geneva Wiskemann of the Michigan Historical Commission, Lansing; and of Richard Hathaway of the Michigan State Library. The staffs of the Michigan Historical Collections and William L. Clements Library, Ann Arbor, always gave efficient and pleasant assistance.

Some of the quantitative data in this study has been manipulated by computer. For indispensable technical help I am grateful to persons at the computer centers of Wayne State University, the University of Pittsburgh, and the University of Rochester. Paul Kleppner and Stanley Engerman tried to give me independent skills with statistics and computers, but they are not responsible for my pidgin literacy in that world.

David M. Harrop brought the manuscript to R. Miriam Brokaw's attention and she has given me wise and kindly advice. Marjorie Putney has been a sensitive and careful editor.

Many more persons should be mentioned here, but the list would grow too long. I am grateful to all and hope they find some value in the result.

RONALD P. FORMISANO

Rochester, New York
November 1970

The Birth of Mass Political Parties

Michigan, 1827–1861

I

The Historical Problem of Party Formation

American society of the first half of the nineteenth century continues to interest historians, political scientists, novelists, poets, and other cultural analysts. Many sense in the period after 1815 the beginning of peculiarly modern experiences and social forms, especially in politics. Modern American political culture took shape in the 1820s and 1830s with the formation of mass party organizations. In most states a mass electorate had internalized party loyalty on so vast and intense a scale by 1840 that a new context for political activity was constituted. Professional politicians had moved in behind Andrew Jackson's 1828 victory to secure substantial power over the processes of government. With their cohorts in the states they worked to create an institutional environment which favored disciplined and cohesive organizations in the competition for majorities in electoral campaigns. Any political majority in a country of so many contrasts would have to be coalitional. Even within regions, states, and localities, the growing heterogeneity of nineteenth century society required that parties would be "coalitional systems" of subcommunities varying by locality. Binding ties of action needed to be developed to rationalize political activity, get political power, maximize the usefulness of power, and provide criteria for the distribution of rewards. By the 1830s, as Richard P. McCormick put it, a "hidden revolution" changed the institutional environment of politics and fostered the growth of pragmatic, electorate-oriented, coalition-building parties, hungry for the spoils of power.[1]

The political chaos of the 1820s is well known. During the disintegration of the Republican establishment of Monroe a bewildering array of

---

[1] Parties as coalitional systems are discussed in Samuel J. Eldersveld, *Political Parties: A Behavioral Analysis* (Chicago, 1964), 89; Richard P. McCormick, *The Second American Party System: Party Formation in the Jacksonian Era* (Chapel Hill, 1966). Also, see the essays by Chambers, Paul Goodman, Frank Sorauf, and McCormick in William Nisbet Chambers and Walter Dean Burnham, eds., *The American Party Systems: Stages of Development* (New York, 1967), 3-116.

elite personalities, factions, cliques, and juntos dominated national and local election contests. Round-robin factionalism gradually gave way to highly institutionalized and ritualized party politics in the 1830s—at least in most areas of the North. Of the intriguing preparty situation almost nothing is known in social terms. The period is often described as one of "personal" or "factional" politics, but these categories are a variation on the "Presidential Synthesis." The structure of society has not been convincingly related to political changes, and social and political history have not come together to provide social analysis of the transition to mass politics. Social group cleavages and patterns of ostensibly nonpolitical group relations beyond the formal contests have been ignored.[2] But these were becoming the bases of loyalty or antipathy to the new mass organizations.

A case study of party formation in Michigan, encompassing a social analysis of party character, political subcultures, and changing voter loyalties, can open a window into American political culture during a seminal phase of its development. The molding of parties in Michigan spanned the crucible years of 1828 to 1837, the beginning of the party system in the nation. During this time Michigan passed from territory to state, and the creation of mass parties closely followed the building of society itself. Demographically speaking, Michigan was a colony of New York, New England, and, increasingly during the period from 1835 to 1860, of Europe. This held great significance for the development of party loyalties.

The strategy of this study is to identify the mass constituencies of the Democratic and Whig parties from 1837 to 1852, and the Democratic and Republican parties from 1854 to 1860; to determine vital differences for voters between the parties; and to discover the rapport between party postures and social group attitudes. These basic steps are needed before understanding may be gained of the impact of mass politics on events or political culture.

Significant political changes unfolded in both the 1830s and 1850s. In the thirties voter loyalties crystallized after a period of resistance to organization, and some social group alignments created then have persisted to the present. In the 1850s, when the Republican party gradually replaced the Whigs, a similar process of party formation occurred. In one sense the ongoing system was only modified, but at the same time significant realignment during 1853 to 1856 made the two periods much alike. The Republican movement was a new departure and was hesitant to establish itself as a party. Republicanism grew to a great extent on

[2] The best attempt to deal with this problem so far has been in Lee Benson, *The Concept of Jacksonian Democracy: New York as a Test Case* (Princeton, 1961), 3-63, 165-207.

preexisting anti-Democratic elements, yet manifested an ethos differing in important ways from its predecessors. Thus the periods 1828 to 1837 and 1853 to 1856 are worthy of intensive study to uncover the original character of the parties and the causes of mass voting patterns.

Shortly after Michigan became a state in 1837 "Democracy" and "Whiggery" took hold as major parties. In 1840 political antislavery intruded as the Liberty party became a third but minor contestant, replaced from 1848 to 1853 by the Free Soil organization. With the exception of 1839 to 1840 the Democrats enjoyed almost continual political hegemony. They succeeded as brokers among a disparate coalition of antievangelical social groups who rejected the moral society which pietist Protestants promoted first through Antimasonry and then Whiggery. Antievangelicalism pervaded the antiaristocratic, laissez faire, and secularist image conveyed by the Democrats. Their coalition also won because of defection from Whiggery of antislavery men. A tendency to schism was one of the symptoms of an antipartyism endemic to the Whig political character.

In the mid-fifties the Whig and Free Soil parties dissolved and recombined in the Fusion, Independent, or, as it came to be called, Republican party. While some voters crossed party lines, much established behavior persisted along Democratic and anti-Democratic lines. The modified system of the 1850s raises complex problems. What changes in voter behavior and what initiatives of party organizers created the new party? Which issues and attitudes now commanded the mass electorate's fealty or hostility? What new relations among social groups, if any, accompanied the political shifts? These questions, in turn, relate to that great historiographical Sargasso Sea of explanations for the Civil War. The triumph of Republicanism in Michigan by 1856 was an early instance of the sectionalization of the North, and therefore led to Lincoln's election in 1860 and to Southern secession. The data presented here, then, should make a small but decisive contribution to the endless combat among historians over the causes of the Civil War. Much scrutiny has been devoted to activities of elite decision-makers who led their sections to war, but analysts have not systematically weighed the conditions in which they acted.

In 1853 cultural and moral issues coming together from different sources caused sharp divisions in the Democracy, and began, at the township, city, and county levels, to transform Whiggery. The most powerful engine of the new movement was anti-Catholicism, as Know Nothingism swept the farms and villages of rural Michigan. In 1854 the anti-Southern outburst occasioned by the Kansas-Nebraska bill joined the already convulsive upheaval that had unhinged traditional loyalties, and the battle for Free (White) Soil gave party leaders the public common

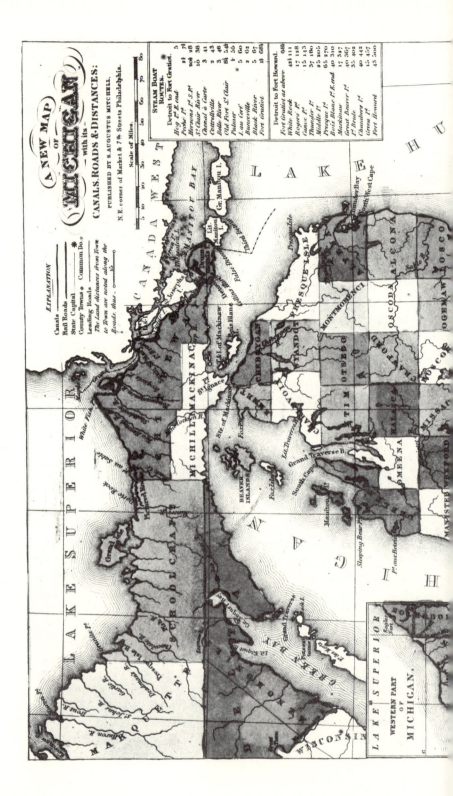

A NEW MAP OF MICHIGAN with its CANALS, ROADS & DISTANCES:

PUBLISHED BY S. AUGUSTUS MITCHELL,

N.E. corner of Market & 7th Streets Philadelphia.

EXPLANATION

Canals ——
Rail Roads ——
State Capital ✦
County Towns ● Common Do. ○
Leading Roads ——
The land distances from Town to Town are noted along the Roads, thus ○ — 15 — ○

Scale of Miles.

5 10 20 30 40 50 60 70 80

STEAM BOAT ROUTES.

Detroit to Fort Gratiot.

Hog I.t F.E. end	5
Peche I.t	7½
Herzons I.t S.Pt	9
St. Clair River	18
Chenal a Carte	38
Cottrelville	41
Belle River	43
Old Fort St. Clair	46
Palmer	54½
L'au Cerf	56
Bunceville	60
Black River	62
Fort Gratiot	67

Detroit to Fort Howard.

Fort Gratiot as above	68
White Rock	111
Rogers Pt	128
Gance Pt	143
Thunder I.t	180
Middle I.t	205
Presque I.t	270
Bois Blanc F.E. end	310
Mackinaw	347
Great Beaver I.t	367
1.t Brule	402
Chambers I.t	443
Green I.t	457
Fort Howard	500

LAKE SUPERIOR
WESTERN PART OF MICHIGAN.

LAKE SUPERIOR

LAKE HURON

LAKE MICHIGAN

MANITOU BAY

GREEN BAY

WISCONSIN

CANADA WEST

MICHILLIMACKINAC

BEAVER ISLANDS

Gr. Manitou I.

Lit. Manitou I.

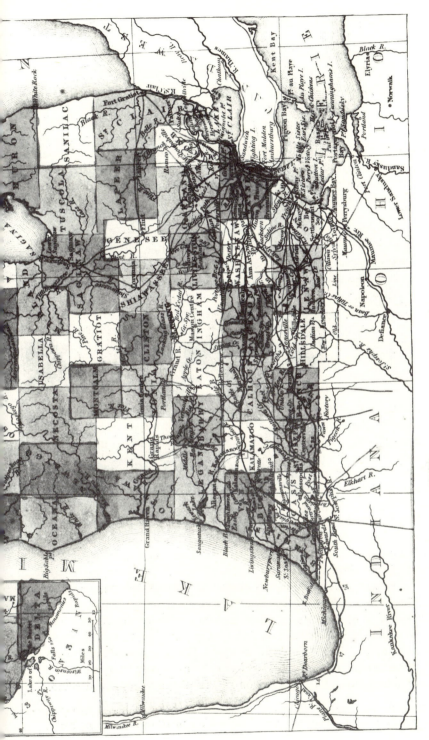

MICHIGAN IN 1850

denominator for a successful anti-Democratic coalition. Under the banner of "Fusion" or "Independency" and sometimes "Republican," the anti-Democrats won the state in 1854 and held a new electoral majority. Religious and ethnocultural cleavages structured the realignment of the 1850s just as they had powerfully shaped the earlier party formations. Michigan Whiggery had been the Christian Party, seeking in many ways to regulate a moral society. Republicanism continued the evangelical quest of Whiggery, and can be considered the Protestant party because of the greater unity it achieved among the several Protestant denominations through anti-Popery. Republicanism's great achievement in building a broader coalition was aided by its blending of moralism with the popular egalitarian compulsion—formerly the property of the Democrats. Popery and the Slaveocracy provided Republicans with foils for a modified antiaristocratic posture and a competitive egalitarian appeal such as the Whigs had never managed to muster against the Democrats.

The Wolverine state has been touted as an example of northwestern Republicanism's intensely antislavery character—"radical Michigan" it has been called in some general studies. But few Michigan Republicans cared about slavery where it did exist. When Democrats stirred Negrophobia against the anti-Southern party, Republicans reassured their constituents that they were the champions of Northern white rights. Among Republican leaders, however, there existed some desire to extend justice to Michigan's own black second-class citizens, by enfranchising them, for example. But most of the party's leadership bowed to white hopes, Democratic and Republican, that caste be maintained in "radical Michigan."

Michigan Republicans stood, nevertheless, in the vanguard nationally of those asserting the prerogatives and political weight of a Northern bloc growing in cohesiveness and backbone. Checking slavery's expansion meant holding firm in the struggle against the South for national power and symbolic representation. Important as anti-Southernism was in Michigan Republicanism, it was just one of several major impulses in a complex movement that lacked social or ideological homogeneity. Its most salient postures and symbols contained overlapping meanings. As a symbol "Slavery" harbored many dragons to be slain by the just.

To avoid or at least lessen misunderstanding about the assumptions of this study,[3] it is necessary to engage now in what Professor Heinz Eulau has aptly called "theorizing activity." The first assumption carries with it the raison d'etre for this work; namely that a case study can reach beyond description and classification of the unique. Properly designed

---

[3] David Potter, "Explicit Data and Implicit Assumptions in Historical Study," in Louis Gottschalk, ed., *Generalization in the Writing of History* (Chicago, 1963), 190-91.

it can join with other such studies to provide bases for broader generalizations. Such local studies permit one to perceive communities in depth—organic entities with their myriad human relationships, their individuality, and their universality. Significance and subtlety in human affairs are not functions of size. As David Potter has said, bringing to mind Pascal's famous structure within which an "infinity of universes" existed: "generalization in history is inescapable and . . . the historian cannot avoid it by making limited statements about limited data. For a microcosm is just as cosmic as a macrocosm. Moreover, relationships between the factors in a microcosm are just as subtle and the generalizations involved in stating these relationships are just as broad as the generalizations concerning the relation between factors in a situation of larger scale."[4]

A second assumption is that a number of variables in their social development and immediate experience strongly influence men's voting and their choice of parties. This is not a euphemism for denying that class or "how a man gains his livelihood" has anything to do with voting. Rather, it recognizes the whole man in his total social environment and a multiplicity of potentially relevant variables whose mix can kaleidoscopically shift over time and place.

These assumptions underlie those modern studies of voting patterns in which political scientists observe many variables relating to individuals. Analysts can know how a person voted and can ask him questions about himself. They can measure an individual's class, for example, by means of such "hard" indicators as occupation and income and can also ask what class he thinks he is in. No such luxurious and helpful tools exist for those conducting studies before the Civil War. Rather, the mass of voters must be viewed from outside, as it were, via a relatively limited, although potentially significant, number of variables. Generalizations about antebellum voting must rest primarily on aggregate data collected for counties, townships, and wards, with the smallest minor civil divisions bringing one somewhat closer to the individual. With aggregate data one does not even see individual voters through a glass darkly; rather, to shift the metaphor, one creates a screen of information about aggregates and reaches through to individuals by inference. Fortunately mid-nineteenth-century settlement patterns in Michigan produced many townships of homogeneous populations or homogeneous politics, permitting reasonably strong inferences to be made regarding the voting of their constituent groups. While the available data and methods do permit inferences to be

---

[4] *Ibid.*, 191. For perceptive comments on the utility of case studies, James C. Malin, "Local Historical Studies and Population Problems," in Caroline Ware, ed., *The Cultural Approach to History* (New York, 1940), and Robert A. Dahl, *Who Governs? Democracy and Power in an American City* (New Haven, 1961), v-vi.

drawn from knowledge of community frames of reference,[5] such inferences do not hold for individual members of social groups who are dispersed throughout the population and are presumably psychically apart from the group, lacking its reinforcement of perception and norms.

Lack of adequate demographic data before 1850 complicates analyzing party formation in the 1830s. Using traditional sources, one must cast a wide net through society, examining many ostensibly nonpolitical activities, to determine which groups transferred their rivalries and antagonisms into party conflicts. The historian must reconstruct the political universe in terms of its political subcultures. The latter might be a group in which class, religion, or ethnicity overlap, but not necessarily. Members generally share primary-group experiences which tend to give them a common view of life and habituated responses to the everchanging political scene. Examination of the values, attitudes, and opinions of the group permits one to discern its belief-system, that is not so much a reasoned, fairly coherent, and perhaps logical "ideology" but rather a hierarchy of values linked by quasi-logical unstructured beliefs.[6] Political subcultures existed before political parties, and they were of various kinds. Some consisted of elite or narrow pressure groups, others were amorphous, dispersed among broad issue publics. Their interaction ranged from cooperation, to coexistence, to struggles for power, patronage, tangible resources, status, and "recognition" of their values. Antagonistic relations between political subcultures will be of most interest here since it appears that they were carried into formal political conflict. Through this complex process of transference, parties as institutions then became reference groups.[7]

[5] See, e.g., Philip H. Ennis, "The Contextual Dimension in Voting," in William N. McPhee and William A. Glaser, eds., *Public Opinion and Congressional Elections* (Glencoe, 1962), 180-211; Austin Ranney, "The Utility and Limitations of Aggregate Data in the Study of Electoral Behavior," in Austin Ranney, ed., *Essays on the Behavioral Study of Politics* (Urbana, 1962), 91-102.

[6] My scholarly debts in this and following paragraphs overwhelm any attempt to enumerate them here. The most immediate are: Philip E. Converse, "The Nature of Belief Systems in Mass Publics," in David E. Apter, ed., *Ideology and Discontent* (Glencoe, 1964), 206-61; Frank J. Sorauf, *Political Parties in the American System* (Boston, 1964); Robert E. Lane, *Political Ideology: Why the American Common Man Believes What He Does* (New York, 1962); Samuel P. Hays, "The Social Analysis of American Political History, 1880-1920," *Political Science Quarterly*, 80 (September 1965), 373-94; Milton M. Gordon, *Assimilation in American Life: The Role of Race, Religion, and National Origins* (New York, 1964).

[7] Two books of influence here were Walter Lippmann, *Public Opinion* (New York, 1965; originally published 1922), and Murray Edelman, *The Symbolic Uses of Politics* (Urbana, 1964). The way in which parties function today as reference groups is described by Robert Lane in *Political Life: Why People Get Involved in Politics* (Glencoe, 1959), 299-300. The literature on reference groups is extensive, with the most outstanding work probably being Robert K. Merton, *Social Theory and Social Structure*, rev. edn. (Glencoe, 1957); for a stock-taking of the subject,

No party ever really conformed to its historical description. The flexibility and pragmatism, the heterogeneous constituencies and lack of ideological rigidity of American parties defies their being captured on paper. In describing the kinds of individuals who are a party's loyal voters and key pressure groups, the historian creates stereotypes, to use the term in its neutral sense. He describes social groups as if they had a common personality or political character. Indeed, a rapport usually exists between a party's character, that is, its image, style, rhetoric, attitudes, and aura, and the political character of its loyalists.[8]

It should be emphasized that elite groups will be neglected here. The pursuit of tangible goals by well-organized minorities or powerful individuals in such controversies as banking, internal improvements, tariffs, land distribution, and territorial expansion will be discussed chiefly in terms of their symbolic meaning for the masses, not in terms of the "allocation of tangible resources" among elites.[9] Historians who believe that the Bank War, states rights, or similar issues gave rise to political parties among the masses are wrongly extending the issue-orientation of limited segments of the electorate to all of it. They assume wide knowledge and intensity on party issues—warranted neither by recent studies of voter issue-awareness nor by what we know about the electorate of 1840.

Many historians admirably immerse themselves in the colorful detail of the politics of the Middle Period only to become victimized by the dramaturgy of Jacksonian politicoes, whose ability to beguile has seduced far more sophisticated analysts of politics than their "common" contemporaries.[10] Our vulnerability lies in the lack of a conceptual

---

now ten years old, Herbert H. Hyman, "Reflections on Reference Groups," *Public Opinion Quarterly*, 24 (Fall 1960), 383-96. Stein Rokkan has written several stimulating works on the historical relationships between social cleavages and party development, e.g., Seymour M. Lipset and Stein Rokkan, "Cleavage Structures, Party Systems, and Voter Alignments," Lipset and Rokkan, eds., *Party Systems and Voter Alignments: Cross-National Perspectives* (New York, London, 1967), 1-64.

[8] Three works that develop the concept of political character in different ways have greatly aided my thinking: Robert E. Lane, "Political Character and Political Analysis," in Heinz Eulau, *et al.*, eds. *Political Behavior* (Glencoe, 1956), 115-25; Robert Kelley, "The Thought and Character of Samuel J. Tilden: The Democrat as Inheritor," *Historian*, 26 (1963-64), 176-205, and "Presbyterianism, Jacksonianism and Grover Cleveland," *American Quarterly*, 18 (Winter 1966), 615-36. Of undoubted importance to this line of thought, too, is the seminal work by David Riesman, Nathan Glazer, and Reuel Denny, *The Lonely Crowd: A Study of the Changing American Character* (New Haven, 1950).

[9] The phrase comes from Edelman, *Symbolic Uses of Politics*, 1-21.

[10] It is in political situations laden with emotion in which the mass public has little or no understanding of issues that governments take bold tacks, such as announcing regulation of business, or warring against monopolies or banks. Since the public which responds has little information or understanding of what goes on,

approach to how group attitudes form, and too heavy a reliance on a liberal-rational judgment of public opinion. According to V. O. Key, Jr., classical treatments of public opinion were disposed "to regard the political system as an atomized collection of individuals, each more or less informed about public issues and possessing views about them. This preconception produces a picture of social conflict organized along issue alignments of individuals," but Key warns that this is only part of any explanation of political controversy: "in some degree cleavages that involve the mass public are in terms, not of conflicting attachments to issues, but of loyalties to competing groups."[11] If Professor Lee Benson is only half correct in his judgment that "historians have not yet generally even *begun* to develop scientific procedures to study past public opinion,"[12] it should not be surprising that their accounts of party formation contain unconvincing accounts of electoral group responses to party battles.

Researchers in elite sources have overestimated the information and interest possessed by mass publics on issues which generated intense elite engagement. It is time that historians confronted the brute fact that "large portions of the electorate do not have meaningful beliefs, even on issues that have formed the basis of intense political controversy for substantial periods of time."[13] Recognition of the citizenry's limitations implies a realism which can complement, indeed intensify, commitment to a Jeffersonian belief in the development of an informed citizenry.

How many accepted explanations of American political episodes need to be rewritten once it is recognized that mass political knowledge has been low and that voting has generally lacked issue orientation? Political scientists have also developed the corollary point that "Party loyalty apparently lacks ideological underpinning." A party's beliefs may attract and unite its activists but issues which are the organization's articles of faith at a given moment may not be revered at all by its mass constituency. Republican and Democratic leaders in the 1950s, for example, divided significantly by issues, but deep ideological cleavages did not separate their constituencies.[14]

---

its response and its gaining of assurance (or feeling a threat) from the announced policy must be based on sociopsychological factors already there, on group attitudes already in existence, *ibid.*, 30-31.

[11] V. O. Key, Jr., *Public Opinion and American Democracy*, 3rd edn. (New York, 1964), 60.

[12] Lee Benson, "An Approach to the Scientific Study of Past Public Opinion," *Public Opinion Quarterly*, 31 (Winter 1967-68), 522-67.

[13] Converse, "Nature of Belief Systems in Mass Publics," 245. See also Daniel Katz and Samuel J. Eldersveld, "The Impact of Local Party Activity Upon the Electorate," *Public Opinion Quarterly*, 25 (Spring 1961), 21-22 (on the electorate's lack of basic political information).

[14] Herbert McCloskey, Paul J. Hoffman, and Rosemary O'Hara, "Issue Conflict

While it is assumed that political knowledge, issue orientation, and articulate belief-systems do not extend significantly beyond elite groups into the electorate, certain assumptions are made regarding the psychological affinities of leaders and followers in parties and other social groups. To some extent psychological congruity is assumed between elites and constituencies: bridges of rapport exist between spokesmen and supporters along a "latent value continuum" which can be inferred from the expressed attitudes of leaders and, when available, followers.[15] The concept of political character rests on this assumption as does the assertion that there is a rapport between a party's character and its loyal constituent groups. All this implies that analysts of traditional documents should search not only for substantive, overt objects of persuasive rhetoric but also for emotions and values appealed to because the rhetorician knows that his readers or listeners are already imbued with them.[16]

These strategies for analyzing party formation and voting will thus use elite sources, but elites will be relatively neglected. Elites, however, played the most important role in creating parties. Social group conflicts did not mechanically generate party organizations. Rather, patterns of conflict among subcultures pervaded the sociopolitical milieu in which organizers worked to build parties. The professional politicians manipulated the institutional environment with ease, but their relative lack of control over the social arena meant that many consequences of their actions would be unintended.[17] Party builders who set out in the 1820s

and Consensus Among Party Leaders and Followers," *American Political Science Review*, 54 (June 1960), 426. "However, we cannot presently conclude that ideology exerts no influence over the habits of party support, for the followers do differ significantly and in the predicted direction on some issues." The latter are of a type in which considerations of "position" and "style" are "mixed," 418.

[15] The quoted phrase is from Edelman, *Symbolic Uses of Politics*, 154-55. Among other works of relevance here are: Lane, *Political Ideology*, 10-11; David Riesman and Nathan Glazer, "The Meaning of Opinion," *Public Opinion Quarterly*, 12 (Winter 1948-49), 633-48, esp. the section "An Approach to Latent Meaning," 644-48; Herbert McCloskey, "Conservatism and Personality," *American Political Science Review*, 52 (1958), 27-45; T. W. Adorno, *et al.*, *The Authoritarian Personality* (New York, 1964; originally published 1950), i; and M. Brewster Smith, Jerome S. Bruner, and Robert S. White, *Opinions and Personality* (New York, 1956).

[16] The preceding sentence is a paraphrase and slight alteration of an observation from Svend Ranulf, *Moral Indignation and Middle Class Psychology: A Sociological Study* (New York, 1964; originally published in Copenhagen, 1938), 60.

[17] The basic studies of the activities of party organizers are: M. Ostrogorski, *Democracy and the Organization of Political Parties: The United States*, ii (New York, 1922); Robert V. Remini, *The Election of Andrew Jackson* (Philadelphia, 1963); and Edward Pessen, *Jacksonian America: Society, Personality, and Politics* (Homewood, Ill. 1969) who discusses the literature and attempts to make a synthesis of works on party organizers, the political system, and the rise of the major parties, 154-247, 374-80. Highly stimulating and important for what it implies

to make political power more effective, more predictable, and more rewarding could not, for example, have anticipated the intense cultural shocks that took place in the 1830s, both within and without American society. Yet the intensification of cultural conflict in the 1830s perhaps made mass party formation easier. The interaction of many causes, some deliberate, some unintended, brought parties and voter loyalties into being.

---

about the motives of party organizers is James Sterling Young, *The Washington Community, 1800–1828* (New York, 1966).

II

Michigan and the Party System

SOCIETY, 1830–1860

In 1818 the first wave of the transportation revolution washed the shores of the Great Lakes as the steamboat *Walk-in-the-Water* sailed from Buffalo across Lake Erie. That same year the first government land office opened in Detroit, and more Eastern emigrants made their way to Michigan Territory. Archaic survivals attended a new society's emergence: in 1824 territorial law still punished witchcraft, and on September 23, 1830, one Stephen G. Simmons was hanged for killing his wife. Michigan's first and last public hanging victim departed after delivering an eloquent "repentance" before a crowded grandstand—gallows and stand having been built for the occasion. Reaction against the event caused the abolition of whipping posts in Detroit. In 1830 the last Indian treaty removing any formal aboriginal obstacle to white pioneering was still twelve years away, but the most important cessions had already been cheaply extracted. Ten years of almost uninterrupted growth and development lay ahead.

In the thirty years before the Civil War a society came into being in Michigan, "Out of the Wilderness" as Professor Willis F. Dunbar put it, and hard upon social growth a new political party system emerged in the 1830s. The new politics came early to this frontier state and was part of the first genuine mass party system ever created. Before looking at Michigan's experience in its broad outlines, it will be useful to explore the character of this market society where the intensity that charged men's pursuit of happiness carried over into politics: "Speculation and politics are the reigning spirit of the times," said the 1839 *History of Michigan* by Charles Lanman, "and they pervade all classes of the population."[1]

Like the rest of the nation in these years, Michigan experienced the transportation and communications revolutions. The state grew in socio-

---

[1] Charles Lanman, *History of Michigan* (New York, 1839), 296-97.

economic complexity, it knew great demographic change with a rapid population increase and an influx of a variety of ethnoreligious groups which produced far-reaching cultural shock. Nevertheless, Michigan society in 1860 resembled that of 1837 in all essentials—the year of its entrance into the Union. This heretical view obviously chooses to stress continuities rather than changes on the social landscape. It also suggests that life goals and styles in 1860 did not differ greatly from those of 1837, that economic and social patterns had more in common than is usually granted when "improvement" or "progress" is emphasized.

Steamboats, canals, cheap Western land, and economic pressures in the East in the 1820s brought settlers to Michigan. Population climbed from 31,640 in 1830 to 212,671 by 1840, an increase of 571 percent, faster than any state or territory in that decade. But the rate of increase fell sharply in the next two decades while population rose to 397,654 in 1850 and 749,113 persons in 1860. This constituted 2.38 percent of the nation's population. Farm land values after 1830 began a steady climb upward, but in 1860 Michigan's still lagged well behind those of New York, Ohio, and even rocky New England.[2]

Although patterns of life were very similar throughout Michigan, yet some socioeconomic developments did depart from prevailing modes. The Upper Peninsula gave the nation its first gold rush, without gold. Copper, and then iron, brought Eastern investors, fortune seekers from all over the Upper Lakes, and miners from Cornwall, Ireland, and the East. In 1860 some 20,000 persons lived on the wild, rich, and beautiful peninsula of tall tales. Perhaps one-half or more of the men worked in mining. The rest were largely employed in lumbering, fishing, or trapping, while a few grew potatoes.[3]

Like mining, lumbering also was essentially peripheral to the mass of society. The Saginaw Valley on the eastern side of the lower peninsula and the Muskegon Valley on the west were well on their way as centers of commercial lumbering by 1860. Their mills, some of them steam powered, employed proportionately large numbers of men in these northern counties. The individual sawmill itself, however, was woven into the fabric of rural agricultural life. It marched across the state with farm settlements, providing lumber for barns, houses, and village homes. Often

---

[2] *Michigan Statistical Abstract* (Lansing, 1966), 6; George J. Miller, "Some Geographical Influences in the Settlement of Michigan and in the Distribution of Its Population," *Bulletin of the American Geographical Society*, 45 (May 1913), 347; J.D.B. DeBow, *Statistical View of the United States: Compendium of the Seventh Census* (Washington, 1854), 40, 47.

[3] Willis F. Dunbar, *Michigan: A History of the Wolverine State* (Grand Rapids, 1965), 365, 369, 375. The Upper Peninsula is discussed in more detail in Chapter XIV.

run by the owner and a "hand" or two the sawmill marked the post-frontier stage of pioneering.[4]

In at least one other important respect the Michigan of 1860 differed from that of 1837: the foreign born had arrived in numbers beyond anyone's expectations. In 1850 almost 14 percent and in 1860 nearly 20 percent of the population was foreign born—150,000 persons. This produced (with other causes) a younger and more male society. Of all the immigrants arriving in the United States from 1820 to 1860 males outnumbered females by a ratio of 3 to 2, and almost one-half of the total was between 15 to 30 years of age. Thus, in Michigan among the total white population, males outnumbered females 388,006 to 348,136 in 1860. The discrepancy was widest in the 30 to 40 age group. It and the 20 to 30 age group, largest numerically, together constituted nearly 32 percent of the total white population.[5]

The image of foreigners concentrated in cities is erroneous for Michigan in 1860: they covered the state, from towns, to farms, to lumber and mining camps. True, the foreign born did account for 45 percent of Detroit's population in 1860, but the 21,349 newcomers there were only 14 percent of the entire foreign group. Taking only Detroit's population as urban, the foreign born were more rural in 1860 since Detroit's 9,927 immigrants in 1850 had constituted 18 percent of the total. Counties with high percentages of foreign born in their population spanned the state in 1860, from the northern mining, lumbering, and fishing counties to the densely peopled southern counties such as Wayne, Oakland, Macomb, and Kent where greater *numbers* of foreigners could be found. The foreign population spread across the state and was overwhelmingly rural and small town, as was the state itself.

Census numbers of farm and nonfarm occupations are not reliable guides to social structure and fail to indicate that Michigan was largely rural. In 1850 the percentage of strictly agricultural jobs was perhaps 60, while it fell in the next decade to 55 or less. Figures based on the population size of towns describe the state as 92.7 and 86.7 percent rural in 1850 and 1860. This measure, although arbitrary, better indicates the society's ruralness.[6]

The preurban and preindustrial character of socioeconomic life can perhaps be appreciated by considering work patterns in the major urban center. DeBow described Detroit in 1850 as one of the "Leading Cities of the United States." The federal census manuscript of social statistics

---

[4] Dunbar, *Michigan*, 358-60.

[5] *Eighth Census of the United States, Population, 1860* (Washington, 1864), I, xxi, 230-31.

[6] *Michigan Statistical Abstract*, 6; *Eighth Census of the United States*, 249; *The Seventh Census of the United States: 1850* (Washington, 1853), 902-03.

listed dozens of "manufacturing establishments" throughout the city, but none employed over 100 "hands." Only 3 worked more than 75 men; in 11 plants over 50 "hands" labored, and most typical of the larger Detroit "manufactories," 19 places employed more than 25 and under 50 men (and women). The largest single employer was the railroad; steam sawmills and lumber yards; makers of sashes, blinds and doors; and machine and foundry shops came next. Moreover, most hands were probably skilled or at least semiskilled workers.[7] (Of course, a large pool of unskilled laborers was otherwise present.) The biggest factory in Michigan in 1860 was not in Detroit, ironically, but just south of it in rural Ecorse Township where the Ecorse Iron Works and Wyandotte Rolling Mills had 80 and 300 men on their payrolls.[8] These mills provide the only approximation of an industrial factory system, and they had come into being in the previous five years. Many occupations in Wayne and other counties, nevertheless, should be considered urban or at least nonfarm. But the structure of manufacturing in Detroit, with a population of over 45,000, gives perspective on socioeconomic patterns in the 15 or so large towns in the state—only 4 of which held over 5,000 inhabitants. These places, or rather the men in their workshops were neither strictly rural nor urban. "Mechanics" came to the towns of Michigan in increasing numbers after 1840, perhaps from Eastern or European cities. They could earn more in Michigan where skilled labor was in demand. Highly mobile, many moved on at faster rates than the rest of a footloose small town population.[9] If urban Michigan was not quite urban, rural Michigan was not solely one big farm.

The agricultural society under discussion here was heavily concentrated in the two southern tiers of counties along the old military roads and the East-West rail lines. Fertile land, rivers, and lakes drew relatively dense settlement into some counties in the third and fourth tiers, but barely halfway up the lower peninsula heavy pine growth, sandy soils, and harsher climate discouraged farmers.[10]

[7] The bound manuscript volumes of the 1850 "Social Statistics of Michigan" are located at the Michigan Historical Commission Archives, Lansing. (Hereafter referred to as MHCom) DeBow, *Compendium*, 399. The table of Michigan occupations in the printed United States Census of 1860 erroneously listed only 50 "factory hands" in the entire state.

[8] See Chapter XIV.

[9] On the mobility of nonfarm occupations in western townships: Mildred Throne, "A Population Study of an Iowa County in 1850," *Iowa Journal of History*, 57 (October 1959), 309-10: William L. Bowers, "Crawford Township, 1850-1870: A Population Study of a Pioneer Community," *ibid.*, 58 (January 1960), 18-24. On high wages in the West: DeBow, *Compendium*, 164; Edgar W. Martin, *The Standard of Living in 1860: American Consumption Levels on the Eve of the Civil War* (Chicago, 1942), 408, 410, 411, 414.

[10] Dunbar, *Michigan*, 350, 358; Miller, "Geographic Influences in Michigan Settlement," 330.

Everywhere in the state from 1835 to 1860 in each year one could find new farms just planted. Although a cross section of farming regions at any point in time would reveal every stage from frontier to commercial farming, almost all shared a basic orientation. The farmers' great goal was to produce cash crops and get rich. "Wealth and honor," said one observer, "are the grand motives of emigration." The habits of thought connected with the constantly advancing value of real property and "the custom of 'dickering,' makes almost every individual a speculator. . . . Everybody seems to know what everything is worth, and what it will sell for."[11] Federal census categories, too, implied mobility and a market psychology. The monetary value of farms, recorded in agricultural censuses for the first time in 1850, has apparently always been understood to mean "estimated current market value of farm land, fences, permanent improvements, and buildings," and did not include estimated value of crops produced, farming implements, machinery, or livestock.[12] These traveled with the farmer-speculator.

Markets beckoned in Detroit, Chicago, New York, or New Orleans. Goods flowed east and west along the Erie axis or south to the Ohio and Mississippi valley. Increasingly in the two decades before the Civil War, Michigan like the rest of the upper Northwest, sent products disproportionately to the East rather than to the South.[13]

Initially goods had to move inside Michigan. In the 1830s and 1850s "railroad fever" raised ecstatic visions of cheap access to markets, but track construction proceeded slowly. It suffered first from collapse of the grandiose internal improvements plan of 1837 in the depression of the late 1830s. Private companies took over in the 1840s, yet by 1850 Michigan possessed only 342 miles of track. Ten years later the mileage had crawled to 800 while Wisconsin, a younger state, built 902 miles in that decade alone. And the canal-building bonanza that affected some Western states left Michigan almost untouched.[14]

Michigan farmers used roads and rivers. The terrain, although sometimes muddy or dusty, was not terribly difficult. In the 1850s the "plank-

[11] Lanman, *History of Michigan*, 297. From Jackson County a pioneer wrote on January 9, 1837: "Speculation! Speculation! . . . a person that has never been in Michigan knows nothing about it. It almost begins to make my fingers itch. Money laid out here will double in one year." Louisa Fidelea Palmer, ed., *The Palmer Letters* (privately printed, 1963), 35. Burton Historical Collection, Detroit Public Library. (Hereafter referred to as BHC)

[12] Thomas J. Pressly and William H. Scofield, *Farm Real Estate Values in the United States by Counties, 1850–1959* (Seattle, 1965), 4.

[13] A. L. Kohlmeier, *The Old Northwest as the Keystone of the Arch of American Federal Union: A Study in Commerce and Politics* (Bloomington, 1938).

[14] Dunbar, *Michigan*, 333, 379, 384-85; Carter Goodrich, ed., *Canals and American Economic Development* (New York, London, 1961), 1-12, 249-55; *Statistics of the United States, 1860* (Washington, 1866), 330.

road craze" created a new speculative mania and temporary boon to internal transportation. Meanwhile, throughout the period, rivers and lakes carried most of the freight. This era remained (in spite of the popular emotions aroused by other ways of travel) "the heyday of river transportation in Michigan."[15]

Thus the transportation revolution came to Michigan only piecemeal. Farm products moved within Michigan in 1860 to a great extent as they had in 1837. Operators in Detroit might be in instant telegraphic communication with Chicago or New York, but Dunbar has put the case well for the everyday impact of the various "revolutions": "Although Michigan had come a long way out of the wilderness by 1860, vast areas of the state were still covered by unbroken forests and isolated hamlets, and a large proportion of the farm homes were often out of touch with the outside world for months at a time—especially during the winter. Rail lines, plank roads, and telegraph wire were remote from many Michigan homes."[16]

Poor local transportation, of course, probably would not prevent Michigan farmers from moving further West with the same facility as other Northwestern migrants. The high geographical mobility of the farm electorate requires comment in connection with the method of this study, which relies heavily on data from the censuses of 1850 and 1860. There is a proverb that a man cannot step into the same river twice. The historian of the nineteenth-century Northwest, similarly, cannot look into the same township twice and expect to see the same population. If one is comparing the voting of townships in 1837 and 1850, for example, their electorates may have changed considerably in that time. This agricultural market society, as noted above, induced high lateral if not vertical mobility. When the seeker of "wealth and honor" met failure or a dead end, he moved on. Studies of mid-nineteenth-century Northwestern townships show that population turnover may have been going on at a tremendous rate. Much impressionistic evidence encourages one to assume this for Michigan. Thus, when one compares the party vote of a township or county in 1837 to its vote in 1850 one compares the party preference of a voting unit, not necessarily of voters, not even in the aggregate.[17]

Despite high geographical mobility the available data is still very useful because most townships formed at an early stage a social character which persisted for a decade or two. Hundreds of local histories sug-

---

[15] Dunbar, *Michigan*, 378-79, 385.

[16] *Ibid.*, 390-91.

[17] Peter S. Coleman, "Restless Grant County: Americans on the Move," *Wisconsin Magazine of History* (Autumn 1962), 16-20; Merle Curti, et al., *The Making of an American Community: A Case Study of Democracy in a Frontier Community* (Stanford, 1959); and the Iowa studies cited in note 9 above.

gest this, as do aggregate data depicting the social composition of Wayne County in 1850 and 1860 assembled from the manuscript population schedules. The turnover among Canton township's native Protestant farmers, for example, may have been high, but between 1850 and 1860 Canton remained a predominantly native Protestant farming community.

Although the myth of the "classless" frontier has died slowly, empirical study has consistently shown that class structures were steadily elaborated after communities passed through a brief communal phase.[18] Postwar county histories provide voluminous testimony to the intensity of the quest for "honor" or distinction. Evidence from Iowa and Michigan counties indicates that most townships began life with a great group of farmers owning farms with a cash value of $1,000 or less. As townships matured the large middle group flattened out, with some increase in the top economic ranks and larger movement to the lowest (see Appendix B).

With these caveats in mind, aggregate voting data over time for townships can provide a basis for making inferences about the party loyalties of social groups. Aside from state and county returns for major elections, this study makes use of voting profiles for townships and wards. Such a profile shows the number, percent, and total vote for parties in each unit in every election year available, from 1835 to 1860. Profiles of some use for 32 counties were assembled.[19] Fairly complete returns for Detroit's wards existed for the entire period, and for several large towns which incorporated as cities in the 1850s, returns by wards were also available.

Mass Party Loyalty, 1835–1852

In the 1830s mass party loyalty on a stable basis came into being for the first time in American history. If a political party is defined as having three major areas of being, namely legislative, organizational, and electoral, then the latter at least had not characterized party structure previously. Studies of the Federalist and Republican parties suggest that they achieved most of their rootedness in the electorate after 1800, and stable, large-scale citizen support proved at best transitory in the individual states. Studies of the "first party system" have not yet provided the data to show the existence of stable voting patterns among freely attached electoral followings.[20]

---

[18] An excellent discussion of the subject and the literature may be found in Ray Allen Billington, *America's Frontier Heritage* (New York, 1966), 97-116.

[19] Returns came from several sources including newspapers, the rich but incomplete collection of election returns in the Michigan Historical Commission, and county courthouses.

[20] Paul Goodman, "The First American Party System," in Chambers and Burnham, eds., *American Party Systems*, 86. The last sentence is a paraphrase from

The second party system—or by this definition the first—created a "party-in-the-electorate,"[21] and thus resembles the political scene today in distribution and intensity of partisanship. Political scientists have shown the great extent to which party loyalty has shaped voting behavior in this century. The "role of basic partisan dispositions" has been called perhaps "the most impressive element" in American political life. While short run influences are not trivial "each election is not a fresh toss of the coin; like all good prejudices, the electorate's basic dispositions have a tremendous capacity to keep people behaving in accustomed ways."[22]

Actually, party loyalty is probably less widespread now than during the nineteenth century when, according to Professor Walter Dean Burnham, the "voting universe was marked by a more complete and intensely party oriented voting participation among the American electorate than ever before or since." Comparing the period from 1854 to 1872 with six subsequent periods between 1878 and 1962 Burnham found stronger party voting by every measure for the earlier years. In Michigan during the Civil War scarcely 15 percent of the potential electorate appeared to have been outside the voting universe. About 7 percent could be classified as "peripheral voters," who participated during "surge" elections of high excitement, while more than three-quarters of the total appear to have been core voters, or party loyalists.[23]

The conditions of electoral mobilization just described came into being in the 1830s. For most of its Territorial Period, from 1805 to 1837, Michigan did not know party politics. In 1819 territorial elections began

---

William Nisbet Chambers, *Political Parties in a New Nation: The American Experience, 1776–1809* (New York, 1963), 45. Recent studies carefully examining the early electorate include David Hackett Fischer, *The Revolution in American Conservatism: The Federalist Party in the Era of Jeffersonian Democracy* (New York, 1965), Carl E. Prince, *New Jersey's Jeffersonian Republicans: The Genesis of an Early Political Machine, 1789–1817* (Chapel Hill, 1967), and Alfred F. Young, *The Democratic Republicans of New York: The Origins, 1763–1797* (Chapel Hill, 1967). They show that party loyalties were shallow and unstable among a comparatively limited electorate.

[21] The phrase is from Frank Sorauf, "Political Parties and Political Analysis," in Chambers and Burnham, eds., *American Party Systems*, 37-38.

[22] Donald E. Stokes, "Party Loyalty and the Likelihood of Deviating Elections," *Journal of Politics*, 24 (November 1962), 689-90; Angus Campbell, Phillip E. Converse, Warren E. Miller, Donald E. Stokes, *The American Voter* (New York, 1960), 121, 121-67 passim; Bernard R. Berelson, Paul F. Lazarsfeld, William N. McPhee, *Voting* (Chicago, 1954, 1962), 15-16, 19-22; Angus Campbell, Gerald Gurin, Warren E. Miller, *The Voter Decides* (Evanston, 1954), 88-111; Angus Campbell and Donald E. Stokes, "Partisan Attitudes and the Presidential Vote," Eugene Burdick and Arthur J. Brodbeck, eds., *American Voting Behavior* (Glencoe, 1959), 355-58, 368.

[23] Walter Dean Burnham, "The Changing Shape of the American Political Universe," *American Political Science Review*, 59 (March 1965), 12-13, 23. Burnham's indicators show only net change, and gross changes could be concealed within the data. However, the indicators all point in the same direction.

in which taxpayers chose a Delegate to Congress every two years. In 1823 voters could also elect a nine-man Council to legislate for the territory. These steps toward self-government often resulted in spirited battles for office among competing Republican factions, but did not bring parties into the arena. Political participation was low. In 1829 Antimasons organized the first party, and the rival Republican factions, whose ideological distinctions have thus far escaped detection, quickly emulated the Antimasons. But these organizational trial runs possessed little continuity, let alone measurable support among voters. The fragmentary state of the data, however, makes identification of voting patterns almost impossible. Before 1835 stable alignments cannot be discerned in a confusing thicket of leadership factions, a growing and barely rooted electorate, and shifting civil division boundaries. Demographic and socioeconomic conditions, undeveloped communications, and political practices all suggest that persisting patterns of voter alignment did not divide Michigan's territorial electorate.[24]

In 1835 the first true Whig-Democratic contest mobilized much of the electorate along party lines.[25] Then after a two year hiatus during which party competition vanished, organizational cadres and the voters finally rallied in 1837. For state and presidential elections virtually all adult white males soon participated. And the vast majority divided along lines that would endure. Nevertheless, party loyalty should not be treated as a "given," but rather as a variable with at least two kinds of fluctuation: defections and conversions. Defecting voters temporarily leave their traditional party to vote for another and return when the specific causes of their departure relax. Converting voters switch their vote and their party allegiance.[26]

Evidence for the party attachment of the electorate by 1837 is of three kinds: aggregate returns, studies of elite affiliations, and contemporary testimony. Returns for the presidential elections from 1840 to 1852 show that voters divided fairly evenly between the Democrats and their combined opponents (Table II. 1). The Democratic vote ranged from 47.2 to 51.0 percent. In off-year contests after 1840 the distribution was not so even. However, the Democratic vote displayed relative stability. The one near landslide of the period (1851) occurred not because of an outpouring of Democratic voters but resulted from a depression in turnout

---

[24] Some returns by counties for territorial elections of delegates to Congress are in the Secretary of State Papers, Great Seal and Archives, MHCom; the county returns for 1823 and 1825 are reprinted in M. Dolorita Mast, *Always the Priest: The Life of Gabriel Richard* (Baltimore, 1965), 207, 259; also useful is the *Detroit Gazette*, BHC.

[25] See Chapters IV and V.

[26] Phillip E. Converse, unpublished lecture given at Inter-University Consortium for Political Research Seminar, Ann Arbor, August 1965.

affecting largely the anti-Democrats. That party loyalty was weaker among the latter is the subject of a later chapter.

TABLE II.1

Major State Elections, Party Vote, 1837–1852

Year	Office	Democrat		Whig		Liberty	
		Vote	*Percent*	*Vote*	*Percent*	*Vote*	*Percent*
1837	Gov.	15,314	51.0	14,546	49.0		
1838	Cong.	16,255	50.3	16,051	49.7		
1839	Gov.	17,037	48.3	18,195	51.7		
1840	Pres.	21,096	47.6	22,933	51.7	321	0.7
1841	Gov.	20,993	55.7	15,449	41.0	1,223	3.2
1843	Gov.	21,392	54.7	14,899	38.1	2,776	7.1
1844	Pres.	27,737	49.7	24,375	43.8	3,639	6.5
1845	Gov.	20,123	50.9	16,316	41.3	3,023	7.6
1847	Gov.	24,639	53.3	18,990	41.1	2,585	5.6
1848	Pres.	30,677	47.2	23,930	36.8	10,393	16.0
1849	Gov.	27,837	54.2	23,540	45.8		
1850	Cong.[a]	29,259	48.7	30,872	51.3		
1851	Gov.	23,827	58.5	16,901	41.5		
1852	Pres.	41,842	50.5	33,860	40.8	7,237	8.7

[a] Equals total of Congressional districts

If returns for major elections are examined by county it is clear that most of those units established a partisan loyalty by 1840. Similarly, inspection of voting profiles for townships in 32 counties throughout the period suggests that most townships, once population stabilized, took on a fairly predictable pattern of vote distribution. Many townships fluctuated widely in the degree to which they preferred a particular party, but major changes of basic disposition usually could be traced to demographic changes.

Another way of inferring party loyalty consists of statistical correlation of party percentage strength over a series of elections. Returns for 30 counties in 1840, for example, were available. The Democratic percentages in each election could be correlated with the Democratic percentages in all other presidential elections. The Pearson coefficients of correlation (Table II.2) suggest the high stability of the 1840-52 period, at least for every four-year interval.

In Wayne, Livingston, and Calhoun counties, interyear correlations for *townships* produced results of overall similarity. These three counties provided a rough sectional sample and different patterns of voting. Wayne, in the east, maintained a consistent Democratic loyalty until 1860. Livingston, north and west, voted Democratic in the 1840s but went Republican in 1856. Calhoun, further west and south, returned a low Democratic vote throughout. The correlations also suggest that the

TABLE II.2

Interyear Correlations of Democratic Percentage Strength of Counties,
1840–1860, Presidential and 1854 Gubernatorial Elections

	1840	1844	1848	1852	1854	1856
1844	.622					
1848	.385	.786				
1852	.345	.810	.858			
1854	.079	.611	.562	.827		
1856	.242	.280	.389	.063	.228	
1860	.106	.603	.551	.589	.066	.482

TABLE II.3

Interyear Correlations of Democratic Percentage Strength
in 3 Selected Counties, 1840–1852

WAYNE COUNTY

	1837	1840	1844	1848	1852	1854	1856
1840	.755						
1844	.642	.672					
1848	.662	.385	.656				
1852	.547	.605	.718	.849			
1854	.364	.227	.546	.801	.837		
1856	.476	.237	.569	.880	.887	.914	
1860	.420	.244	.496	.834	.902	.856	.912

LIVINGSTON COUNTY

	1844	1848	1850	1852	1854	1856
1848	.556					
1850	.802	.634				
1852	.706	.653	.668			
1854	.519	.662	.588	.471		
1856	.489	.484	.730	.498	.704	
1860	.593	.563	.696	.667	.385	.797

CALHOUN COUNTY

	1840	1844	1848	1852	1854	1856
1844	.622					
1848	.385	.786				
1852	.345	.810	.858			
1854	.079	.611	.562	.957		
1856	.242	.280	.389	.787	.787	
1860	.106	.603	.551	.786	.870	.708

basic Democratic and anti-Democratic divisions of the electorate in the
1840s probably continued into the 1850s. One result of the turmoil of
the 1850s may have been to *increase* the tendency to identify with a
major party.

Political researchers using aggregate data often rely on measurement of split ticket voting as an index of party loyalty. Burnham has suggested that the 99 percent levels of straight ticket and complete ballot voting that he found in the nineteenth century "may have been partly an artifact of the party ballots then in use." Michigan law provided that voting "shall be by ballot in writing, or on a paper ticket, containing the names of the persons for whom the elector intends to vote."[27] Newspapers, or their printing presses, were vital to party organization because they usually distributed printed ballots, often of bright colors, to their party's faithful. The convenience of such ballots undoubtedly encouraged straight ticket voting. Ticket splitting did occur, however, and political observers regarded it as a deliberate display of independence of party.[28] However, in township after township, county after county, from the late 1830s on, manuscript and newspaper tallies of votes given for groups of federal, state, or local offices, presented in tabular form, usually looked like an intricate design consisting of vertical columns of numbers. Some idiosyncratic breaks in the symmetry could be observed, but the overwhelming impression was of straight ticket voting, especially in rural townships.[29]

Elite behavior also suggests a high degree of party loyalty. Men mentioned frequently in newspapers as political activists broadly represented party leaderships. From 1848 to 1856 in Wayne County of the 743 men who appeared as active in one or more elections only 174 changed their allegiance and only 11 shifted more than once.[30] When one considers that the Republican party replaced the Whig and Free Soil parties during these years the overall stability is more impressive. Professor Alexandra McCoy's study of Wayne County's economic elite observed the party loyalty of 97 elite members from 1837 to 1854. McCoy found that the elite displayed almost uniform party loyalty up to 1854. Only two of these prominent men switched parties.[31]

No wonder contemporaries described "heredity in politics" as "stronger even than in religion" and that "It was expected as a matter of course that partisan politics would descend from sires to sons with unbroken regularity." One pioneer told of how a strong Jackson man typically had carried his Democratic principles from New York state into the Michigan

[27] Burnham, "American Political Universe," 18; Thomas M. Cooley, ed., *The Compiled Laws of the State of Michigan* (Lansing, 1857), I, 107.

[28] *Kalamazoo Gazette*, Nov. 10, 1838, microfilm, Michigan State Library, Lansing. (Hereafter referred to as MSL) *Detroit Free Press*, Nov. 15, 1847; *Detroit Advertiser*, May 9, 1850.

[29] Appendix A lists newspaper and manuscript sources of election returns for counties by townships and wards.

[30] Dorothy Fisher, "Personnel of Political Parties in Wayne County from 1848 to 1878" (unpublished M.A. thesis, Wayne State University, 1935), 38.

[31] Alexandra McCoy, "Political Affiliations of American Economic Elites: Wayne County, Michigan, 1844, 1860, As a Test Case" (unpublished Ph.D. dissertation, Wayne State University, 1965), 96.

woods where he raised his sons: "It was natural for his young family, to claim to be Democrats in principle, in their isolated home."[32]

Finally, campaign styles prevalent in Michigan by the late 1830s also bolster the proposition that intense partisanship characterized the disposition of the mass of voters. Parades, wagon trains, marches, rallies, singing, floats, transparencies, flags, and a variety of quasi-military activities directed toward mobilizing opposing "armies" implied mass party loyalty.[33] Such practices assume that the hosts to be marshalled for voting were already committed partisans.

IMPACT OF THE LIBERTY AND FREE SOIL PARTIES

The Liberty party's entrance into the political lists in 1840 did not disturb the unity of the 1837-52 period because the new party drew its votes overwhelmingly from Whiggery. Thus, Democratic and anti-Democratic divisions remained about the same, much to the advantage of the Democrats. Whigs, naturally did not take a calm, analytical view of this. Astute Whig observers recognized that "political abolitionists" came from both parties but that "the majority in our state, heretofore has been [sic] of the opponents of the Locos."[34] Indeed, one major Libertyite goal was to seize the balance of power between parties. Whigs were thus more vulnerable and Libertyites expected more from Whigs. Many had been Whigs, their old party had pretensions to morality while the Democrats had always been pro-Southern, pro-slavery, and of dubious virtue. Liberty leaders felt justified in punishing the Whigs even if the loss of votes and elections did not push them to antislavery.[35]

[32] Edward W. Barber, "The Vermontville Colony: Its Genesis and History," *Historical Collections, Michigan Pioneer Society*, 28: 236-37. (Hereafter referred to as *MHC*) William Nowlin, *The Bark Covered House: Or Back in the Woods Again* (Detroit, 1876), 121-22; for the author's attitude to his father, 202-04. In Monroe in 1852 the boys of the town had their own rallies, parades, and political meetings "same as the men. . . . Each political party among the boys controlled its company of soldiers." "Auld Lang Syne," *An Incidental History of Monroe* (Merrill), 12. For an example of party loyalty conceived of as being as strong as or stronger than one's "own blood," John Stuart to Kate Stuart Baker, Dec. 12, 1850, in Helen S. M. Marlatt, ed., *Stuart Letters of Robert and Elizabeth Sullivan Stuart, 1819–1864* (New York, 1961), I, 166.

[33] Richard Jensen, "American Election Campaigns: A Theoretical and Historical Typology," paper delivered to the Midwest Political Science Conference, Chicago, 1968, 2, 2-10. Contemporary comments often implied an enduring division of the electorate, e.g., Robert Stuart, Nov. 19, 1841, to William Woodbridge, Woodbridge MSS, BHC.

[34] William Woodbridge, Aug. 25, 1843, to Hon. Willie P. Mangum, Woodbridge MSS, BHC. See also *Detroit Advertiser*, Nov. 6, 1840, Oct. 18, 1841, and Sept. 19, 1842.

[35] Theodore Foster to Birney, Ann Arbor, Dec. 14, 1841, ed. Dwight L. Dumond, *Letters of James Gillespie Birney, 1831–1857* (New York, London, 1938), II, 644; Arthur L. Porter to Birney, Detroit, Oct. 4, 1844, *ibid.*, 846-47; Theodore Foster to Birney, Oct. 16, 1835, *ibid.*, 979-80. Also, Ann Arbor, *Signal of Liberty*, Nov. 17,

The aggregate state vote from 1837 to 1841 suggests that most abolition votes came from the Whigs. In major elections from 1837 to 1840 Whigs kept pace with and surpassed the Democrats, but fell drastically behind in 1841, as the Liberty vote climbed to 1,223. The Whig vote fell from 22,933 to 15,449 (Table II.1). Obviously, in addition to defections and conversions, nonvoting also caused the Whig decline. In the 1840 Congressional voting, 17 counties out of 31 gave one or more votes to the Libertyites. Of these 17, 13 had voted Whig in 1839. By 1841 only two of those 13 remained Whig. In the others the Liberty vote had increased and the Democrats now enjoyed a majority or plurality.

Many causes produced Whig nonvoting in 1841. Before the election one Democrat observed that the Whig party "manifests a most astonishing apathy and I do not believe they can drag their force to the polls." The first Whig President, William Henry Harrison, had taken office only to die soon after in April 1841. His successor, John Tyler, dismayed Whigs everywhere by revealing himself to be more of a States' rights Southern Democrat than a Whig. Michigan Whig leaders reacted to Tyler's "apostasy" with rage, disgust, and frustration.[36]

In Michigan itself political apathy received a boost from hard times, while Whiggery had been racked by internal feuds and had been deprived of its most prominent leader. The party controlled the legislature in 1841 but could not agree on a choice for United States Senator. After an intraparty fight, the Democratic minority joined one Whig faction to elect William Woodbridge, incumbent Whig governor elected in the Whig triumph of 1839. The departure of the popular Woodbridge could not have helped Whig morale. Meanwhile the Bank of Michigan, which the Whigs had made state fiscal agent, failed, and many Whigs privately predicted that the "monster's" mishaps would cost the party votes.[37]

The Liberty party's presence probably increased nonvoting among Whigs. Since they were more vulnerable to political antislavery, it follows that more Whigs than Democrats would be caught undecided between their old party loyalty and the abolition appeal, and might resolve their indecision by not voting.[38] Many of the Whigs who failed to vote

---

1841, Nov. 7, 1842, May 15, July 17, 1843, June 17, 1844, microfilm, Ann Arbor, Michigan Historical Collections. (Hereafter referred to as MHCol)

[36] Robert M. McClelland, Oct. 7, 1841, to John S. Bagg, letters from the John Sherman Bagg MSS in the Huntington Library. George Goodman, Niles, Sept. 8, 1841, to W. Woodbridge, Woodbridge MSS, BHC. The Woodbridge Papers contain many examples of Whig distress with Tyler. Also, Austin Blair, Jackson, Dec. 15, 1841, to A. T. McCall, Austin Blair MSS, BHC; and *Detroit Advertiser*, Nov. 3, 1841.

[37] Floyd Streeter, *Political Parties in Michigan, 1837–1860* (Lansing, 1918), 39-40; Franklin Sawyer, Ann Arbor, Jan. 16, 1840, to Woodbridge; Richard Butler, Mt. Clemens, Feb. 9, 1841, to Woodbridge; same to same, Dec. 26, 1840, Woodbridge MSS, BHC. *Detroit Free Press*, Feb. 4, 1841.

[38] On cross pressure situations and withdrawal see Lane, *Political Life*, 199-201.

in 1841 probably voted Liberty in 1844. In 12 counties in 1844 the Liberty party received more than 6.5 percent of the vote, its statewide percent. In only 3 of the 12 counties did the Democratic percentage strength decline from 1840. In 2 of these, Genesee and Kalamazoo, the Democratic percentage fell slightly while the Whig tumbled much more (Table II.4). In only one, Van Buren, did the Democrats lose more percentage points than the Whigs between 1840 and 1844.

TABLE II.4

Party Percentages in 1840 and 1844 Presidential Elections in Counties Giving the Liberty Party 6.5 Percent or More in 1844

			Dem.	Whig	Liberty
	Oakland	1840	44.9	50.1	
		1844	52.1	40.9	6.9
	Washtenaw	1840	44.9	55.1	
		1844	48.2	44.4	7.3
EAST	Hillsdale	1840	46.1	53.9	
		1844	48.0	42.7	9.3
	Jackson	1840	42.7	57.3	
		1844	43.9	41.1	15.0
	Eaton	1840	40.5	59.5	
		1844	44.4	48.4	7.2
	Lapeer	1840	45.6	54.4	
		1844	50.8	40.3	8.9
	Genesee	1840	42.6	57.4	
NORTH		1844	42.5	46.0	11.5
	Shiawasee	1840	36.0	64.0	
		1844	40.1	45.1	14.4
	Ionia	1840	45.2	54.8	
		1844	45.5	47.8	6.7
	Kalamazoo	1840	43.8	56.2	
		1844	40.7	45.8	13.6
WEST	Van Buren	1840	58.0	42.0	
		1844	52.3	40.8	6.9
	Ottawa	1840	52.1	47.9	
		1844	66.3	24.0	9.7

In most townships Whig and Liberty voters can be regarded as the approximate sum of anti-Democratic strength, particularly in units where, were it not for the abolitionists, Whiggery would have enjoyed a majority. The most common pattern observed was the Liberty party taking votes from Whigs. The social bases of this will be explored later.

In 1848 the Liberty party merged into a broad political antislavery movement which nationally brought together Conscience Whigs, New York's Barnburners, and a variety of supporters from the antislavery-abolition spectrum of politics. In Michigan prominent Democrats for the first time joined political antislavery. The national Free Soil Party nominated Martin Van Buren, former Democratic president, to head the coalition's ticket. It appeared that Michigan Democrats with antislavery tendencies were being given strong incentives to set aside party loyalty. At first Michigan politicians expected that Van Buren's candidacy would help the Whig nominee, General Taylor, and Whig leaders encouraged Free Soilism. However, it became clear that "multitudes of Whigs also were joining" Free Soil,[39] and regular Whigs called for a halt to any efforts to aid the independents. In some areas, however, Whigs and Free Soilers formed coalitions.

More Michigan Democrats do appear to have defected to Free Soil in 1848 than had ever deserted earlier to the Liberty camp. Yet it is surprising how few Democrats did vote Free Soil. Of course, the Democrats were running Michigan's favorite son, Lewis Cass, for President, and this must have offset somewhat the pull of Van Buren. Open Whig-Free Soil fusion in some districts also repelled Democrats from Free Soil.

The Democratic percentage of the state vote fell by 2.5 percentage points between 1844 and 1848, while the Whig fell by 7 points. The number of Democratic votes rose by 3,000 with the Whig falling by 400. In 1852, with Van Buren absent from the ticket and the sectional crisis quiet, the Free Soil vote declined sharply. The Whigs increased their percentage strength between 1848 and 1852 far more than the Democrats: they had far more to regain. County and minor civil division returns show the same patterns, with this difference: slightly increased Democratic defections occurred mostly in units already disposed to cast some antislavery votes. Whig defection or conversion to Free Soil still greatly surpassed that of the Democrats.

Thus, in the period from 1837 to 1852 most of the electorate identified with a party, and most voters obeyed the norm of party loyalty. Antislavery parties upset very little the gross divisions of voting strength because they drew votes largely from the Whigs. In 1844 probably 90 percent of Liberty men were ex-Whigs and in 1848 perhaps 80 percent or more of Free Soilers were ex-Whigs. The general continuity of party loyalty simplifies the task of identifying Whig and Democratic social groups.

[39] William Woodbridge, Oct. 2, 1848, to N. W. Coffin, Boston, Mass., Woodbridge MSS, BHC. Democratic editor Wilbur F. Storey had earlier feared that free soil promoters in Michigan "desire above all to carry the state for General Taylor." Storey, Jackson, July 31, 1848, to John S. Bagg (confidential), Bagg MSS, Huntington Library.

III

Economic Interest, Elites, Classes, and Parties: 1837–1852

> Do not allow yourself to be gulled into bitterness towards
> what is falsely called "aristocracy"—this is a cant term used
> by demagogues to effect vile purposes—"monopoly" is
> another. . . . There is neither "aristocracy" or "monopoly"
> in this country: the best and firmest friends of popular rights
> are found among those who have property enough to be
> independent, and who can never in this land have enough
> to sever their interest from those of the people—they are
> more reliable, because they are rarely seekers for office and
> therefore rarely resort to falsehood. The interests of property
> are here, the interests of all—for property is so generally
> diffused that all are interested in its preservation and
> inviolability.—George F. Porter to Fred B. Porter,
> September 15, 1851[1]

Through the long ascendancy of Progressive history in the first half of the twentieth century[2] an economic determinism, sometimes unconscious, declared that economic conflicts brought parties into being and caused rival economic groups to align in opposing parties. Leaders and masses were assumed to choose their parties by the lights of a fairly rational perception of their interest as members of a class or economic group. Some historians offering this kind of interpretation emphasized different classes as the most significant, but all tended to present variations on a theme: Democrats came from the poor and Whigs from the rich classes. It then followed that Democratic ideology and party programs challenged the status quo, calling for the radical, democratic, and humanitarian, while Whiggery, opposing change, was conservative, aristocratic, and property minded.

Many features of "Jacksonian Democracy" have undergone substantial shifts in interpretation.[3] But at least since James Schouler, a patrician

---

[1] George Porter claimed to have been a Federalist but was now a "democrat." The family was Whig and abolitionist in sentiments. John S. Porter MSS, MHCol.

[2] John Higham, Leonard Krieger, and Felix Gilbert, *History* (Englewood Cliffs, N.J., 1965), 171-97.

[3] For a review of changing interpretations see Charles Grier Sellers, Jr., "Andrew Jackson Versus the Historians," *Mississippi Valley Historical Review*, 44 (March 1958), 615-34; Higham, *History* 216-18; and Alfred Alexander Cave, *Jacksonian Democracy and the Historians* (Gainesville, 1964).

liberal of the 1880s[4] to the 1950s, most analysts agreed more or less on
the class composition of parties. In 1919 Dixon Ryan Fox introduced
quantitative data to demonstrate empirically the relationship between
class, or at least wealth, and party in the period from 1828 to 1852.[5] The
distinguishing feature of what Fox and many later writers called their
"statistical" attempts to show "correlations" between class or wealth and
party consisted of their observing for a number of political units (usually
counties) only two variables: party vote and some aggregate index of
wealth. Indeed, such work can be described generally as single-factor
analysis, since it operated on the unexpressed assumption that an economic variable was the only one of any relevance to voting. Time and
again counties or wards would be shown to have voted according to their
relative wealth; at least most units observed would adhere to the pattern
asserted. Yet there always seemed to be, in each study, "exceptions" to
the general tendency of poor Democrats and rich Whigs. The explanations for these deviant cases were conspicuous for their lack of
credibility.[6]

Class conflict between Democrats and Whigs probably reached its
apogee not in 1832 or 1840 but in 1945 with the publication of Arthur
Schlesinger, Jr.'s, *The Age of Jackson*, which contained one of the most
thoroughgoing economic interpretations of politics and parties to be
found in any study of the era. Schlesinger presented no quantitative data,
relying instead on the work of Fox and others to argue that Frederick
Jackson Turner had misled scholars in emphasizing that the wellsprings
of Jackson's party could be found on Western farms and frontiers.
Rather, rising industrialism in the East caused urban workingmen and
their intellectual spokesmen to provide the main drive of the Jacksonian
coalition. This thesis, along with the general tide of revisionism, provoked studies of the voting habits of urban workingmen in the 1830s and
1840s. William A. Sullivan contended that Philadelphia workingmen did
not support Jackson and the Democrats, Edward Pessen found the same
for Boston workingclass wards, while Robert T. Bower disagreed with

[4] James Schouler, *History of the United States of America Under the Constitution*, IV: *1831–1847, Democrats and Whigs* (New York, 1889). Schouler was one
of the first to give such a full description of the class composition of parties. Cf.
Horace Greeley, *The American Conflict* (Hartford, Chicago, 1864), I, 168; Henry
Wilson, *Rise and Fall of the Slave Power in America*, I (Boston, New York, 1872);
and Herman von Holst, *Constitutional History of the United States*, II: *1828–1846,
Jackson's Administration Annexation of Texas* (Chicago, 1879), 330-405, 696, 697.

[5] Dixon Ryan Fox, *The Decline of Aristocracy in the Politics of New York,
1801–1840* (New York, 1919), 116-17, 420-22, 438-39. Fox had been influenced
by Frederick Jackson Turner.

[6] For a detailed analysis of such monographs see Ronald P. Formisano, "The
Social Bases of American Voting Behavior: Wayne County, Michigan, 1837-1852,
As a Test Case" (unpublished Ph.D. dissertation, Wayne State University, 1966),
17-40.

both Pessen's method and conclusions for Boston.[7] These works did service by making "labor's" support for Jackson and the Democrats, which had usually been taken for granted, a moot question. But they still either paid unconscious homage to economic determinism or failed to demonstrate that urban workingmen constituted a self-conscious political subculture during the 1830s. Meanwhile, as many orthodoxies of Progressive history came under attack in the 1950s, critics began to question the allegedly "radical" and humanitarian program of Jackson's party, and to deny the significance of economic conflicts.[8] Much of the revision seemed to be directed at establishing a point made long before by Ralph Waldo Emerson. Anticipating our contemporaries Bray Hammond and Richard Hofstadter, Emerson said, "However men please to style themselves, I see no other than a conservative party. You are not only identical with us in your needs, but also in your method and aims. You quarrel with my conservatism, but it is only to build up one of your own."[9]

The revision of the 1950s seconded Emerson in stressing similarities between the parties. Democrats seemed to be men poorer than Whigs who wished to become rich. As Democrats lost much of their reputation as radicals and humanitarians, historians still tended to place them below the Whigs in socioeconomic status, even as, in some studies, class lines between parties began to blur.[10] About 1960 revision entered a new phase as Richard P. McCormick and Lee Benson explicitly challenged the axioms of economic determinism and class divisions between parties. McCormick showed that broad upper and lower economic groups in New York's electorate in the 1820s and in North Carolina's from 1835 to 1856 behaved very much like one another at the polls.[11] In 1961 Ben-

[7] William A. Sullivan, "Did Labor Support Andrew Jackson?" *Political Science Quarterly*, 62 (December 1947), 569-80; Edward Pessen, "Did Labor Support Jackson?: The Boston Story," *Political Science Quarterly*, 64 (June 1949), 262-74; Robert T. Bower, "Note on 'Did Labor Support Jackson?: The Boston Story,'" *Political Science Quarterly*, 65 (September 1950), 441-44. See Bernard Berelson, H. Gaudet, Paul F. Lazarsfeld, *The People's Choice* (New York, 1948). Carl Neumann Degler, "Labor in the Economy and Politics of New York City, 1850-1860: A Study of the Impact of Early Industrialism" (unpublished Ph.D. dissertation, Columbia University, 1952), criticized Fox's method of analyzing voting in city wards, 296, 330, 331, 333.

[8] Higham, *History*, 213-14.

[9] Quoted in Arthur I. Ladu, "Emerson: Whig or Democrat?" *New England Quarterly*, 13 (September 1940), 439. Bray Hammond, *Banks and Politics in America from the Revolution to the Civil War* (Princeton, 1957). Richard Hofstadter, *The American Political Tradition and the Men Who Made It* (New York, 1948).

[10] Higham, *History*, 216-18.

[11] Richard P. McCormick, "Suffrage Classes and Party Alignments: A Study in Voter Behavior," *Mississippi Valley Historical Review*, 46 (December 1959), 397, 398-400, 401, 402; Lee Benson, *Turner and Beard: American Historical Writing Reconsidered* (Glencoe, 1960), 153-59.

son published *The Concept of Jacksonian Democracy*: *New York as a Test Case* and sought to reorder the priorities of the debate. His New York parties had drawn their leaders and mass support from roughly the same socioeconomic groups; ethnic and religious cleavages influenced the party loyalties of social groups more than economic differences. In considering six variables, Benson did not ignore economic or sectional differences (intrastate), but assigned them lesser influence; under different conditions they could become relatively more important.[12]

Benson's and McCormick's work, for many scholars, exposed the implicit and often unconscious assumptions of their predecessors and freed students of Jacksonian parties from the economic determinism underpinning almost all previous explanations of mass voting. It is possible of course, that this generation is substituting new implicit assumptions, new determinisms, in place of the old. But detecting voting patterns should be the kind of problem to which methods can be applied which contain built-in checks upon unrecognized assumptions. The systematic observation of social variables of known or suspected relevance to political life offers the best hope of analyzing the mass electorate.

The standard work dealing with Michigan antebellum politics is Floyd B. Streeter's *Political Parties in Michigan, 1837–1860*, published in 1918 and typical of the economic determinism described earlier. Although Streeter paid considerable attention to ethnic and religious elements in political life he tended to reduce these variables to mere dependencies of economic class. For example, Baptists voted Democratic and Episcopalians voted Whig but Streeter related nothing in their religio-cultural background to their politics. Baptists, however, were mostly "rural" and in "moderate financial circumstances" while Episcopalians "represented the wealthy and conservative class." Democratic voters generally were "poor and uneducated people in the cities and rural districts, though a number of well-to-do had also been attracted to it"; the "vast majority" of Whigs rather "were the well-to-do" and conservative men, or those who for some reason upheld the interest of this class. Among them were many bankers, merchants, and financiers in the cities and large landowners in the country."[13] At no point did Streeter confront the problem of explaining the Democratic loyalty of "a number of well-to-do" or why some men of no wealth apparently supported Whiggery against their economic interests. In the 1830s, according to Streeter, poor radicals dominated the Democratic party and enacted "radical" legislation designed to benefit the lower classes.

[12] Benson, *Concept.*
[13] Streeter, *Political Parties*, 4-6. Streeter stressed three "reasons for division of voters into political parties": place of origin, amount of wealth and social position, and sectional interests. The first and third actually dovetailed into the second.

ECONOMIC ISSUES OF THE 1830s

In 1839 the Democratic editor of the *Kalamazoo Gazette* offered a very different appraisal of his own party's recent legislative achievements. He said that they "illy suited" a new state and "much of it has been destructive and ruinous." The legislators since 1835 had failed to consider the interests of the *whole* state and had engaged in "a general scramble for sectional and private benefits. And to effect their purposes, a system of log-rolling, buying and selling, gambling and finessing, huxtering, and compromising, has been resorted to . . . which has been degrading to themselves, mortifying to their constituents and ruinous to the State."[14] Neck-deep in depression, expecting defeat soon at the polls, possibly embittered for personal reasons, the *Gazette's* editor obviously exaggerated. Yet his analysis, the like of which rarely appeared in print, approximated far better than Streeter's what happened when political entrepreneurs found themselves possessed of political power, alluring economic opportunities, and responsible to an electorate possessing little understanding of public matters. What information went out to "the people" was filtered by poor communications and constricted by partisan blinders. In any event, Democratic politicoeconomic legislation cannot be construed to be radical or lower class oriented. The one piece of socially conscious legislation promoted by Democrats during the early period of party development was a debt exemption law which allowed workers, artisans, and others in debt to keep that part of their personal property needed to make their living. The law established criteria of what was "necessary." The Democracy promised such a law in its 1841 state platform, although Democratic legislators subsequently did not support it unanimously.[15] Other than this law, Democrats showed little interest in the poorer classes.

If basic differences between parties had resulted from conflicting economic interests one might expect that such cleavages would have become manifest during the constitutional convention of 1835, as Michigan passed from a territory to a state. In New York, according to Marvin Meyers, the "most incendiary issues" of the two Jacksonian decades (1826-1846) were "banking and corporations, public debt, and public works"; and these issues caused partisan splits in New York's conventions of that era.[16] Yet in Michigan's 1835 convention, economic issues

---

[14] *Kalamazoo Gazette*, July 27, 1939, microfilm, MSL.

[15] Paul A. Randall, "Gubernatorial Platforms for the Political Parties of Michigan, 1834-1864" (unpublished M.A. thesis, Wayne State University, 1937), 37. The Whig *Detroit Advertiser* recognized the need for the law but criticized the Democratic version for going "too far," Feb. 15, 1842; *Detroit Free Press*, Feb. 21, 1842.

[16] Marvin Meyers, *The Jacksonian Persuasion: Politics and Belief* (Stanford,

barely threw off a spark of conflict. Although the Whig contingent was small (only about 10 percent of the delegates), it protested loudly over other issues. But the record of the debates contains few hints about what Whigs thought about political economy. Whigs and Democrats apparently shared that enthusiasm for public works which a traveler in Michigan had noticed even in 1833, when projects as grandiose as a railroad from Detroit to Chicago were talked about, not to mention a canal from Maumee (Toledo) to Lake Michigan.[17]

The convention decided without disagreement to have the constitution enjoin the legislature to encourage internal improvements. Similarly, it provided that the legislature could pass no act of incorporation unless by a two-thirds majority in each house. No strong sentiment for or against this measure materialized.[18] Nine delegates voted for a sweeping ban on corporations "with special privileges," but 56 voted against it. Nineteen delegates favored authorizing some kind of state bank, including prominent Democrats as well as leading Whigs such as William Woodbridge.[19] Significantly, an attempt to make the private property of corporation stockholders liable for the debts of the corporation, a measure not usually encouraging to business enterprise, failed without a roll call vote.[20]

Michigan's internal improvements plan of 1837 cannot be viewed as a class or interest group issue in relation to parties. Historians have often assumed that in state politics Democrats opposed internal improvements while Whigs promoted them. Carter Goodrich has warned that this idea should be viewed with caution and pointed to Michigan as one case where those positions, as Streeter described them,[21] were reversed. Yet even this needs to be qualified. The Michigan parties never differed significantly on internal improvements and both generally favored them. The Democrats, a majority party responsive to demands from Democrats in all sections, tried to build railroads and canals in the north, south, and center all at once. It may have been the only way to get an improvements program through the legislature. The *Advertiser* and some Democrats eventually argued that transportation facilities should be built

---

1957), 236. For a corrective to Meyers' view that the Whig and Democratic parties descended directly from the Federalist and Republican see Shaw Livermore, *The Twilight of Federalism* (Princeton, 1962).

[17] Harold M. Dorr, ed., *The Michigan Constitutional Conventions of 1835–36: Debates and Proceedings* (Ann Arbor, 1940), 55-420, 462, 539. (Hereafter referred to as *Debates*) Charles Fenno Hoffman, *A Winter in the West* (New York, 1835; Ann Arbor, 1966), 137.

[18] *Debates*, 606, and passim.

[19] The vote was 19-57, *Debates*, 391, Appendix A, roll call 87.

[20] *Debates*, 393. A measure requiring payments in specie on notes and bills secured by land failed 27 to 48.

[21] Streeter, *Political Parties*, 9.

where people were, not through empty forests.[22] Throughout the North-west the "interplay of regional and local rivalries" in improvements, as Harry N. Scheiber has observed, caused partisan politics to disappear. Members of state legislatures would vote "for nothing which does not pass through their own county." So Michigan, like Indiana and Illinois, adopted a program overextending its resources.[23]

Whigs began to criticize the program after the panic of 1837 and complications developed attending the state's notorious Five Million Dollar Loan. Taking power in 1841, Whigs cut back the program.[24] In turn the Democrats continued the limited Whig policy and began nego-tiations to sell the railroads to private investors. In 1845 both parties promised to sell the roads, and soon Democratic governor Alpheus Felch began selling the roads at bargain prices. Some Democrats raised pro-tests against "monopolies" but sentiment to unload the roads by then pervaded both parties. Opposition came mainly from local interests.[25] Party positions on improvements thus varied little and changed with circumstances. The improvements mania respected no party or class lines. Farmers and merchants in all sections viewed railroads as their stairway to prosperity.[26]

[22] Carter Goodrich, *Government Promotion of Canals and Railroads, 1800–1890* (New York, 1960), 266. Streeter, *Political Parties*, 10-13. Harold B. Hoffen-bacher, "Michigan Internal Improvements, 1836-1846" (unpublished M.A. thesis, Wayne State University, 1937), 10-12, 25-26.

[23] Harry N. Scheiber, "Urban Rivalry and Internal Improvements in the Old Northwest," *Ohio History*, 71 (October 1962), 228, 234-35.

[24] One Whig legislator told Woodbridge that the cut back on railroads would have no effect on the election of 1840. Henry B. Lathrop, Jackson, to William Woodbridge, July 2, 1840, Woodbridge MSS, BHC. Lucius Lyon to Gen. John McNeil, Jan. 24, 1840, "Letters of Lucius Lyon," *MHC*, 27: 531.

[25] Goodrich, *Canals and Railroads*, 144-46, 326. William L. Jenks, "Michigan's Five Million Dollar Loan," *Michigan History*, 15 (Autumn 1931), 619, 622-23. Austin Blair to A. T. McCall, Jan. 8, 1846, Austin Blair MSS, BHC. Henry T. Backus, Whig legislator, thought the "wire workers" reluctant to sell the railroads which they deemed "the nursery of their power." Backus to William Woodbridge, Feb. 21, 1846, Woodbridge MSS, BHC.

[26] George Rogers Taylor, *The Transportation Revolution, 1815–1860*, IV: *The Economic History of the United States* (New York, 1951), 91, 100, 344-45, 375-77. For an example of an axiomatic belief in transportation improvements, Comfort Tyler, Centreville, to Woodbridge, Feb. 3, 1840, Woodbridge MSS, BHC. It might be instructive to study who was awarded public work contracts and the political activities of this group. See, e.g., the Memorial, Dec. 28, 1839, Woodbridge MSS, BHC, of 15 contractors engaged in building the Clinton-Kalamazoo Canal, asking the Governor-elect not to stop or cut back on that work; and from the contractors on the same project, "Petition, Mt. Clemens, July 28, 1842, to John Barry," the Democratic governor, in "Executive Records, Petitions," MHCom. Also fruitful for this line of inquiry would be the tremendous volume of correspondence relating to the appointment of commissioners to the Internal Improvements Board during 1840 in the Woodbridge MSS.

It has frequently been assumed that most entrepreneurs and promoters in the old Northwest were largely Whigs.[27] Yet even a cursory look at enterprise in Michigan during the 1830s reveals the heady involvement of Democrats in growth-related business enterprises. Counting on the wealth promised by a continuing influx of settlers, entrepreneurs established new banks, promoted towns, and turnpike, canal, and railroad companies. Democrats controlled the state government from 1835 to 1839 and most county and town governments as well. Being strategically placed more Democrats than Whigs may have been involved in promotion of internal improvements.[28]

Banking certainly attracted many Democrats, both before and after Michigan's costly "Wild Cat" episode. Legend has it that "radical" Democrats democratized banking. The realities were different. In 1837 the state had 16 chartered banks. The Democratic legislature passed a General Banking Act permitting "freeholders who had a limited amount of capital to start a bank." But this "killer of monopolies" spawned an illegitimate brood of wildcat banks, mainly because of an untimely suspension of specie payments which applied to the new banks as well as the old. Forty-nine new banks existed by April 1838, with a nominal capital of $3,915,000. "Most of them flooded their communities with worthless notes and then failed."[29]

Several items block interpretation of this episode as an unfortunate result of a Democratic assault on economic privilege. If the 16 chartered banks in 1837 represented "entrenched capital" or monopoly, then these things were nonpartisan. Both Whigs and Democrats owned the "old" banks: in 1836 the Democratic legislature had chartered 9 of them. While Governor Mason simultaneously vetoed applications for charters from steamboat companies and other corporations, arguing against potential monopolies, he had not vetoed any bank charters. Old and new banks had both Whig and Democratic officers, stockholders, and debtors, and out of state Whig and Democratic capitalists had interests in Michigan banks.[30]

[27] See, e.g., Glyndon Van Deusen, *The Jacksonian Era, 1828–1848* (New York 1959), 96.

[28] On Democratic involvement in railroad, turnpike, and canal building: John T. Mason to Stevens T. Mason, Nov. 7, 1836, and stock certificates of S. T. Mason, Nov. 1836 and March 24, 1837, Mason MSS, BHC; *Free Press*, April 18, 21, 1837; record of meeting, May 22, 1837, John R. Williams MSS, BHC; John Sherigian "Lucius Lyon: His Place in Michigan History" (unpublished Ph.D. dissertation, University of Michigan, 1960), 34-67, for the affairs of a particularly active businessman and Democratic leader in western Michigan; also Edsel K. Rintala, *Douglass Houghton: Michigan's Pioneer Geologist* (Detroit, 1954), 67, 84-85, 87.

[29] Streeter, *Political Parties*, 32-33.

[30] William G. Shade, "The Politics of Free Banking in the Old Northwest, 1837-1863" (unpublished Ph.D. dissertation, Wayne State University, 1966), 13-14. Professor Shade contributed freely of his expert advice to this section.

The General Banking Act provided that no more than 12 freeholders in any county could organize a bank, with a minimum of $50,000 capital, 36 percent of which had to be paid in in specie. Persons possessing the capital required for such a venture in Michigan in 1837 were not poor. Most of the new banks' capital was land which would never have the productive capacity claimed for it; some of it was encumbered. The banks misrepresented their capital, overextended themselves, and brazenly defrauded the populace. No one has ever shown that "the masses demanded that banking should be free."[31]

A suggestive fictional portrait of a wildcatter appeared in 1837, created by a social commentator, Mrs. Kirkland, in her *A New Home: Who'll Follow?*—an account of life in Michigan in the 1830s. She satirized the typical wildcat banker in her story of one Harley Rivers, of "Tinkerville." Rivers was poor, but not "of the poor classes." A typical popular villain, he fancied himself a gentleman, had never worked for a living, and had squandered two fortunes. Rivers redeemed himself from poverty by setting up the Bank of Tinkerville, making "money of rags," and moved East to "live like a gentleman on the spoils of the Tinkerville Wild Cat."[32]

A systematic inquiry into the identity of wildcatters would unearth characters like Rivers, no doubt, as well as respectable Whigs and Democrats. The *Kalamazoo Gazette* said that "in the associations" created under the bank law "many members of the legislature and their *particular friends*, figured conspicuously, as Presidents, Directors, Cashiers, stockholders and borrowers." The legendary "Bank of Brest" probably qualifies as the most notorious of the wildcats; located, according to its sponsors, in the "thriving metropolis" of Brest, which was and is a thriving forest. At least one of its stockholders was a Democratic politician. Origen D. Richardson, elected Lieutenant Governor by the Democrats in 1841, promoted the 1837 Bank of Oakland with several other Democrats.[33]

[31] Streeter, *Political Parties*, 33. The claim rests ultimately on the reminiscences of Alpheus Felch, banking commissioner in 1837-38. Professor Shade in his study of free banking has exposed the origins of the myth. See Alpheus Felch, "Early Banks and Banking in Michigan," *MHC*, 2: 114; H. M. Utley, "The Wildcat Banking System in Michigan," *MHC*, 5: 221; and Herbert Randall, "Alpheus Felch: An Appreciation," *Michigan History*, 10 (April 1926), 166.

[32] C.M.S. Kirkland, *A New Home: Who'll Follow? or, Glimpses of Western Life* (New York, 1837), 191-200. I have used the 1850 edition, BHC.

[33] *Kalamazoo Gazette*, July 27, 1839, film, MSL. *Advertiser*, Sept. 30, 1841. Democrat Calvin Britain held stock in the Brest bank. Edwin O. Wood, *History of Genesee County, Michigan* (Indianapolis, 1916), 314, 519-21; *Michigan Biographies*, 75, 329, of Democrats launching banks in frontier Genesee County. The names of the men incorporating banks and other corporations, e.g., the "Walled Lake Steam Mill Company," during 1836 can be found in *Michigan House Journal, 1835-36*, 188, 192-93, 196, 206, 216, 226, 236-37, 247, and passim.

The *Monroe Times* (Democratic) congratulated the townspeople of Brest on their new bank and noted that the town has risen "to wealth and importance in a surprisingly short time." One has to choose between awarding the editor a vast gullibility or a ready sense of humor. The *Detroit Free Press* welcomed a flock of wildcats while the *Pontiac Balance* (Democratic) greeted the Bank of Oakland as an "antimonopoly triumph."[34] *Free Press* editor John Bagg implored a friend to loan him money in 1836 for unrivaled investment opportunities. His description of the latter reveals much about the ties between editors, legislators, land speculation, new towns, and new banks. "You must be aware," wrote Bagg:

that from my situation with this press, I am easily enabled to form acquaintances with members of the Legislature. They are men of good judgement and most of them have laid the foundations for fine fortunes in real estate. They are very friendly to me—more perhaps on account of my situation than anything else—and would very willingly do me a favor in affording me facilities for investing money in lands in different parts of the state. Many of them are anxious to have me invest something in their *embryo cities—so as to get an occasional puff from the state paper, and it provokes me much* to see the fine opportunities I enjoy for making money—if I had the capital to avail myself of them.[35]

By the time the wildcats failed and their frauds were exposed the populace had already begun to experience depression. Rich, poor, merchants, farmers, laborers, and artisans, all suffered from the wildcats. Speculators were so despised that "the people would hang them if they could."[36] Yet the public did not seem to associate wildcats with any one party. Both parties accused each other of harboring all bankers. The Whigs published a list of bank officers which said, in effect, that 69 percent of them were Democrats. The Democrats released a list claiming that 55 percent of bank officers were Whigs. These claims, as William G. Shade has observed, tended only to confirm that bankers could not be associated with any one party.[37]

The Whigs originally raised no clamor against the banking law, but as the financial debacle descended Whig legislators introduced a resolution declaring it unconstitutional.[38] This opportunism contrasts with

[34] *Times* quoted in *Free Press*, Aug. 28, 1837; others from *Free Press*, Sept. 13, Sept. 27, 1837, and Aug. 17.

[35] Italics in original, John S. Bagg, Detroit, to I. H. Bronson, Feb. 21, 1836, Bagg MSS, Huntington Library.

[36] Austin Blair to A. T. McCall, July 21, 1841, Blair MSS, BHC. See also Lawton T. Hemans, *Life and Times of Stevens Thomson Mason* (Lansing, 1920), 377-78; the Hemans biography, while flawed, is one of the best books on antebellum Michigan politics available.

[37] Shade, "Free Banking," 33, 34-35.

[38] Joseph Gantz, "A History of Banking Legislation and Currency in Michigan, 1835-1865" (unpublished M.A. thesis, Wayne State University, 1936), 18. *Adver-*

Whigs otherwise consorting rather openly with the Bank of Michigan. The party's 1837 gubernatorial candidate, Charles C. Trowbridge, was its cashier, later its president.[39] Governor Woodbridge's administration (1840-41) relied heavily on Bank personnel and facilities. Bank officials and stockholders served as chairmen of the Senate Finance Committee, United States Senator, Auditor General, and State Treasurer. It became the state's fiscal agent and took over management of the Five Million Dollar Loan.[40]

This liaison hurt the Whigs. In 1840 the Bank of Michigan and the Farmers' and Mechanics' Bank provided the state with reliable currency, though both had suspended specie payments; in 1841 their notes joined their predecessors in ignominy. From all over the state, even from George Dawson's Whig *Advertiser*, came denunciations of the Bank of Michigan for protecting the investments of absentee controllers at the expense of local interests. The 1841 Whig State Convention, while blaming Democrats for the misdeeds of all other banks, virtually admitted that the party had erred in relying on the Bank.[41] The Bank's failure angered many persons in 1841, poor and "monied." It also benefited rich individuals who had access to political power to protect their interests, but the Bank was not the tool of a cohesive "wealthy and commercial" class in the Whig party. How can such an interpretation cope with Democratic chieftain Lewis Cass being one of the Bank's largest stockholders?[42]

The Democrats also had a "monster," indeed, at least two. A group

---

tiser, July 14, 1836. Elsa Holderreid, "Public Life of Jacob Merritt Howard" (unpublished M.A. thesis, Wayne State University, 1950), 32-33.

[39] Democrats reacted mildly to Trowbridge's candidacy. The *Free Press* regarded him as a good banker but unqualified for office. Democrats, it explained, were "not hostile to banks per se" and a "moderate connection" with banks did not disqualify a man. *Free Press*, Sept. 18, 20, 1837. Although Whigs called them "locofoco" for years, Michigan Democrats did not deserve the label, which connoted total hostility to all paper money facilities. For understanding of real locofocos, see Edward Pessen, *Most Uncommon Jacksonians: The Radical Leaders of the Early Labor Movement* (Albany, 1967).

[40] *Free Press*, Jan. 24, 1840, Jan. 25; see Woodbridge MSS, BHC, 1840-41, esp. correspondence between Woodbridge and Robert Stuart.

[41] MS of Peter Beckman, St. Louis University, on James F. Joy, Chap. I. Juliana Woodbridge to William Woodbridge, Jan. 26, 27, and Gideon Gates, Romeo, to Woodbridge, June 29, 1841, Woodbridge MSS, BHC. The latter is a good description of the depression. Thomas Rowland, Detroit, to Woodbridge, Jan. 25, 1841, and Robert Stuart to Woodbridge, Jan. 29, 1841, Woodbridge MSS, BHC, discuss Dawson. Stuart said that Dawson was "worse than mad" and feared he would "destroy us root and branch—he is worse than any locofoco, for he is all brimstone." Also Robert Stuart to Thomas Dunlap, President U. S. Bank, Pennsylvania, Feb. 13, 1841, Department of Treasury Papers, Letter copy book, 1840-1848, MHCom. Randall, "Gubernatorial Platforms, Michigan, 1834-1864," 20-37.

[42] Robert Stuart, Detroit, to Woodbridge, July 16, 1841; Henry T. Backus to Woodbridge, July 6, 1841; Richard Butler, Mt. Clemens, to Woodbridge, July 9, 1841, Woodbridge MSS, BHC. Shade, "Free Banking," passim.

of Democrats led by John R. Williams had incorporated the Michigan State Bank in March 1835. The Democratic state administration used it for deposit of state funds; shortly, after the 1837 depression began, the bank failed. The scene enacted between the Whigs and the Bank of Michigan virtually repeated the embarrassment earlier of the Democrats.[43] The Farmers' and Mechanics' Bank was more successful: John R. Williams also had led in founding this bank. Williams was one of Detroit's wealthiest men who enjoyed a long public career in the Democratic party. He had been president of the Bank of Michigan but resigned when control of the Bank shifted eastward to the Dwight family of New York. That transaction touched off a legal battle between the Dwights and Williams, marked by his being jailed three times in 1829.[44]

The Farmers' and Mechanics' Bank eventually became a "pet"—a federal deposit bank of the Jackson administration—after John Norvell, one of its directors, "assured the treasury department of its solvency and of the high percentage of its stockholders (90 percent) who had Democratic views." Not only did Democrats nurse their own monsters but in 1831 Lewis Cass had helped the Bank of Michigan obtain a government deposit and become a "pet bank." Later, in 1837, John Norvell urged Treasury Secretary Levi Woodbury to sue the Bank of Michigan if it could not meet its drafts. George Bancroft, Massachusetts Democrat, joined Cass in intervening on the Bank's behalf. Bancroft was a relative of the Dwights and held stock in several of their enterprises.[45]

ELITES

Obviously both parties contained many men of wealth, enterprise, and power. Party loyalty and economic competition sometimes joined together in the motives of these frontier condottiere; they also could disregard party when mutual profit was at stake. But the upper classes did not act as a unit in politics. There was at least widespread tacit acceptance of the economic, social, and political system. Party programs never

[43] Clarence M. Burton, Gordon K. Miller, and William Stocking, eds., *The City of Detroit, Michigan, 1701-1922* (Detroit, 1922), I, 640. Kinsley S. Bingham believed the Michigan State Bank failure hurt the Democrats more than the wildcat episode, Bingham to Alpheus Felch, March 30, 1839, Alpheus Felch MSS, BHC. (Parts of the Felch MSS are in the Michigan Historical Collections.) According to Professor Shade the nonlocal stockholders of the State Bank were Albany Regency men. For its incorporation see *Territory of Michigan, Acts Passed at the Extra and Second Session of the Sixth Legislative Council, 1835* (Detroit, 1835), 155.

[44] Burton, et al., eds., *Detroit*, I, 634-35. Silas Farmer, *History of Detroit and Michigan, I: General* (Detroit, 1884), 860-61.

[45] Harry N. Scheiber, "George Bancroft and the Bank of Michigan, 1837-1841," *Michigan History*, 44 (March 1960), 83-88, 88-89; 1833 fragment of letter of John Norvell to S. T. Mason, n.d., Mason MSS, BHC.

threatened the distribution in society of property or power. Political life certainly provided access to both for ambitious or "well situated" men, while political and economic elites appeared to be, and encouraged the belief that they were, relatively open, competitive, and divided in party preferences.

If the Democracy possessed many political entrepreneurs, it also enjoyed status derived from political control of the territorial establishment fashioned with care by Lewis Cass in halcyon Republican days. When Captain Marryat visited Detroit in 1837 he observed that "the society is quite equal to that of the eastern cities"; he met some of the "pleasant people" at the home of Michigan's Democratic governor, Stevens T. Mason. Both Whigs and Democrats often commented in these years on the "respectability, talent, and influence" of many Democratic politicians. On the other hand, Whigs too possessed wealth and status, and seemed more disposed to social snobbery.[46]

Several recent studies of leadership groups in Wayne County permit more systematic assessment of the party preferences of men at the upper levels of economic and political life. These works vary in the rigor of their methods, but all push beyond any impressionistic sample.

An earlier survey of politically active men in the 1840s and 1850s found no significant differences in occupation between Whigs and Democrats. The two groups consisted simply of men listed in newspapers over the years as engaging in party affairs and included both top and secondary leaders. Occupation alone is not a reliable guide to wealth, class, or status, but since Wayne was the most commercially advanced county, obvious divisions among the business class there are significant.[47]

A more recent study of the occupations, wealth, birthplace, religion, age, and length of time in Wayne County of 100 Whig and Democratic leaders in 1844 concluded that leaders could not be distinguished by socioeconomic background. Similar classes provided leaders for both parties. Democratic leaders included some of the wealthiest men in the county, particularly landowners.[48]

[46] Frederick Marryat, *Dairy in America*, ed., Jules Zanger (Bloomington, 1960), 133; Arno L. Bader, ed., "Captain Marryat in Michigan," *Michigan History*, 20 (Spring-Summer 1936), 169; Gen. Jos. W. Brown, Tecumseh, to Lucius Lyon, Feb. 1, 1835, Lyon MSS, William L. Clements Library, Ann Arbor (Hereafter referred to as Clements); Thomas Rowland to Woodbridge, Jan. 14, 1842, Woodbridge MSS.

[47] Fischer, "Personnel of Political Parties," 10. For systematic consideration of the limits of occupation as an indicator of economic mobility, wealth, and income, see Stuart Mack Blumin, "Mobility in a Nineteenth Century American City, Philadelphia, 1820-1860" (unpublished Ph.D. dissertation, University of Pennsylvania, 1968), 60-82.

[48] Lawrence Howard Sabbath, "Analysis of the Political Leadership in Wayne County, Michigan, 1844" (unpublished M.A. thesis, Wayne State University, 1965), 75, 128, 135. On the lack of significant class differences between Whig

Alexandra McCoy's 1965 doctoral dissertation on Wayne County's economic elite in 1844 and 1860 is a carefully controlled investigation which used both wealth and economic role as indicators of class and status. The elite group of 97 in 1844 had a Whig majority: 60 Whigs (62 percent), 5 Libertyites (5 percent), 28 Democrats (29 percent), and 4 unknown. Although the elite preferred Whiggery, no simple economic determinism accounted for this, and surely failed to explain the anti-Whig minority among elite members. McCoy tested several variables and sorted out subgroups (e.g., Democratic landowners) for closer examination.[49]

Economic role had some relation to party choice. Merchants and non-specialized entrepreneurs tended to be predominantly Whigs (87 percent) as did manufacturers (68 percent), while landowners (as with farmers among party leaders) showed a Democratic preference (66 percent). Yet rationally calculated economic interest did not seem to have determined men's choice of party. Party programs offered few clues; men with the same interests preferred different parties. The nonspecialized nature of business enterprise, moreover, made the positing of a fixed "interest" unrealistic for most men.[50]

Ethnocultural and religious group correlations with party preference yielded more suggestive relationships than those for economic role. Yankees were the largest single ethnic group among the elite (47 percent), and 84 percent of all elite Yankees were Whigs. But a minority of Yankees, from New England and New York, made up the largest ethnocultural group within the Democracy—32 percent. Religious affiliation, however, decisively separated Yankees. With one exception "Yankees who were not Democrats were not Presbyterians," while 76 percent of elite Presbyterians were Whigs, and 61 percent of all Whigs were Yankee Presbyterians. This finding was particularly impressive, ac-

---

and Democratic party leaders in Newburyport, Massachusetts, in 1850, see Stephan Thernstrom, *Poverty and Progress: Social Mobility in a Nineteenth Century City* (Cambridge, Mass., 1964), 53. W. Wayne Smith, "Jacksonian Democracy on the Chesapeake: Class, Kinship, and Politics," *Maryland Historical Magazine*, 43 (March 1968), 55-67, also did not find class to be a significant distinction between opposing party elites. For a summary of the literature analyzing party leaderships, Edward Pessen, *Jacksonian America*, 251-54; Pessen properly emphasizes the similarities of party leaderships. A preliminary study of Rochester, New York, party leaders under my direction has found a tendency for Whigs to be both lower and higher in class and status than Democrats; the latter were overwhelmingly middle class while the Whigs tended to be upper class or not quite in the establishment at all, Albert C. E. Parker, "Inter-Party Differences in Rochester, New York, 1834-1843: A Preliminary Study of a Political Elite," unpublished paper, 1969.

[49] McCoy, "Economic Elites, Wayne County, 1844, 1860," 97-98. She discusses her method, 51-52, and criteria of selection, 55-67.

[50] *Ibid.*, 101-20.

cording to McCoy, because "religion presents a much more clear-cut designation than economic role. Many who were merchants or capitalists were also landowners, but no one was a Presbyterian and an Episcopalian simultaneously." In searching for an explanation of the Yankee Presbyterian Whig preference McCoy observed that Presbyterians promoted moral reform to which Whiggery was far more sympathetic than the Democrats. Presbyterians and Whigs alike pursued a kind of "Yankee reformism," but Democrats seemed hostile to such "reformist zeal" —propositions which will be explored in some detail below. McCoy concluded that "opposing party types were characterized by different religious affiliations and economic roles" and that men's political choices depended on complex social conditioning rather than on narrow economic interest; examination of personal and family relationships showed that "class interest among the elite operated in the same way as party loyalties in the community as a whole; class solidarity tended to lessen party cleavage [on elite levels] in the same way that party loyalty among all economic strata blurred class antagonisms."[51]

Whatever small comfort McCoy's data offers to those who would see the Whigs as the party of the rich and special interest groups, it presents further obstacles to the perhaps already impossible view of the Democrats as poor radicals. Yet scholars who developed their economic conflict view of Democrats and Whigs did not create it from nothing. Jacksonian rhetoric, for one thing, provided a powerful stimulus to their model of party conflicts and constituencies. Democrats throughout the country generally trumpeted antiaristocratic and antimonopoly rhetoric to a much greater extent than did the Whigs, using a class conscious vocabulary and terminology borrowed from the true radicals of the day.[52] These rhetorical habits infected Michigan Democrats more so than their Whig opponents. The existence of this verbal militancy, especially in the

[51] *Ibid.*, 160-61, 173-83, 199; also 193-95, 197. Typical of political differences dissolving before the prospect of profit was the launching of the Cass Farm Company in 1835, "one of the largest real estate enterprises" in Detroit's history, formed by Whig and Democratic businessmen. Burton, et al., eds., *Detroit*, I, 341; George E. Catlin, "Oliver Newberry," *Michigan History*, 18 (Winter 1934), 13-14. Charles C. Trowbridge and Lewis Cass enjoyed a close business and personal relationship both before and after Trowbridge ran for governor as a Whig in 1837. Several letters in the Cass MSS, Clements, show this. See, e.g., C. C. Trowbridge to Cass, May 29, 1837, and same to same, Aug. 24, Sept. 6, 1838. Most interesting is the letter in which Trowbridge, formerly a Democratic Republican but not an active politician, first mentioned his candidacy to Cass, who was in Paris. Trowbridge speculated about the coming election, passing it off as if it were a sporting event in which gentlemen and friends happened to find themselves on opposing sides, C. C. Trowbridge to Cass, Aug. 14, 1837, Cass MSS, Clements.

[52] For a sensible assessment of party rhetoric, Pessen, *Jacksonian America*, 224-33. Joseph L. Blau, ed., *Social Theories of Jacksonian Democracy: Representative Writings of the Period, 1825-1850* (New York, 1954), is misleading in conception, but provides examples of the rhetoric from which the Democrats borrowed.

mid-1830s, allowed earlier historians to marshal plausible if superficial evidence for their hypotheses about the class composition of the Democrats and their radicalism.[53] Although the words functioned as a smokescreen for clever, opportunistic men, one still confronts the problem of why Democrats chose to stage the mock drama of their political warfare so heavily against "monopoly" and "aristocracy" while Whigs tended to deplore such rhetoric as socially divisive, unhealthy, and phoney. Subsequent chapters should shed some light on why Whigs employed a more integrative rhetoric.

Democratic political appeals in Michigan do not seem to have differed as much from those of the Whigs as in other areas of the North. The Antimasons contributed to radicalizing political language in Michigan as they did in New York.[54] The Democratic Republicans acquired antimonopoly and egalitarian verbiage from Eastern workingmen's parties and the Antimasons made it fashionable. This style of political declamation peaked in the mid-thirties and then began to pass into rather empty ritual. In 1837 a new Democratic newspaper demonstrated how tame the antiaristocratic strain could become. In its maiden issue the *Detroit Morning Post* proclaimed its solidarity with "workingmen," its opposition to monopolies and to a caste system creating "artificial classes of rich and poor." The *Post*, however, was no rabble-rouser, and insisted that the rights of all be protected, including the rights of property and success. "Because an individual is wealthy, or elevated in office, it does not necessarily follow that he is to be denounced or humbled. . . . Some of the most true, self-sacrificing friends of the [Democratic] cause are to be found among them."[55]

Reexamination of the politicoeconomic issues of the 1830s has failed to discover any Democratic "radicalism" and has shown, rather, a lack of vital differences between the two parties. Crucial distinctions in Whig and Democratic attitudes and style on economic matters may have existed, but not the kind previously alleged. Democrats engaged heavily in entrepreneurial pursuits, but that Democrats were newer capitalists "on the make" in Michigan is yet to be demonstrated.[56] The economic elite in Wayne County was predominantly Whig but not because that party simply reflected its economic interest.

Too little is known about political and economic elites and their rela-

---

[53] For examples see editorials in the *Monroe Times* and *Detroit Free Press*, 1834 to 1836, and Stevens T. Mason's messages, George N. Fuller, ed., *Messages of the Governors of Michigan* (Lansing, 1925), I, 137-38, 140-41, 142.

[54] See Chapter V, and Benson, *Concept*, 9-46.

[55] July 3, 1837.

[56] Ronald P. Formisano, "The Detroit Markets Controversy," *Detroit Historical Society Bulletin*, 25 (December 1968), 4-8.

tion to parties. More studies of the McCoy type are needed.[57] Skeptics may retort that while everything is not known, enough information exists to describe the distribution of power and resources in American society. But why, for example, were Presbyterians so disproportionately numerous among the elite? Could an examination of the Protestant ethic and its relation to certain occupational groups as well as to the successful, tell us more of the world view of these men, their party choices, and their political behavior generally? There are no easy answers. Invoking the "Protestant ethic," for example, does not explain the disproportionate presence of the nonpuritanical Episcopalians among the elite. More knowledge on such questions will give better insight into the causes of party choice and political behavior generally.

MASS VOTING BEHAVIOR

Among the masses significant differences in party preferences for socioeconomic groups are less detectable than among elites. This finding does not seem to have resulted from the state of the available data, but rather from the relative insignificance of class or economic group lines in forming party cleavages. The small Wayne economic elite had a Whig tendency, but the vast middle and lower classes were closely divided in party preference. Given the limited size of the economic elite the Whigs could not have been a major party without the support of thousands of "common men."

In the first party contest in 1835, the Whigs polled from 40 to 49 percent of the vote in several eastern and more populous counties. In 1837, 14,546 men or 49 percent of all Michigan voters chose Whiggery, well before the effects of the depression began to be felt in Michigan. In 1839 and 1840 the Whigs carried the state as more voters turned out (proportionately) than in any other election from 1835 to 1852. In 1840 79 percent of the potential national electorate voted, and 84.9 percent of Michigan's potential electorate swarmed to the polls. Of 44,350 voters in 1840, 51.7 percent went Whig.[58]

The great majority of voters in the 1830s were rural farmers, and many of these were still hacking their way out of the forest. Census data for 1850 taken from several sample counties shows the overwhelming majority of voters to have been middle and lower class, so in 1840 the vast middle range probably stood even lower in the socioeconomic scale.[59]

---

[57] Sociologists and political scientists have provided provocative historical works on some of these problems, e.g., E. Digby Baltzell, *The Protestant Establishment: Aristocracy and Caste in America* (New York, 1964), and Dahl, *Who Governs?*

[58] McCormick, "New Perspectives on Jacksonian Politics," 292.

[59] See Appendix B and below.

Although farmers generally were poorer in 1840, probably more were self-employed than in 1850. Indirect evidence for this comes from the scarcity of labor then. One prosperous new farmer wrote in 1837: "My greatest difficulty is to find men to work for they are nearly all farmers themselves." In the spring of 1837 Charles Trowbridge observed that "the opening of navigation has brought us immense crowds of *old fashioned* emigrants, with their wives and babies and wagons and spinning wheels and a hundred dollars to buy an eight-acre lot for each of the boys." In 1843 a traveler estimated that with "first quality" land selling at $1.25 an acre and with timber nearby it would take $600 "at farthest" to buy the necessaries of farming and "independence."[60] Both before and after hard times began to set in, roughly half of this electorate in 1837, 1838, 1839, and 1840 voted Whig.

Urban and rural differences had no apparent effect on party loyalties. Any inquiry into urban-rural voting patterns, however, must begin by questioning whether the classifications are meaningful for antebellum Michigan. Moreover, many workers and employers in the early or mid-nineteenth century may have been first or second generation migrants from farms. Whether they lost their rural perspectives as rapidly as is often assumed is a moot question. Even long time town dwellers may have remained rooted in economic and social patterns which were pre-industrial, prefactory, and preurban.[61]

Detroit's electorate best approximated urban voting in Michigan, but its population was never large during this period: 6,000 in 1835 and 12,000 in 1845. In 1838 the City of the Straits had 4 banks, 4 foundries, 2 breweries, and several small metal and woodworking factories. Detroiters owned 47 lake vessels and commercial interests led the economy. The port functioned as a jobbing center for merchants in the interior and its industry produced for the hinterland. Before the rise of Chicago the town served as a key center for the general eastward flow of grains and wool and the westward flow of manufactured goods. In 1849 William Candler found Detroit to be "a thriving, manufacturing" city with "shipping of all sorts and descriptions—steam tugs, huge schooners, and

---

[60] Louis Leonard Tucker, ed., "The Correspondence of John Fisher," *Michigan History*, 45 (September 1961), 231. Catherine Stewart, *New Homes in the West* (Nashville, 1843, Ann Arbor, University Microfilms, 1966), 10-11. Hoffman, *Winter in the West*, 112, 128. C. C. Trowbridge to Lewis Cass, May 29, 1837, Cass MSS, Clements.

[61] Recent studies of Philadelphia argue that up to 1860 the pace of the industrial revolution there moved in deliberate stages, with older methods of production persisting as market relationships and the scale of production changed, Blumin, "Mobility in Philadelphia, 1820-1860," 34, 38-39; also Sam Bass Warner, Jr., *The Private City: Philadelphia in Three Periods of Its Growth* (Philadelphia, 1968).

a few square-rigged ships, with here and there a steamer churning white waves in her wake."[62] The 1840 federal census takers counted 1,009 persons engaged in commerce, manufacturing, and the learned professions, accounting for roughly 11 percent of Detroit's population; this was perhaps 30 percent of the potential electorate.[63]

While all this made for an electorate more urban than elsewhere in Michigan, it did not create political subcultures based on occupational groups related to an urban-industrial structure. Mechanics, the group most often mentioned next to farmers in political discourse, do not seem to have possessed a separate political consciousness. Many were self-employed and this type seems to have predominated among the leadership of Detroit's Mechanics' Society, which included prosperous businessmen and professionals. The Whigs regarded the mechanics as loyal to them and in 1843 conspicuously nominated a prominent member of the Mechanics' Society for state representative.[64]

There is only one example, conspicuous by its rarity, suggesting the kind of artisan self-consciousness and occupational group solidarity more common in the East or Europe. In September 1839 a group of journeymen printers lost faith in the goodwill of their employers, the owners of the *Detroit Morning Post* (mentioned earlier). Accordingly, the printers set up a clandestine sheet called the *Rat Gazette*, whose purpose was to report on the unfairness of employers generally, but especially those of the *Post*. The printers claimed that the *Post's* owners, Democrats all, had not paid them for honest work and habitually made money by cheating honest men.[65] Unfortunately this episode was short-lived and it does not seem to have been typical of Detroit.

The city's party vote closely followed the even balance of the state vote, with Whigs winning in 1838, 1839, and 1840, running slightly better there than statewide in the last two years. The Whigs did not carry

[62] Almon E. Parkins, *The Historical Geography of Detroit* (Lansing, 1918), 131-32, 184, 316-17. On emigration in 1826, 1834, 1835, and 1836, see Gordon W. Thayer, ed., "The Great Lakes in *Niles' National Register*," *Inland Seas*, II (Fall 1955), 208; *ibid.*, 14 (Spring 1958), 56-57; *ibid.*, (Summer 1958), 163-64; *ibid.*, 15 (Winter 1959), 313. Burton, ed., *Detroit*, I, 336, 339. Candler letter of July 20, 1849, quoted in Henry E. Candler, *A Century and One: Life Story of William Robert Candler* (New York, London, 1933), 141, 148.

[63] Detroit occupations for 1840 can not be found in the federal census but were printed in the *Free Press*, Dec. 1, 1840; see also George N. Fuller, *Economic and Social Beginnings of Michigan, 1807-1837* (Lansing, 1916), 182, and *Michigan Manual, 1838* (Lansing, 1838).

[64] Julius P. Bolivar MacCabe, *Directory of the City of Detroit, 1837* (Detroit, 1837); *Detroit Directory, 1845*, 109; *Detroit Advertiser*, Oct. 4, 1843, Nov. 4, 1845.

[65] (Detroit) *Rat Gazette*, Sept. 1839, BHC. This may have been the only issue ever published.

Detroit again in state or federal elections during the next 12 years. Still, Whiggery retained a sizable part of Detroit's vote in Presidential contests.

TABLE III.1
Party Percentage Strength, Detroit, 1837–1852

Year	Office	Total Vote	Dem.	Whig	Liberty
1837	Gov.	1,645	51.0	48.7	0.3[a]
1838	Cong.	1,497	49.7	50.2	—
1839	Gov.	1,588	48.7	51.3	—
1840	Pres.	1,484	46.9	52.3	0.8
1841	Gov.	1,169	59.2	37.4	3.4
1842	St. Sen.	1,206	56.1	40.9	3.0
1843	Gov.	1,340	51.4	47.2	1.4
1844	Pres.	1,932	50.3	47.8	1.9
1845	Gov.	1,411	51.2	45.0	3.8
1846	Cong.	1,716	56.7	42.7	0.6
1847	Gov.	1,542	56.6	41.2	2.2
1848	Pres.	2,663	51.5	45.4	3.1
1849	Gov.	1,792	60.2	39.8	—
1850	Cong.	2,614	55.6	44.4	—
1851	Gov.	2,228	68.9	31.1	—
1852	Pres.	4,428	54.8	41.1	4.1

[a] Independent Democrat

There were other large towns in Michigan, such as Pontiac, Jackson, and Grand Rapids, but election returns for them in the 1830s and 1840s are either incomplete or usually available as aggregate returns for the particular village and its surrounding rural township, a condition which theoretically as well as practically argues against attaching too much significance to any discoverable town-country voting differences.

It was possible to grade townships within particular counties according to the relative degree of "urbanness" in 1837-40 by using data in the 1840 United States census, the far more complete data in Blois's *Gazetteer of Michigan, 1837*, and information from county and township histories. This process, crudely though exhaustively pursued, revealed no relationship between level of development and party strength.[66] The 1850 federal census manuscript of population schedules provided a more precise measurement in the descriptions of occupations of individuals. Every potential voter went into two major occupational divisions, "farm" and "urban," and the percentage of each provided a relative measure of rural or urban voters. These data were assembled by township for six counties (Wayne, Eaton, Ingham, Kalamazoo, Barry, St. Joseph), selected because they spanned the settled part of the state

[66] An exhaustive study of Wayne County is reported in Formisano, "Social Bases of Voting: Wayne County, 1837-1852," 126-28, 461.

from east to west in 1850. A seventh group of towns included the "banner" party units (top Democratic and anti-Democratic units) in the counties of Washtenaw, Oakland, and Hillsdale. The great majority of the townships were, of course, overwhelmingly rural; 97 were 60 percent rural or more. There was great variation of party strength among them. In 10 of the entire 107 townships considered, 40 percent or more of the potential voters pursued nonfarm occupations. Four of these units had strong Democratic party percentages, 3 had anti-Democratic means, and 3 did not have strong party characters, as Table III.2 shows. Further, the coefficients of correlation between rural and Democratic Party strength in the townships in every county but one were low and insignificant (Table III.3).

TABLE III.2

"Urban" Towns and Democratic Mean in 6 Michigan Counties, 1850

Township	County	Percent Urban	Percent Democrat
Lansing	Ingham	79.9	62.0
Springwells	Wayne	68.0	53.0
Hastings	Barry	60.0	65.0
Constantine	St. Joseph	56.0	52.0
Monguagon	Wayne	51.0	60.0
Plymouth	Wayne	49.0	38.0
Hamtramck	Wayne	48.0	70.0
Sturgis	St. Joseph	46.0	38.0
Lockport	St. Joseph	44.0	49.0
Milford	Oakland	43.0	38.0

Within the basic categories of farm and urban were 17 subgroups, (8 farm and 9 urban) used here as an occupational status scale. Potential voters in townships were ranked on the scale according to the description of their occupation and the amount of real estate they owned.[67]

[67] The farm owner categories are not completely arbitrary, but are not based on statistical procedures. However, they were decided upon after several trial runs of townships were made classifying farm owners by property; e.g., the $1,000 and $3,000 figures were common and obviously popular ways of classifying a farm in round figures.

Farm

1. Laborers
2. Tenants, renters
3. Farmers with land $ 500 or less
4. " " " $ 501-$1,000
5. " " " $ 1,001-$3,000
6. " " " $ 3,001-$5,000
7. " " " $ 5,001-$9,999
8. " " " $10,000 and up

Urban

1. Unskilled
2. Semiskilled
3. Skilled
4. Service
5. Sales
6. Clerical
7. Managers, officials
8. Professionals
9. Proprietors

The Rural Lower Classes might have included individuals from several of these groups, but after experimenting with various combinations and taking into account other evidence it was decided that the bottom 3 farm groups (1-3), and the bottom 2 urban (unskilled, semiskilled), best represented the rural lower classes (RLC). When the towns of the 6 counties and the banner units are ranked by their Democratic mean percentages, 1848-52, and rural lower class percentages listed in a parallel column, simple observations suggest no relationship between the two variables. The Pearson correlation coefficients for Democratic means and rural lower class percentages and Democratic means and rural percentages are also, with one exception, all low and insignificant (Table III.3).

TABLE III.3
Democratic Mean, 1848–1852, in 6 Michigan Counties and
Banner Units Correlated with Rural Lower Classes and Ruralness, 1850

	Rural Lower Classes	Rural
Wayne	.158	.332
Ingham	.200	.724
Eaton	.316	.261
Barry	.207	.239
Kalamazoo	.165	−.121
St. Joseph	−.210	−.083
Banner units	.212	*(not computed)

One of the ten commandments of American history, pervading even the most divergent schools of interpretation, has been that small, independent farmers constituted the backbone of the Democratic Party, virtually anytime, anywhere. Countless textbooks and secondary works have made such an assertion particularly for the antebellum period. But in Michigan small independent farmers showed no consistent attachment to the Democrats—in many rural areas they voted heavily anti-Democratic.

In southwestern Wayne County where the Huron River, as Charles Hoffman described it in 1833, "waddles onto the lake, as little excited by the flocks of ducks which frolic on its bosom, as an alderman after dinner by the flies that disport upon his jerkin,"[68] lay 3 townships where farm owners with farms worth $1,000 or less constituted the great majority of potential voters: 76 percent in Sumpter, 71 in Taylor, and 67 in Romulus. The 3 had similar socioeconomic structures; none had many farm laborers or tenants. Since no large farms were present, men who owned farms worth under $500 were probably not tenants, as was the possibility in other towns with large farms where small property own-

[68] Hoffman, *Winter in the West,* 126.

ers may have worked their land and someone else's as well. No man in the 3 towns owned a farm worth over $3,000. Sumpter had a Whig-Free Soil mean (1848-52) of 53 percent; Taylor was the strongest Whig township in the county with a 63 percent straight Whig mean; and Romulus had a Democratic mean of 60 percent.

The phenomenon of small farmers dividing between the parties was not confined to southern Wayne County. Searching through the other 6 counties and banner units 27 townships (in Ingham, Barry, and Eaton) could be found in which farmers owning farms worth $1,000 or less constituted 60 percent or more of the potential voters. Eleven of these units had Democratic means of over 55 percent, 9 of 45 to 55 percent, and 7 less than 45 percent. Thirteen had Democratic mean percentages of 50 or less. Clearly, a great many small farmers throughout Michigan, probably just under half at the least, voted anti-Democratic.

For a long time the frontier has been regarded as the special breeding ground of Jacksonian Democrats, but frontier areas throughout Michigan obviously produced wide variations in party loyalty. Most of the farm communities discussed above were just beginning to move out of the frontier stage and subsistence farming, and were increasingly tied into a market economy. These units were not the raw frontier but were not far removed from it. Even Wayne County in many areas in the late 1830s still received many pioneers.[69] Farmers worth under $1,000 were not necessarily lazier, or inefficient, or unproductive compared to other farmers, nor did they necessarily occupy poor lands. In 1850 they tended to be men whose farms had been more recently settled. (See Appendix B.)

The data thus far have been marshalled to establish a negative point: disproportionate voting support for the Democrats from the lower classes did not exist. For example, the problem can be seen in microcosm in three Wayne County units: Livonia, Plymouth, and Canton. These townships were the 3 richest in the county, no matter what measure of prosperity was used. They lay side by side where the flat land west of Detroit begins to roll and look greener. All 3 had comparatively large proportions of middle-class farmers, and Plymouth had large groups of skilled workers. Farmers with farms worth over $3,000, rare elsewhere, constituted 9 percent of Canton's potential voters, 8 percent of Livonia's, and 17 percent of Plymouth's. Except for the skilled workers in Plymouth, the towns bore a striking resemblance to one another in socioeconomic character. According to the traditional model of interpretation all 3 of these towns should have voted anti-Democratic. Plymouth and Livonia obliged, with Democratic means (1848-52) of 39 and 38 percent. Canton, however, was one of the Democracy's strongholds in Wayne with a

---

[69] Nowlin, *The Bark Covered House*, 29-46.

64 percent party mean. Could it have been possible, although Canton gave a consistent Democratic majority, that most of its prosperous farmers voted anti-Democratic with the Democratic vote consisting of an unbroken array of the lower classes plus a small portion of the upper occupations? Given the data presented so far this was possible though unlikely. It was not the case. Newspapers and county records provided the names of Democratic party leaders and activists and township officers. The schedules of the 1850 census gave their real property ownership. All of those investigated owned farms worth $1,000 or more, usually more. Archibald Y. Murray, a Democratic county leader and Supervisor of Canton in 1836, 1837, 1841, 1844, and 1852, owned more real estate than any other man there in 1850: $18,750. More typical was David D. Cady, Supervisor in 1846, 1853, 1854, and 1855, who owned real estate valued at $4,800. These men were among the original settlers of the town, like the Kinyons, Stevens, and Andrews families, who were also Democrats. They came mostly from New York state in the 1820s and 1830s, prospered quickly, and were staunch Democrats.[70] Thus, the question arises as to why the prosperous farmers of Canton, unlike their neighbors in Livonia and Plymouth, voted Democratic.

To this point only socioeconomic variables have been considered. But what of religious, ethnocultural, or other kinds of variables of potential relevance to party cleavages? Other data are available, though hardly complete. What is quantifiable is limited, but when 2 noneconomic variables are correlated with Democratic percentages in the 6 selected counties and banner units, the results (Table III.4) show an inconsistent relationship between Democratic voting and the foreign born, and quite insistently argue for a negative relationship between Yankee background and Democratic voting.[71]

---

[70] *United States Census of State of Michigan, 1850, Population Schedule,* microfilm. Party delegates listed in *Free Press,* Nov. 1, 1836, Oct. 14, 1837, June 16, 1840. Town officials in Farmer, *Detroit,* II, 1255-57.

[71] A final test of this data was made using multiple regression analysis, measuring the effect on the Democratic voting percentage of 7 variables in all 95 townships of the 6 sample counties considered together. The 7 variables were the percentages of potential voters who were (1) Yankee or New England born, (2) foreign born, (3) urban, (4) mid-Atlantic states born (not New York), (5) New British, (6) farm laborers and tenants, and (7) rural lower classes. It was possible to determine the relationship of each variable to changes of Democratic percentages; both logarithmic and arithmetic measures were obtained. However, the primary goal was conceived of simply as measuring the relative strength of correlation of each variable with the Democratic percentage within the universe of 95 townships. Partial and simple correlation coefficients show that 2 of the ethnocultural variables, Yankees and foreign born, were correlated significantly with Democratic strength. The only impressive finding again emerged as the negative association between Yankees and Democrats. For providing indispensable help in making this analysis I am indebted to Professors Robert W. Fogel and Stanley L. Engerman, and to the University of Rochester Computer Center.

TABLE III.4

Democratic Means, 1848–1852, Correlated with Percent of Foreign Born
and Yankees in 6 Michigan Counties and Banner Units, 1850

	Foreign Born	Yankees
Wayne	.561	−.422
Ingham	.490	−.621
Eaton	−.318	−.318
Barry	−.069	−.349
Kalamazoo	.386	.018
St. Joseph	−.052	−.388
Banner units	.195	−.534

Socioeconomic differences did not significantly affect party divisions
in the electorate. Both masses and elites agreed on the basics of political
economy. Parties quarreled over how to manage the economy and the
role of the state in it, but they were quite opportunist and internally divided on such affairs. The parties' mass supporters tended to follow the
positions on economic issues marked out by national and state leaderships. The electorate took its partisan passions seriously, but these did
not originate in class antagonism and much less in different views of
political economy. As to the latter, Whigs and Democrats did possess
diverging ideologies which must be seen in the broader context of their
antipathetic world views of man and society.

Ethnocultural and other social cleavages may have had a strong
impact on party loyalties, as seems very likely with Yankee ethnicity.
The findings for elites and masses at this point encourage exploration of
ethno-religious variables. The presence of sharp ethnic and religious conflict, like intense party competition, cut vertically through class groups
and inhibited class resentments.[72] Whatever the cohesion of the upper
classes beyond party disputes, the lower classes were sharply divided.
Mass politics did not raise any threat to the political-economic order, and
the kinds of cleavages underlying mass party loyalties probably insulated
the social order from any serious challenge, let alone abrupt change.

[72] A recent study of temperance, sabbatarianism, and other moral reformisms
in early nineteenth-century England concluded that these movements should be
interpreted in terms of "culture-conflict," which blurred class conflict: "England
was thus 'sewn together by its inner conflicts.'" Brian Harrison, "Religion and
Recreation in Nineteenth-Century England," *Past and Present*, 38 (December
1967), 98-125.

IV

Party, Antiparty, and Political Character

> Don't be too fastidious, when party is strong almost anything
> that is done is right.—William L. Marcy, 1830[1]

> If parties in a republic are necessary to secure a degree of
> vigilance to keep public functionaries within the bounds of
> law and duty, at that point their usefulness ends. Beyond
> that they become destructive of the public virtue.
> —William Henry Harrison, Inaugural, 1841

The cultural and social dimensions of the emergence of mass parties
are only beginning to be understood. Institutional changes related to
politics have attracted able examination,[2] but what happened in society
as groups and subcultures massively identified their hopes and fears for
self and government with the new organizations? How did parties become reference groups in the 1830s? What value conflicts, generated by
which existing lines of social cleavage, infused party contests in the
electorate? To answer these questions one begins not with the inevitable
identification of voting patterns, but with a description of how Whigs and
Democrats responded to *party*, that is, to party and organization as such.

In the 1830s political leaders and their personnel built modern, mass
parties, bringing a new phenomenon into American life and the necessity
of adjusting to it by all who would participate in politics. Not all did so
happily. Hostility against division and faction in American society had
been habitual, especially in New England's Puritan derived culture, and
the stigma of divisiveness attached to the foreshadowings of party in the
1790s. George Washington's farewell warning against the baneful effects
of party spirit was only one of many manifestations of antipartyism to
accompany primitive Republican and Federalist organizing. Researchers
have not appreciated, however, the persistence of antiparty and its

---

[1] Quoted in Alvin Kass, *Politics in New York State, 1800-1830* (Syracuse
1965), 29.

[2] For example: Richard P. McCormick, *The Second American Party System*
(Chapel Hill, 1966); Roy Nichols, *The Invention of the American Political Parties* (New York, 1967). An excellent study which develops some ideas parallel to
those here is Richard Hofstadter, *The Idea of a Party System: The Rise of Legitimate Opposition in the United States, 1780-1840* (Berkeley, Los Angeles, 1969).

impact on party formation in the 1830s, especially on Whigs. The very idea of "party" still symbolized something which many disliked almost instinctively.[3]

Wherever a competitive, two-party system took hold by 1840, party loyalty assumed a major role in the behavior of political activists, legislators, and administrators, and above all among the mass electorate. Most voters identified with a party and the ethos of party loyalty assumed so vast a behavioral impact as to constitute a qualitative change in our political patterns. In Northern states Whigs usually completed their organization after Democrats; their constituencies often were less stable, less reliable. The Democrats, we have been told, were excellent politicians. The Whigs, by comparison, have looked like bumblers, self-defeaters. Actually, impressionistic evidence on Whig parties throughout the North reveals many symptoms of Whig antipartyism: lack of organizational ability, poor discipline, and chronic factionalism.[4] This was no accidental phenomenon. Rather, it gives us clues to essential differences in the political characters and social origins of Whigs and Democrats.[5]

In Michigan antiparty feelings help explain why, after 1840, Whigs became the minority party, especially in nonpresidential years. It ac-

---

[3] Key, *Public Opinion*, defines a reference symbol, 63. On antiparty in eighteenth-century England see Caroline Robbins, " 'Discordant Parties': A Study of Acceptance of Party by Englishmen," *Political Science Quarterly*, 73 (December 1958), 508-59; in eighteenth-century America, Bernard Bailyn, *The Origins of American Politics* (New York, 1968).

[4] Nichols, *Invention of American Political Parties*, 321. Robert V. Remini, *The Election of Andrew Jackson* (Philadelphia, 1963), 94, 181-204. McCormick, *Second American Party System*, 266, 322, 324. James Staton Chase, "The Emergence of the National Nominating Convention" (unpublished Ph.D. dissertation, University of Chicago, 1962), 362. E. Malcolm Carroll, *Origins of the Whig Party* (Durham, 1925), 173-74. State and regional studies include: Henry R. Mueller, "The Whig Party in Pennsylvania," *Columbia Studies in History, Economics, and Public Law*, 101: 2 (New York, 1922), 36-38. John Julius Reed, "The Emergence of the Whig Party in the North: Massachusetts, New York, Pennsylvania, and Ohio" (unpublished Ph.D. dissertation, University of Pennsylvania, 1953), 33, 142, 348, 376; David M. Ludlum, *Social Ferment in Vermont, 1791-1850* (New York, 1939), 118, 126, 130-32. Charles M. Thompson, *The Illinois Whigs Before 1846* (Urbana, 1915), 42-43. Adam A. Leonard, "Personal Politics in Indiana, 1816 to 1840," *Indiana Magazine of History*, 19 (1923), 153, 154, 266, 269; R. C. Buley, *The Old Northwest: Pioneer Period 1815-1850* (Indianapolis, 1950), II, 187-88; Martin B. Duberman, *Charles Francis Adams, 1807-1886* (Boston, 1961), 48, 56, 65; a recent history of a state Whig party begins with a chapter on "Tardy Whiggery," John Volmer Meering, *The Whigs of Missouri* (Columbus, 1967), 1-27.

[5] For a more extended treatment of the concept of political character see my "Political Character, Antipartyism, and the Second Party System," *American Quarterly*, 21 (Winter 1969), 685-88. The following works among others have been quite helpful: M. Brewster Smith, Jerome S. Bruner, and Robert W. White, *Opinions and Personality* (New York, 1956); Edelman, *Symbolic Uses of Politics*; Lane, *Political Ideology*; and Herbert McCloskey, "Conservatism and Personality," *American Political Science Review*, 52 (1958), 27-45. See also works listed in Chapter I, note 9.

counts in part for the greater tendency of Whigs not to vote and to be more vulnerable to the appeal of a moralistic third party. Both parties, of course, included a great variety of men, but in each a certain type predominated or clustered. Many Democrats give the impression of being manipulative types, men with a proclivity for organization. Although Jacksonian Democrats professed a passion for laissez faire in government and society, they combined this with a pragmatic ability to submit to organization, to an authority which functioned at least as much by oligarchic as by majority rule.

The prevalence of Yankee Protestantism and pietism in Michigan Whiggery, to be discussed at length in later chapters, accounts for Whigs having a disproportionate share of antiparty men. Whig antipartyism drew sustenance from the evangelical, moral reform, benevolent, and Christianizing strains lacing Whiggery in Michigan—as in other Northern areas. Men who had a strong devotional tendency, who devalued institutional commitments, in religion or elsewhere, did not have organizational malleability. As party builders they floundered because they could not easily compromise—a trait that is necessary to the maintenance of broad-based political coalitions. They tended to follow an ethic of ultimate rather than of political responsibility.[6]

"Wire-pullers" certainly existed in Whig ranks. Indeed, in both parties men could be found who could organize yet who constantly expressed hatred for "dirty politics," bargaining, and compromise. The coexistence of these strains reflected a tension present in Yankee Protestant culture from the beginning: between liberty and authority, conscience and power. This kind of tension seems to be higher in some historical periods than others, especially during times when society is ordering, organizing, and reorganizing. After the War of 1812, Americans went on something of an organizational spree which displayed an increased national consciousness induced by war experiences, improved transportation and communication, and rising immigration and urbanization. Parties, as Roy Nichols and others have observed, were the organizational counterparts of the corporation in business. But the new responses in politics ran into opposition from men who saw party as a threat to their individuality and autonomy.

Puzzles of the Party System

As the Democratic and Whig parties became reference groups for different political subcultures in Michigan, large numbers of men participated in parties and in voting as political language, actions, and goals

[6] Max Weber, "Politics As a Vocation," H. H. Gerth and C. Wright Mills, eds., *From Max Weber: Essays in Sociology* (New York, 1958), 115.

were invested with symbolic meanings. This was a gradual process, as was party organization. Historians sometimes get confused about whether organization caused voter participation or vice versa, missing the point that both are interdependent. Preceding were general causes of political differentiation and interest, operating through society and making parties "emotionally significant reference groups" for most of the electorate.[7]

Voter participation in Michigan was low until 1837 when it began to boom toward the 84 percent plus outpouring of adult white males in 1840. Both parties ran very close races from 1837 to 1840, but after 1840 a different pattern emerged. McCormick has observed that after 1836 "in most states Whigs put forth their best efforts and made their strongest showings in the presidential contests."[8] (See Table II.1)

In 1841 the Whig total fell from almost 23,000 in 1840 to 15,449. Many short-run influences were at work in 1841 to help reduce the Whig vote: apathy produced by Harrison's death and Tyler's apostasy; feuds in the state party; failure of the Bank of Michigan which the Whigs had made the state's bank of deposit; and cross-pressures created by the presence of the Liberty Party, inducing more Whigs than Democrats to withdraw from a choice. Yet this pattern was repeated after large turnouts in 1844 and 1848. Something more was involved. Surveying Whig defeats in Wayne County in 1841 and 1842 the Whig *Detroit Advertiser* said it was impossible to rally Whigs unless for a national contest. Groping for an explanation the editor blamed Tyler for Whig apathy: "So strong is their sense of treachery, and so deep their resentment, that many of them utterly refuse to take any further part in political action." In 1843 also "the Whigs . . . staid [sic] at home." And anticipating a low turnout in 1845, the paper noted that "the Whigs are usually the largest losers at such times." In 1847 the Grand Rapids *Grand River Eagle*

[7] An example of confusion on this point in an otherwise excellent article is provided in Richard P. McCormick, "New Perspectives on Jacksonian Politics," *American Historical Review*, 65 (January 1960), 300, 301. On organization and participation, Daniel Katz and Samuel J. Eldersveld, "The Impact of Local Party Activity Upon the Electorate," *Public Opinion Quarterly*, 25 (Spring 1961), 1-24. See also Chambers and Burnham, eds., *The American Party Systems*, esp. Frank J. Sorauf, "Political Parties and Political Analysis," 33-55.

[8] McCormick, *Second Party System*, 326. While explaining lower Whig turnout is of concern here, the problem might also be conceived in terms of explaining *higher Democratic turnout*. Organization and social causes probably both contributed. Michigan's Democratic Party had a much greater number of ethnic voters in its ranks than Whiggery. According to Robert Lane, "the seat of ethnic politics is the local community." Jobs, protection, and public service have customarily been distributed "in some relation to the voting strength of the various regional, national and religious groups in the community." This helps explain why "the difference in turn-out between local and national elections is almost always substantial for non-ethnics, but is usually much smaller for ethnic groups." *Political Life*, 239.

lamented the same phenomenon.⁹ The implication seemed to be that there was something about the character of Whigs that helped account for this behavior.

Antipartyism best describes this Whig trait, as it helps to explain the halting development of parties. Many causes made party organization a difficult, gradual undertaking. Communication problems alone were enormous in a frontier state. Yet something deeper caused the hostility to parties per se and made a Democratic organizer worry about "the wavering" and "non-commital, of whom (God grant) we may have but a few hereafter." When party divisions began to determine township elections, Democratic organizers rejoiced as much at the electorate aligning itself by party as they did at victories.¹⁰ After the first Democratic-Whig contest in the April 1835 election the Whigs disappeared for two years. Then, from 1837 to 1840 party lines again extended throughout the state and into all manner of elections. Many reactions to this process were at least ambivalent, if not hostile. Many pioneer reminiscences recall the first party contest in their township or village and exhibit unconscious pride in the resistance their communities showed to party divisions.¹¹

ANTIMASONRY'S CONTRIBUTIONS

Our understanding of antiparty in the age of egalitarianism begins with an analysis of the "Blessed Spirit," Antimasonry. Evangelical Protestantism's aversion to Masonry had much in common with its hostility to party organization. In fact, the structure of evangelical antipathies to Masonry, party, Popery, and Democracy, paralleled and overlapped. Evangelicals saw all these institutions as threats to the freedom of conscience of their members.

If the Antimasons did not hate parties for the same reasons that they hated Masonry, they certainly transferred much of the rhetoric they used in damning the one to damn the other. Parties, like Masonry, set up cen-

⁹ Nov. 14, 1842, Nov. 16, 1843, Nov. 5, 1845, Nov. 4, 1847; Marshall, *Western Statesman*, Oct. 28, 1841; Jackson, *American Citizen*, Nov. 5, 1851, film, Jackson Public Library.

¹⁰ George R. Palmer, Detroit, to Hon. L. Lyon, Dec. 1, 1834; E. Winslow, Detroit, to Lyon, Jan. 10, 1835; John McDonell, Detroit, to Lyon, Feb. 14, 1835, all in Lucius Lyon MSS, Clements. Monroe, *Michigan Sentinel*, March 7, 1835, film, MSL.

¹¹ A.D.P. Van Buren, "Michigan in Her Pioneer Politics," *MHC*, 17: 240-41. Enos Goodrich, "Early Atlas—A Pioneer Sketch," *ibid.*, 414. *History of Washtenaw County, Michigan* (Chicago, 1881), II, 244-45. *History of Kalamazoo County, Michigan* (Philadelphia, 1880), 363-64. In Mackinac County party lines were not "drawn tight" until 1839, Reuben D. Turner to Ross Wilkins, May 26, 1840, Ross Wilkins MSS, BHC. Wood, *History of Genesee County*, I, 211-12.

tralized organs of authority which thought and judged for the individual. They demanded allegiance necessitating the harnessing of free judgment, and, if need be, the violation of conscience. Within the framework of secular politics, Antimasonry can be seen as a populist form of the Antinomian spirit in politics.

The movement embodied, too, the evangelical impulse to Christianize America, that ubiquitous energy radiated by New England Protestantism to create the moral, homogeneous, commonwealth. Coming into being at the beginning of the period during which parties acquired power, Antimasonry ironically emitted perhaps the strongest feeling of antiparty of any political movement in the United States. It was, in a sense, an antiparty party! Yet one which unintentionally acted as a catalyst in establishing the second party system.

There is a strong continuity from evangelical pressure groups, to Antimasonry, to Whiggery in Michigan. Most Michigan evangelicals aligned first with Antimasonry and after its demise moved into Whiggery. Editors of Michigan's two Antimasonic newspapers, the *Detroit Courier* and Ann Arbor, *Western Emigrant*, became Whigs, and their papers unfurled the Whig banner under different names. In 1833 the *Courier* listed 28 Wayne County Antimasonic leaders from different towns who served on committees of correspondence. Checking on their later party affiliation in 1835-37, 18 of the 28 could be identified: 17 had become Whigs, 1, a Democrat.[12]

Though he had not been an Antimason, the Whigs' 1839 candidate for governor had accepted an Antimasonic nomination for office in 1833. The Whig candidate in 1841, however, Philo C. Fuller, had been a "whole hog" Antimasonic leader in western New York before coming to Michigan.[13] Shifting county and township boundaries, a fast growing population and electorate, and lack of election returns make generalizing about rank and file Antimasonic voters too speculative. But the two towns in Wayne County giving the most votes, in number and percent, to the Antimasons in 1833 were Whig strongholds later in the 1830s. A cluster of eastern Michigan townships near the juncture of Wayne, Oak-

---

[12] Antimasonic list: *Detroit Courier*, April 10, 1833. Whig lists: *Detroit Journal and Courier*, Jan. 21, Feb. 13, March 5, 1835; *Detroit Advertiser*, Oct. 25, 1836. Democratic lists: *Detroit Free Press*, Aug. 21, Oct. 19, Nov. 1, 1836, and July 25, Aug. 14, Sept. 20, Oct. 11, 12, and Nov. 6, 1837. Also Ann Arbor, *Western Emigrant*, March 16, 1831, film, MSL, listed 58 delegates to the Antimasonic Territorial Convention, many of whom later became Whigs and none of whom, so far as I knew, became Democrats.

[13] *Free Press*, Oct. 1, 1841. Harriet A. Weed, ed., *The Autobiography of Thurlow Weed* (Boston, 1883), I, 347-48. Also, Ann Arbor, *Michigan Argus*, March 12, April 2, 1835, MHCol. Men who became both Whigs and Democrats at first opposed Antimasonry for violating "peace and good order," *Monroe Michigan Sentinel*, Feb. 21, 1829, film, MSL. Many, however, later professed some kind of Antimasonry.

land, and Washtenaw counties, constituted a miniature "Burned-Over District" where Antimasonry, antislavery, temperance, and revival activity flourished, and where the anti-Democratic vote was later high.[14]

One reason Antimasons were less likely to become Democrats was that, as elsewhere, Masons and Democrats seemed to be allies. Lewis Cass, Michigan's foremost Democrat, had been a Mason since 1816 and first Grand Master of the state lodge formed in 1827. Lucius Lyon, Democratic Republican candidate for Territorial Delegate in 1833, support of whom the Democrats made a test of party loyalty, was also a Mason. He refused to answer Antimasonic demands to repudiate the order.[15]

The complexity of Antimasonry cannot be denied, nor can the centrality of its evangelical drive. Historians have usually recognized the movement's complexity, if not their own bafflement. Antimasonry called for Masonry's destruction because it was secret, aristocratic, unrepublican, privileged, infidel, and immoral. Behind these charges, historians have seen many motives and causes: class resentments, status anxiety, country-city antagonism, denominational rivalries, paranoia, hopes for a better life, and anger at misfortune and failure. They have also emphasized how anti-Jackson politicians moved in quickly to give this uprising of true believers some very opportunistic twists and turns.[16] Yet in Antimasonry's early stages, a religious dynamic provided most of its drive. The movement originated, after all, in western New York's "Burned-Over District," the most preached to, proselytized, revived, and reformed area in all of Yankee Christendom.[17]

[14] *Courier*, July 10, 1833. The vote of several townships is in the *Emigrant*, July 31, 1831. See Chapter VIII.

[15] Lou B. Winsor, "Masonry in Michigan," *Michigan History*, 20 (Autumn 1936), 287-89. *Emigrant*, March 6, 1833. The *Emigrant*'s successor, the *Michigan Whig*, claimed in 1835 that Washtenaw's Whig candidates for constitutional delegates had been Antimasons and that most of the Democrats had been Masons, April 2.

[16] Charles McCarthy, "The Anti-Masonic Party," *Annual Report of the American Historical Association, 1902*, I (Washington, 1903). Dixon Ryan Fox, *The Decline of Aristocracy in the Politics of New York, 1801-1849* (New York, 1919), 337-51. Whitney R. Cross, *The Burned-over District* (Ithaca, 1950), 113-25. Weed, ed., *Thurlow Weed*, I, 210-354.

[17] Cross, *Burned-over District*, 117. McCarthy, *Anti-Masonic Party*, 540-41. Chase, "Emergence of National Nominating Convention," 195-98. Leslie A. Griffen, "The Anti-Masonic Persuasion" (unpublished Ph.D. dissertation, Cornell University, 1951), 174-80, 186-93, 198, 206-07, 209-10, 212-13 and 332-54. Other studies emphasizing Antimasonry's moral religious roots: Ludlum, *Social Ferment in Vermont*, 102-07; Arthur Loyd Collins, "The Anti-Masonic Movement in Early Missouri," *Missouri Historical Review*, 39 (October 1944), 45-46; J. Cutler Andrews, "The Anti-Masonic Movement in Western Pennsylvania," *Western Pennsylvania Historical Magazine*, 18 (December 1935), 255-56; Duberman, *Charles Francis Adams*, 46, 47.

As New York emigrants poured into Michigan in the 1820s, Antimasonry lost little time in spreading there.[18] Antimasons in Michigan as in New York seem to have promoted themselves as well as morality. Antimasonic leaders in Detroit headed benevolent and reform societies and promoted railroads, banks, and land companies. A leading Antimason developed the town of Ann Arbor and other enterprises. New York and Michigan Antimasons shared not only a concern for the mundane, but both also showed themselves capable of political pragmatism. From the beginning of its career in Michigan, Antimasonry was accused of opportunism. Gradually, the charge became true as the crusaders bent their zeal to a desire to win by nominating popular candidates who were not whole-hog Antimasons.[19]

Michigan Antimasonry impresses one most, however, with its evangelical and moralizing style. The Antimasonic *Detroit Courier* and Ann Arbor, *Western Emigrant* were essentially moral reform journals. Many Antimasonic leaders staffed the interlocking directorate of Christian benevolence. Henry R. Schoolcraft, a Democrat, caught the quasi-messianic cast of Antimasonry when he wrote that it was a "kind of 'shibboleth' for those who are to cross the political 'fords' of a new Jordan."[20] At their first territorial convention, at Farmington, January 1, 1829, Antimasons declared that Masonry was a "perpetual conspiracy against morality, Christianity, and republicanism." Their "Address" recited a typical litany of Masonic evil-doing and ended with praise for those recusant Masons who had "come out and washed themselves from the pollution" and who had "confessed their sins and the sins of that society; they have made atonement to the community."[21]

Antimasons hammered away incessantly at themes tied to the anti-Democratic nature of Masonry. But Antimasons also recognized, at least implicitly, that Masonry threatened Protestantism by serving many persons "in place of a church, to the exclusion of Christianity." Thus Antimasons exhorted that "no man can perform the duties of a

[18] Even fugitive Masons joined the trek, Jackson, *American Citizen*, July 11, 1855, film, Jackson Public Library.

[19] Benson, *Concept*, 14-27. *Courier*, Nov. 13, 27, 1833. Russell E. Bidlack, *John Allen and the Founding of Ann Arbor* MHCol, *Bulletin*, 12 (1962). *Michigan Sentinel*, May 23, 1829. Philo C. Fuller to H. Howard, July 3, 1837, Department of Treasury Papers, Letters 1836-1862, MHCom, shows Fuller's interest in the Erie and Kalamazoo Railroad Company of 1836.

[20] Henry R. Schoolcraft, *Personal Memoirs* (Philadelphia, 1851), 324. The entry quoted was written about 1830. Many Antimasons in Washtenaw County supported temperance, a favorite evangelical cause, *Emigrant*, Jan. 1, 20, 1830, April 27, 1831. I have seen two privately owned copies of what was probably Michigan's first temperance newspaper, the *Michigan Temperance Recorder*, published in the thirties. A descendant of the editor said that his ancestor was a lifelong Antimason.

[21] *Michigan Sentinel*, Jan. 10, 24, and Feb. 21, 1829.

mason and of a Christian."[22] They saw the order as an anti-Christian heresy, a delusion which gripped men's minds and hearts. For the evangelical, God's good grace should be in the heart. Masonry ensnared men by secrecy, ritual, oaths, regalia, magical devices, and dogma. Hence, the great fanfare given seceding Masons, similar to the rejoicing that had always greeted religious conversions—each one a soul saved, each one evidence of God's hand. Long after the excitement subsided a Baptist leader still bent on exposing "the pretended religious character" of Masonry said that though a Christian owed his "first and special attention to the 'household of faith' " Masonry reversed this and required its members to give their allegiance to "worthy brother[s]. *The brother that takes this oath of allegiance virtually renounces his allegiance to Christ.*" (Italics mine)[23]

Although the Antimasons failed to elect their candidates for Territorial Delegates, they helped stimulate changes in political organization and rhetoric. In 1831 the Antimasons ran against the regular Republicans, who, the Antimasons charged, were "loaded with Masons," and against a splinter group of "Democratic Republicans," who claimed to represent true Jacksonianism as well as the "Workingmen's Party" and even boasted of being "antimasonic." The regulars won the three-way race, but the Democratic Republicans, with their eclectic, pragmatic approach to image and rhetoric, represented the wave of the future.[24]

The minority Democratic Republican faction of 1831 led the way in creating Democratic Party apparatus and discipline with its rewards and punishments. As early as 1829 an incipient Democrat urged that party lines be "drawn taut, and no man put in nomination who is not a thorough whole hog party man." Ebenezer Reed argued that Michigan Democrats would have no influence in Washington until they had a strong local party.[25] The Democratic Republicans began moving in this direction in 1831, launching the *Detroit Free Press* which advocated states rights and limited government, the emerging Jacksonian creed.[26]

[22] Antimasonic 1831 Territorial Convention "Address," *Emigrant*, May 18, 1831. The quotations are from Cross, *Burned-over District*, 117, and Griffen, "Anti-Masonic Persuasion," 131. See also, Ludlum, *Social Ferment in Vermont*, 92, and *Emigrant*, April 27, June 29, 1831.

[23] *Michigan Christian Herald*, April 14, 1848. The major sources for my generalizations are the *Courier*, 1833 to 1835, *Emigrant*, 1829 to 1834, and many letters in the Woodbridge MSS and John Allen MSS, BHC.

[24] *Emigrant*, March 16, 23, May 18, and June 29, 1831. The Democratic Republican and Workingmen's candidate, John R. Williams, was one of Detroit's most prosperous landowners and businessmen.

[25] Letter of Ebenezer Reed, Dec. 27, 1829, printed in Friend Palmer, *Early Days in Detroit* (Detroit, 1906), 325-27.

[26] Harold M. Dorr, "Origin and Development of the Michigan Constitution of 1835: A Study of Constitution Making" (unpublished Ph.D. dissertation, University of Michigan, Ann Arbor, 1933), 168. *Emigrant*, March 23 to 30, May 18, 1831.

The national administration boosted party development by conducting something of a purge in 1830-31, egged on, apparently, by the emergent Democratic-Republican clique. Among those purged as unreliable party men were Judges William Woodbridge, Henry Chipman, and James B. Witherell, all of whom became Whigs. A "batch of new party men," as Woodbridge later complained, replaced them.[27] The 1833 delegate election pushed ahead the trend to party politics as the Antimasons and National Republicans made their last organized efforts. The Democrats nominated Lucius Lyon, making support of him the "test of every man's faith and principles."[28] While the *Free Press* announced that "the time has arrived when the perfect and permanent organization of the democracy of Michigan should no longer be delayed," a Central Committee began to campaign for Lyon and to make it clear that office holding depended on full support of the party. One critic said that the Committee intended to regulate "all appointments whether coming from the Executive of the United States or of the Territory, and have proclaimed to the world that no man can receive any office . . . without . . . procuring from them an endorsement that he is a 'true Democrat dyed in the wool.' "[29] Lyon won the election and partisans such as Reed attributed victory to organization and Jacksonian principles: "the cry was Jackson and Democracy—and I have no doubt our majority is much larger in consequence of our 'hanging out the Banner on the outer wall.' "[30]

The Democrats apparently followed up on their promise to base appointments on party loyalty and the Central Committee continued during the winter of 1833-34 to enlist "all true friends of the Cause of Democracy." Andrew Mack of the Central Committee assured a hesitant Stevens T. Mason that the Committee's intent was "not mere party control, or the obtaining of office," but the "application of the principles of our party to our institutions, and . . . our contemplated state constitution."[31]

The Democratic Republicans issued an address "To the Farmers, Mechanics, and other Working-Men," which the *Emigrant* blasted as the trickery of Masons and a "powerful aristocracy," April 7, 27, 1831.

[27] Letters of Ebenezer Reed, Jan. 24 and 26, 1830, in Palmer, *Early Days in Detroit*, 327-28. On Witherell's removal see Clarence Edwin Carter, ed., *The Territorial Papers of the United States*, XII: *The Territory of Michigan, 1829-1837* (Washington, 1945), 127-32, 138, 144-47. William Woodbridge, Springwells, to Lewis Cass, Jan. 13, 1834, Woodbridge MSS, BHC.

[28] Convention proceedings in "Letters of Lucius Lyon," *MHC*, 27: 488. For Antimasonic "Address," *Courier*, May 8, 1833.

[29] Last quotation from Stevens T. Mason, Detroit, to John T. Mason, March 1, 1833, Mason MSS, BHC. *Free Press*, Feb. 6, 1833. C. K. Greene to Lucius Lyon, Jan. 25, 1833, Lyon MSS, Clements.

[30] Reed to Elijah Hayward, St. Joseph, July 25, 1833, in Carter, ed., *Territorial Papers*, XII, 603-04.

[31] For a complaint about removal, Richard Butler, Mt. Clemens, to Woodbridge,

These activities of the Democrats transformed them, in Antimasonic eyes, into "public enemy number one." The Democrats, it appeared, had an organization remarkably like the Masonic; it represented an old evil in new dress.

The *Courier's* denunciation of the Democratic-run Territorial Council early in 1834 illustrated vividly its association of Democrats with a host of traditional villains. It compared the Council to the "infidels of France," "Jacobin revolutionaries," and "Jesuitical inquisitors." It was "Masonic" and a "political inquisition." The Central Committee, a "contemptible cabal," congregated "weekly to inquisitorialize (the word is new but suggestive) delinquents to the holy cause." This "Hydra-headed faction" insinuated "political dogmas" to establish "omnipotency of party." The *Courier* warned that a "secret, machinating, irresponsible espionage is going on, backed by a cabal of aspiring demagogues, whose exclusive and darling object aims at total subversion of . . . genuine republicanism."[32] The *Courier's* outburst displayed very well its anticonspiratorial and countersubversive frame of mind.

It also illustrated how Antimasonic rhetoric suggested to any Protestant with an imagination that Masonry resembled Popery, the original anti-Christ. The Antimasonic mind is, of course, well known for its imagination, but deduction need not be relied on for this point. The *Courier* was quite explicit regarding the "bigoted, malignant, and intolerant spirit" of Popery.[33] Many Antimasonic leaders used anti-Catholicism in missionary work. Raising the spectre of Popery helped mobilize support in the Protestant Crusade.[34] Like Antimasons in New York, Michigan Antimasons recognized, at least in 1833, that French Catholics voted for their enemies. After the Whig party took over the evangelical cause, both the old French and the new immigrant Irish and German Catholics voted heavily against Whiggery, largely because of its evangelical identifications.[35] Thus, the evangelicals' anti-Catholicism gradually merged with their antiparty and anti-Democratic feelings.

The Antimasons ironically acted as unintentional catalysts in estab-

---

March 16, 1834, Woodbridge MSS, BHC. Andrew Mack to Stevens T. Mason, Dec. 18, 1833, Mason MSS, BHC.

[32] *Courier*, July 31, Oct. 2, 1833, Jan. 29, 1834. For an excellent analysis of related themes see David Brion Davis, "Some Themes of Counter-Subversion: An Analysis of Anti-Masonic, Anti-Catholic, and Anti-Mormon Literature," *Mississippi Valley Historical Review*, 47 (September 1960), 205-24. See also Richard Hofstadter, *The Paranoid Style in American Politics* (New York, 1965), 17.

[33] McCarthy, "Anti-Masonic Party," 544; *Courier*, Sept. 3, 1834.

[34] See the Report of the Michigan Education Society, *Courier*, Oct. 15, 1834; also Sister Evangeline Thomas, *Nativism in the Old Northwest* (Washington, D.C. 1936), 41; and Ray Allen Billington, "Anti-Catholic Propaganda and the Home Missionary Movement, 1800-1860," *Mississippi Valley Historical Review*, 22 (December 1935), 361-84.

[35] *Courier*, July 10, 1833. See Chapter IX.

lishing parties. Conventions were a device well-known to evangelicals whose benevolent societies had been holding them for years. Antimasons called the first Territorial Convention in 1829 and the National Republicans and then Democratic Republicans soon followed their example. The same pattern developed nationally. Organizers in the Republican party, especially the Van Burenites, had been working for a national convention throughout the late 1820s. The Antimasons broke the ice for the rising professionals. The convention system, once established, as Ostrogorski observed, provided the foundation for party apparatus. In the classic style of political paranoids obsessed with conspiracy, the Antimasons imitated the enemy. What has not been sufficiently stressed is that they anticipated the enemy.[36]

Despising "party usages" Antimasons helped nurture them by insisting on clarifying party lines. They brought an absolutist, moralizing temper into politics. Their demand for unequivocal allegiance forced men into positions they would not otherwise have taken. This, perhaps, caused the complaint that Antimasons were the "political prescriptive ones" [sic]. In 1828 a New York critic charged that "their motto is down with every man that is a Mason and *they who will not cry out against them.*" (Italics mine)[37]

In the manner of revivalists, Antimasons insisted on a narrow choice between right and wrong and on the necessity of "coming out" for right. This "all who are not with us are against us" attitude encouraged party politics. Antimasons unintentionally helped set precedents for what became known as party "regularity," and infused the idea with moral sanctions. Thus, they aided the Democrats in erecting the first commandment of party discipline and making it into, in Ostrogorski's words, a "moral constraint." Of course the Democrats worked more deliberately and more systematically to fashion in-group party perspectives of religious intensity.[38]

[36] Ostrogorski, *Democracy and Organization*, II, 59-63; Hofstadter, *Paranoid Style*, 32-33; Davis, "Themes of Counter-Subversion," 233.

[37] McCarthy, "Anti-Masonic Party," 373. Lewis B. Sturges, Norwalk, Ohio, to W. Woodbridge, Nov. 7, 1833, Woodbridge MSS, BHC. See also Ludlum, *Social Ferment in Vermont*, 116. J. B. Bryan, Pampila, New York, to John Bryan, Washtenaw County, Nov. 3, 1828, John Bryan MSS, MHCol.

[38] Ostrogorski, *Democracy and Organization*, II, 67-69. Levi Beardsley, a New York Democrat, observed Antimasonry's polarizing tendencies, *Reminiscences* (New York, 1852), 226, 227. The Democrats' single-minded promotion of party as an institution claiming first loyalty has been well documented. See, e.g., Leonard D. White, *The Jacksonians: A Study in Administrative History, 1829-1861* (New York, 1954), 13, 14, 302, and Kass, *Politics in New York*, 28, 29, 31, 32, 33. Many examples of the New York Van Burenite-Jacksonian deliberate inculcation and rigid practice of party norms could be produced from these and from a fine recent study, Michael Wallace, "Changing Concepts of Party in the United States: New York, 1815-1828," *American Historical Review*, 74 (December 1968), 453-91, which emphasizes Van Burenite success in overcoming the old "consensus ideal" by marrying "party" to "democracy."

DEMOCRATS AND ANTIPARTY

Despite the *relative* ease of Democratic organization, antipartyism obstructed Democratic organizers too. Potential or active Democrats tended to have more generalized and secular antiparty attitudes. They tended to object to certain aspects of the party system, such as regular nominations, implying de facto acceptance of the *system*. The 1833 Democratic convention itself testified implicitly to the presence of anti-party feeling by sounding highly defensive about its actions. The 1837 State Democratic Convention, similarly, still deemed it necessary to devote several resolutions to exhorting Democrats to unity through observance of party regularity and established party "usages."[39]

Catherine Mason, sister of Michigan's first Democratic governor, complained in 1836 that candidates for office needed only to belong to the *"strongest party."* The degree to which party feeling was being carried, she said, was a great evil and "It has already in a measure usurped the place of patriotism." The Democratic Young Men of Wayne County in July 1837 agreed to support the Democrat's regular nominations, but with evident reluctance. They resolved to acquiesce in the "system" of regular nominations, "but at the same time *do insist* that competence, integrity of purpose, and purity of character are important considerations in choosing candidates." Many Democrats apparently agreed with Catherine Mason that "Partyism like many other 'isms' has been carried too far."[40]

Because many potential supporters did not see a party as an unmixed blessing, the Democrats had to work to establish party regularity. Democratic leaders, aware of resentment against unwarranted party intrusions, knew that some occasions demanded at least a show of nonpartisanship. In the 1835 Constitutional Convention, Democratic leader John Norvell insisted that he had set aside all "mere party views" to consider only Michigan's interest. In the angriest exchange of the Convention he and the unofficial leader of the Whig minority accused one another of bringing party spirit into the Convention.[41]

In 1833 Stevens T. Mason, a Democrat who would be elected gover-

[39] Paul A. Randall, ed., "Gubernatorial Platforms for the Political Parties of Michigan, 1834-64" (unpublished M.A. thesis, Wayne State University, 1937), 12-13. For an example of secular antipartyism see James Fenimore Cooper, *The American Democrat*, 1st published 1838 (New York, 1931), 170-73.

[40] C. Mason to S. T. Mason, Nov. 27, 1836, Mason MSS, BHC. *Free Press,* July 25, 1837. Neal M. Gaffey, White Pigeon, to Lyon, March 14, 1835, Lyon MSS, Clements. See also Charles W. Whipple, Pontiac, to Woodbridge, Dec. 2, 1839, Woodbridge MSS, BHC, and Isaac Bronson to Lyon, Sept. 10, 1837, Lyon MSS, Clements.

[41] Harold M. Dorr, ed., *The Michigan Constitutional Conventions of 1835-36: Debates and Proceedings* (Ann Arbor, 1940), 254-60.

nor by party vote in 1835 and 1837, criticized parties with gusto. In March he described the Democratic Convention and Central Committee:

The unfortunate people of Michigan have set over them a Regency more formidable than the famous Albany Regency itself, and have only to bow their heads to be trampled on by Andrew Mack, David C. McKinstry, John P. Sheldon, and Elliott Gray.

The . . . Convention has instituted these gentlemen . . . to regulate all appointments. . . . 'Tis said that governments are republican only in proportion as they embody the will of the people, and execute it; but if these gentlemen are to be our dictators, and their decisions . . . should be the will of the people, deliver me from New York politics.[42]

Personal considerations probably influenced Mason's attitude. He resented the Committee's intention to regulate *him*—he was Acting Governor—and the Convention had bypassed his friend Austin E. Wing, a National Republican incumbent whom Mason hoped would be re-elected as delegate. By April, Mason still hoped for Wing's election, but his opinions regarding parties had undergone an about-face. William Woodbridge had accepted the Antimasonic nomination but not their platform. Mason thought that this candidacy would hurt Wing's chances and he criticized Woodbridge's claim "to represent the people and not a party." Mason called that "the language of an individual who means to represent anyone rather than those who elect him." Mason was now "satisfied" that parties must exist and would be the last to discourage party spirit "when properly controlled. It is the surest plan of keeping people awake to their rights, and whenever I see a man declaiming against party spirit, and professing to be for the *people alone*, I always think that he is for slipping quietly along, serving his own interests, and flattering himself that no one can see it." Mason now held attitudes more characteristic of Democratic organizers who, in their more sublime moments, no doubt engaged in similar rationalizations which transformed necessity into preference and power into principle.[43]

Antimasons and Whigs, on the other hand, indulged in few comforting thoughts about parties. Woodbridge assumed a nonpartisan stance in 1833 partly because he was, unofficially, a National Republican trying to unite Antimasonic and National Republican voters. His nonpartisan posture would appeal particularly to Antimasons and Republicans who distrusted parties and who would be reassured by his claims that he had

---

[42] S. T. Mason to John T. Mason, March 1, 1833, Mason MSS, BHC.

[43] Same to Same, April 16, 1833, Mason MSS, BHC; Ostrogorski attributed the rise of parties to an "unhealthy politico-social condition," *Democracy and Organization*, II, 66-67. James Sterling Young suggests that party building was part of an attempt to establish mechanisms for effective government, circumventing antipower cultural attitudes and the formal and informal checks on the exercise of power established by the early custodians of American government, *The Washington Community, 1800-1828* (New York, 1966), 179-210, 250-54.

never been "the slave of any party" and that he would hate being forced into office "by the mere operation of a party."[44] Lucius Lyon could not have used such words in accepting the Democratic nomination.

During the pre-Convention campaign of 1835, the Whigs challenged the Democrats in two major ways: by counterorganizing and by denouncing Democratic organization and discipline as evils. Even some Democrats doubted the wisdom of electing delegates to a constitutional convention on a party basis.[45] Democrats met the Whig challenges and ambivalence in their own ranks with more assertive demands for regularity. All over the state Democratic organizers heralded the virtues of party. The Ann Arbor, *Michigan Argus* asserted that "the regular nominations" were the party's "chief strength" while Lenawee Democrats warned that "the doctrine of 'No Party' in these times of corruption and intrigue should meet with no acceptance, as every man is bound to join the party of the government and of the constitution."[46] "*Union, harmony, self-denial, concession,*" trumpeted the *Niles Gazette and Advertiser,* "*everything for* CAUSE, *Nothing for men*—should be the watchword of the Democratic Party." In 1836 Niles Democrats, though objecting to being forced to "swallow any measure," nevertheless said "we feel our duty to the party paramount to almost every other consideration."[47]

In the major political events of the mid-thirties—the Constitutional Convention of 1835, the Convention of Dissent which refused Congress's terms of admission (1836), the Convention of Assent which accepted (1836), and the presidential election of 1836—the Democrats acted far more as a party than their opponents. This resulted from several causes: Democrats held power and could reward and punish; impending statehood promised patronage and other benefits to loyalists; and Democrats had more positive attitudes to organization.[48]

Indeed, as their party became solidly established, Democrats characteristically regarded party loyalty as a supreme virtue. In 1837 and sporadically thereafter, some Democrats rejected party nominations and supported independents, but in few cases between 1837 and 1852 did this result in a loss for the Democrats. As a Macomb County Whig observed in 1839, splitting Democratic ranks was "in opposition to

---

[44] Woodbridge to John W. Davis, March 9, 1833, Woodbridge MSS, BHC.

[45] *Michigan Sentinel,* Jan. 24, Feb. 14, 1835.

[46] Aug. 27, 1835.

[47] *Niles Gazette,* Oct. 3, 1835, and Aug. 24, Sept. 21, 1836.

[48] *Michigan Argus* "Extra," Nov. 1836, MHCol. Democratic factionalism did exist. There is extensive evidence of its intensity and persistence, as e.g., in Lucius Lyon's correspondence, especially for 1838-39: "Letters of Lucius Lyon," *MHC,* 27: 510, 512, 514, 516, 517, 519, 520, 521, 524, 525-26. What is remarkable is not that some Democratic activists supported the Whigs (as in 1839) but that Democrats consistently overcame the factionalism of their many ambitious chieftains to present a relatively united front.

all good rules in that party." In 1840 a meeting of Dearborn Democrats equated party loyalty with religious fidelity. Abandoning a party, it said, because of "alleged mistakes, misconduct or corruption," by those who professed its principles, "could only find its parallel in the folly and wickedness of the person who would change his religion, in consequence of the delinquencies of the minister appointed to enforce its obligations."[49]

Party ideals never gained such prestige among the opposition. The evangelical disposition ensured that Whig spokesmen would hesitate to offer the party itself as an object of reverence, rather that they would tend to undervalue or reject the ethics of party loyalty.

WHIGS AND ANTIPARTY

Both the National Republicans and Antimasons apparently lay dormant or dead when news of the new Whig Party's surprising victory in New York City's 1834 spring elections came to Michigan. (National Republicans seem to have become both Whigs and Democrats, but it is very difficult to say in what proportions.) Tentative Whig organizations did not begin until late 1834, and effective, permanent organization did not begin until 1837. The Democrats' hold on power would have put any opposition under a handicap. Whig organization proceeded especially painfully because of the inhibitions inherent in the political character of the Whigs.

The *Detroit Courier*'s conduct from 1833 to 1835 illustrated how evangelicals both resisted and accommodated themselves to "party." In 1833 the *Courier* propagated Protestantism and a puritanical code. It advised its readers, for example, to shun intemperance, keep the Sabbath, and avoid the theater, that "sink of vice." (Significantly, a prominent Democrat, David C. McKinstry, opened Detroit's first theater in 1833.) The *Courier* warred upon Masons, Catholics, parties, and Democrats. Gradually, however, it sacrificed its hatred of parties to its hatred of Democrats, and muted its evangelicalism and anti-Catholicism. During 1834 the *Courier*'s secularization paralleled its preparation to embrace Whiggery. On September 24 editor Franklin Sawyer, Jr., called for "efficient organization" and soon branded "political indifference" as the "crying sin of the day." Although opposed "to the drilling tactics of tory-ism," he declared that "Organization cannot begin too soon."[50]

[49] William Dusell, Macomb Co., to Woodbridge, July 8, 1839, Woodbridge MSS, BHC. *Free Press*, Feb. 29, 1840. "Remarks of Benjamin S. Bagg, 1840," John S. Bagg MSS, BHC, is a speech idealizing party loyalty by a Young Democrat.

[50] *Courier*, Feb. 19, Sept. 24, Oct. 8, Nov. 19, 1834.

Sawyer and his co-editor, Charles Cleland, at least accepted organization as a necessary evil, though Cleland still warned in January 1835 against "the success of the party [becoming] more important than the causes over which they first arose." George Corselius, editor of the *Ann Arbor Michigan Whig* and a sincere Antimason, took far more time to resign himself to "party."[51] Corselius could not get by "This word organization [which] has a harsh, unpleasant sound. It calls up to our view free minds bound in fetters, drilled, disciplined, like the foot soldiers of a marching regiment—accustomed to act what others think and obey what others command."[52] In January Corselius still thundered against "party discipline" and "counterorganization" as *unnecessary* evils. He advocated "people met in primary assemblies" rather than "men working in the collars." All parties smacked of "Van Buren politics . . . a gigantic system of slavery and corruption." They suppressed dissent as heresy and demanded unthinking submission.[53]

Washtenaw County Whigs shared Corselius's sentiments. In January of 1835 they met to oppose the "arbitrary, intolerant, and uncompromising course of those with whom party is all, the Common Weal nothing," and to oppose the "disposition to impose the odious collars of an odious political discipline on Freemen." Their "Address" attacked the Democrats chiefly for establishing a "consolidated national party" based on "a cordon of affiliated clubs" ruled by a central junto. The most remarkable thing about this "Address" was its deprecation of party names, including "the term 'Whig.' " In 1837 the Washtenaw Whigs asked the electorate to choose between Whig "liberty of Freemen" versus Democratic "slavery of party."[54]

The 1837 Whig state "Address" devoted more than half its attention to an attack on Jacksonian party organization *as such*. While criticizing specific Democratic "usages" such as the spoils system, it attacked also such general attributes of parties as "compactness" and centralized authority.[55]

In the early stages of party development the antipartyism of Whig party builders affected their actions as well as their rhetoric. In 1835 Jackson County Whigs outdid perhaps even Washtenaw Whigs in their

[51] *Courier*, Jan. 7, 1835. George Corselius, "Diary, 1833," entry for Aug. 1, MHCol.

[52] Ann Arbor, *Michigan Emigrant*, Aug. 14, Nov. 13, 1834, film, MSL. After detailing five very demanding conditions on which he would consent to cooperate with "The Whigs," Corselius added, "I know my propensity to run into extremes," "Diary, March, 1834—Nov. 1838" MHCol. See also the "Prospectus" of the *Michigan Whig* in the *Emigrant*, Dec. 11, 1834.

[53] *Michigan Whig*, Jan. 15, 1835.

[54] *Michigan Whig*, Jan. 29, Feb. 12, 1835. Ann Arbor, *State Journal*, Oct. 26, 1837. On Whig antipartyism in Lenawee County in 1835, Gen. Jos. W. Brown, Tecumseh, to Lyon, Feb. 1, 1835, Lyon MSS, Clements.

[55] *Advertiser*, Aug. 17, 1837.

attempt to have a party without organization or "usages." After defending their meeting by admitting that "many of us were originally opposed to organization" and "were driven into the necessity of organizing by the Van Buren men," the Jackson Whigs told of how "a motion was made that the Convention pledge themselves to go to all reasonable lengths in support of the candidates who may be nominated by the Convention—delegates from several parts of the room spoke against it as having too much Van Burenism, and the Convention refused to entertain it."[56]

Antiparty feeling, combined with the Ohio boundary dispute and Whig lack of power, helped prevent effective Whig organization before 1837. The rudimentary Whig organization of 1835 disappeared after the election of convention delegates. In the fall elections of state officials the Democrats faced no organized party. Indeed, the opposition claimed to invoke no "spirit of party" and to have selected men "without regard to party, men who had not made a business of politics, and who, if left to their own choice, would prefer remaining in the walks of private life." During 1836 Charles Cleland wondered "Where are the Whigs!" while in the presidential election the opposition billed itself as a state rights party. After the Democratic victory one Whig paper claimed that no one had voted "as Whigs" but that the issue had been between the Democrats and a "genuine state rights party."[57]

As late as April 26, 1837, Whig partisans lamented that "no regular Whig organization existed." Shortly, however, Whigs organized, all the while criticizing parties and denouncing Democrats for having such a thing. In time such claims disappeared. Yet even after the party had been in existence a decade, and had acquired traditions, loyalties, "moral constraints," and all the hunger for success of its opponent, antipartyism survived. After the pitched party battle of 1844 a Whig could still say that he believed party distinctions "in great measure but a name." And William Woodbridge continued to campaign for Whiggery while decrying the very idea of party. In an 1844 speech he said that he had never tried to hide his Whig "associations" but added that he had always tried "to at least rescue myself from the enslaving prejudices of Party as to leave my mind free to act for the best interest of the Country."[58]

Whigs rationalized that they were only temporarily involved in a

---

[56] *Michigan Whig*, April 2, 1835.

[57] *Detroit Journal and Advertiser*, Sept. 29, 1835. C. Cleland to Woodbridge, July 26, 1836, Woodbridge MSS, BHC. *Journal and Courier*, Nov. 12, Dec. 6, 1836. Other examples of antipartyism: prospectus of the Adrian, *Michigan Whig*, Aug. 22, 1838; 1839 Jackson Whig County Convention, *Jackson Sentinel*, Oct. 2, 1839, MSL.

[58] John J. Abbott, Detroit, to Woodbridge, Dec. 25, 1844, Woodbridge MSS. The speech is a MS dated 1844. Woodbridge's image of being above parties seems to have been a key element of his popularity with Whigs, J. M. Edmunds, Ypsilanti; to Woodbridge, Oct. 3, 1844; on Whig organization, *Circular*, June 28, 1837, Woodbridge MSS, BHC.

necessary evil and could still feel superior to their opponents. In 1849 after a crushing Whig defeat, Rufus Hosmer, a Whig editor, showed his detachment from party in a postmortem on the election. He attributed defeat to many Whigs balking at the party's gubernatorial candidate (a Free Soiler):

the body of the Whig party can never be driven into the support of an unpalatable nomination by the mere force of party discipline. The character of the party is such that no organization however perfect can serve to keep it in the traces, unless the nominations are acceptable.

Our opponents are differently constituted, or to say the least, they possess in their ranks fewer of that class of independent men who vote, or refuse to, less upon the dictation of party leaders, than upon the conviction of their reason and the dictates of their own judgment.[59]

In 1851 the Whigs made their poorest showing in a state election; with no third party drawing off votes they still managed to get only 41.5 percent of the vote. The activity of the Whig nominee for Lieutenant Governor typified Whig antipartyism as it related to such an election. George Hazelton recalled how he had not been in the state when nominated, had not wanted the nomination, expected defeat, and did not campaign.[60]

In the late thirties the paradox of continuing Whig antagonism to party in the midst of party-making was due to a complex of motives and conditions. Some Whig leaders probably felt a personal need for self-justification in order to quiet their own doubts and guilt. Their protestations also reassured their evangelical followers that they could use and vote for a party and remain uncontaminated by its "usages." Some certainly wanted to exploit general antipartyism to Whig advantage (relying perhaps on the electorate's recognition of the Democrats as the politician's party par excellence).

LIBERTY PARTY AND ANTIPARTY

Since the Liberty Party drew heavily from Whig ranks, it is not surprising that antiorganization and antiparty attitudes flourished amid Libertyites. Men likely to be abolitionists were also likely to be religious men, moralists in politics, men of principle not expedience, men sure of their rightness, and therefore less flexible, less compromising.

It is well known that the abolitionists had great difficulty in organizing a political party in 1839-40, in "changing the character of the anti-

[59] *Advertiser*, Nov. 9, 1849. Among Wayne County's economic elite in 1844 Democrats were "more political" than Whigs, in proportion to their numbers; 55 percent of the Whigs and 64 percent of the Democrats engaged in political activity, McCoy, "Wayne County Economic Elites, 1844, 1860," 99.

[60] *MHC*, 21: 391, 413. For an analysis of the "spirit of obstinate independence" governing the Whigs—in contrast to the Democrats—see Ann Arbor, *Signal of Liberty*, July 17, 1843.

slavery movement from a religious to a political base." The Garrisonians reached extremes in their opposition to organization, but the sentiment pervaded abolitionist ranks. James Birney, Liberty Party candidate for president in 1840, "had more active opposition from his antislavery friends than from rival parties." Besides Garrisonians, "many Christian abolitionists" deplored the shift to a political base.[61] Abolitionist anti-institutionalism has also been analyzed well by David Brion Davis. What has not been recognized are the antiparty and antipower attitudes of the abolitionists which practically insured their lack of success in a party movement. The executive committee of the Michigan State Anti-Slavery Society, in explaining why it had not deemed it wise to put up candidates for office in 1839, put the matter succinctly: "we repudiate the spirit of party intolerance as but another name for the spirit of SLAVERY."[62]

Even after Michigan abolitionists reluctantly organized, their anti-political attitudes retained a firm hold, evident particularly in the "one idea" that thoroughly dominated the party from 1841 to 1846. This can be seen the better because of the efforts of two leaders who tried to work against the grain. Theodore Foster and Guy Beckley, editors of the abolitionist *Signal of Liberty* (Ann Arbor), worked hard to convince other abolitionist leaders to broaden the party's platform to attract antislavery Whigs. The lure of "many tens of thousands of religious men, who now vote with the Whigs," exerted a strong pull on the pragmatic Foster. He realized, at least implicitly, that it was the moral-religious character of the Liberty Party which prevented its acting with more flexibility. He regarded it as a political disaster that "most of our leaders and political speakers have been and are *ministers*—not statesmen or politicians. Hence their blindness to anything but the one idea."[63]

A recent systematic study of Michigan abolitionist leaders reached conclusions strongly agreeing with Foster regarding the religious character of Liberty leadership. The most important characteristic of Michigan abolitionist leaders, according to Gerald Sorin, was that the great

[61] Betty Fladeland, *James Gillespie Birney* (Ithaca, 1955), 175, 188. Gilbert Hobbs Barnes, *The Antislavery Impulse, 1830-1844* (New York, 1964), 171-76. Louis Filler, *The Crusade Against Slavery* (New York, 1960), 150-59.

[62] Jackson, *Michigan Freeman*, Oct. 23, 1839, also Sept. 16, 1840, MHCol. "As a kind of surrogate religion, antislavery had long shown tendencies that were pietistic, millennial, and anti-institutional," David Brion Davis, "The Emergence of Immediatism in British and American Antislavery Thought," *Mississippi Valley Historical Review*, 49 (September 1962), 229. See also *Signal of Liberty*, June 23, Aug. 4, 1841, Feb. 5, 1844.

[63] Theodore Foster to Birney, Ann Arbor, Feb. 13, 1846, in Dumond, ed., *Birney Letters*, II, 1002; Guy Beckley and Theodore Foster to Birney, Ann Arbor, Feb. 9, 1846, 999-1000; Theodore Foster to Birney, March 30, 1846, 1009; Theodore Foster to Birney, Aug. 1, 1846, 1025-26. Fladeland, *Birney*, 258-60. John E. Kephart, "A Pioneer Michigan Abolitionist," *Michigan History*, 45 (March 1961), 38-40.

majority of them were "actively and intensely religious"; 21 of the 35 top leaders were either pastors, deacons, or elders. Michigan abolitionists "had been exposed to the revivalism of the era" and "were motivated by a reawakened religious impulse."[64]

In the Liberty Party, then, the antipolitics and antipartyism of evangelical origins can be seen in concentrated form (as they existed more diffusely in Whiggery). But neither in the Whig nor Liberty parties did the political character of the evangelical completely dominate. If the dominant type in Whiggery's evangelical wing and in the Liberty Party was the "moralizer in politics," there were present in both parties men of instrumentalist, inside-dopester, and manipulative tendencies. Certain men, too, combined ability to organize with chronic revulsion from "politics."[65] Libertyites were typically men of a strong devotional rather than institutional commitment to religion. Such men did not have that ability to compromise which is necessary in politics. Their temperaments did not dispose them toward making bargains. Their contempt for "politics" was an integral part of their resistance to parties. For many of them a choice between two evils was no choice at all. For this reason the great evangelist Charles G. Finney said that "No man can be an honest man, that is committed to a political party." Perhaps this caused a pious Detroit carpenter to refuse to vote in the city election of 1832 and to record in his diary: "I'll none of sin."[66]

SOURCES AND STRUCTURE OF ANTIPARTY

While the existence of antiparty has been shown its sources have been only partly exposed. Similarly, James Sterling Young, in *The Washington Community, 1800–1828*, examined the influence of antipower attitudes on the early governing establishment and their inhibiting effect on party development, but he did not explore the sources of antipower dispositions.[67]

Antipartyism in the early national era has been observed often by

[64] Gerald Sorin, "The Historical Theory of Political Radicalism: Michigan Abolitionist Leaders As a Test Case" (unpublished M.A. thesis, Wayne State University, 1964), 78, 88.

[65] Riesman, et al., *Lonely Crowd*, 191-217. Austin Blair, Dec. 6, 1841, to A. T. McCall, Blair MSS, BHC. See also Geo. F. Porter, Detroit, to Fred B. Porter, Sept. 15, 1851, J. S. Porter MSS, BHC.

[66] Finney quoted in Charles C. Cole, Jr., *The Social Ideas of the Northern Evangelicals, 1826-1860* (New York, 1954), 152. Fred Landon, ed., "Extracts from the Diary of William C. King, A Detroit Carpenter in 1832," *Michigan History*, 19 (Winter 1935), 67. See also William G. McLoughlin, Jr., *Modern Revivalism* (New York, 1959), 117.

[67] Bernard Bailyn has begun this formidable task in *Origins of American Politics*. John H. Bunzel, *Anti-Politics in America* (New York, 1967), deals with related themes but has not been helpful for this study. See J. R. Pole, *Political Representation in England and the Origins of the American Republic* (New York, 1967).

historians. Indeed, there is reason to believe that its pervasiveness and strength have been underestimated, and a tendency has grown to attribute an acceptance and conception of party and its functions to Federalists and Republicans that they simply did not possess.[68] Recognition of antiparty's impact in the 1830s should lead to greater appreciation of its role in the earlier period.

Yet by the 1830s general antipartyism had diminished as party-builders consciously set about organizing party structures based on the convention system and deliberately extolled the virtues of party. Evangelical antipartyism affected parties most in the 1830s, yet it is also clear that nonevangelicals also resisted party and that antiorganizational attitudes obstructed all types of party men. A general reservoir of anti-politics and antiorganization existed to which both major parties appealed when it suited them.

Antiparty thinking tended to be related to ideas about government that began with society rather than the individual, with the corporate organic whole rather than its atomic parts. If this thought pattern assumed a hierarchy of classes, it also assumed social harmony, not conflict. Men who desired society unified by shared moral codes tended to assume that government and society possessed organic unity. Party organization contradicted these assumptions and mocked the idea that government existed to promote the commonweal and by sufferance of the commonality. "Party" suggested the promotion of the particular, artificial, and selfish, unnaturally and unconstitutionally, in a broad, non-legal as well as legal sense. Parties implied a failure of the ideals of the Founding Fathers, an unnatural and unnecessary growth on the socio-political order.[69]

Antiparty was associated with community, tradition, and deference. Politics and party were associated with the opposite of these things. Men socialized into tradition and community would be more likely to be anti-

---

[68] For a lucid antidote to the "functional" view of parties in the 1790s see Franklyn George Bonn, Jr., "The Idea of Political Party in the Thought of Thomas Jefferson and James Madison" (unpublished Ph.D. dissertation, University of Minnesota, 1964).

David Hackett Fischer, *The Revolution in American Conservatism: The Federalist Party in the Era of Jeffersonian Democracy* (New York, 1965), helped greatly with this chapter. However, acceptance of party as a "positive good" (193) was not as complete as Fischer implies. See, e.g., Robert V. Remini, *Martin Van Buren and the Making of the Democratic Party* (New York, 1959), 139-41; Martin Van Buren, *Inquiry into the Origin and Development of Political Parties in the United States* (New York, 1867), 6; McCormick, *Second Party System*, 355; Harvey C. Mansfield, Jr., "Whether Party Government Is Inevitable," *Political Science Quarterly*, 80 (December 1965), 518.

[69] Very helpful here were Fischer, *Revolution in American Conservatism*, 3, 9, 17; Rowland Berthoff, "The American Social Order: A Conservative Hypothesis," *American Historical Review*, 65 (April 1960), 495-514; Shaw Livermore, Jr., *The Twilight of Federalism*, 1-15.

party than men alienated or relatively detached from society—marginal types. The party leader could be a new man, not necessarily a natural leader of society. Parties could place in power men of obscure connections as organizations became the major vehicle for entrepreneurship through politics. Parties, indeed, may have stimulated the rampant egalitarian beliefs and expectations of the "age of the common man," as well as many of the common man's resentments, by opening new ways for the lower and middle classes to occupy or identify with traditionally high-status positions. While these propositions, surely, could benefit from additional investigation it does seem likely that parties gave the death blows to the deference politics of the aristocratic state republics of the early national period.[70]

The origin of evangelical antipartyism in New England Protestantism seems fairly clear. Long after the Massachusetts Bay Christian Commonwealth disintegrated, a puritan-derived compulsion continued to propel drives for cultural and moral homogeneity in the community. Antiparty probably was more intense among evangelicals imbued with a "sense of solidarity," the belief that "the good of each is bound up with the good of all," the outlook that the community was a moral whole, and the desire to work for the moral integration and regulation of society. One of the best expressions of this attitude was given by the Ann Arbor Society for the Promotion of Temperance in 1832, several of whose members were Antimasons and later Whigs: "Resolved, that we look upon our interests, our rights, all our earthly hopes and means of future happiness as identified with the well being of community, and that we regard the injuries done to community by intemperance as encroachments on our public and individual rights which as good citizens we consider it our duty to resist."[71]

The evidence for the hypothesis that evangelical antiparty derived from and was associated with New England Protestantism and its town-culture is admittedly impressionistic. A rare example of an explicit connection of antipartyism with New England customs appeared in an 1855 newspaper history of Jackson, Michigan. The first town election was

---

[70] Compare with Bailyn: "Parties, to almost every political writer of the early eighteenth century, were indisputably evil. The ancient ideal of an organic policy whose parts, operating independently within their assigned spheres, fitted together harmoniously persisted . . . Party rivalries signified illness within the body politic, malfunctions within the system," 36-37. Lynn L. Marshall, "The Strange Stillbirth of the Whig Party," *American Historical Review*, 72 (January 1967), 445-68. J. R. Pole, "Historians and the Problem of Early American Democracy," *American Historical Review*, 67 (April 1962), 626-46. Benjamin W. Larabee, "Microanalysis," in Edward N. Saveth, ed., *American History and the Social Sciences* (New York, 1964), 370-79. Paul Goodman, "The First American Party System," in Chambers and Burnham, eds., *The American Party Systems*, 56-89.

[71] Ralph Barton Perry, *Puritanism and Democracy* (New York, 1944), 327; Ann Arbor, *Emigrant*, Feb. 1, 1832, film, MSL.

described: "the manner of voting then was as in New England to ballot separately for each office until a choice was made, and then for another; thus in rotation until all were filled. . . . . It was the caucus as well as the election of the people, and altogether more democratic than the present system, as it enabled voters to vote for men instead of 'the ticket.' "[72] A more systematic study would identify antiparty and party types in a given political universe, investigate the cultural heritage, beliefs, and social positions of both types, and compare them. Tentatively, however, the hypothesis is strongly supported by several studies of evangelical leaders of New England background. Historians have seen, for example, "a profound distrust for the major political parties among the [evangelical] ministry and their devoted followers." To many evangelicals *party* in politics resembled Romanism in religion, namely, submission of individual reason and conscience to a central authority. Parties inevitably produced at least an "implicit subjection of mind and opinion." Horace Bushnell expressed succinctly this evangelical attitude to parties: "It is the worst form of Papacy ever invented."[73]

Evangelicals condemned Popery, parties, Masonry, and the Democrats for very similar reasons. Not all evangelicals everywhere did this, but for a great many, apparently, the sectarian rhetoric of militant Protestantism served to lambast Masonry, parties as such, and the Democrats, in that order. For some evangelicals in Michigan in 1833-34 all three seemed to overlap and merge. Of course the archetypical destroyer of freedom of conscience was the Roman Church.

Metaphors such as "political church" or "party dogma" have long been meant to suggest similarities between religious and political behavior. Today such words usually lack a pejorative meaning, though they might be ironic. But this was not the case with evangelicals in the 1830s. Their use of these metaphors in politics suggested the kinds of evils they associated with Popery or Masonry. Masonry, for example, in presuming to be a substitute religion, imposed duties on the individual superseding those of conscience and religion. A political party presumed to mediate between the individual and God.

This, then, was the structure of evangelical antipartyism which helped

---

[72] *Jackson American Citizen*, July 11, 1855. Pole, *Origins of Representation*, 38-54, on the town in New England and its strong sense of corporate identity in social and political life.

[73] Bushnell quoted in Cole, *Northern Evangelicals*, 153. See also, John R. Bodo, *The Protestant Clergy and Public Issues, 1812-1848* (Princeton, 1954); Timothy L. Smith, *Revivalism and Social Reform in Mid-Nineteenth Century America* (New York, 1957); William G. McLoughlin, "Pietism and the American Character," *American Quarterly*, 17 (Summer 1965), 176. The word "party" in a religious context had long had a pejorative meaning, referring usually to artificial distinctions within the universal Christian Church, Winthrop S. Hudson, *American Protestantism* (Chicago, 1961), 3, 45-47.

shape Antimasonry and Whiggery and helps to explain many of the traits of Michigan Whiggery *in comparison with* the Democrats. The Whig Party had less organizational ability, indeed, was less predisposed to organize.[74] Whigs tended to vote less than Democrats in nonpresidential elections and were more prone to schism. Whigs tended to devalue party loyalty and the ethics of party discipline, while the Democrats preached the inherent virtue of correct party behavior. Whigs ironically combined a contempt for "politics" with a tendency to overreact to political events. Evangelical antipartyism as described above can be regarded as a subsystem of beliefs about society, government, and religion. General antipartyism was a strong force among some of the electorate, along with antipower attitudes and the party-a-necessary-evil syndrome of accommodation. It affected Whigs, Democrats, and probably some apathetics, often as an inarticulate fear, anxiety, or prejudice. Apathy, however, was not caused by antipartyism. The latter's significance came from its prevalence among those who somehow participated in the political process even if only on its fringes. We shall know more about the sources of general antipartyism when we know more about antipower and antipolitical attitudes in American culture.

[74] Richard Hofstadter, *The Age of Reform* (New York, 1955), 214-15, 254-69, discussed the antiorganizational tendencies of Yankee Protestant Progressives. Samuel P. Hays has noted the attacks on parties in the early twentieth century from cosmopolitan elites, "Political Parties and the Community-Society Continuum," in Chambers and Burnham, eds., *American Party Systems*, 176-77.

V

Alien Suffrage and Party Formation

> This is the evil most to be dreaded—the loss of property may
> be retrieved or remedied but what is to become of a people
> where the great landmarks which distinguish virtue from
> vice, honor from dishonesty, and worth from baseness are
> obliterated.—Thomas Rowland to William Woodbridge, 1841

When Michigan Democrats and Whigs fought their first party contest
the great issue dividing them was alien suffrage, a matter of practical
politics and of deep emotional impact. Most Democratic leaders would
have allowed noncitizens, otherwise qualified, to vote after one or two
years' residence, while Whigs insisted on limiting voting to citizens. The
controversy gradually exposed the nativism, anti-Catholicism, and
impulse toward cultural homogeneity permeating the ideology of an
influential group in Whiggery. It engaged the pride and self-esteem of
native and foreign born groups, yet what it indicated about the character
of parties has been ignored, although the "history" of the issue has been
duly recorded.[1] Alien suffrage was more than a struggle for power: it
expressed a range of informal ethnocultural and religious conflicts, reinforced in some persons by class attitudes.

Michigan's alien suffrage fight sent repercussions throughout the
Northwest. The same issue became an effective dividing line between
Whigs and Democrats in two other Western states in the 1840s. As Iowa
and Wisconsin moved from territories to states, controversy over alien
voting helped shape nascent Whig and Democratic parties during periods
of constitution-making. Earlier, in Illinois from 1838 to 1841, Democrats and Whigs fought over alien suffrage in election campaigns, legislative halls, and the state supreme court.[2]

The Michigan episode perhaps held greater significance because of its
timing. In 1835 the familiar issues of Democratic-Whig strife were alive

---

[1] Streeter in *Political Parties* did not discuss the issue in relation to party development, 1-45, but in a later chapter on "The Foreign Element," 165-67, and
in relation to Democratic factions, 27-28, rather than Whig and Democratic
differences.

[2] For discussion of alien suffrage in the 1840s in Illinois, Wisconsin, and Iowa,
Ronald P. Formisano, "A Case Study of Party Formation: Michigan, 1835," *Mid-
America*, 50 (April 1968), 85-88.

and at hand, not ritual themes as they had become by the 1840s. No formal Whig party had existed anywhere before 1834, and the mid-1830s were the crucible years of the party system. As the party system made its debut in Michigan, with no old issues or constitutions to complicate party struggles, Democrats and Whigs battled intensely not over banks, *the* Bank, corporations, or other politicoeconomic issues, but over whether or not noncitizens should vote. The beginning of the two-party system came at a time characterized more than anything else by "growth." In 1835 Michigan euphorically sped along with the rest of the nation toward the Panic of 1837. The rate of population increase alone must have raised great expectations: 31,640 in 1830, to 212,671 by 1840. New land offices opened in 1831 and 1836 (ever westward), as land sales shot up (fed partly by speculation). Pioneers poured into virgin lands in all parts of the state, west and east. By 1834-35 railroad building was under way. The *Monroe Michigan Sentinel* soon knew of "scarce an individual in our community who is not engaged in anticipation or reality, in splendid speculations in Real Estate—and who is not moreover ready to shoulder, at one fell swoop, a Railroad, a Canal, or some other great project of local or general improvements."[3] Boom times did not cause the alien suffrage fight, but it seems safe to say that prosperity, rapid growth and flux, and the presence of recently uprooted and upwardly mobile persons helped intensify such a conflict once it began. It was a good example of status and cultural politics.[4]

Democratic leaders first enfranchised all inhabitants for the election of delegates and then prepared to write alien voting into the new constitution. These actions alone virtually caused the Whigs to build a party. The Democrats swamped the Whigs in the election, but probably no *party* fight would have occurred at all in 1835 were it not for alien voting. Neither the state election of 1835 nor the Presidential contest of

---

[3] George N. Fuller, *Economic and Social Beginnings of Michigan, 1807-1837* (Lansing, 1916), 63, 66-67, 70-71, 79-82, 86-87, 535. Almon Ernest Parkins, *The Historical Geography of Detroit* (Lansing, 1918), 170-90, 286-91. *Abstract of Returns of the Fifth Census, 1830* (Washington, 1832), 42. *Monroe Michigan Sentinel*, Aug. 1, 1835, 3, microfilm, MSL.

[4] Richard Hofstadter, "The Pseudo-Conservative Revolt (1955)," and "Pseudo-Conservatism Revisited: A Postscript (1962)," in Daniel Bell ed., *The Radical Right* (New York, 1964), 99, and 84-85. Nationally, the prosperous mid-1830s experienced a sharp increase in nativism and anti-Catholicism beginning about 1834-35, Billington, *The Protestant Crusade*, 85-141, and see esp. Ray Allen Billington, "Anti-Catholic Propaganda and the Home Missionary Movement, 1800-1860," Mississippi Valley Historical Review, 22 (December 1935), 361-84. It was after 1830, of course, that Irish Catholics and Germans began arriving in large numbers. One Michigan Protestant saw in 1833 the "Catholic question . . . becoming of so much interest all over the U.S.," M. E. Stuart to Z. P. Grant, Sept. 18, 1833, in Marlatt, ed., *Stuart Letters* I, 15.

1836 brought forth comparable contests.[5] Yet the parties of 1837 were the parties of 1835; that is, party loyalties crystallized in 1835 and most persons who voted for a particular party in 1835 probably continued to vote for that party in subsequent elections. Probably not many voters made their party choice on the alien suffrage issue alone. It is difficult to be precise, but the issue expressed deeper, preexisting social antagonisms which determined party choice for groups accounting for perhaps 40 to 60 percent of the electorate.

Systematic data on the composition of Michigan's population in the 1830s does not exist, but considerable impressionistic evidence testifies that about two-thirds came from New York and New England. Most New Yorkers came from counties bordering the Erie Canal, particularly in western New York, an area heavily colonized by Yankees. Thus, Michigan has been considered by many as a daughter of New England. Long before that, however, French Canadians had farmed and fished on the lake shores and river banks for several generations. In 1837 they numbered an estimated 10,000 to 12,000 out of a total white population of over 170,000. The Catholic French were not "aliens," of course, however alien their culture and religion may have seemed to many Yankee Protestants streaming into Michigan with very definite ideas about who were "foreigners" and who were not. Of the total native population perhaps 15 to 20 percent were "affiliated" Protestants of some kind: in 1837 the Methodists claimed 10,000 actual members, the Baptists 3,230, the Presbyterians and Congregationalists about 1,000, and the Episcopalians under 500. European immigrants, mostly Irish Catholics and German Catholics and Protestants, coming in growing numbers, did rank as aliens. Irish and Germans probably constituted the bulk of the 3,561 "aliens" recorded in an 1834 census—just over 4 percent of the population. That figure should be taken as a bare minimum, as other sources indicate that the numbers of aliens listed for many counties were far too low. According to Blois's 1838 *Gazetteer*, the total foreign born in 1837, including actual aliens and first generation immigrants, may have made up 15 to 20 percent of the population, and perhaps 20 to 30 percent of the electorate.[6]

[5] During 1836 Michigan was in the unique position of having a state government but being out of the Union because of a quarrel with Congress and Ohio over her southeastern boundary. This helped inhibit party growth. Clark F. Norton, "Michigan Statehood: 1835, 1836, or 1837?" *Michigan History*, 36 (December 1952), 321-50.

[6] The 1834 census is in Clarence Edwin Carter, ed., *The Territorial Papers of the United States*, XII: *The Territory of Michigan, 1829-1837* (Washington, 1945), 1018-21. On population sources: Fuller, *Economic and Social Beginnings*, 468-80, 493; J. Harold Stevens, "The Influence of New England in Michigan," *Michigan History*, 19 (Autumn 1935), 321-54; John A. Russell, *The Germanic Influence in*

Alien suffrage stimulated the hopes and fears of at least three politically significant groups: evangelicals, antievangelicals, and non-British immigrants. Evangelicals generally feared the influence of foreigners and Catholics as destructive of the values they promoted. Alien voting horrified them. In contrast Democratic Party leaders tended to be pluralist, secular, and nonauthoritarian in morals and religion. They trafficked easily with minority or out groups since their lack of self-righteousness made them more flexible. For these and other reasons non-British immigrants allied with the Democrats. Alien voting did not simply divide natives and immigrants. The Democrats pushing alien voting were mostly natives while the opposition included some foreign born. However, Irish Catholics and most Germans had a natural antipathy for the evangelicals. The Whigs feared that alien suffrage would greatly increase the power of their enemies and give too much influence in American society to groups that they wanted acculturated before political assimilation. To Whigs, who did not use such words, acculturation usually meant conformity to Anglo-Protestant models of behavior.

To the nascent Whig Party, alien voting was the overriding issue. What became a standard repertory of campaign charges filled the air from Detroit to Lake Michigan, but the most substantive and symbolic issue dividing the parties was alien voting. Not only did it open a chasm between Whigs and Democrats, but it also caused the only significant and intense division among Democrats themselves.

In firm control of the Territorial Legislative Council, the Democratic Republicans took the first step toward alien voting when the Council called for a referendum on statehood in 1832 and enfranchised all "inhabitants," white, male, and 21. Since 1819 voters had been white, male "citizens of Michigan Territory," one-year residents, and payers of a county or territorial tax. Now all noncitizens, nontaxpayers, even nonresidents could vote. Only 3,007 voted, while in the territorial election the year before 4,435 votes were cast. The majority for statehood was 627. Governor George F. Porter questioned the legitimacy of an election conducted with so broad a franchise, but Porter died in 1834 and Stevens T. Mason, young and impetuous, became Acting Governor. When Congress failed to pass a Michigan enabling act, Mason began to insist on

---

the *Making of Michigan* (Detroit, 1927), and John T. Blois, ed., *Gazeteer of the State of Michigan, 1838* (Detroit, 1838), 155-58. In 1834 Detroit's population of just under 5,000 contained nearly 1,000 aliens about 800 of whom were Irish, letter of Rev. Robert Turnbull, Nov. 8, 1834, M.E.D. Trowbridge, *History of Baptists in Michigan* (1909), 45. On the need for revising upward estimates of foreign-born voters based on population returns see George A. Boeck, "A Historical Note on the Uses of Census Returns," *Mid-America*, 44 (January 1962), 46-50.

Michigan's right to become a state and encouraged those Democrats who wanted to write a constitution without Congressional authorization.[7]

During 1834 no other party challenged the Democratic Party. There had been occasional calls for counterorganization, and an April 4 meeting in Detroit protested Jackson's removal of deposits from the Bank of the United States. Whig organization appears to have moved first from talk to action on December 18, in Detroit. Now the Bank was ignored except by implication. The Whigs concentrated instead on Michigan's "Tories" who had introduced spoils—"this stupendous system of corruption"—into Michigan. They accused the Democrats of being creatures of Martin Van Buren's Albany Regency. "This odious party machinery" was now about to impose a constitution on the people.[8]

References to New York held obvious meaning for the many emigrants from the Empire State. Political nativism had swept through New York City in 1834 after the unsuccessful attempt of the Whig candidate for mayor to enlist immigrant support. Thus, at the outset a classic pattern of the second party system emerged: Whig candidates facing heterogeneous electorates tried pluralist appeals, inviting even Irish Catholics to back them; but most of the invitees would decline; then nativism would gather force at secondary levels within Whiggery and outside of it. In 1834-35 in New York City the Native American Democratic Association formed and ran independent candidates. In November 1835 its Congressional entry polled 8,000 votes against Tammany's 10,000. Thereafter the NADA gradually fused with Whiggery. Michigan's nascent Whigs read New York newspapers. William Woodbridge learned from a New York friend that "we in this city have got to submit to be ruled by the dregs and outcasts of Ireland"; illiterate greenhorns who voted for "the party" were "increasing in us at the rate of 3 to 400 per year."[9] Considerations such as these may have led a Michigan Whig to tell Woodbridge that he thought constitution-making not very important"

[7] Act of February 16, 1819, *Laws of the Territory of Michigan, 1833* (Detroit, 1833), 35-36. Harold M. Dorr, "Origin and Development of the Michigan Constitution of 1835: A Study of Constitution Making" (unpublished Ph.D. dissertation, University of Michigan, 1933), 182-87, 201, 215, 224-29. Fuller, ed., *Messages of the Governors of Michigan*, I, 93. For Whig acquiescence during 1834, *Detroit Journal and Michigan Advertiser*, Nov. 5, 12, 1834, and Ann Arbor, *Michigan Emigrant*, July 24, 1834, Sept. 11, film MSL.

[8] *Detroit Courier*, March 5, 1834, April 2. *Detroit Journal and Michigan Advertiser*, April 9, 1834. Streeter, *Political Parties*, 6. *Michigan Emigrant*, Aug. 14, 1834. *Resolutions of Whig Meeting, 1834*. Dec. 18, an address of the Detroit General Whig Committee, BHC, also printed in *Journal and Michigan Advertiser*, Dec. 24, 1834.

[9] Leo Herskowitz, "The Native American Democratic Association in New York City, 1835-1836," *New York Historical Society Quarterly*, 46 (January 1962), 42-45, 55. Elihu White, New York, to Woodbridge, Nov. 8, 1834, Woodbridge MSS, BHC. Cf. Dixon Ryan Fox, *The Decline of Aristocracy in the Politics of New York, 1801-1840* (New York, 1919), 375n.

except "the qualification of electors" which was "of vast moment, a pivot on which the whole turns."[10]

Late in December the Territorial Council began considering legislation for holding a convention. John McDonell, a Democratic chieftain, sent a copy of the bill to Lucius Lyon, Territorial Delegate to Congress, to emphasize to Lyon the importance of alien suffrage: "The right of suffrage in this bill is based upon the ordinance of Congress of 1787. And it is best it should be so in order to give the democracy in the territory the ascendancy." McDonell even hinted that if Congress tried to admit Michigan without alien suffrage then he and his friends might "be compelled to adopt the nullification doctrine."[11]

On January 22 the Council enfranchised aliens and "Indians and persons of color" who paid taxes. But the next day, disenfranchising nonwhites, it provided that free, white, male inhabitants over 21 and three months resident, could vote, and that only United States citizens be elected delegates. Opposing final passage of the bill was a minority of 5 of the 13 Council members, 2 Democrats and 3 Whigs, who also voted to restrict the suffrage to citizens and to grant it to nonwhites. The bill concerning alien voting became known as the "Doty Bill," after one of its architects, Democrat James Duane Doty.[12]

To some extent the Doty Bill resulted from pressures from below. After its passage a Detroit Democrat boasted that: "during the present sitting of our circuit court I have been perhaps the sole means of adding about 400 names to the ranks of Jefferson Democracy in Wayne Co.—it is strange that 500 Irishmen should be found in this county most of them freeholders and little more than 50 naturalized citizens. The Legislative Council were kind enough to pass a law in consequence of the course we pursued enabling them to vote at the next convention."[13]

The Doty Bill immediately became for the Whigs a symbol of alien corruption and "of devotion to party at the expense of truth, honor and honesty." The Democrats had the weight of rational argument against them: *"Their only hope is founded upon . . . giving to foreigners . . . the*

[10] Simon Perkins, Nov. 26, 1834, to Woodbridge, Woodbridge MSS, BHC.
[11] John McDonell to Lyon, Dec. 29, 1834, Lyon MSS, Clements.
[12] Party affiliations in two cases are based on informed guesses: Daniel S. Bacon (D-Monroe); Abel Millington (W[?]-Washtenaw); George Renwick (W-Washtenaw); Samuel Satterlee (W-Oakland); John Stockton (D[?]-Macomb); *Michigan Biographies*, 55, 463, 549-50, 614; *Portrait and Biographical Album of Oakland County, Michigan* (Chicago, 1891), 881. Renwick, Millington, and Satterlee had all been Antimasons, which reinforces the probability of Millington's Whiggery, Ann Arbor, *Emigrant*, June 29, 1831, film, MSL, *Monroe Michigan Sentinel*, May 16, 1829, 1, film, MSL. Territory of Michigan, *Acts Passed at the Extra and Second Session of The Sixth Legislative Council* (Detroit, 1835), 74-75, 76, 77, 174. Dorr, "Origin of the Michigan Constitution," 216, 234-35.
[13] Michael L. Kesley, Detroit, to Lyon, Jan. 29, 1835, Lyon MSS, Clements.

privilege of voting away the rights of American citizens."[14] (Italics in original)

The prospect of alien voting intensified and released Whig nativism, anti-Irish and anti-Catholic attitudes, feelings that already existed. If one believes contemporary Democratic newspapers, the Whigs spent most of their time scheming to discriminate against foreigners and to create an authoritarian union of church and state that would suppress Catholics. After the election defeat, Whig newspapers did unleash their hostilities. But before that, Whig attitudes were apparent in seemingly detached discussions of Catholic convents, "Irish bullies," and in objections to foreigners voting who had not renounced allegiance to foreign powers, one power implicitly being the Roman Pope. When the constitutional convention failed to restrict liberty of conscience by providing that it not excuse "acts of licentiousness" or practices inconsistent with peace and safety, the *Journal and Courier* warned that all kinds of religious exotics could come to Michigan: Hindus, Mormons, "Bacanalian revels" [sic], and "Convents with all their impurities, priests with all their power to do evil may exert an influence destructive to the public virtue." This attitude had not developed overnight, but exposed a mentality in the editor, and to some extent in his audience, prepared to read and believe anti-Catholic fantasies in what Ray Allen Billington called "the greatest of the nativistic propaganda works," Maria Monk's *Awful Disclosures of the Hotel Dieu Nunnery of Montreal* (1836).[15]

During the first months of 1835 the Whigs established committees of correspondence, held township, county, and territorial conventions, nominated candidates, and organized to get out the vote. Wayne and Washtenaw counties led the way, followed closely by surrounding out-state areas.[16] Meetings in Wayne's Plymouth, Greenfield, Nankin, and Dearbornville townships all protested the Doty Bill. In Hamtramck an "Assemblée Française" said the bill was "contraire à la constitution des Etats Unis." In Springwells Whigs justified their organizing with resolutions devoted almost entirely to showing the injuries done to "American freemen" by alien voting. The Whig Wayne County convention rapped Tory hypocrisy in giving aliens the vote but denying them election as

[14] G. Kinwiock, Detroit, Feb. 5, 1835, to John Allen, John Allen MSS, BHC.

[15] *Michigan Emigrant*, Sept. 11, 1834, 3, Oct. 16, 2. *Michigan Whig*, Feb. 17, 19, 26, and March 5, 1835, discussed religion, temperance, and politics. *Detroit Journal and Courier*, July 29, 1835, on convents and priests. Billington, *Protestant Crusade*, 99. See also George Paré, *The Catholic Church in Detroit, 1701-1888* (Detroit, 1951), 347-51, and Dorr, "Origin of the Michigan Constitution," 212.

[16] Woodbridge, Jan. 5, 1835, to Henry T. Backus, Woodbridge MSS, BHC. Lewis Allen, Sharon, Jan. 9, 1835, to John Allen, M. Wright, Saline, Jan. 29, 1835, to Allen, John Allen MSS, BHC. George Corselius, "Diary, 1834-1838," entries for Dec. 19, 20, 29, 1834, and Jan. 24, April 1, 1835, MHCol, also described Whig organization in Washtenaw County.

delegates. This became a common Whig theme throughout the state, coupled with pleas to immigrants not to become the "tools" of the Democrats.[17]

The Wayne County convention declared itself in favor of a tax paying suffrage qualification. I have found no other instance of Michigan Whigs publicly advocating property or tax qualifications. In two cases Whigs privately favored a suffrage based on a "stake in society," but in both cases the men also were ardent nativists. Class and cultural attitudes blended in their thinking. Democrats in Detroit, furthermore, acquiesced to a taxpaying suffrage for city elections. Indeed, on March 21, 1835 the Legislative Council turned back, 6 to 5, a move to extend the right of suffrage in Detroit. Democrats voted on both sides. The Ann Arbor *Michigan Whig* admitted that some Whigs as well as some Democrats probably favored "in the abstract" some kind of property representation in government. No one, however, publicly advocated this in Michigan in 1835. Conservative Whigs—and Democrats—either kept silent or out of politics. In March the Whig Territorial Convention declared its "unqualified opposition" to property qualifications of any kind.[18]

In Washtenaw County, as in Wayne, the suffrage issue easily dominated the campaign. While the *Michigan Whig* argued almost continuously against alien voting, the Democratic *Michigan Argus* steadily accused the Whigs of being illiberal bigots. Whig township meetings and the county convention all played upon the immigrant "tools" theme.[19]

The Whig Territorial Convention's "Address," issued from Ann Arbor March 5, described in detail a Democratic plot to write alien voting into Michigan's constitution. The Tories welcomed Congress's failure to admit Michigan and would sacrifice the state's interests for the sake of alien voting. The Whigs called for citizen voting and insisted that any

[17] The Springwells resolutions are on a MS dated Dec. 1834, in the Woodbridge MSS in his handwriting, BHC. Plymouth, *Journal and Courier*, Jan. 21, 1835, Greenfield, *ibid.*, Feb. 4. Nankin, Dearbornville, *ibid.*, Feb. 18. Hamtramck, *ibid.*, March 5. Wayne County, *ibid.*, March 4.

[18] William Woodbridge, n.d., 1832, to Gov. George B. Porter; Henry P. Powers, Monguagon, Oct. 5, 1835, to Woodbridge, Woodbridge, MSS, BHC. Woodbridge and Powers are the two men referred to. *Territory of Michigan, Journal of the Sixth Legislative Council, Second Extra Session*, 141-42. *Michigan Whig*, Jan. 1, 1835. *Detroit Journal and Courier*, March 4, 1835, Feb. 4.

[19] Ann Arbor, *Michigan Argus*, e.g., Feb. 26, March 5 and 12, 1835, MHCol. *Michigan Whig*, Jan. 8, Feb. 5, 19, 22, March 19, 28. Township and county conventions, *ibid.*, Jan. 23, 1835, Feb. 19, Feb. 26, March 5, 19. Macomb County Whigs, *ibid.*, Feb. 5. It has been possible to examine Whig reactions in depth only in Wayne and Washtenaw counties, but the evidence there and at the territorial level that alien voting was the salient issue is overwhelming. In 1834, of Michigan's population of some 87,000, over 30,000 were in Wayne and Washtenaw combined. Another 22,000 were in nearby Oakland and Monroe.

constitution be submitted to the electorate for approval. The Address's only reference to the Bank of the United States amounted to hoping that the Bank issue would die and be forgotten.[20]

The suffrage issue did not play as crucial a role in the Democratic campaign. Democratic newspapers and conventions, at least, gave it far less attention. Many implicitly supported it while some deliberately ignored it, preferring to appeal to voters to prevent the latent "elements of a deep-rooted Aristocracy" from gaining power.[21] On the other hand, several Democratic meetings explicitly stood by the Doty Bill. Lenawee County Democrats issued an "Address" filled with rhetoric denouncing privilege and intolerance, and hailing "those who have sought asylum among us from oppression and tyranny in foreign lands, as our own brethren and friends, who are equally entitled with ourselves to the enjoyment of liberty, property, the elective franchise, eligibility to office, and all the other blessings which flow from our free institutions."[22] In the Democratic Territorial Convention's "Address" alien suffrage easily ranked as the dominant local issue. The bulk of the address reviewed party history from 1787, tracing a continuous line from Federalists to Whigs, aristocrats all! It blamed Whigs for making the election "a party question," forcing Democrats to campaign to insure that the constitution be written according to principles of a "pure representative democracy." The Democrats also defended their actions in the dispute Michigan was having with Ohio over the "Toledo strip" boundary, but gave far more attention to constitutional arguments for suffrage. Although they eulogized immigrants at length, their resolutions did not explicitly favor alien voting.[23]

The Democrats' warm words for foreigners, however sincere, contrasted sharply with the stiff, cold gestures of the Whigs. The latter did hold meetings for "Foreign Emigrants" and Wayne County Whigs claimed that they embraced "all the various religious denominations."[24] Whatever success Whigs enjoyed in this area of image-building, after the April 4 election it must have crumbled as Whig ultra-evangelicals and nativists opened fire on foreigners and Catholics. The *Journal and Courier*, believing that aliens had decided the election, blamed Tory demagogues for selling American birthrights to "fugitives from justice, ignorant beings besotted with vice." "Party demagogues . . . are holding

[20] *Detroit Journal and Courier*, March 25, 1835.

[21] *Monroe Michigan Sentinel*, Jan. 31, 1835, 7.

[22] Saline, Dexter, Salem, Sylvan meetings, *Michigan Argus*, March 5, 1835, March 12, Feb. 26. The Democratic Young Men of Washtenaw, and of Detroit, and Jackson County Democrats made no reference to the bill, *ibid.*, April 2. Lenawee County Democrats: *Michigan Sentinel*, Jan. 24, Feb. 14, 1835.

[23] *Michigan Argus*, Feb. 12, 1835.

[24] *Detroit Journal and Courier*, Feb. 25, 1835, March 4, April 1. *Michigan Whig*, March 5 and 19. See also, *Michigan Argus*, March 5, 1835.

out every encouragement to the vilest of the outcasts of Europe, to swarm upon our shores, take possession of our polls and control our elections." The paper charged that Catholic priests and young seminarians had campaigned for Van Burenism. The original French Catholics had been good citizens, but "new men" (the Irish) led by a "whole host of church functionaries" had now come to overthrow "our social system." Although 1,433 votes were polled in Detroit, the city contained, according to the *Journal*, only 450 legal voters: the rest were "Foreign Paupers" and "Catholic Mobs." Henceforth political parties should not be distinguished "by any other names than 'Americans' and 'Foreigners.' "[25]

In an equation common to evangelical thinking the paper later asserted that Americanism was synonymous with Protestantism. "All that we prize in the blessings of equal rights and . . . freedom of opinion in politics or religion is the result of Protestantism." Romanism inevitably conflicted with free inquiry and liberty of conscience. Now Van Burenism and Popery had joined in an unholy alliance to convert American freemen into slaves.[26]

In Washtenaw County the *Michigan Whig* said that about "400 aliens —British and German Subjects" voted the Jackson ticket "almost to a man." The editor had seen foreign Jackson voters "drawn up to the polls and handled like sheep in hurdles. . . . A man who votes without intelligence had best stay at home and lend his clothes to the demagogue to be stuffed with straw and walked up to the polls."[27] The *Whig* also warned Catholics that any attempt to gain political influence would raise a storm against them. The Catholics' "*foreign connections*, and the power of their priests, expose them to the constant vigilance of the friends of liberty."[28]

The Whig postelection bitterness suited the extremity of their defeat as they elected no less than 4 and no more than 9 of 89 delegates.[29] Yet study of election returns by counties and townships shows that this election was the first modern *party* conflict in Michigan and that the Whigs ran considerably better than their failure to elect many delegates suggests. They captured as much as 49 percent of the vote in some older eastern counties, where strong party voting prevailed. Comparison of 1835 returns with later elections in various townships indicates that party loyalties were fairly well established in 1835. In Monroe County, Democrats ran unopposed, but that was an exception. Whig candidates

---

[25] *Detroit Journal and Courier*, April 8, 1835.

[26] *Ibid.*, April 15, 22.

[27] The paper's name was now the *Michigan Whig and Washtenaw Democrat*, April 9.

[28] *Michigan Whig and Washtenaw Democrat*, April 16, also March 7, June 11.

[29] This estimate is based on information in the various sources below.

gained mean vote percentages of about 48 in Washtenaw, 45 in Oakland, 44 in St. Clair, 40 in Macomb, and about 45 in Wayne. Four Wayne townships went Whig in 1835 and 2 of them remained Whig strongholds for the next 16 years, as did several in Washtenaw, Oakland, and Lenawee.[30]

Lack of township returns for most counties and lack of party identification of some candidates makes it difficult to assess the extent to which party voting prevailed. Not all candidates ran as party men. Given the fragmentary nature of the data, it still suggests that the counties and towns with the sharpest party divisions were also the most populous, the most socially and economically complex, and possessed the best-developed communications facilities.[31]

THE CONSTITUTIONAL CONVENTION OF 1835

Although one observer thought that "party feeling has governed exclusively" in the election, delegates assembled in convention frequently protested their nonpartisanship, and charges of "bringing party spirit" into the convention brought angry denials. The delegates voted in a variety of alignments on different issues, and the Democratic majority, on key votes, often polled about 20 less than might have been expected.[32] This happened during the elective franchise fight. That debate lasted five days, two more than consumed by any other issue.[33]

Wayne County's Democratic delegation, led by John R. Williams, Alpheus White, and John Norvell, unofficial Democratic leader and chairman of the franchise committee, gave strong support to alien suffrage. In 1834 Wayne County contained five times as many aliens as any other county. By 1837 perhaps 20 percent of Wayne's population and

[30] The returns are in: Secretary of State, Great Seal and Archives: Elections, 1835-36, Box 35, MHCom. Township returns for Wayne, Oakland, and Lenawee are included. Washtenaw Township returns, *Michigan Whig and Washtenaw Democrat*, April 16, 1835. An indication of party voting occurs when each group of party candidates receives very similar—sometimes identical—totals. Some of the county totals showing no party vote may hide township returns which do. The village of Monroe experienced party voting in the election of town officers as early as March 2, 1835, *Monroe Michigan Sentinel*, March 7, 1835. Modern studies, too, show a relationship between length of residence and party voting; see, e.g., Alan L. Clem, *Precinct Voting: The Vote in Eastern South Dakota* (Vermillion, South Dakota, 1963), 236.

[31] Fuller, *Economic and Social Beginnings*, 95-243, 535-36, and map showing township organization by 1837, lxi. Blois, *Gazetteer of Michigan, 1838*, passim. *Compendium of the Sixth Census* (Washington, 1841), 94, 331.

[32] Henry R. Schoolcraft, *Personal Memoirs* (Philadelphia, 1851), 511. Dorr, ed., *Debates*, 278.

[33] Dorr, "Origin of the Michigan Constitution," 271, 277. Hemans, *Mason*, 152-77. Streeter, *Political Parties*, 27-28. Charles Lanman, *The Life of William Woodbridge* (Washington, 1867), 51.

30 percent of its potential electorate was foreign born. Throughout the antebellum period the Wayne Democrats showed themselves sensitive to the feelings of Irish and German newcomers through campaign rhetoric, flattery on Saints' Days, minor patronage and nominations, and symbolic gestures. With their offer of alien suffrage they made their most striking gesture of the period, one of immediate political value and of lasting symbolic importance.[34]

Numerous in Wayne County, too, were the Old French who early became strongly attached to the Democrats, in large part because their religion and folkways ensured antagonism against evangelicals. Not directly affected by alien voting, their position on it is difficult to determine and probably was somewhat ambiguous. They shared with non-British immigrants a sense of separateness from most natives as well as repulsion from evangelicals. But one gets the impression that they did not closely identify with non-French immigrants. It would not be long before they became rivals of the Irish and Germans for favors within the Democratic Party. Sympathy and uneasiness toward the immigrants, antipathy for the evangelicals, and Democratic Party loyalty probably all complicated their position.[35]

John Norvell initially presented a franchise article enabling white, male inhabitants over 21 and residents for 6 months to vote. As an opposition bloc holding out for citizen voting developed, Norvell's forces moderated their position by extending residency to 2 years. The first struggle came over attempts to strike the word "white" from the article. Democrat Ross Wilkins of Lenawee asked: "Paper is white and snow is white, yet how many men [are] white as paper or as snow?" Negroes are men, he said, and "all men are created free and equal." But Wilkins and most supporters of nonwhite suffrage opposed alien voting. This pattern of attitudes appeared throughout the North, as Professor Chilton Williamson has observed. Persons favoring Negro suffrage usually were Whigs and tended to be nativist. Similarly, Norvell's Democrats fell into a larger pattern: foremost in urging alien voting, they led in opposing Negro suffrage and in voicing race prejudice. When the Wilkins amendment lost (63-17), the antialien Democrats heavily supported it. The few identifiable Whigs, however, contrary to the pattern described, joined the majority against.[36]

---

[34] Carter, ed., *Territorial Papers*, xii: *Michigan, 1829-1837*, 1018-21. On White see [Richard R. Elliott], *MHC*, 26: 268. On Williams, Farmer, *Detroit*, ii, 1031. Democrat Michael Stubbs, an Irish Catholic from Washtenaw, supported alien voting, *History of Washtenaw County, Michigan* (Chicago, 1881), 644-45.

[35] See Chapter IX. Lewis Beaufait, a French Democratic delegate from Hamtramck, supported alien voting.

[36] Darius Comstock, William H. Welch, and Edward D. Ellis also spoke for nonwhite voting and opposed alien voting, *Debates*, 155-56, and Appendix A, roll

Norvell's group took orthodox Democratic states rights ground in arguing that states had full power to determine who could vote and that a person was first a citizen of a state and secondly of the United States. Norvell claimed his policy would promote prosperity by encouraging immigration. It embodied the "highest liberality of American institutions": exclusion of foreigners would mean incorporating "prejudices and aristocratical distinctions into the constitution."[37]

Whig spokesman William Woodbridge argued that the article violated the federal Constitution and usurped Congress's power of defining citizenship. In Woodbridge's view the community which made law for itself could only be a culturally homogeneous community. A representative democracy, he said, should represent only "the members of the community . . . its elemental parts . . . these only, who are of this Anglo-American family; in a word, its citizens." Newcomers needed at least 5 years to learn about "our complicated system of government." To qualify as a citizen and voter a man must have more than "general intelligence" and an "abstract devotion to liberty. . . . *His habits must* likewise have been formed upon our model."[38]

Opposition Democrats expressed less ethnocentrism than Woodbridge and emphasized their concern for abuse of the ballot and devaluation of citizenship resulting from alien voting. Few delegates, however, spoke as bluntly as Democrat David White, of Whiteford, Monroe County. Foreigners came to Michigan "as paupers . . . absolutely destitute, and entirely ignorant," and were led "like cattle to the polls."[39]

The antialien Democrats offered a compromise on May 27 but it failed 31 to 53,[40] and the same day a slightly modified article passed, requiring residency of 2 years in the country and 6 months in the state, declaration of intentions, and an oath "renouncing all allegiance to any foreign prince, potentate, or state." This part passed 51-33. A second part, enfranchising all inhabitants resident on April 4, 1835, passed 68-14.[41]

---

call 17. For Democratic anti-Negro speeches, *Debates*, 157-59, 161-62, 163. Chilton Williamson, *American Suffrage: From Property to Democracy, 1760-1860* (Princeton, 1960), 261-67.

[37] *Debates*, 193-218.

[38] *Debates*, 226, 228. Many of these arguments appeared in Whig sources listed above. The Whig editor of the 1838 *Gazetteer of Michigan* clearly shared Woodbridge's view of social "amalgamation" under Yankee influence, 158-59.

[39] *Debates*, 184-92, 173-80, 220. A Democratic newspaper described "Gen. David White" in 1834 as a "wealthy and intelligent landholder" under whose auspices western New Yorkers had settled Whiteford, *Michigan Sentinel*, Sept. 6, 1834.

[40] The Manning amendment would have enfranchised citizens after 6 months residence and inhabitants resident at the time of the Constitution's adoption, *Debates*, 249, 253-54.

[41] *Debates*, 265-66. The vote on both parts was 55 to 27. Mason apparently proposed the formula at meetings in Norvell's home attended by Crary, Wilkins, McDonnel, and Adam, MS note in Stevens T. Mason MSS, BHC, dated May 26, 1835. *Michigan Sentinel*, June 6, 13, 1835.

On June 4 Woodbridge and 3 other Whigs formally protested, calling alien voting unconstitutional, unrepublican, and unjust. Their "Protest" expressed anxiety over the undermining of cultural homogeneity and the loss of ancestral virtues. The coming of so many European foreigners, with different social and political habits "seems to have given a different character to our economical and social intercourse. The sober frugality and republican simplicity, which marked the manner of our ancestors, seems fast fading away before a . . . too suddenly enfranchised foreign population."[42]

The *Journal and Courier*, predictably, choked with rage over the "disgrace." The "slaves of a HIRELING DEMAGOGUE" had passed the franchise, a man who "spends his time in bar-rooms and grog-shops."[43] The *Michigan Whig*, presenting lengthy arguments against the article, predicted that it might be reconsidered. One Monroe Whig shared this optimism and wrote to Woodbridge that "Already such a feeling [is] abroad . . . as cannot fail to assure its reconsideration."[44]

Reconsidered it was, due to the refusal of a minority of some 20 Democrats to reconcile themselves to alien voting. The minority was stronger than its numbers because it included several influential Democratic leaders, men such as Robert McClelland, Lucius Lyon, and John Barry. Opposition Democrats hailed from all parts of the state. Outside the convention at least 3 Democratic newspapers opposed alien voting: Edward Ellis's *Michigan Sentinel*, the *Lenawee Republican*, of Lenawee County in the southeast, and the *White Pigeon Statesman*, of St. Joseph County in the southwest.[45] Lucius Lyon, who would be elected one of Michigan's first Senators in November, moved behind the scenes before the convention met to undercut alien voting. He asked John Forsyth, Jackson's Secretary of State, to send him literature dealing with "laws now in force for the naturalization of Foreigners," explaining that there were many foreigners in Michigan "and as the people are about forming a State government these laws are very much needed."[46]

[42] *Debates*, 510-15. Compare these Whig anxieties with what Marvin Meyers said were characteristic Democratic anxieties, *The Jacksonian Persuasion*, 3-15.

[43] June 3, 1835.

[44] May 28, 1835, June 4, 11. James Quincy Adams, Monroe to Woodbridge, (June 17, 1835) Woodbridge MSS, BHC.

[45] Barry would soon be elected state senator, then governor in 1841. McClelland was later congressman, governor, and United States Secretary of the Interior. Even before the election the Monroe Democratic convention said it favored a constitution "which will guard, in its purity, the elective franchise," *Michigan Sentinel*, March 14, 1835. The *Michigan Whig* complimented the *Sentinel* and *Republican* "for their upright American course on the elective franchise question" and congratulated the *Statesman* for criticizing Norvell's tactics, July 2, 1835.

[46] Dorr, "Origin of the Michigan Constitution," 213-15. Lucius Lyon, New York, April 3, 1835, to John Forsyth, in Carter, ed., *Territorial Papers*, XII, 891. E. Byron Thomas, "Political Ideas and Activity of John Stewart Barry, 1831-1851" (unpublished M.A. thesis, Northwestern University, 1935), 21-22.

The Democratic majority, perhaps fearing that the minority might oppose the entire constitution, perhaps also fearing that Congress would refuse to accept it, brought forth a compromise on June 17. It limited voting to citizens of 6 months' residence and enfranchised only those inhabitants resident at the time of the signing of the constitution, substantially the same compromise formula proposed earlier.[47] Edward Ellis reported happily to his readers that "brethren of the same principle" had compromised by means of an "honorable concession, to some extent, of the *majority* to the views of the minority."[48]

Although some Democrats sought to disguise it,[49] the franchise fight had badly split the party. In December Lucius Lyon wrote to a friend in New Orleans about it discussing the necessity of setting up safeguards against immigrant voters, and expressing the belief that the Michigan fight had "occasioned a split in the Jackson party which in all probability cannot be healed." Lyon was only partly right. Some of the same men who opposed one another on alien voting had again crossed swords as the legislature in November voted to select United States senators.[50] Yet the Democrats remained sufficiently united to carry the state in 1835, 1836, and in 1837 against a revived Whig opposition.

The last struggle over Michigan's 1835 enfranchisement of aliens was yet to come. In the spring of 1836 Michigan remained unorganized as a state but technically out of the Union because she refused to accept the loss to Ohio of land she regarded as hers. Congress spent many hours discussing the question until April 1836, when the Senate fashioned a compromise by which Michigan would get her Northern Peninsula and lose the "Toledo Strip" to Ohio. During the closing moments of debate, Henry Clay and other prominent Whigs turned their attention to the alien voting clause in Michigan's constitution. The Senate was about to make Michigan's admission conditional on assent to the boundary proposals from "a convention of the people of Michigan." Clay asked to

---

[47] Democratic fear of Congress was proposed by Woodbridge on his copy of the June 4 "Protest," Woodbridge MSS, BHC, and is suggested by the defensive tone of Lucius Lyon, John Norvell, and Isaac Crary, Washington, D.C., Dec. 31, 1836, to Hon. F. Thomas, Chairman, Judiciary Committee, in Carter, ed., *Territorial Papers,* XII, 1218-22.

[48] *Michigan Sentinel,* June 20, 1835; *Debates,* 393-94. *Michigan Whig and Washtenaw Democrat,* June 25, July 2, 1835.

[49] See, e.g., *Michigan Argus,* July 2, 1835.

[50] In urging Louisiana to protect itself from aliens, Lyon ironically echoed Norvell's state rights position by asserting that Congress could not interfere if Louisiana chose to require 15 years' residence or to prohibit foreigners from voting altogether, "as women and boys are," Lucius Lyon to Col. Geo. W. Boyd, Dec. 25, 1835, in L. G. Stuart, ed., "Letters of Lucius Lyon," *MHC,* 27: 468-69. Floyd B. Streeter attributed Democratic factions to economic and sectional differences, "The Factional Character of Early Michigan Politics," *Michigan History,* 2 (January 1918), 165-91.

substitute for that phrase: "by the free white male citizens of the United States" residing in the state. This failed by one vote, 22 to 23. Although the party identification of a few senators is elusive, almost every identifiable Whig voted with Clay. Silas Wright led the overwhelmingly Democratic majority on this issue. Clay then attacked Michigan's constitution directly, proposing that if Michigan accepted Congress's terms her constitution would be approved by Congress "except that provision . . . by which aliens are permitted to enjoy the right of suffrage." Although Clay lost some of his support as this measure failed, 14 to 22, the minority was still mostly Whig and the majority for alien voting still heavily Democratic. Clay's support on both votes came from all sections. His tactics, the debates show, fit into a larger strategy of Whig attempts to embarrass the Jacksonians in an election year.[51] The Whigs who voted to eliminate alien voting in Michigan probably wanted most to aid their party. Whether or not their votes individually acquired symbolic importance or had an impact on their constituencies is a subject for further study. This chapter of Michigan's alien voting controversy received little notice in Michigan, but the 1835 convention debate and the general positions of the parties were long remembered.[52]

Most Democrats in Michigan, it seemed, willingly joined together in appeals designed to capitalize on Whig nativism. Letting aliens vote was different. The minority opposing it probably acted from a variety of motives: fear of loss of power and status to intraparty rivals strengthened by alien votes; nativism; fear of a "native backlash" against Democrats; constitutional scruples; and genuine doubts as to the wisdom of noncitizen voting. The public Democratic opposition to alien voting usually lacked the nativism and anti-Catholicism often expressed by Whigs.

Whatever the internal strains within parties in 1835, their general public postures, their official and unofficial images were quite different regarding foreigners and Catholics. Whig newspapers continued to rage against them into 1836. The Democratic state convention in August

[51] *Congressional Globe*, 24th Cong., 1st Sess., Dec. 1835-July 1836 (Washington, 1836), III, 276, 268. Calhoun, Crittenden, and White still voted with Clayton on the second vote. Buchanan had a lengthy speech justifying alien voting read into the *Globe*, "Appendix," 330-32. Party affiliations are from *Biographical Directory of the American Congress, 1774-1961* (Washington, 1961). For the general political context see Charles M. Wiltse, *John C. Calhoun: Nullifier, 1829-1839* (Indianapolis, New York, 1949), II, 223-36, 278-95, and Van Deusen, *Jacksonian Era*, 96-98, 110-11.

[52] Extensive reading of newspapers and manuscripts for the period 1836 to 1852 has produced only one reference to the Senate debates, *Report of the Committee on State Affairs, to Whom Was Referred a Joint Resolution Proposing an Amendment to the Constitution in Relation to Qualification of Voters*, Doc. No. 6, State of Michigan, *Documents Accompanying the Journal of the Senate, 1843* (Detroit, 1843). The Democratic author stressed Whig opposition to and Democratic support of alien voting during these debates.

1835 reaffirmed its friendship for foreigners and Catholics and denounced Whig papers for creating "a spirit of Jealousy and distrust between native born citizens and foreigners," accusing Whigs of systematic efforts "to connect religion and politics" which subverted Republican institutions.[53]

The actions of leaders and parties in 1835 probably came to have symbolic meaning for many voters, as, for example, William Woodbridge and the Whig "Protest." Eight years later, after Woodbridge had served a year as governor and three years as United States Senator, a Whig voter wrote to him that "Your public life as far as I am acquainted has been pleasing to the people in particular and *the course which you pursued at the forming of our state constitution was worthy of your head and heart.*" (Italics mine) In 1847 Detroit's Native American newspaper, *American Vineyard*, came out for Zachary Taylor for President and Woodbridge for Vice President in 1848. It printed the 1835 "Protest" in full to show why it supported Woodbridge. Ironically, many Democratic newspapers throughout the 1840s, indeed as late as 1852, also printed the 1835 "Protest," but for a very different reason.[54]

Because parties were just coming into being, the alien suffrage fight and its aftermath contributed significantly to forming voter loyalties and establishing party traditions. Henceforth, words and actions of party leaders would be seen by many in the context of these traditions, and that context would lend to words and actions symbolic meaning often running far deeper than appearances. Both parties and leaders began to "stand for" certain things.

The alien voting fight held profound drama for certain ethnocultural groups and engaged group antagonisms of growing significance in American society. While the issue directly affected practical political interests, it was also a matter of cultural politics, arraying on opposite sides subcultures already hostile to one another. Such a party fight at such a time powerfully shaped the character and images of parties and the response of voters.

EPILOGUE: THE CONSTITUTIONAL CONVENTION OF 1850

In 1850 Michigan again held a Constitutional Convention. The public style, image, and rhetoric of Whigs and Democrats had changed in 15 years, yet the convention debates reveal that alien voting still constituted a salient dividing line. Social pressures had not abated but increased.

[53] *Michigan Argus*, Sept. 24, 1835.
[54] John B. Hough, Bristol, Lapeer Co., to Woodbridge, Nov. 28, 1843, Washington, D.C., Woodbridge MSS. *American Vineyard*, April 23, Dec. 14, 1847, BHC. Edelman, *Symbolic Uses of Politics*, proved stimulating in the development of these conclusions.

Population data suggest only a small part of the group dynamics at work. In 1850 over 54,000 persons, or 13.8 percent of the population, had been born in foreign countries. Foreigners may have constituted 20 to 30 percent of the electorate. How large the "foreign" or "ethnic" population was once the unassimilated of the second and third generation were counted, and those foreigners included who had illegally crossed borders, can only be guessed. Although immigrants were scattered across the state, many non-British newcomers lived in urban and rural concentrations. The disproportionate ratio of males to females among immigrants meant that the percentage of the electorate that was foreign certainly exceeded the percentage of foreigners in the entire population. Far more impressive to the native mind in 1850, however, were the group immigrations of the late 1840s which brought whole colonies of Dutch to western Michigan and of Germans to the Saginaw Valley. Native images of these settlements, sometimes quite distorted, formed an important backdrop to the debates in the 1850 convention.[55]

In the short campaign before the May 6 election of delegates no "Doty Bill" excited the Whigs, and county nominating conventions appear to have been routinely dull. The Democratic *Grand Rapids Enquirer* did not expect party lines to be drawn and the *Advertiser* claimed that "no party issues are necessarily involved in the canvass."[56] Turnout and interest were low, and the *Free Press* said there was "more [ticket] splitting than we have ever known."[57] But the off-year Democratic charm was not to be broken. Some 80 or 81 Democrats gained election, 16 or 17 Whigs, and 3 Free Soilers.[58]

The Democrats brought a franchise article to the convention that gave the vote to every white male citizen of 21 years who had resided in the state 6 months, and to "every white male inhabitant who was permitted to vote under the previous constitution of this state, and their male descendants." Some Democratic delegates then offered amendments, most of which extended the suffrage further. One large group favored letting every inhabitant of 2 years' residence vote; another seemed will-

[55] Streeter, *Political Parties*, 44; Dunbar, *Michigan*, 350-58; Russell, *Germanic Influence*, 56-59; DeBow, *Compendium*, 50, 61, 350, 599. Daily Advertiser, *Directory for the City of Detroit, 1850* (Detroit, 1850).

[56] For Wayne and Kalamazoo county conventions, *Advertiser*, April 19, 26, 1850. *Free Press*, May 8, 1850; *Advertiser*, April 12, 1850.

[57] *Free Press*, May 7, 1850; Wayne County returns are in the *Advertiser*, May 17, 1850.

[58] *Free Press*, May 13, 1850, said 18 Whigs were elected but named only 10. *Advertiser*, May 10, said 16 Whigs won office but named only 13. Frederick W. Stevens, *Michigan Constitutional Convention of 1850* (n.p., n.d.), 12, gave the number of Whigs as no more than 10. I checked the various lists in *Michigan Biographies*.

ing to enfranchise every inhabitant (otherwise qualified) with only a minimal residence requirement of weeks or months.[59]

As in 1835 a small minority of Free Soilers demanded black suffrage, and charged Democrats with being inconsistent in professing liberality but restricting it to whites. Joseph Williams, a Whig Free Soiler, gave a long, passionate speech and taunted the Democrats: "Let the naturalization laws of the United States be the test; or let gentlemen go for universal suffrage, and admit all men to the rights of electors." But the call for black suffrage was again only a brief interlude and apparently not of concern to most Whigs and Democrats.[60]

Alien suffrage in 1850 provoked no full-scale debate as in 1835, nothing comparable to the set speeches and dramatic exchanges of William Woodbridge and John Norvell. The "conservatives" as before, however, were both Whigs and Democrats. They argued that Michigan should not violate United States naturalization laws, that newcomers needed at least 5 years to learn how to read and write English, that special enfranchisement of "inhabitants" discriminated against later arrivals, that localities needed to be protected against floods of foreigners who could take control of them, and one Whig asked why "our young men" should not vote at 16 years of age.[61]

The fear of nonassimilated foreigners had increased by 1850 because of the immigrant concentrations in the Saginaw Valley and western Michigan. "It is well known," said one Democrat, "that there has been a large emigration from Germany and Holland to our State for the last three or four years, and that these emigrants have clustered together, and are not dispersed among our citizens." Another prominent Democrat observed that when foreigners mixed they rapidly become assimilated, "But do gentlemen know that to be the case where large colonies are formed without any mixing of American population; colonies of thousands; and when they come in and settle the way they do, giving the American citizens no access to them, and under the control of their religious protectors to so great a degree that you can have no influence with them."[62]

In general, conservatives showed a sensitivity for the feelings of for-

[59] State of Michigan, *Report of the Proceedings and Debates in the Convention to Revise the Constitution of the State of Michigan, 1850* (Lansing, 1850), 278-79. (Hereafter referred to as *Report.*)

[60] *Report*, 485-86. See also 284-96, 490-91, for discussion of colored suffrage. "Colored" was the term current among blacks and abolitionists.

[61] Remarks of Sutherland (D), *Report*, 279; Hascall (D), 279; Gale (W), 280; N. Pierce (W), 282; Beeson (D), 283; White (W[?]), 490; Hanscom (D), 493.

[62] *Report*, 496; 489. Another Democrat pointed to thousands of foreigners who could not speak English, knew nothing of the laws, and who were under leaders "who can control their votes by thousands," 493.

eigners that was a tribute to the latter's voting strength. A Democrat from Wayne County, however, opposed alien voting with words that since 1835 symbolized nativist attitudes. Henry Fralick said aliens would vote our rights away; even "the best class of foreigners" did not want the suffrage cheapened: "It is too much like driving cattle to market. They are imposed upon by designing demagogues." Fralick, an atypical Democrat, came from Plymouth, an anti-Democratic stronghold where Yankees, Whigs, and abolitionists flourished. In 1853 Fralick, as state representative, was a leader of the drive for an antiliquor Maine Law, which many of his fellow townsmen also desired. He held many local offices, was a respected businessman, and a Congregationalist.[63]

Fralick voted against alien suffrage but few Democrats joined him. Some of those who objected to the 2-year limit wanted to enfranchise inhabitants of two and one-half years who had declared their intention of becoming citizens. Editor John S. Bagg, a delegate, exhorted Democratic waverers to be true to Democratic traditions by championing liberal suffrage and naturalization laws. The clique of Whigs and Free Soilers present, he said, had no responsibility "except to artfully and deceptively defeat the measure."[64]

One Whig, at least, was trying artfully to defeat the measure. Henry T. Backus, appropriately William Woodbridge's son-in-law, led the opposition to alien voting with a subtle game. After opposing all Democratic measures expanding noncitizen voting, Backus tried to attach amendments going beyond the limits of Democratic generosity, probably in an effort to turn Democratic moderates against the entire article. His proposal to make every elector eligible for election to state offices also pointed out a Democratic inconsistency which Whigs had complained of since 1835. Democrats warded off Backus with cries of Native Americanism and Whig insincerity.[65] In its final form the franchise article gave the vote to all white male citizens of 21, to every inhabitant permitted to vote in 1835, to every inhabitant resident on January 1, 1850, and all inhabitants resident for two and one-half years in the state who had declared their intention of becoming citizens—as well as to every "civilized" Indian not a member of a tribe. The key vote was 59 to 31, with 10 abstentions, mostly Democrats. The *Free Press* correspondent in Lansing said the Whigs voted against the article 2 to 14. The available sources indicate that at least 1 Whig voted for the measure and no more than 2; 13 or 14 Whigs definitely opposed it. At a minimum, then, 76

[63] *Report*, 281. Rev. R. C. Crawford, "Memoir of Hon. Henry Fralick," *MHC*, 18: 318-20.

[64] *Report*, 487.

[65] *Report*, 499, 501, 505. Backus presented a petition from H. Eisnack and 20 other "naturalized citizens" asking that the vote not be extended to foreigners until they were "regularly naturalized," 381.

percent of the Whigs opposed the article and 71 percent of the Democrats supported it.[66]

As the convention came to an end, the *Free Press* reporter reviewed Whig activities in the convention and said that on three major issues the Whigs had voted along party lines. First, they had voted for a new districting system for the state legislature, allegedly because they expected to gain seats thereby. Second, they voted against admitting newly organized counties, allegedly because they feared these counties would elect Democrats. Finally, the "last general vote of a partisan character given by the Whigs" was on the franchise article, where they displayed a "deep-seated hatred" for the foreign born. "In fact, every action of the Whig delegates touching the qualifications of voters, indicated the strongest desire to disfranchise and alienate from our institutions and common country all foreigners."[67]

If the foregoing could be accepted at face value, then alien voting could be considered the most salient electorate oriented issue dividing the parties in the convention of 1850. Before that claim could be made, however, systematic analysis of voting in the convention, and public reaction, would have to be made. Votes on such issues as debt exemption, for example, would have to be analyzed and compared to the divisions, by party, on other issues.[68]

If alien suffrage was not the most salient issue dividing parties in the 1850 convention, it was at least one vital point of divergence between them, one that exposed elements of their deeper character, and one that still retained emotional intensity and symbolic importance.

[66] *Report*, 505; *Free Press*, Aug. 7, 1850. For contradictory claims regarding the episode: *Free Press*, July 24, 1850; *Advertiser*, July 30, 1850.

[67] *Free Press*, Aug. 7, 1850.

[68] The debt exemption article excluded $500 worth of personal property and the individual property of married women from execution. It passed by a vote of 52 to 21: 5 or 6 Whigs opposed it and 15 or 16 Democrats. *Advertiser*, Aug. 2, 1850; Lena London, "Homestead Exemption in the Michigan Constitution of 1850," *Michigan History*, 37 (December 1953), 385-406. In the convention Wilbur F. Storey, Democratic editor, fought for an article forbidding the teaching of a mechanical trade to convicts with a flourish of "proletarian rhetoric." His biographer commented: "Ironically during the next thirty years, there was to be no more hated employer in the newspaper business than this same Wilbur F. Storey who until the day he died fought a bitter and successful campaign against the typographical union." Justin F. Walsh, *To Print the News and Raise Hell: A Biography of Wilbur F. Storey* (Chapel Hill, 1968), 42-43.

VI

Moral Society v. Laissez Faire Ethics: Evangelicals

> Come all ye Yankee Farmers
> Who'd like to change your lot;
>
> . . .
>
> Come follow me and settle in Michigania.
>
> Then There's your land of Blue Laws
> Where deacons cut the hair
> For fear your locks and tenets
> Should not exactly square;
> Where beer that works o' Sunday
> A penalty must pay,
> While all is free and easy
> In Michigania.
> —Emigrants' Traveling Song, 1837[1]

The alien voting fight of 1834-35 threw into relief some of the value conflicts imbedded in party cleavages. The traditional interpretation of party formation placed vital issues along a politicoeconomic spectrum, with conservative Whigs and radical Democrats at opposing ends. This view must be modified and placed in historical context by recognition of the centrality of Whig-Democratic clashes on an authoritarian-laissez faire spectrum. On a set of issues connected with government regulation of ethics, morals, and beliefs, Whigs tended to favor and Democrats to resist control. The Democrats supported that traditional liberalism which has promoted the separation of law and morality. The Whigs leaned toward an authoritarianism demanding compliance with certain community norms—just as they favored a paternalist national government acting to promote economic development. The Democrats preferred fewer restraints on individual and presumably enlightened self-interest and tended to reject the Whigs' integrative approach, whether in morals, religion, culture, or national political economy. These diverging traits of party ideology and program proceeded from a different underlying world view of self, society, and government.

Ralph Waldo Emerson, who believed that "Morality is the object of

---

[1] Refrain and fourth verse, quoted in W. G. Doty, "Ann Arbor," *Michigan History*, 7 (July-October 1923), 197.

government," came to disapprove of Democrats because "they did not base political action on morality, or shape their politics toward the promotion of individual culture."[2] On the first count, the Whigs should have been Emerson's party. In Michigan, at least, they tended to back legislation to enforce moral integration of the community. While some believed that the individual heart was "the source and fountain of human action that must be purified before we can realize the beau ideal which is set forth in our system,"[3] Whig evangelicals nevertheless accepted legal coercion as a necessary supplement to the persuasive techniques available to bring about the moral society.

The evangelical v. antievangelical conflict in Michigan should be seen in the perspective of a dispute at least as old as the republic. Beginning in the 1790s, Protestant leaders provoked by frontier hedonism, disestablishmentarianism, French revolutionary naturalism, Jeffersonian deism and rationalism, free thought, lack of God's "representation" in government, and other demons, began trying to reclaim America for the deity. Although frontier revivals marked high fever points, New England theocrats, some of whom during these years fashioned an "Arminianized" or "revival Calvinism," provided the drive and most of the organizing intelligence of the campaign. After the War of 1812 a proliferation of national benevolent societies managed by interlocking directorates spread across the land hoping to: put a Bible in every home; promote missions; preserve the Sabbath; support Sunday schools; save the Indians; extirpate demon rum; wage peace; revive backsliders, and much more. The organizing mania reached a crescendo in the mid-1820s, just before the Reverend Ezra Stiles Ely issued his now famous call for a "Christian Party in Politics," and just before the "evangelical united front" began its 1828-29 "Great Offensive" to save the Mississippi Valley from Popery.[4]

[2] Arthur I. Ladu, "Emerson: Whig or Democrat?" *New England Quarterly,* 13 (September 1940), 433. Daniel Bell, *The End of Ideology: On the Exhaustion of Political Ideas in the Fifties* (New York, 1960), while stimulating and useful here, is not always informed accurately on nineteenth-century America; but see "Status Politics and the New Anxieties," 103-21.

[3] Thomas Rowland to Woodbridge, May 10, 1842, Woodbridge MSS, BHC.

[4] Bodo, *Protestant Clergy;* Cole, *Northern Evangelists;* Timothy L. Smith, *Revivalism and Social Reform in Mid-Nineteenth Century America* (New York, 1957); Bernard Weisberger, *They Gathered at the River* (Boston, 1958), 3-19; Franklin Hamlin Littell, *From State Church to Pluralism* (New York, 1962); Ludlum, *Social Ferment in Vermont,* 30-52; Richard Hofstadter, *Anti-Intellectualism in American Life* (New York, 1964); Clifford S. Griffin, *Their Brother's Keepers: Moral Stewardship in the United States, 1800-1865* (New Brunswick, 1960); see the use of "evangelical" by John L. Thomas, *The Liberator: William Lloyd Garrison* (Boston, 1963), 57-69; Joseph L. Blau, "The Christian Party in Politics," *Review of Religion,* 11 (November 1946); Gilbert H. Barnes, *The Antislavery Impulse, 1830-1844* (New York, 1933); Anne C. Loveland, "Evangelicalism and 'Immediate Emancipation' in American Antislavery Thought," *Journal of*

Although scholars have given the evangelicals considerable attention, the full impact of their activities has not been appreciated. No one, for example, has suggested that the evangelical agitation should be regarded as a long-run cause of political party development. Yet, Christian politicizing helped prepare the electorate for its reception of parties and affected the manner of their reception, once political elites set about building parties. Revivalism, the engine of the movement, helped launch successive waves of moral ultraism; the evangelical campaign generally escalated the level of moral tension in society, and perhaps more importantly, articulated and sharpened the value conflicts of subcultures. These social cleavages became conditions having a significant determining effect on mass party divisions once political elites began to build parties.

As evangelicals laid spiritual siege to the West, the revival impulse took political form in Michigan as Antimasonry rose in righteous wrath. After Antimasonry died politically its spirit went marching on in the evangelical wing of the Whig party. It also carried on in benevolent societies heavily staffed by ex-Antimasons and Whigs. Thus, the Whig party succeeded Antimasonry as a more secularized "Christian Party" and became the evangelicals' best hope to Christianize America. The benevolent societies interlocked not only with one another but also with Whiggery.

Presbyterians more than any other denomination occupied leadership positions in benevolence, reform societies, and Whiggery. By the late 1830s Presbyterianism appeared to be in almost open alliance with Whiggery. The Michigan Synod repeatedly made policy statements intended for the ears of rulers and politicians.

THE ANTIEVANGELICALS: SECULARISM AND LAISSEZ FAIRE ETHICS

The Democracy should bear in mind that we are now entering upon a new era in our political history—we are casting aside the exploded doctrine of supporting *men* instead of *measures*—we are just bringing into operation the plan of a general organization for the furtherance of sound, liberal, Democratic principles; we are taking ground against the baneful influence aimed to be attained by a union of Church and State—and we are taking a bold and dignified stand against an irresponsible faction. . . . [the Aristocracy][5]

So spoke the *Monroe Michigan Sentinel* on the eve of the April 1835 election. The editorial sharpened its appeal to class resentments by charging Democratic opponents with sneering at "the idea of a farmer or mechanic being called upon to assist in framing a Constitution."

Southern History, 32 (May 1966), 172-88; Charles I. Foster, *An Errand of Mercy: The Evangelical United Front, 1790-1837* (Chapel Hill, 1960).

[5] *Monroe Michigan Sentinel*, April 4, 1835, film, MSL.

Along with its egalitarianism, however, the *Sentinel* emphasized party organization and antievangelicalism. Democrats conspicuously denounced "Aristocracy," but almost every politician in Michigan used that negative reference symbol. None favored "aristocracy," at least not in public. The task of historical analysis is to find out, if possible, what meanings the symbol held for various groups. "Union of Church and State," for example, meant evangelical authoritarianism to many. Content analysis of these terms could be quite useful; meanwhile, one gets the clear impression that the idea of aristocracy often included among its meanings the idea of evangelical hegemony in frontier Michigan.

From the beginning of Whiggery, Democrats reacted to the evangelical-authoritarian impulses they saw infusing that party. An ungrammatical Ypsilanti Democratic Republican described a Whig meeting in his town in December 1834. Two men from Detroit and one minister directed the proceedings and

exorted the people everyone to join the Coldwater Society and by the arbitrary Laws they exorted to be enforced upon the people was the two plain not to be [mis]understood by all discerning the one was a violent anti Mason from the first Commencement of anti ism the other as great a Gambler and Corrup Shavour as Michigan afords, it is evident that some of the Ministers together with the antis have mingled themselves with the Coldwater Society to gain [ascendancy] over the Republican party.[6]

Not all Democrats were antievangelical. Some, such as Ross Wilkins, a prominent Democrat and Methodist preacher, could be described as pietist if not evangelical. Yet an aversion to "arbitrary laws" regulating moral conduct probably repelled such men from Whiggery. As will be seen, native Protestant Democrats tended to belong to nonevangelical denominations which had compartmentalized views of religion and secular affairs. Democrats, too, far more than Whigs, simply cared less about religion. This helped make for tolerant, pragmatic attitudes. As Nathaniel Ward of Ipswich, a seventeenth-century Puritan, said, "A person who is willing to tolerate any religion . . . either doubts of his own or is not sincere in it." The difference between Ward and religious men who are also tolerant is, of course, that the latter regard doubt positively, as a useful humanizing process of self-examination. The Democrats remind one of the *politiques* who emerged during sixteenth-century France's Wars of Religion, men concerned with finding a secular common denominator of coexistence between warring religious groups.[7]

[6] Oliver Whitmore to Lucius Lyon, Dec. 16, 1834, Lyon MSS, Clements. See also Ann Arbor, *Michigan Argus*, Nov. 9, 1837; other Democratic newspapers which are good sources of Democratic antievangelicalism are the *Kalamazoo Gazette, Jackson Patriot,* and *Detroit Free Press.*

[7] Ward quoted in Hudson, *American Protestantism*, 13. Leonard L. Richards' analysis of a "traditionalist" mentality touches upon themes connected with secular-

The 1835 Constitutional Convention debated several issues concerning religion and government, consuming as much time in this area as in any other except the elective franchise. On religious, moral, and ethical questions Whigs, as represented by William Woodbridge, expressed substantially evangelical attitudes. Democratic attitudes tended to be secular, latitudinarian, and pragmatic. While tolerant and relaxed on religious and moral matters, Democrats felt strongly about being told what to do. They knew very well what they did not want. The convention adopted a Bill of Rights that was aggressively secular. Three sections of Article I guaranteed freedom of conscience, separated church and state, and granted equal political and civil rights for individuals of "any opinions or belief concerning matters of religion." The first clause was submitted originally as "Every man has a right to worship Almighty God according to the dictates of his own conscience, provided such worship does not lead to acts of licentiousness, or to a breach of the peace." Democratic leader John Norvell moved successfully to strike out the words after "provided," saying he wanted to take no chances of putting a loophole in the constitution through which sectarian animosities might operate.[8]

When a delegate made the seemingly innocuous proposal that clergymen be invited to give a daily invocation, many delegates quickly objected. John Norvell said he opposed any mingling of religion with politics which might be the first step toward union of church and state—creeping theocracy, as it were, by way of a daily prayer. William Woodbridge, on the contrary, welcomed a prayer to foster solemnity among the delegates and a "direct perception of the power of God . . . [by] a direct appeal to His overruling Providence." A daily prayer would show respect for patriotic customs and, he claimed, for "the public sentiments of the American people."[9]

Evangelicals had long sought to purge the practice of dueling from American society; they were especially outraged by election of duelists to public office—for example, Andrew Jackson. Pietists contended that honoring a duelist gave public sanction to the evil. In the Michigan convention a Quaker delegate proposed that any person fighting or seconding a duel be excluded from voting or election to office. Norvell warned that such a measure gave the legislature too much power. The convention might as well go further, he said, "and exclude all who may utter such language calculated to provoke such a challenge. *If they undertake to deprive a man of his rights for resenting injury . . .* they may go to the

ism as defined here, *"Gentlemen of Property and Standing": Anti-Abolition Mobs in Jacksonian America* (New York, 1970), 131-50.

[8] Dorr, "Origin of the 1835 Michigan Constitution," 271-72. *Debates,* 598, 289-90.

[9] *Debates,* 119-20, 130-32.

end of the chapter of discretion, and make every little irregularity such an offence." (Italics mine) He did not approve of dueling, however, and thought if death resulted it should be treated "as a crime." His rather ambivalent disapproval notwithstanding, Norvell was defining dueling as a matter of personal judgment in which the law should not interfere. Until someone was killed, personal codes of honor took precedence over law. Woodbridge expressed a characteristic Whig desire to regulate such "personal" matters. He found dueling a barbaric "relic of the feudal system; a means of gratifying the angry and malevolent passions, which had nothing but custom to sanction it."[10]

In an exchange over freedom of the press Woodbridge and Norvell clashed again. The question was whether in libel cases, if it appeared to a jury that the matter charged as libelous was true, and "published with good motives and for justifiable ends, the party should be acquitted." Norvell moved to strike out the "good motives" and "justifiable ends" clause. He wanted no jury to "determine the intentions of any man, when liberty of the press was concerned"; men in politics should be willing to bear abuse from the press. Woodbridge objected to such unrestrained personal freedom, pointing out that slander cases reached not only political men but everybody, holding nothing sacred. Norvell's amendment left "open the door for the gratification of the most malignant and vindictive feeling, and gives the malicious libeler the assurance that he shall go free." Certainly the character of public men should be "freely canvassed," but Woodbridge wanted limits on the "outpourings . . . of such things as were fit only for the bar room."[11] The opposition of Norvell and Woodbridge on these issues, and the values implied, did not represent all Michigan Whigs and Democrats, but did express central tendencies in their parties.

The article on education adopted by the 1835 convention pointed the early educational policy of the state in a secular direction and thwarted evangelical pressures to establish denominational alternatives. The education system fashioned in the convention, largely the work of Democrats Isaac E. Crary and John D. Pierce, reflected the secular view. Church leaders did not object to a state university, but also wanted church colleges. Pierce, who became the state's first Superintendent of Public Instruction, maintained that the state's should be the only system, at least until well established. Some Democrats, however, regarded sec-

10 Cole, *Northern Evangelists*, 104; *Debates*, 267-68, 269. The new state did, however, provide stiff penalties against dueling, State of Michigan, *Revised Statutes, 1837-38* (Detroit, 1838), 621.

11 *Debates*, 292, 295. Compare Woodbridge's language here with the Anti-masonic *Emigrant's* earlier in favoring capital punishment: "Released from one powerful restraint, the bad passions might spring up into a growth threatening the . . . human race; the moral government of the world would have within itself a principle of self-destruction," May 9, 1832; and see below.

tarian colleges as undesirable per se, as "anti-republican . . . monopolies favoring a particular class of religionists," where free opinion was suppressed and studies were pursued "squinting at the adopted tenets of Clerical usurpation." The *Michigan Sentinel* said they also tended "to sap the foundation of our liberties" by diverting resources from primary schools.[12] Since 1827 Baptist, Methodist, and Presbyterian leaders had been asking the Legislative Council to allow them to incorporate colleges. The Council permitted incorporation but had withheld from them the degree granting power and had required that they be open to members of any denomination and subject to state inspection.[13] After 1835 Pierce urged the continuation of this policy by the state on the grounds that church colleges would draw off students and money from the new university. Pierce believed the university should be secular and opposed a department of theology, but offered a concession to churchmen in a professor of theology who would teach the "evidences" of divine existence and the bases of Christianity. In seeking neutral ground the Superintendent held that "There is a medium between bigotry on the one hand and atheism on the other. The success of the University would depend on adoption of a 'medium course.' "[14]

In 1836 the Baptists renewed agitation for a college and their state convention appointed a committee to lobby and raise funds. They eventually lost hope in the face of what one minister called a "prevalent antipathy among politicians against denominational movements, in supposed efforts to secure a sectarian control of the educational interests of the country." The Detroit Presbytery protested, that "no action of civil government on the Subject of Education, however liberal can *fully* meet the moral wants of a community," and in 1838 the Presbyterians launched the most serious effort of the sects to gain a college charter.[15] After detailed plans for a manual labor school at Marshall had been made, Whig legislative leader Jacob M. Howard presented a bill for its incorporation. A Whig majority overcame a Democratic minority which

---

[12] Feb. 14, 1835.

[13] Willis F. Dunbar, *The Michigan Record in Higher Education* (Detroit, 1963), 55. Willis F. Dunbar, "Public Versus Private Control of Higher Education in Michigan, 1817-1855," *Mississippi Valley Historical Review*, 22 (December 1935), 390-91

[14] Quoted in Dunbar, *Michigan Record*, 57-58. It tells much of Pierce and his relationship to these value conflicts that although he began his career as part of the benevolent crusade, he had also been a Freemason and in 1830 had left a Congregational pastorate in Oneida County, New York, because of Antimasonry. In connection with this, see his "Sermon, Delivered New York, 1829, 1830," John Davis Pierce Papers, MHCom, which is a long discussion of the nature of "prejudice." See also, Arthur B. Moehlman, *Public Education in Detroit* (Bloomington, Ill., 1925), 55.

[15] Dunbar, *Michigan Record*, 36-38. Quotation in M.E.D. Trowbridge, *History of Baptists in Michigan* (1909), 49.

argued that granting college charters would result in a proliferation of weak colleges. The majority wanted rather to encourage volunteers in the cause of education, regarded competition in education as healthy as in commerce, and claimed that a state monopoly ran against religious and political opinion which desired the "New England system." In 1839, resorting finally to logrolling, the legislature incorporated both a Presbyterian and Catholic school.[16] Significantly, neither school ever managed to become established as a going concern, but at the time of their incorporation their symbolic probably outweighed their practical importance.

Although many interpretations of Democratic ideology have stressed its laissez faire political economics, in Michigan state affairs neither Democrats nor Whigs could be regarded as laissez faire. The national platforms of the Democrats in the 1840s, however, rested on a conception of a "negative liberal state"; Whig "positive liberalism," on the other hand, favored using government to influence moral and economic growth.[17] Michigan's parties from 1837 to 1845 followed their national party's line on economic issues. During that period Whigs favored: a national bank, a distribution bill, a general banking act, a uniform national currency, and lake harbors appropriations. They opposed a sub-Treasury and the annexation of Texas. Michigan Democrats favored a sub-Treasury and Texas annexation, and of the measures approved by the Whigs supported only lake harbors appropriations.[18]

Despite these formal differences on national policy, it is difficult to find differences between the parties on state economic matters, in policy or practice. In 1837, 1839, and 1841 the parties made few concrete proposals. In 1845 both parties endorsed a long list of reforms in the state's political and judicial system, and their platforms were almost identical. Both always claimed to be the most capable administrators of a limited and "economical" government.

One episode in the 1830s revealed more than any other the similarity between the parties in political economy. In 1838 Whig and Democratic legislators granted a state bounty of 2 cents on every pound of beet sugar manufactured in the state. Townsend E. Gidley, a Whig

[16] Holderreid, "Public Life of Jacob Merritt Howard," 38; Dunbar, *Michigan Record*, 36-39, 111-13; Dunbar, "Public Versus Private Control," *Mississippi Valley Historical Review*, 22: 397-98.

[17] Benson, *Concept*, 104-09. Charles Foster observed that for the evangelicals "Political prosperity depended upon moral prosperity. The weaker the government, the less power it had to control the passions and interests of its subjects, the more it was endangered by evil customs." *Evangelical United Front*, 179-80.

[18] Randall, "Gubernatorial Platforms, Michigan, 1834-1864," 1-70. The period of party formation could be considered to have closed by 1845, if not before. On the strength of national legislative parties, Joel H. Silbey, *The Shrine of Party: Congressional Voting Behavior, 1841-1852* (Pittsburgh, 1967).

fruit grower from Jackson, introduced the bill, reporting it out of committee with Whiggish blessings. To be independent of other states, he said, Michigan needed "to encourage the agricultural and manufacturing interests, and . . . the manufacture of beet sugar may not be as extensively produced for the next few years as the interests of the state require without the patronage of the state government."[19]

This act benefited the White Pigeon Beet Sugar Manufacturing Company, owned chiefly by Democratic leader John S. Barry, a representative from St. Joseph County in 1838. Senator Lucius Lyon, Barry's political and business friend, also began trying to produce beet sugar at this time. Although the White Pigeon Company obtained a conditional loan of $5,000 from the state it was unable to meet its terms. In 1840-41 Barry went to France to study the making of beet sugar and decided it was not feasible in Michigan. More significant than the failure of the industry to take root, however, was the obvious ease with which Whigs *and* Democrats set aside laissez faire doctrine. The *Detroit Free Press* often blurted out Democratic orthodox objections to special privilege or government granted favors to business. In 1839, however, as the legislature extended the loan to Barry's company, the editor admitted "that the general principle of giving the direct aid of the State to individual enterprise is not sound, but there are exceptions to the rule, and we consider this case a striking one. By loaning $5,000 on good security to test the experiment, it may be the means of securing to the State, hundreds of thousands in a few years."[20]

Democratic laissez faire conflicted with Whig activism not so much in political economy but rather over issues involving religion and morals. More will be seen of how evangelical Whigs would have involved the state in regulating morals and promoting Christianity. Michigan Democrats insisted such matters were personal and equated any man's appointing himself judge "over other men's conscience" with bigotry and intolerance. In 1843 the Ann Arbor, *Michigan Argus* clearly stated the Democratic position: "We regard a man's religious belief as concerning only himself and his Maker."[21]

[19] Sidney Glazer, "Early Sugar-Beet Industry in Michigan," *Michigan History,* 28 (July-September 1944), 406. *Michigan House, Documents Accompanying the Journal, 1838* (Detroit, 1838), 573.

[20] L. Lyon to Sherman McLean, May 26, 1839, "Letters of Lucius Lyon," *MHC,* 28: 523-24; Glazer, *Michigan History,* 17: 406-14; E. Byron Thomas, "Political Ideas and Activities of John Stewart Barry, 1831-1851" (unpublished M.A. thesis, Northwestern University, 1935), 15; John S. Barry, Constantine, to W. Woodbridge, March 4, 1840, Woodbridge MSS, BHC; Sue Imogene Silliman, "A Prince in Puddleford," *Michigan History,* 13 (Spring 1929), 258, 259; *Free Press,* March 25, 1839.

[21] *Detroit Morning Post and Craftsman,* March 16, 1839; *Michigan Argus,* Feb. 1, 1843.

WHIG BENEVOLENCE AND EVANGELICALISM: PIETY AND POWER

In 1831 Charles C. Trowbridge described the new Governor of Michigan Territory to a friend. Governor and Mrs. Porter, he said, impressed him as agreeable, informed, and *proper* persons, yet Trowbridge was disturbed: "Neither of them are pious, however. How few there are in the seat of power who are—and how earnestly we ought to pray that the influence of station and character might be brought to bear in the great work of the gospel."[22]

Six years later Trowbridge became the Whig Party's first candidate for governor. He helped manage the Bank of Michigan and his financial ability, it may be assumed, brought him nomination in a time of threatening economic crisis. Just as important, however, was Trowbridge's identification with benevolence. He had served as Detroit alderman and mayor, director of the Detroit and St. Joseph Railroad, founder of the Historical and Algic societies, and member of various Bible and Missionary societies. A fellow Protestant Episcopal Church member described him as an influential church leader whose interest "in religious matters was great." He belonged to an elite which ran Michigan's benevolent system, a network "controlled through a series of interlocking directorates by a small number of Presbyterian and Congregational ministers and laymen," but which included several Episcopalians.[23]

The benevolent system interlocked with Whiggery. Three representative benevolent societies in 1833 were the Detroit Temperance Society, the Wayne County Bible Society, and the Michigan Sunday School Union. Together they had 47 offices which were filled by only 31 men. There was most overlap at top levels. Thus, Eurotas P. Hastings, a prominent Presbyterian and Whig, presided over both the Temperance and Bible Societies and was a director of the Sunday School Union. Lists of other officers of other societies in the 1830s reveal a similar pattern.[24] Of the 31 officers of the 3 organizations, the later party affiliations of 22 were: 4 Democratic, 18 Whig.

The Michigan Education Society, a branch of the American Education Society, devoted itself to raising funds to train missionaries. John Allen,

[22] C. C. Trowbridge, Hamtramck, to Henry R. Schoolcraft, Oct. 23, 1831, in Carter, ed., *Territorial Papers*, XII, 360.

[23] James V. Campbell, "Biographical Sketch of Charles C. Trowbridge," *MHC*, 4: 478-91. Arthur R. Kooker, "The Anti-Slavery Movement in Michigan, 1796-1840: A Study in Humanitarianism on the American Frontier" (unpublished Ph.D. dissertation, University of Michigan, 1941), 87.

[24] *Detroit Courier*, March 6, 1833, Feb. 26, 1834, April 3, 1838. Pauline Joan Ullrich, "The Impact of New England Influences Upon the Formative Stages of the Non-Political Institutional Developments in Michigan During the Late Territorial Period" (unpublished M.A. thesis, Wayne State University, 1942), 47, 48, 52, 55-56, 59, 84. Kooker, "Anti-Slavery Movement," 84, 85.

enterprising founder of Ann Arbor, presided over the MEA in 1834. Allen, an Antimason and later Whig, was not a communicant in the Presbyterian church, but his immediate family founded the First Presbyterian Church of Ann Arbor. The Education Society was perhaps the most conspicuously anti-Catholic of Michigan's benevolent groups. Playing upon fears of Popery was a chief means of raising funds and also of reducing internal strife among Protestants.[25] Evangelicals saw the blight of Popery in every manifestation of Catholic presence, as this letter from Michigan in *Home Missionary* testified: "In Detroit the Catholics are building a most spacious and splendid cathedral. At Bertrand in Berrien County or nearby, they have a college, and all southwestern Michigan and northern Indiana are being scoured to obtain Protestant children to educate. The villages on the whole line of our railroads are beginning to be filled by Papists; and wherever they pitch their tents and gain an influence, immorality, intemperance, and crime stalk abroad unblushingly."[26]

The vigil against Popery enlisted the Presbyterians as much as any evangelical denomination, and their deep commitment to anti-Popery was interwoven with their strong sociopolitical interests. The historian Dixon Ryan Fox observed that New England influence on politics in western New York was exercised primarily through the Presbyterian Church.[27] The same might be said of Michigan, adding that Presbyterians there included many Congregationalists; members of these denominations wielded political, economic, cultural, and social influence far out of proportion to their numbers. As a pressure group and through individuals Presbyterianism for a time dominated the Whig Party and state government. Inheriting the puritan tradition of "the necessary interrelationship of civil and religious life,"[28] Michigan Presbyterians and Congregationalists were the most active carriers of that New England culture in which religion pervaded all spheres of life.

The Presbyterian-Whig association manifested itself in many ways.

---

[25] Bidlack, *John Allen and the Founding of Ann Arbor*, 22-23. Allen founded Ann Arbor to make money. He invested in sawmills, railroads, and land companies. Later he became a Democrat, but his ardent Whiggery of the 1830s is evident in the John Allen MSS, and Woodbridge MSS, BHC. *Courier*, Oct. 15, 1834; Ray Allen Billington, "Anti-Catholic Propaganda and the Home Missionary Movement, 1800-1860," *Mississippi Valley Historical Review*, 22: 361-84. McLoughlin, *Modern Revivalism*, 38.

[26] Quoted in Thomas, *Nativism*, 41. Charles Hoffman observed in 1833 that Catholics had the largest congregation in Detroit, *Winter in the West*, 112. Fears of Popery in the West were expressed by a New York Seventh Day Baptist minister on a tour of the Northwest (including Michigan) in 1843, James Leander Scott, *Journal of a Missionary Tour* (Providence, 1843; reprinted Ann Arbor, 1966), 91, 138.

[27] Fox, *Yankees and Yorkers*, 210.

[28] Blau, *Review of Religion*, xi, 25.

Whig meetings, such as the Whig Young Men's State Convention of 1837, were often held in Presbyterian churches.[29] Meeting for public purposes in church buildings was not unusual in a newly settled area where few spacious buildings existed. But Presbyterian churches provided Whigs with a familiar and hospitable setting. Detroit Whigs had other buildings available, yet frequently found the Presbyterian Session Room convenient, as did the benevolent societies. The Presbyterian *Michigan Observer* was published in Detroit at the offices of the Whig *Advertiser*. During the 1838 campaign the *Observer* printed a sermon which asked church members to vote against the incumbent Democratic administration of "profane men" who "contemned" God and trampled on His laws. Democratic papers across the state criticized the *Observer's* departure from religion to politics and charged Presbyterian ministers in various localities with the same offense. In 1840 the *Free Press* said that the sound of Harrison songs emanating from the Presbyterian Session Room indicated the "union of a religious sect with a political party," giving urgency to the Democratic slogan of "Political, Civil, and Religious Liberty."[30] Years later an old Detroiter reminisced about the political activities of Reverend George Duffield of Detroit's First Presbyterian Church: "in whig politics the doctor could not get all to follow him. In the log cabin, hard cider campaign some of his democratic members . . . threatened to nail up their pew doors—Major Kearsley, Jonas Titus and others—if he did not stop preaching politics, because for six Sundays [he had not prayed for President Van Buren]. The Dr. said if that was so he did not know it. He meant as in duty bound to pray for all who needed prayer and he knew of no one who needed it more than Martin Van Buren."[31]

During the campaign Democrat Lucius Lyon described Whig policy since 1839: "Jacob M. Howard was nominated for congress by the Whigs . . . in pursuance, I suppose, of the central policy which has concentrated all offices, all appointments, all patronage and all power here in the city of Detroit in the Presbyterian Church and in the Bank of Michigan ever since that party got the ascendancy."[32] (Lyon, an Episcopalian, promoted that church's fortunes.)

In 1840, Democrats denounced most the alleged alliance of Whiggery and banks, but in 1841 religion was discussed more openly. The Democratic gubernatorial candidate, John Barry, was known to be a skeptic,

[29] *Advertiser*, Oct. 1837, passim; Aug. 2, 1843, for First District Convention in Clinton Presbyterian Church.

[30] *Free Press*, Dec. 3, 1838; *Michigan Argus*, Nov. 1, 8, 1838; *Kalamazoo Gazette*, Nov. 17, 1838. *Free Press*, Oct. 1, 1840.

[31] Reverend W. Fitch, "Reminiscences of Detroit," *MHC*, 5: 538.

[32] L. Lyon to T. H. Lyon, Sept. 13, 1840, "Letters of Lucius Lyon," *MHC*, 27: 537.

although during the campaign his supporters claimed he was a Unitarian. The *Marshall Western Statesman* (Whig) said that Barry entertained "infidel principles" while the *Advertiser* charged that as a state representative Barry had sat in the legislature and made "coarse jokes" about the birth of the Savior. Late in the campaign the Whig *Jonesville Expositor* added that Barry was not only a "scoffer at religion" but had also "horsewhipped a minister." The *Free Press* counterattacked with an assault on the Presbyterian-Whig entente cordiale. If Barry were elected, promised the paper, he would not "aggrandize one particular sect." In the past two years the Presbyterian denomination of Detroit "has had a Governor, an Auditor General, two United States Senators, one Representative in Congress, the Commissioner of Internal Improvements, the Collector of Customs for the Port of Detroit, [and] several Regents of the University selected from it."[33]

The *Free Press* continued to appeal to a popular sentiment regarding Whigs and Presbyterians that seems to have been present from the time the Whigs took power in the winter of 1839-40. In February 1840, Eurotas P. Hastings wrote to Governor William Woodbridge recommending the Reverend Ira M. Mead for University Regent. Hastings thought Mead "well *qualified*" but doubted the political wisdom of the appointment. "As he is a Presbyterian minister it may seem under the present state of the public mind an unfit selection."[34]

Meeting in Ann Arbor in 1830 Michigan Presbyterians had beseeched "God with united heart and voice to come down and make the infant Territory, a land of Temperance, of bibles, and of revivals." In the next decade Presbyterians did not leave it to God to Christianize Michigan, however, but acted in society in His behalf with greater zeal than any other religious group. Presbyterians who staffed benevolent societies and those who brought Godly influence to bear in politics were following their church's urgings and ideals. The ministers of Detroit's First Presbyterian Church, particularly, were forceful men who dominated the Detroit Presbytery and Michigan Synod. Reverend John P. Cleavland in the mid-1830s plunged boldly into sociopolitical issues. One churchgoer described an 1836 sermon of his as "an exceedingly well written *political discourse*" proper for an election day which "touched upon

---

[33] *Free Press*, Sept. 12, 1841. The *Advertiser* failed to reply to these charges. *Kalamazoo Gazette*, Nov. 5, 1841; *Western Statesman*, Sept. 9, 23, 1841; *Expositor*, Oct. 28, 1841.

[34] Eurotas P. Hastings to W. Woodbridge, Feb. 13, 1840, Woodbridge MSS, BHC. The Whigs nominated Rev. Hiram L. Miller, of Saginaw, for Lieutenant Governor in 1847; "familiarly known as 'Priest Miller'" he was a Presbyterian pastor and "one of the first ordained preachers to impart Christianity among the settlers." James Cooke Mills, *History of Saginaw County, Michigan* (Saginaw, 1918), 124-25.

everything but religion." Prodded by Cleavland, the Synod in 1835 declared slavery "a sin before God and man [which] ought to end immediately." The Presbyterians also branded the "use, manufacture and sale of ardent spirits" as morally wrong, and the use of tobacco as "offensive to personal and domestic requirements." Sabbath desecration was a "principle cause of darkness and declension." In the mid-1830s the Synod even condemned war and declared conscientious objection to be a Christian duty.[35]

The Synod took a conservative turn after 1837, partly because of the effects of the Old School-New School schism. Although most Michigan Presbyterian churches went New School, they became, according to Lewis G. VanderVelde, more conservative in trying to prove their orthodoxy. The departure of Cleavland from the Detroit church for a university post symbolized the shift. George Duffield replaced him and brought a moderate evangelical influence to the Synod. Duffield had been, ironically, a New School "rebel" of the 1830s and a former assistant of Charles G. Finney. But Duffield saw such causes as abolition as "ultra reforms." The Synod paid less attention to slavery and war after 1838 and more to Sabbath-keeping and education.[36]

Yet neither the Synod nor many individuals lost their evangelical drive; even the desire to preserve the Sabbath kept them embroiled with sociopolitical issues. Individual Presbyterians and Congregationalists, moreover, continued to lead in "ultra reforms." Duffield himself gave ardent support to temperance. He also distinguished himself in advancing education, denouncing Popery, and upholding capital punishment. Although distrusting abolitionists, he reacted to Southern offenses to the North, such as the Fugitive Slave Law, with high indignation and resentment. Whatever his reservations, Duffield was easily the leading evangelical in Michigan.[37]

[35] *Monroe Michigan Sentinel*, Sept. 18, 1830. Church-goer quoted in Kooker, "Anti-Slavery Movement," 120-21. John Comin and Harold F. Fredsell, *History of the Presbyterian Church in Michigan* (Ann Arbor, 1950), 62, 69, 74-76. See also, Presbyterian Church, Detroit, "Minutes of the Detroit Presbytery, 1828-1840," I, 3-4, 115, 143-44, 145, 155, 173-74, 179, MHCol.

[36] Lewis G. VanderVelde, "The Synod of Michigan and Movements for Social Reform, 1834-1869" (n.d., typewritten MS, BHC), 6, 9-12. Lewis G. VanderVelde, "The Diary of George Duffield," *Mississippi Valley Historical Review*, 24 (June 1937), 22. Smith, *Revivalism and Social Reform*, 26, 53, 108-09. Lewis G. Vander-Velde, ed., "Notes on the Diary of George Duffield," 31.

[37] *Ibid.*, 62. On Presbyterian activity in antislavery and temperance: Kooker, "Anti-Slavery Movement," 148-49, 84-85; and Birney to *The Signal of Liberty*, Detroit, Sept. 29, 1841, and Lemoyne S. Smyth and others to Birney, Lyons, Ionia Co., Aug. 22, 1845; Dumond, ed., *Birney Letters*, II, 633, 634, 962-63. In 1839 the Detroit Presbytery heard an antislavery address by the Reverend Marcus Harrison and then took up a collection "for the cause," "Minutes of the Detroit Presbytery, 1828-1840," I, 393.

THE PARTIES AND MORALITY

By 1835 temperance sentiment prospered in Michigan, but the strongest regulation of the liquor traffic yet achieved was simple requirement of licenses, with fines for those selling ardent spirits without a license. Temperance reform seemed to grow with revivalism. One senses in Michigan, as elsewhere, interconnections between all the burned-over enthusiasms and teetotaling.[38]

Detroit acquired its first temperance society in 1830, and in 1834 the Common Council attempted to reduce the number of "groceries" selling liquor by instituting high license fees. Liquor dealers simply continued to do business as usual, a response which continued to be one of the major ways in which "wets" would frustrate "dry" schemes. Still, the temperance thrust gained momentum and began to seek goals characteristic of the movement elsewhere. Many temperance societies moved, for example, to demand total abstinence; and they increasingly focused attention on state legislation as they shifted their hopes of success from moral suasion to legal coercion. It was not accidental that this shift took place in the 1830s as the cultural shock of many incoming and imbibing Irish and Germans merged with existing concern for the intemperate natives. The intensification of subcultural conflict between pro and anti temperance groups helps account for shifts, as Joseph Gusfield put it, from assimilative reform to coercive reform.[39]

Also, temperance in Michigan resembled the crusade elsewhere by the conspicuousness of evangelicals. Reverend Duffield, Presbyterians generally, and the editors of the Baptist *Michigan Christian Herald* and *Michigan Observer* led in the agitation. The Whig Party, not surprisingly, was far more sympathetic to temperance than the Democrats. Antimasonry, of course, had been strongly temperance minded. Yet temperance never emerged as a party issue on a statewide basis through 1852, and in elections where it did become an issue it did not last long. Temperance cut across both parties, or rather politicians in both paid lip service to prevent its becoming a formal issue. Nevertheless, unofficially, Whiggery contained more genuine temperance zeal. Among officers of

[38] Floyd B. Streeter, "History of Prohibition Legislation in Michigan," *Michigan History*, 2 (April 1918), 292-93. Temperance reformation, as David Ludlum observed, often preceded revivals and prepared hesitant sinners for conversion by giving them proof of worthiness to be saved, *Social Ferment in Vermont*, 68-69. Revivals also prepared the way for temperance.

[39] John Allen Krout, *Origins of Prohibition* (New York, 1925), 167-76; Joseph R. Gusfield, *Symbolic Crusade: Status Politics and the American Temperance Movement* (Urbana, 1963), 69-70; Farmer, *Detroit*, i, 838-39; John Fitzgibbon, "King Alcohol: His Rise, Reign and Fall in Michigan," *Michigan History*, 2 (October 1918), 775. For examples of temperance activity in 1835, *Michigan Sentinel*, Jan. 13, 31; *Michigan Whig*, Feb. 12. See also, Cole, *Northern Evangelists*, 116.

the societies, too, the names of prominent Whigs were far more conspicuous than those of Democrats.[40]

Eastern Michigan Whigs particularly during the formative campaigns
of 1837 to 1840, showed their temperance streak by suggesting often
that the Democrats were intemperate, hence immoral, and unfit for
office. In 1837 they talked incessantly of a scandal wherein the Democratic legislature had ostensibly appropriated funds for "stationery"
which had gone for alcohol.[41] Long after the 1830s an old resident of
Dearborn recalled what Democratic county conventions had been like:
in those days, he said, the hurly-burly of a town-meeting was "a puritan
Sunday" in comparison. "Dray loads of refreshments in kegs and bottles
came from Detroit." Dearborn offered "greater individual freedom" than
Detroit. "There were no policemen nor jail in Dearborn in those good
times."[42]

One incident of the 1830s made a particularly strong impression on
the temperance minded. In 1837 Governor Mason and a large group of
dignitaries gathered at Mt. Clemens to celebrate the groundbreaking of
the Clinton and Kalamazoo Canal. A Baptist minister in 1873 recalled
quite vividly that "Whiskey flowed profusely." After a sumptuous dinner
"came the toasts, with speeches and responses. It was a day of democratic glory. All were hilarious with joy and whiskey. Distinctions were
abolished. All were on a level."[43] Another pioneer later recalled the
scene in similar fashion. This man's memory changed the libations to a
more exalted "abundant supply of champagne" but agreed that there had
been much "toasting and drinking"; the celebrants "did not act as though
the champagne had added to their brains or sense. I am proud to say that
a governor would not do such things now."[44] The repressed envy in this
indignation is hard to miss. Not just temperance was being offended,
however, but also that sense of moralistic propriety so characteristic of
small town Protestant New England and its colonies in the Middle West.
Intemperance caused a blurring of social distinctions, and lack of regard
for natural distinctions between ranks was to the New Englander, even
on the frontier, somewhat immoral.

[40] McCoy, "Wayne County Economic Elite, 1844, 1860," 133-34. *Constitution
and By-Laws of the Detroit Young Men's Temperance Society* (Detroit, 1835),
3-4; Farmer, *Detroit*, I, 838-39; *Free Press*, Nov. 23, 1841; *Michigan Observer*,
March 19, 1839; the latter is the only copy of that paper I have seen. Of 10 officers
of the Detroit Temperance Society in 1844, 4 were well-known Whigs and only 1
was a prominent Democrat, *Advertiser*, Feb. 3, 1844.

[41] *Advertiser*, June 16, 29, 30, Aug. 1, Sept. 15, 18, 26, Nov. 15, 1837. Parties in
western Michigan also sought to turn temperance sentiment to their advantage,
Kalamazoo Gazette, Aug. 26, 1837, *Jackson Sentinel*, April 22, 1837, May 26, 1838.

[42] F. A. Gulley, "Old Dearborn Families," Historical and Genealogical Sketches,
typewritten MSS, BHC.

[43] Rev. Supply Chase, "A Pioneer Minister," *MHC*, 5: 59-60.

[44] *MHC*, 14: 553-54.

Despite these incidents the Democracy was not unambiguously identified as antitemperance or intemperate. The party included some men
genuinely favorable to temperance, but the leadership generally took the
innocuous position that: intemperance was very bad, temperance was
good, but laws to enforce temperance were very bad. An 1838 report of
Democratic legislators "of the House Committee on Ardent Spirits,"
however, could not have endeared the Democrats to temperance zealots.
Written in response to petitions from temperance societies to prohibit
licensing, about three-fifths of the report reminded the petitioners of the
beneficial uses of alcohol. The committee eventually arrived at the
"dreadful evils of intemperance," but, it went on, any food or drink used
immoderately could become "fatal poisons." A prohibitory law "could
not be well enforced, and would perhaps be entirely nugatory." Let man
use all things without abuse, "and deadly poisons will be harmless, like
the dews of heaven."[45]

In 1840 the Whigs, now in control of the legislature, submitted a quite
different report. It recommended no temperance law, but Munius
Kenny's report read like a temperance tract. Kenny was an antislavery
Whig from Washtenaw County, a farmer, lawyer, and founder of the
Washtenaw Mutual Insurance Company. He listed not the beneficial uses
of alcohol, but rather the evils it caused: misery, poverty, wasted time.
Indeed, Kenny could find no benefit "to offset against the evils it inflicts
upon the community . . . no bright spot to relieve the dark shade of the
picture." Some men argued, said Kenny, that "compelling men to be
moral . . . is always odious, and savours of church and state." He answered that every law on the books, even those punishing murder, compelled men to be moral. Against the "private rights of individuals, to buy
and sell as they please," Kenny upheld the rights of the community: "this
giving up of private rights so far as they come in conflict with the general
good, is the very principle which holds society together." Still, Kenny
bowed to a public opinion which would not yet support any law even if
enacted.[46]

During the 1840s many local temperance revivals flared sporadically
in the wake of circuit riders and all manner of exhorters in alliance with
piety, loneliness, fear, and the backwoods. Michigan was swept by the
Washingtonian movement in 1841, a popular, secular temperance drive
appealing to egalitarianism and the reformed drunkard. In 1843 temperance crusader Augustus Littlejohn roused western Michigan; Alonzo

---

[45] *Michigan House Journal, 1838* (Detroit, 1838), 212, 232, 307, 387, for petitions. *Michigan House, Documents Accompanying the Journal, 1838* (Detroit,
1838), 460-61, March 6, 1838, A. W. Buel, Chairman.

[46] *Michigan Biographies*, I, 464. State of Michigan, *Documents Accompanying
the Journal of the House of Representatives, 1840* (Detroit, 1840), II, No. 61,
552-54.

Hyde toured Michigan and Lyman Beecher came to Detroit in 1845 for the cause. In 1849 C. C. Colton, General Riley of Rochester, and the famous Father Theobald Mathew of Ireland all barnstormed Michigan fighting demon rum.[47]

During the early forties temperance forces increasingly demanded that government cease to license the sale of ardent spirits. "License" came to symbolize not just a legal but a moral condition as well. Many persons expected that withdrawal of licenses would prohibit the sale of alcohol.[48] Accordingly, in 1845 the legislature passed a local option law letting each local government vote on licensing. Towns which thereafter voted no license became dry depending on general community support for enforcement. "No license" failed utterly in Detroit. The city voted in 1846 for no license, 1,070 to 230. City revenue fell, but dealers continued to sell and the absence of a fee encouraged a new group of small sellers to enter the market. By 1847 voters recognized the impracticality of no license and voted for licensing to be resumed. Elsewhere, temperance men tried to elect officials who would enforce "no license."[49]

Agitation revived in the late forties, with churches forming "temperance leagues" and the Sons of Temperance, a nationwide fad, gaining in popularity. The Detroit Sons even began publishing a newspaper in 1850, the *American Gleaner and Temperance Advocate.*[50] As temperance fires burned brighter in 1849 the Whigs sought to win votes by accusing the Democratic candidate for governor, John Barry, of selling whiskey at his place of business in St. Joseph County. Barry and the Democratic press denied the charge, and their response showed sensitivity to temperance feeling.[51] In 1852, the Whigs again attempted to turn "drys" against the Democrats. A mysterious "Temperance Party"

[47] Fitzgibbon, "King Alcohol," 742-45; A.D.P. Van Buren, "Our Temperance Conflict," *MHC*, 13: 393-96. The *Advertiser* covered temperance activities particularly well in 1841. For a discussion of the Washingtonians, *Michigan Christian Herald*, April 1, 1841.

[48] *Michigan Temperance Advocate* (Marshall), Jan. 15, 1842, Vol. 2, No. 6. Samuel W. Durant, *History of Oakland County, Michigan* (Philadelphia, 1877), 74. *Christian Herald*, June 17, 1844, report of State Temperance Society resolving to effect abolition of the license system. L. W. Osgood to John S. Barry, Jan. 30, 1845, Executive Records, Complaints, MHCom.

[49] Fitzgibbon, "King Alcohol," 775; Farmer, *Detroit*, I, 1839; *Advertiser*, March 7, 1846, March 3, 1847. The Monroe charter election in 1845 turned on the question of licensing, *Advertiser*, March 7, 1845. License and no-license forces in Plymouth, Wayne County, nominated tickets cutting across party lines, *Free Press*, April 26, 1847.

[50] *Michigan Christian Herald*, March 16, 30, May 4, Nov. 23, 1849. *Detroit Tribune*, March 7, 9, 1850. Albert Baxter, *History of the City of Grand Rapids* (New York, 1891), 199.

[51] *Advertiser*, Nov. 5, 1849; *Free Press*, Nov. 2, 1849; *Centreville Western Chronicle*, Nov. 3, 1849; J. S. Barry, Constantine, to J. S. Bagg, Oct. 5, 1849, and same to same, Oct. 22 and Oct. 24, 1849, Bagg MSS, Huntington Library.

on the eve of election circulated a mixed slate of candidates which was, however, top heavy with Whigs and included only those Democrats, according to the *Pontiac Jacksonian,* "whose election was morally certain long before the election." What effect this tactic had, if any, is difficult to measure. The victorious Democratic candidate for governor in 1852, Robert McClelland, had, at any rate, promised that if the legislature passed a Maine Liquor Law he would "sanction the bill."[52] Once again the issue remained neutralized.

The attitudes of the Whig and Democratic parties to abolitionism, which was so much an outgrowth of evangelical revivalism, also demonstrate their evangelical and antievangelical tendencies. No single attitude, however, fully characterized either party, and both contained much hostility and sympathy for abolitionists. The problem of identifying their central tendencies can be simplified here by omitting all the various shades of antislavery-abolition and confining attention to abolition, i.e., the embracing of some kind of immediatism or the willingness to join antislavery societies or vote Liberty after 1840.

In Michigan organizers of antislavery societies and the Liberty Party tended to be involved in benevolent and moral reform causes. Indeed, the Liberty Party formed a splinter group of the Whig-Presbyterian-evangelical subculture. Presbyterian Whigs led in founding the state antislavery society. They dominated the Detroit Antislavery Society, too, but not all of them made the painful move to political abolition; many stayed in Whiggery to work for their goals. This begins to explain the Whigs' ambivalence to abolition, even after the latter began to hurt the party quite seriously. Thus, too, Democratic hostility for abolitionist "fanatics" becomes understandable, even if Democrats claimed to be "antislavery in principle."

Whigs initially tried hard not to offend abolitionists. Most Whig newspapers in the 1830s, although they would have preferred to ignore abolitionists, gave them cautious publicity and something of a hearing.[53] After the Liberty Party began drawing off Whig votes, the editors changed tactics. Before elections they would court and harangue, but after the election delivered unmixed chastisements on abolitionist heads. In 1844 Whigs reached peaks of outrage against abolitionists when they saw their chance to elect Henry Clay to the Presidency narrowly defeated by abolitionist defection in New York. Michigan Whig leaders

[52] *Pontiac Jacksonian,* Oct. 6, Nov. 17, 1852; *Free Press,* Oct. 25, 1852; *Coldwater Sentinel,* Oct. 29, 1852. Detroit Post and Tribune, *Zachariah Chandler: An Outline Sketch of His Life and Public Services* (Detroit, 1880), 85-86, mentioned the temperance ticket as a bona fide operation.

[53] Kooker, "Anti-Slavery Movement," 148, 149, 182, 183. E.g., *Advertiser,* June 22, 30, July 2, 16, 19, 25, Aug. 6, 25, Nov. 16, 1836.

in their campaign resorted to the desperate trickery of the "Garland forgery," publicizing a false report that Liberty presidential candidate James Birney had accepted a local Democratic nomination in Saginaw County and was in secret alliance with the Locos. Abolitionist rancor toward Whigs grew mightily because of this, while Whigs unleashed after the election a flood of vituperation against abolitionists whom they blamed for the election of Polk on a platform of Texas annexation.[54]

Even before the culmination of Whig-Liberty antagonism in 1844, connection with abolition could obstruct an otherwise loyal Whig's getting a nomination or appointment. Having been a member of an antislavery society or having liberated views regarding blacks was a political liability, while voting for the Liberty Party undoubtedly was political suicide within Whiggery.[55]

Whatever the grievance between the two, abolitionists recognized that far more of a chance existed to bring Whigs "to antislavery ground" than the Democrats.[56] Public Democratic sympathy for abolitionists was rare indeed, and hostility was common. In the 1830s Democrats ignored or scorned abolitionists. Seldom did Democratic newspapers mention abolitionists without simultaneously stirring Negrophobia. Democratic editors moved quickly from Southern slavery to discussion of free blacks in Northern society and their various threats to whites.[57] In 1836 the Democratic legislature considered censuring "abolition societies and the acts of certain individuals calling themselves abolitionists" which were "in direct violation of the compact of the Union, and destructive to the tranquility, and welfare of the country." The final version omitted mention of "abolitionists" but they could hardly have missed the point. Thus, when in 1838 the legislature refused to table petitions dealing with

[54] E.g., Ann Arbor, *Michigan State Gazette*, Aug. 13, 20, 1840, *Jonesville Expositor*, Oct. 28, 1841, *Advertiser*, Sept. 19, 1842; Fladeland, *Birney*, 235, 237, 246-47; *Advertiser*, Jan. 16, 1845; Junius Tracts, *Political Abolition*, No. 5 (New York, 1844); *Free Press*, Nov. 1, 2, 1844.

[55] This is clear from what is taken for granted in letters discussing Robert Stuart and his past affiliations: Robert Stuart to W. Woodbridge, June 3, 1841; same to same, July 31, 1841; Stuart to John C. Calhoun, July 31, 1841; and William Johnston, Michilimackinac, to Woodbridge, Sept. 14, 1841, Woodbridge MSS, BHC. Patronage could also be used, as it was in the Democratic Party on one occasion to quiet "antislavery" opposition in the party: A. Felch, D. A. Noble, R. McClelland, and 13 others, Monroe, to John S. Barry, Governor, Dec. 22, 1842; Titus Babcock, Monroe, to John S. Barry, Jan. 7, 1843, Executive Records, Governor's Papers, MHCom; typescripts are in the Barry MSS, BHC.

[56] "The *Advertiser* and Detroit clique stand chiefly in the way," Theodore Foster to Birney, Sept. 29, 1845; same to same, Oct. 16, 1845, Dumond, ed., *Birney Letters*, II, 972-73, 980. A. G. Crittenden, M. D., Saline, to Woodbridge, Dec. 26, 1844, Woodbridge MSS, BHC.

[57] *Detroit Morning Post*, Nov. 9, 1837, Dec. 7, 1837; *Free Press*, Sept. 9, 1835, Jan. 31, 1838.

slavery by large majorities (thereby refusing to enact its equivalent of Congress's "Gag Rule"), this did not mean broad sympathy for the petitions. (The few supporters of a "gag" were, significantly, Democrats, while the legislators who had been willing to present the antislavery petitions were Whigs.)[58] In 1844 Democratic legislators brusquely replied to abolitionist petitions asking the state to protect fugitive slaves, advising the petitioners to read the federal Constitution. If they had, they would not have invited the legislature to disregard an act of Congress.[59]

Whig rapport with abolitionists emerged in the agreement of both groups on other moral causes. Two threats to morality by the Democrats in the early 1840s raised evangelical ire: the first and most conspicuous of these was Sabbath desecration. While temperance and abolition are today perhaps the best known evangelical causes, the campaign to preserve the Sabbath was as characteristic and at times as prominent a focus of evangelical energies. No other question did more to place the Whigs clearly on the side of morality and religion.[60]

The controversy in the United States over Sabbath-keeping went back most immediately to an 1810 act by Congress permitting post offices to remain open and mails to be carried on Sunday. In 1825 Congress required post offices where mail was delivered on Sunday to stay open and rekindled the controversy. In 1828 evangelicals created the General Union for Promoting Observance of the Christian Sabbath and in 1829 they petitioned Congress remonstrating against the Sunday mail laws. A Kentucky Jacksonian, Richard M. Johnson, replied to the petitions in his famous report to the Senate in 1830 which defended Sunday mails and was a "classical defense of the American system of separation of church and state."[61]

Sympathetic historians of Michigan Presbyterianism have remarked that the Synod in the 1830s seemed to think that "Christian civilization itself depended on keeping the Sabbath after the Puritan fashion." The Synod advised the churches to exercise "immediate, steady, uncompromising discipline" over violations of the holy day. Violations were: "to journey or transact any secular business, or give or receive social visits . . . or to own stock in establishments, such as Stage Companies, Rail-

[58] Kooker, "Anti-Slavery Movement," 125-26. *Michigan House Journal, 1838,* 46-47. Democratic and Whig Congressional candidates replied to abolitionist questioning in 1838: *Advertiser,* Oct. 8, 20, 1838, *Free Press,* Sept. 27, Oct. 8, 9, 11, 1838; see also Woodbridge to Arthur L. Porter, Michigan Anti-Slavery Society, Oct. 14, 1839, Woodbridge MSS, BHC.

[59] State of Michigan, *Documents of the Senate and of the House of Representatives, 1844* (Detroit, 1844), House Doc. No. 13.

[60] Stewart, *New Homes in the West,* reported that "The desecration of the Sabbath, in many places, calls aloud to the dispensers of religious instruction, to rise up, with divine revelation in their hands," 14.

[61] Bodo, *Protestant Clergy,* 39-48; Cole, *Northern Evangelists,* 107-08.

roads, Steamboats, etc., which are employed in violation of that holy day."[62] Further, it was wrong to elect rulers who violated the Sabbath by example or legislation.

The outstanding example of rulers violating the Sabbath in Michigan was the Democratic state government's permitting railroad mail cars to run on Sunday. Presbyterians and other evangelicals, especially the Baptists, petitioned the legislature to stop the "running of the cars," but the Democrats took little notice.[63] William Woodbridge, as Whig candidate for governor in 1839, took a personal interest in Sabbath violation by the state, and the new Whig legislature decided to rescue the state from sin. On March 13, 1840, the House passed, 26 to 16, a resolution prohibiting any locomotive, passenger, or freight car to run on any state railroad on "the first day of the week," except to fulfill the terms of any existing contract for transporting government mail. Three days later Sabbatarians tried to pass a stiffer law. True M. Tucker, a Whig from St. Clair County, added an amendment which fined any person "traveling on any public or private road . . . on the Sabbath day" $50, with fine money to go for support of Sabbath schools. Tucker's proposal failed, but so irritated one Democratic legislator, Charles P. Bush, that he proposed that the state pay the cost of any person's business suffering because the cars were *not* to run on Sunday. After other attempts to weaken and strengthen the measure, the original repassed the House, 25 to 19.[64]

The House's action had been preceded by a committee report in which Munius Kenny again put the Whigs squarely on the side of the angels and in which he recommended "some prompt and efficient legislation" to prohibit the cars running on the Sabbath. "That christianity [sic] is the common law of this country, is a fact not to be questioned." Sabbath observance was one of the great Christian duties: "No christian nation has guarded effectually against the prevalence of vice and immorality, who have not required the sanctification of the Sabbath."[65] Kenny conceded that the state had an obligation to meet federal mail contracts, but

[62] Comin and Fredsell, *History of Presbyterian Church*, 67, 69, 74-76. Vander-Velde, "Synod of Michigan and Social Reform," 16-19. In 1832 a farmer wrote to his native England that "The laws of this territory strongly prohibit working on the Sunday and are well enforced." Tucker, ed., "Correspondence of John Fisher," *Michigan History*, 45: 224.

[63] *Acts Passed at First Session of the Legislative Council, 1824*, 6. *Michigan House Journal, 1838*, 309. *Michigan Christian Herald, 1839*, passim. The legislature scandalized the *Michigan Observer* in 1839 by allowing their last session before adjournment to last into the Sabbath, Hemans, *Mason*, 464.

[64] Robert Abbott informed Woodbridge that "labor has been performed at the depot in the city, and on the road on Sundays," March 25, 1839, Woodbridge, MSS, BHC. *Michigan House Journal, 1840* (Detroit, 1840), 356-57, 478-81.

[65] State of Michigan, *Documents Accompanying the Journal of the House of Representatives, 1840*, II, Doc. No. 49, 467, 468.

said it was not necessary to forward passenger and freight cars with the mail.

In the original vote passing the Sabbath bill (26-16), 19 Whigs and 7 Democrats voted for it, 10 Whigs and 6 Democrats voted no, and 2 Whigs and 4 Democrats abstained.[66] Thus, House Democrats split while about two-thirds of the Whigs favored the bill. A systematic study of legislative behavior could identify the evangelical and antievangelical blocs in both parties. It is enough here to distinguish the central tendencies of the parties. A Whig legislature stopped the cars from running in 1840 and a Democratic legislature, on February 15, 1842, instructed the commissioners of internal improvements to have one passenger train run over the Central Railroad every Sunday. No freight cars would run and no work except mail carrying would be done, but the Democrats set the passengers and cars rolling again.[67] The *Advertiser* observed "the first step taken by the new Democratic legislature . . . directing cars to run on the Sabbath. Any exhibition of regard for that day, would have been set down as heresy by the locofoco ultraists." The Presbyterian Pastoral Letter of 1842 noted the "visible and growing profanation" of the Sabbath, and attributed this partly to the "evil example" set by the legislature.[68]

The capacity of Democrats to encourage evil doers must have seemed limitless to evangelicals when in 1843 a Democratic legislature amended and loosened the laws relating to adultery and fornication which had made those sins criminal offenses in Michigan.[69] The Whig First District Convention opposed repeal of the "adultery laws" and accused the legislature of committing an "outrage upon the moral sense of the community." The abolitionist *Signal of Liberty* proclaimed "Adultery Legalized." The Whig State Convention condemned the outrage which struck "at the foundations of our social system and can only be sanctioned by

[66] Roll call vote in *Michigan House Journal, 1840,* 442; party identification, *Advertiser,* Dec. 28, 1839.

[67] *Michigan House Journal, 1842* (Detroit, 1845), 331-32. The vote indicated some Democratic opposition. A motion to postpone failed 31 to 17, and the House passed the proposal 27 to 24. On February 17 the Democratic-run Senate adopted the measure as a joint resolution without a roll call vote. That hardy antievangelical John Norvell was among those voting for the cars to run, *Michigan Senate Journal, 1842* (Detroit, 1842), 278.

[68] *Advertiser,* Feb. 17, 1842. VanderVelde, "Synod of Michigan and Social Reform," 16-19, and *Michigan Christian Herald,* March, 1842. For abolitionists on Sabbath desecration, *Signal of Liberty,* Sept. 1, 1841, March 2, 1842, March 16, 1846.

[69] The record is confusing, but see *Michigan House Journal, 1843* (Detroit, 1843), 163-64, 177, 178. The repeal seems to have passed Jan. 24, 1843, by a vote of 29 to 16. On Feb. 5, 1844, the legislature approved an act "to punish persons criminally who are guilty of seduction or adultery." It punished the begetting of children and "carnal knowledge" not sanctified by marriage, *Advertiser,* Feb. 26, 1844.

those who are interested in having it passed as a relief measure."[70] The Democrats did not, of course, come out in favor of sin, but this was another example of the Whig tendency to desire government to regulate morality and of the Democratic to prefer laissez faire.

So it was with capital punishment, which a few delegates to the 1835 constitutional convention proposed be abolished. For the next 10 years this issue stirred debate. Party lines were even less clearly drawn on this question than on those discussed above, but evangelicals and Whigs did occupy the vanguard of opposition to abolition, and antievangelical Democrats led in the fight for it.

Agitation for removal of the death penalty gathered steam in the 1843 legislature. When the House passed an abolition bill, the *Advertiser*, some Whig legislators, and Reverend Duffield, lined up against abolition. In 1844 the House buried abolition in committee reports, but in 1846 "a determined group of reformers" carried elimination of capital punishment. The Democratic legislator who drafted the repeal law was Charles P. Bush, the same one who found Sabbatarianism so irritating.[71] The *Advertiser* and the Presbyterians protested the repeal. The Synod officially condemned it in 1846 and continued to do so and to petition for reinstatement of the death penalty until after 1860. Duffield persisted in delivering sermons arguing that God "has ordained there shall be such a thing for the welfare of society." The *Michigan Christian Herald* claimed that crime had increased since abolition of the death penalty.[72]

The capital punishment controversy illustrates the frequently symbolic nature of the evangelical and antievangelical conflict. Capital punishment virtually did not exist because there had been only one execution under the territorial government and none since. De facto abolition already existed in the 1840s. Charles Bush and George Duffield nevertheless disagreed about matters vital to them: whose values would be acknowledged as legitimate by the state; whose values should predominate in society?

[70] The First District and State Conventions are in the *Advertiser*, Aug. 2, 1843, and Sept. 4, 1843. The Wayne County convention attacked "licentiousness and crime," *Advertiser*, Oct. 4, 1843. *Signal of Liberty*, April 10, 24, May 1, 1843.

[71] *Michigan House Journal, 1843*, 158, 177, 178, 194, 198, 210; *Advertiser*, Feb. 1, 6, 1843; Albert Post, "Michigan Abolishes Capital Punishment," *Michigan History*, 29 (January-March 1945), 44-46, 47-49. The committee on capital punishment in the 1844 House submitted a majority report favoring abolition and a minority report opposing it, both signed by Democrats, State of Michigan, *Documents of the Senate and House of Representatives, 1844* (Detroit, 1844), House Doc. No. 22, and House Doc. No. 23. Bush was a "successful business man, and his farm of 1,700 acres in Livingston County was one of the best in the state," *Michigan Biographies*, 142.

[72] VanderVelde, "Synod of Michigan and Social Reform," 25-26. *Advertiser*, Jan.-March, 1848, passim, and esp. Feb. 19, 1848. *Michigan Christian Herald*, Jan. 29, 1849. Post, *Michigan History*, 29, 49.

So it was with other matters. Duffield and the evangelicals may not have really believed that a train running on Sunday was rending the social fabric, though it undoubtedly set a bad example. It did, however, represent the attitude of the state to their God and their values, which they believed to be the true American heritage. Elected officials were men designated by the community to represent it before man and God. That "representation" should not be sinful. With symbolic issues it does not matter if the law is violated by parts of the community, particularly by the subterranean, unseen, or unlived-with. Form counts more than substance for those who are looking for recognition, either for themselves or their values. It matters that the letter and spirit of the law exist, bestow sanction, and indicate the approved direction of society.

Twenty-five years after the Michigan Synod first denounced intemperance Duffield gave a 25th Anniversary Address in which he expressed exactly this evangelical compulsion to find symbolic recognition. In the midst of a lengthy history of the trials of temperance reform in Michigan, the Doctor said he saw the day advancing "when the example and position of the Synod of Michigan . . . will be vindicated and honoured by the applause of a temperate community; when intemperance and the use of intoxicating drinks shall be confined to the secret dens of an illegal and disgraceful traffic, and when the enemies of temperances reform . . . shall find no sympathy or countenance or apologists any longer in the church."[73]

In the Whig-Democratic cleavages outlined above one can see to some extent classic polarities over man, society, and government. For the Democrats, man was an end in himself—(white) man provided the measure. Ideally the law should free the individual for self-realization. Walt Whitman was a young Democrat when he editorialized in 1846 that "We generally expect a great deal too much of law." Government did not exercise anything like the influence for good or evil that people imagined. "We have grown in the way of resting on it to do too many things which ought to be done by individuals, and of making it answer for much that society alone (for government and society are distinct) is in truth the responsible author of." Whitman would support a "true measure to prevent crime or to reform" (vaguely), but he vastly preferred that "we would hunt immorality in its recesses in the individual heart, and grapple with it here, *but not by law*." Whitman's antievangelicalism here hit Democratic chords in valuing the individual over society or govern-

---

[73] Address delivered on October 13, 1860, *Free Press*, Oct. 14, 1860. "Protestantism regarded the State as a religious institution, and saw its end and aim in the protection of the Christian commonwealth and the moral law," Ernst Troeltsch, *Protestantism and Progress: A Historical Study of the Relation of Protestantism to the Modern World*, first published in English, 1912 (Boston, 1958), 106.

ment and in compartmentalizing the latter two entities. (In political competition, however, Democrats subordinated the individual to party regularity and valued the whole over its individual members.) For Whigs, man tended not to be an end in himself. Norms and values existed independently and absolutely. If necessary the law should require community conformity to objective criteria. Drawing a rigid line between government and society had no place in their thinking. They tended to see one as the expression of the other. Whigs valued society over free expression of the individual, although their vision of society was not that of any social order, but rather an historically and culturally rooted vision of an organic society with specific ethnocultural and religious traditions.[74]

[74] Whitman's *Brooklyn Daily Eagle* editorial of March 27, 1846, is reprinted in Blau, ed., *Social Theories of Jacksonian Democracy*, 133. These antimonies are discussed in an essay on constant assumptions underlying ideological polarity, Silvan Tomkins, "Left and Right: A Basic Dimension of Ideology and Personality," Robert W. White, ed., *The Study of Lives* (New York, 1963), 389-411. See also the opposition between "Community" and "Democracy" discussed by Robert E. Lane, *Political Ideology*, 226-27; though Lane has been of great help throughout, his formulations in this case lack critical detachment from American liberal ideology.

VII

The Whigs and the Moralization of Politics

The Whig Party constituted the evangelicals' best hope to Christianize America through politics. Even if the party passed only a few pieces of "Christian" legislation, its sympathy for moral causes would make its being in power reassuring to evangelicals, who took comfort from the piety of Whig leaders. William Woodbridge, for example, though not a pious man, usually took positions conveying rapport with religious values. Public men maintain their leadership, according to Professor Murray Edelman, by "taking the roles of publics whose support they need. The official who correctly gauges the response of publics to his acts, speeches, and postures, makes these behaviors significant symbols evoking common meanings for his audience and for himself and so shaping his further actions as to reassure his public and in this sense 'represent' them."[1] Whigs thus represented evangelicals; many shared with them the perception of political activity in a providential framework, recognizing the intervention of God in secular affairs. This, like the desire to Christianize society, continued the puritan tradition in modified form.

Whig managers interested in power also realized that for the party to win elections it must temper its evangelicalism and enlist broad support. Party leaders self-consciously enlarged its appeal and image after 1836. Still, the Whig campaign of 1837-40 (the preparation for different elections in these years may be regarded as almost continuous) is best characterized as a form of political revivalism. During the late 1830s politics became moralized, even as issues between the parties became less explicit. Tension rose and never did more voters come to believe that the political drama presented a clear confrontation of good and evil, right and wrong.

[1] Edelman, *Symbolic Uses of Politics*, 188.

"WOODBRIDGE AND REFORM"

The central Whig slogan of 1839, "Woodbridge and Reform," sounded like an evangelist's call to camp meeting. Yet "Reform" undoubtedly also suggested release from discontents located in purely secular causes. After the boom expectations of the mid-thirties which lasted in some quarters up to 1837, financial dislocations and depression spread rapidly so that by 1838 even an optimist reported that "poor Michigan is suffering the horrors of the rack." In 1839 still another shock wave of "The Big Bust" hit Michigan. Land values and commodity prices fell, immigration slowed, and most disastrously, the financial system's collapse denuded the state of currency, causing hardship among all classes. The degree and quality of suffering among different groups is not clear. Unemployment apparently was not a problem. What does seem to have been total was the pervasive psychological reverse.[2] To observe, however, that emotional and material discontent, bred of depression, affected political perceptions in 1837-40 is not to say that voters turned out the Democrats in 1839 because they blamed them for the depression. The election data in Chapter II do not at all support that explanation. The mobilization of opposing electoral armies in fierce competition, high turnout, and the closeness of the vote in 1839 and 1840 do not imply that voters held political parties responsible for the vicissitudes of socioeconomic conditions in a market society. There is little evidence even to indicate that governments were held responsible in that way in the early nineteenth century. Nevertheless, material conditions undoubtedly influenced many of the Whig perceptions discussed below, especially those emanating from the late 1830s. For most, the economic scourge only paralleled the political blight already upon them. The aim here, at any rate, is to recognize the essentials of an outlook which persisted in bad times and good.

"Woodbridge and Reform" undoubtedly appealed strongly to the

---

[2] Compare the Letters of C. C. Trowbridge, Detroit, to Lewis Cass, Paris, May 29, 1837, and Aug. 24, Sept. 6, 1837, Cass MSS, Clements; the first said "Our farmers were never so well off as this spring. The year 1836 was one of abundant harvests—prices were very high, and every farmer was benefitted by this state of things. . . . There is as much bustle in our streets as ever although money is so scarce nobody has failed here and all wear cheerful faces." Dunbar, *Michigan*, 321-43, has a good account of boom and bust. Nowlin, *Bark Covered House*, 65-67, described hard times in 1836-37; W. Woodbridge, to Isaac Van Olinda, Sept. 5, 1839, still lamented the "total derangement of our currency," Woodbridge MSS; W. Anderson to Woodbridge, Dec. 24, 1841, Woodbridge MSS, described hard times for farmers in Washtenaw County; but for signs of recovery, George Goodman, Niles, to Woodbridge, Sept. 8, 1841, Woodbridge, MSS, BHC, and Austin Blair, Eaton Rapids, to A. T. McCall, July 18, 1842, Blair MSS; currency problems seem to have been chronic, Blair to McCall, July 1, 1847, Blair MSS, BHC.

revivalist mentality. "Reform" held meanings in 1839 which we cannot appreciate today because in its political sense the word holds a largely secular meaning for us. But even in a political context then, the word loosed inevitable religious connotations, especially to a rural public familiar with revivals.

Sidney Mead's examination of nineteenth-century revivals helps clarify this point. The revival, he said, encouraged a cycle of sin and salvation, or, a habit of backsliding and reforming: "The revivalist emphasis that Christ came to save sinners had the effect of encouraging the Church to nurture flagrant sinners in its bosom in order that they might be 'gloriously saved.' " The individual welcomed revivals as a means to personal reform and salvation, a casting out of sin. Mead suggested an obvious political parallel on the community level: "The stock answer to decline and apathy in a local church was to import a forceful revivalist to 'revive us again!' just as the stock answer to troubles in the country was the importation [or election] of a morally impeccable plumed knight in shining armor to lead a great crusade for spiritual renovation and to throw the rascals out."[3]

Surely "Woodbridge and Reform" suggested these things to portions of the electorate in 1839, particularly to the evangelical sector. Many private statements of Whigs support that inference. Stephen V. R. Trowbridge, prominent Oakland County Whig and a Presbyterian elder, in urging Woodbridge to be a candidate in 1839, said "It is high time the reckless irreligious and awful men in power here should be put down." He prayed to Providence to spare Woodbridge's life so that he would be a candidate and Trowbridge assured him that God would join the battle.[4]

A Presbyterian minister who preached for the Whigs in 1839 and 1840 told Woodbridge in 1841 that he had viewed the recent period in state government under Democratic control as a time of encroachment of ambition and "corruption."[5] Another Whig surveyed the blasted fortunes of the party in 1842, following Harrison's death, Tyler's defection, and state defeat, and revealed the intense religious meaning that "Woodbridge and Reform" and "Harrison and Reform" had contained for him.

[3] Sidney E. Mead, "Denominationalism: The Shape of Protestantism in America," *Church History*, 23 (December 1954), 309-10. Perry Miller went further: "the dominant theme in America from 1800 to 1860 is the invincible persistence of the revival technique. . . . By its basic premise, revivalism required—indeed demanded—that between outbursts there come lulls, which would shortly thereafter be denounced as 'declensions.' " *The Life of the Mind in America: From the Revolution to the Civil War* (New York, 1965), 7.

[4] Stephen V. R. Trowbridge, Birmingham, to Woodbridge, June 25, 1839, Woodbridge MSS, BHC.

[5] Marcus Harrison, Jackson, to Woodbridge, Jan. 12, 1841, Woodbridge MSS, BHC.

He was desolate because his long cherished hope of "practical reform in the Gov't—of the glorious triumph of right over might—the establishment of honest[y] and merit and the overthrow of corruption and crime —of a bright political millenium has died within me. It went to the grave of Harrison and I despair of reformation."[6]

One evangelical Whig described the state of affairs that had existed under Democratic rule as "Barefaced and Unblushing Infidelity . . . and instead of Rulers being a Terror to Evil doers they have become Encouragers." Phineas Fullerton, an evangelist living in Redford, Wayne County, said that he had seen the "public trust betrayed, our Treasuries Robed and our government well nigh subverted." But by the "Interposition of that God who holds the destinies of all men in his hands" the reins of the state had been placed in Woodbridge's hands ensuring salvation.[7]

ACTIVE PROVIDENCE

The notion of an active God who intervened in secular affairs is a crucial aspect of early nineteenth century Whig thinking which has escaped us in a secular age. When a revival visited a community, evangelists attributed it to God's becoming immanent in each individual, and each person could reform himself only by God's grace coming to him. Evangelical Whigs viewed political reform similarly. They readily attributed the vicissitudes of politics to the pleasure or displeasure of God.

Phineas Fullerton envisaged Woodbridge's election in 1839 as part of a Providential plan. He believed that the "powers which be are ordained of God, some fore judgement and some for Mercy, and as we for years past have been chastised with Scorpions I now trust and I humbly hope that the same God which has afflicted is now returned with Bowels [sic] of Mercies. . . . I feel that Heaven has owned and blest the Whig cause in Michigan."[8]

An Ann Arbor Whig editor pursued virtually the same theme as he rejoiced over the salvation of 1839. No state, he wrote, ever achieved "a more sublime moral and political triumph than Michigan." He had never "felt more devoutly grateful to an over-ruling Providence than for the present signal exhibition of his favor. . . . At one time we had thought that a curse had been pronounced upon us as a people for the listlessness

[6] H. Mower [?], Kalamazoo, to Woodbridge, May 3, 1842, Woodbridge MSS, BHC.

[7] Phineas Fullerton, Reford, to Woodbridge, Jan. 30, 1840. Fullerton enclosed a copy of his own work, *The Christian Luminary*, an anti-Catholic tract. Michael Katz has pointed out that in the lexicon of contemporary reform school founders "reform" implied a "total transformation of character," *The Irony of Early School Reform: Educational Innovation in Mid-Nineteenth Century Massachusetts* (Cambridge, 1968), 186.

[8] P. Fullerton to Woodbridge, Dec. 3, 1839, Woodbridge MSS, BHC.

with which we tolerated the official iniquities of our rulers; but instead of a curse, we have received a blessing."[9] Governor Woodbridge's Thanksgiving Proclamation of 1840 echoed the salvation theme and more importantly reassured the religious with his language that a man of piety properly expressed their gratitude to God.[10] Woodbridge seems to have successfully bestowed his regime with an aura of piety. One Jackson County Whig wrote him that "there is a God whose eyes run to and fro throughout the whole earth to show himself strong in behalf of the upright; and I doubt not that you function under full conviction of such a belief." He knew that Woodbridge put his confidence "in Him whose divinity guides the end of all human action."[11]

Heaven could own the Whig cause, but an angry God could also chastise the Whigs for pride and worldliness. Detroit Postmaster Thomas Rowland, a Whig, interpreted William Henry Harrison's death as such a punishment. An "all wise and benevolent God," he said, ordered all things.

If we have offended God by vainly claiming to ourselves the glory of our late astonishing and unparalleled triumph as a political party hailing it as the result of our skill and sagacity, and cast off for the time our dependence on him and put our trust in an arm of flesh, it is in accordance with his ordinary dealing that we should receive our punishment in the very thing wherein we have offended, so that "our pleasant vices are made whips to scourge us." Hence in the loss [of] our idolized President and the humiliation and destruction of our great Whig party [were we punished].[12]

In Rowland's piety appear the sources of antipolitical and antiparty sentiment. That piety encouraged the devaluation of personal loyalty to a political leader or party. Parties were secular and by nature profane, and pietists readily saw the danger of placing too much reliance upon men or of becoming infatuated with party spirit. Such men as Rowland already possessed an alternate set of values which took precedence over such obvious things of the world. They weighed party itself as counting for very little as a secular institution. It was but one agent which God might choose to fulfill His plan for America. After the bitter Whig defeat of 1844 one Monroe Whig leader wrote to Woodbridge of his concern for the "great Moral, as well as political Evil" threatening the country: "Our Fathers thought . . . that America was destined by Divine Providence to act an efficient and most conspicuous part in the regeneration

[9] Ann Arbor, *State Journal*, Nov. 13, 1839; see also *Jonesville Expositor*, Nov. 19, Dec. 3, 1840.

[10] *Free Press*, Oct. 26, 1840.

[11] Benjamin J. Mather, Jackson, to Woodbridge, Feb. 24, 1841, Woodbridge MSS, BHC.

[12] Thomas Rowland, Detroit, to Woodbridge, Jan. 25, 1842, Woodbridge MSS, BHC.

of true Liberty and Religion in the World. Can it be that all our Hopes are so soon blasted? Will not God in a way that we cannot now comprehend, yet cause America to become the Joy and Praise of the whole Earth?"[13]

POLITICAL REVIVALISM

Although the Whigs organized late, once they began in 1837 they conducted a continuous campaign until 1840 that was a kind of political revivalism. Whig political picnics resembled camp meetings, Whig rhetoricians spoke a political idiom resembling that of the evangelist, and the party caught an enthusiasm in those years which can be compared only to that of the extended revival.

In the dark days of 1836 Charles Cleland, Whig editor and former Antimason, prayed: "God grant that there may yet be a redeeming spirit in the people and that it may break forth . . . ere it is too late to save the Republic."[14] Cleland must have thought that the "redeeming spirit" was breaking forth by 1837, and if not then, certainly by 1839, as Whigs went to the polls in unprecedented numbers, in a pitch of enthusiasm sweeping the electorate which, by all accounts, has seldom if ever been matched in American politics.

Whig mass meetings were thoroughly "Arminian" in political theology. They gathered together without distinction of party all those who opposed Democratic misrule and wanted to cast out the rascals. People just going to meetings became a processional extravaganza. Families loaded themselves on wagons, joined together with other wagons or persons on foot or horseback, and trooped in cavalcades to political rallies, prepared to spend the day. The ladies packed food and many men packed hard cider. The meeting was rally, picnic, and revival all rolled into one. The First District Whigs held such a rally in 1840 and their central committee recommended that all who could should "bring with them, a trencher of Pork and Beans, Johnny Cake, and other Log Cabin fixings." Ladies were invited and "their fixens, the Committee leave to themselves, as they are always in good taste."[15]

A Democratic observer of a Kalamazoo County Whig meeting criticized it for its "mock religious ceremony" and, perhaps in hyperbole, suggested how successful the Whigs were in blending religion and politics. He had observed the "infuriated excitement of inebriated revelings" and wondered how the Whigs expected to elect Harrison "by the sense-

[13] Oliver Johnson, Monroe, to Woodbridge, Nov. 20, 1844, Woodbridge MSS, BHC.

[14] C. Cleland, Detroit, to Woodbridge, July 26, 1836 Woodbridge MSS, BHC.

[15] Circular, July 1, 1840, Woodbridge MSS, BHC. See also Hemans, *Mason*, 491-92.

less display of pictured banners and the exhibition of cider barrels, mammoth balls of johnny cakes, [and] *by their blasphemous imitation of the Holy Supper of our blessed Savior in giving parched corn and hard cider* to their devotees saying, 'drink ye all of it.' "[16]

The Whigs were playing upon the appeal of the folkways of New England as well as upon religious symbolism and succeeded in incorporating both into their campaign. Hard cider not only energized Whig rallies but also served as a nostalgic culture symbol. Years later a Whig recalled that in 1840 "Log cabins and coonskins were familiar things, but the hard cider was merely a reminiscence of by-gone days in New England."[17] Whigs indignantly rejected the Democratic charge that alcohol caused the Whig fervor. William Woodbridge gave a more sublime interpretation: "It is worse than purile vanity to pretend that Whig enthusiasm of the day has its origins in the Grog-shop! . . . We see a moral power at work which must and will hurl from their seats the bad men who now occupy the high places of our national government."[18]

Religious enthusiasm in politics made for an intensity of partisan politics that stirred the electorate as it had never been stirred before. Silas Beebe watched the Detroit city election in 1838 and then told his diary that "such a fuss, rumpus and a rioting I never witnessed in a state election. The hand-bills, flags, procession, and a band of music with a marshal mounted on a richly caparisoned horse with gilt trappings." Beebe left before "the election waxed hottest, but learned that there was fighting, broken heads and bloody noses" and a Whig victory.[19]

The "mighty democratic uprising" of 1840 resulted in great measure from political revivalism and the moralization of politics. Thomas Rowland said that "the politics of our time can be compared to nothing so fitly as the great Norwegian Maelstrom which carries into its vortex everything that comes within its influence, so that a man can scarcely think or speak of anything else."[20] Decades later a politician told about the political heat of 1840 and "the topic of the day—whig politics": "whatever else a man might have, in that wonderful year of 1840, he was sure to have an extra supply of politics. And it was politics of a kind which, like Josh Billings hornet, always meant business. If two strangers met each other in the woods, they could not be together five minutes before they would be discussing this all absorbing theme. [The campaign

[16] *Free Press*, June 19, 1840.

[17] Edward W. Barber, "The Vermontville Colony," *MHC*, 28: 238.

[18] William Woodbridge, Detroit, to Isaac Van Olinda, New York, Aug. 22, 1840; also John M. Woodbridge to W. Woodbridge, Feb. 21, 1840, Woodbridge MSS, BHC.

[19] Quoted in Hemans, *Mason*, 446-47.

[20] Thomas Rowland, Uniontown, Pa., to Woodbridge, July 19, 1840, Woodbridge MSS, BHC.

had] so much of the stirring and dramatic in it."[21] Shortly after the campaign a young man recorded in his diary that "Never was a political campaign carried on with such zeal. . . . Every nerve was strained and every means tried which a fruitful imagination could choise [sic]."[22] Political life of such intensity, conviction, and moral drama, where the participants see in party conflict the collision of great moral principles, results from the moralization of politics. Robert Lane has described a situation of low political tension as one in which "politics has not been moralized" and a low level of participation exists. According to Lane low tension and participation have existed when parties and issues have not been invested with strong moral feeling and when political leaders are not seen as moral heroes and villains. This reduces the stakes in elections and makes political commitment "a rather loose affair that can be dissolved as the situation may require. It permits ticket splitting, switching, and a rapid adjustment when the opposition party wins."[23]

The *reverse* of all this held in Michigan in the period from 1837 to 1845. Historians have often said that by 1840 Whigs and Democrats seemed most alike, yet in 1840 Whigs and Democrats themselves perceived the greatest differences between one another and thought most intensely of their side as "us" and of opponents as "they." Broad symbolic groups had been created and parties had become emotionally significant reference groups.

For these and other reasons the election of 1840 needs to be re-examined. The Whigs did not simply copy their campaign methods from the Democrats and hypocritically masquerade as common folk. Any interpretation of the 1840 election built around the hypothesis that politicians are opportunists advances little beyond common sense. In Michigan, Whig party character and campaign style had roots as much in Whig and Antimasonic precedents as in Democratic. Its style was influenced by Yankee culture and evangelical religion. The Whigs had politicized both, and not overnight. As early as 1836 Michigan Whigs consciously set about broadening and secularizing their then predominantly evangelical image. In the process militant evangelicalism was tempered and diffused to make the party more inclusive of diverse social groups. The Whig *Detroit Journal and Courier* admitted in 1836 that "our party prints are too much addressed to the ultras of [our] own party, with whom no further argument is necessary; and not at all fitted to win the assent of moderate men, much less to make converts from the opposition." The first object of a minority, therefore, was to win the

[21] A.D.P. Van Buren, "The Log Schoolhouse Era," *MHC*, 14: 322. Also, Wood, *History of Genesee County*, I, 212, 219.

[22] Henry Chase, "Journal, 1826-48," Chase MSS, BHC.

[23] Robert E. Lane, *Political Ideology* (New York, 1962), 344.

uncommitted. Arguments "which weigh most with confirmed advocates of the party" were "least fitted for that purpose."[24] Already in 1835 the *Advertiser*, for example, had tentatively begun to practice this preaching and became increasingly moderate in 1836, dropping, for example, nativist, anti-Catholic, temperance, and religious articles and editorials, and giving more space to occupational groups such as farmers, businessmen, mechanics, and others. Indeed, after 1836, Whig editors, like Whig county and state conventions, became politicized enough to begin protesting their friendship for foreigners and their religious tolerance. Egalitarian rhetoric had arrived on the scene somewhat earlier; in New York, for example, Democratic Republicans had picked it up from such opponents as the People's Party, Antimasons, and Workingmen. In Michigan, Whigs in the late 1830s acquired enough of the eclecticism and pragmatism of Democrats to shape an image broad enough to win elections. Whig success in 1839 and 1840 lay in the creation of an image diffuse enough to include nonevangelicals and yet to retain reassurance for evangelicals.

[24] *Advertiser*, Nov. 15, 1836; the *Jackson Democrat* attributed Whig success to an appeal that had been quite secular, Nov. 14, 1839, which indicates both Whig image-broadening and the *Democrat*'s own perceptual framework.

VIII

Religious Groups and Parties: 1837–1852

Let no one, however, think that all the early settlers were by
any means religious. But it is true that they all possessed so
much respect for religion, and so much regard for the feelings
and sentiments of their neighbors who were religious, that
their outward conduct was on the whole favorable to morality
and religion in the community.—Reminiscence of Concord,
Jackson County[1]

Though our drink is always gay,
There are ever those who nag,
and we shall be indigent.
May those who nag us be confounded,
and never be inscribed among the just.
                    —*Carmina Burana*

Religion as a group experience and source of values profoundly
influenced political behavior in nineteenth-century America. This has not
always been apparent to twentieth-century historians with secular perspectives. They have often missed the interplay between religion and
party preferences, not in terms of formal creeds coinciding with party
ideologies but rather from religion shaping basic orientations to self,
society, and government. This mode of analysis sees religion neither as
the ultimate cause nor as a disguise for real causes. It recognizes instead
that religion joined with cultural background, socioeconomic conditions,
and many other causes to influence party choice.

In contrast to ethnicity, religion is more articulate. That is, ethnicity
may be studied in folkways, traditions, group experience, and symbols
of identity. Religion usually provides more explicit texts whose reason
for being is to address themselves to defining values. Religious belief systems articulated for many social groups the group attitudes and values
resulting from complex processes of socialization in which religious
teachings are but one element. "Religion" here clearly does not mean
fine-spun theology, or specific doctrines and institutions. Rather, it im-

[1] Melville McGee, "The Early Days of Concord, Jackson County, MHCol, 21:
431.

plies common group dispositions which provide ways of interpreting experience and strategies of coping with it.[2]

Party loyalties in Michigan in 1835 to 1852 appear to have been strongly associated with religious differences. Protestants and Catholics, churched and nonchurched Protestants, and evangelical and nonevangelical Protestants diverged significantly in their voting. A majority of native, churched Protestants voted Whig. Native evangelical Protestants voted heavily anti-Democratic (Whig, Liberty, or Free Soil). Methodists, however, were closely divided with a probable Democratic list. Catholics disproportionately supported the Democrats. Most polarized, perhaps, were evangelical Protestants and foreign Catholics.

Presbyterians, Congregationalists, and Baptists are characterized here as evangelicals, and the other major denominations as nonevangelical. These labels convey the dominant temper of each, but the evangelical groups contained many nonevangelicals, and vice versa. Denominational rubrics convey only clues to vital dispositions cutting across different churches. Gerhard Lenski's sociological study of religious values in Detroit in the 1950s can clarify this point. Lenski found that denominational distinctions bore little relation to variations in political behavior. However, two broad, opposing religious postures, "doctrinal orthodoxy" and "devotionalism," did carry over into politics. Doctrinal orthodoxy generally neutralizes religious beliefs in political life because it "fosters a more compartmentalized type of religious belief and experience." On the other hand "devotionalism seems to encourage its adherents to think in terms of the 'oneness of life' and to disregard the popular distinctions between that which is religious and that which is secular; but orthodoxy appears to have the opposite effect." The Michigan evangelical and nonevangelical cleavage resembles Lenski's dichotomy, and it follows closely the "puritan" and "nonpuritan" alignment Lee Benson found in New York in the 1840s.[3]

The 1850 census manuscript of social statistics lists each church by denomination in every township, and gives the number of "accommodations" for church buildings. The number of seats thus provides a relative measure of denominational strength called "religious preferences." These

---

[2] A classic work is H. Richard Niebuhr, *The Social Sources of Denominationalism* (New York, 1929). See also Benton Johnson, "Ascetic Protestantism and Political Preference," *Public Opinion Quarterly*, 26 (Spring 1962), 35-46, esp. 44-45; and Robert Kelley, "Presbyterianism, Jacksonianism and Grover Cleveland," *American Quarterly*, 18 (Winter 1966), 622-23. Robert W. Doherty has examined the social differences related to doctrinal splits within the Quakers in 1827, *The Hicksite Separation: A Sociological Analysis of Religious Schism in Early Nineteenth Century America* (New Brunswick, 1967).

[3] Gerhard Lenski, *The Religious Factor: A Sociological Study of Religion's Impact on Politics, Economics and Family Life* (Garden City, 1961), 182-87. Benson, *Concept*, 207.

are computed by finding the percentage of total seats held by each denomination.[4] For example, Redford had three Methodist churches with a total of 450 seats, 250 Baptist seats, and 150 Dutch Reformed. Its Methodist preference thus was 53 percent, and so on. The "religiosity" of each unit made the preferences more meaningful. This is the ratio of all church seats to population. Redford's 850 seats constituted 52 percent of its total population in 1850.

Several considerations prevented the data derived in this way from being processed and correlated with other demographic and voting indices. The number of seats did not measure membership. Many if not most communicating members of Protestant churches were women and children. Towns listing no churches in the census often had persons attending services in nearby towns. A "Methodist" church may, in a poor rural area, have been attended by Baptists, or others. Towns remaining thinly settled or lacking a village center may have been peopled with religious men. The census manuscript of population lists many "clergymen" in towns with no churches, and county histories often tell of "societies," classes, or organizations lacking buildings. Thus, a religious index based on seats is several times removed from the adult male electorate of voters. Merely quantifying the available data for religion gives it concrete substance it does not possess.

PROTESTANTS AND CATHOLICS

Rather simple tabulations suggest that a majority of churched Protestants voted Whig. Whig-Free Soil areas in 1850, compared to Democratic, had far more Protestant church seats. In the 5 counties which cast the highest Democratic percentage in 1852, there were 6,250 Protestant seats. In the 5 lowest Democratic counties there were 9,390 Protestant seats. The aggregate population of the Democratic counties was over 6,000 persons larger than the anti-Democratic. Church seat data for townships and available election returns permitted a similar comparison of high and low Democratic towns in 12 counties in 1850 and 1852. In only two western counties, Cass and Calhoun, and one eastern, St. Clair, did the Democratic towns have more Protestant seats. In Wayne, Washtenaw, Oakland, Macomb, Jackson, Kalamazoo, Branch, Allegan, and St. Joseph, the number of Protestant seats in anti-Demoratic townships heavily exceeded those in Democratic units.

Catholics, according to contemporaries throughout the period, voted

---

[4] Philip A. Nordquist, "The Ecology of Organized Religion in the United States: 1850" (unpublished Ph.D. dissertation, University of Washington, 1964), first used this method with county data.

heavily Democratic.[5] The 5 counties with the highest Democratic vote in 1852 had (in 1850) at least 15 Catholic churches with 5,240 seats, compared to 2 Catholic churches with 800 seats in the 5 most anti-Democratic units. Data permitting comparison of party, religiosity, and Catholic preference was available for 8 towns in 5 different counties. Except for one town, all voted strongly Democratic year after year. Most of the Catholics in these towns were in the lower classes: many, such as the frontier poor of Westphalia and Grattan, were upwardly mobile.[6]

TABLE VIII.1

Michigan's "Catholic" Townships, 1850:
Democratic Percentage Strength and Wealth

	Dem.	Cath. Pref.	Relig.	Mean Value	RLC
Hamtramck, Wayne County	68	100	25	$2,700	54
Grosse Pointe, Wayne County	76	78	83	1,661	47
Ecorse, Wayne County	55	100	32	1,121	60
Northfield, Washtenaw County	63[a]	100	134	1,807	42
Dexter, Washtenaw County	63[a]	100	21	1,011	
Harrison, Macomb County	68	100	41	1,917	
Grattan, Kent County	56	100	31	795	
Westphalia, Clinton County	95	100	65	696	

[a] 1852 return

Neither voting nor census data permits observation of urban Protestant and Catholic voting in any large town other than Detroit. The 1850 census gave no useful data for Detroit wards, but the publisher of the 1853 Detroit Directory compiled a census "Showing the several National and Religious Divisions" by ward. Percentages of religious groups derived from the census are based on population and underestimate the proportion of foreign-born and Catholic voters. The returns also lumped together a "scattered population" of 4,600 persons living in hotels and rooming houses. Yet the census is remarkable for its day and provides a relative measure of Protestant-Catholic density. The three most Catholic wards (Four, 57 percent; Eight, 47 percent; Seven, 46 percent) were also the most Democratic. Although there was a strong negative relationship between Protestantism and the 1852 Democratic vote ($-.667$), Protestants were divided in their party loyalty.[7]

[5] W. Hickey, Office of the Secretary of the Senate, to William Woodbridge, Aug. 13, 1844, Woodbridge MSS, BHC. *Advertiser*, Nov. 12, 1844, Nov. 6, 1852. *Free Press*, Feb. 11, 1853. This claim is based on much more supporting evidence in newspapers and manuscripts.

[6] *History of Shiawasee and Clinton Counties, Michigan* (Philadelphia, 1880), 533-35. *History of Kent County, Michigan* (Chicago, 1881), 755-60.

[7] *Johnston's Detroit Directory and Business Advertiser, 1853-54* (Detroit, 1853), xiv.

EVANGELICALS

That Whig-Free Soil units contained large numbers of Protestant church seats reflected in large part the heavy anti-Democratic voting of evangelical denominations. Evangelicalism or Arminianized Calvinism cut across nineteenth-century churches. Indeed, Timothy L. Smith has identified "Four significant strains of thought and feeling [which] flowed freely across denominational lines": Traditionalism, Orthodox Calvinism, Evangelical Arminianism, and Revival Calvinism. Smith applied the term "evangelical" to Arminians who "claimed the allegiance of a vast army of Methodists of all sorts, the German Wesleyan sects, the Friends, many New Lutherans, the Cumberland Presbyterians, and the Free Will Baptists."[8]

Smith used "evangelical" as most historians have, to connote simple, single-minded, emotional religious behavior. Here the word has been used rather to describe Revival Calvinism, benevolence, moral reform, theocratic thinking, and devotionalism. Orientation to this strain emerged as having a vital relation to politics. The feature of evangelical Calvinism holding most salience for political behavior was concern for the moral and social welfare of the community. This attitude might have emphasized individual reform as a means to social ends, but the goal of the moral society distinctively marked evangelical values in their political bearing.[9]

The evangelical credentials of Presbyterians have been well established. Little need be added except to note that Presbyterian piety was not confined to leaders. From the prosaic record of Dearbornville's Presbyterian Church, for example, from 1834 to 1860, emerges the emphasis members placed on pious behavior. Dismissals or threats of excommunication resulted from such offenses as intemperance or the "frequent habit of using profane language," such as "By God."[10] Other local records tell of revivals, concern with slavery, and reveal the Calvinist obsession with God's governance and their self-image as His agents for the moral regeneration of society.[11]

Congregationalists before 1842 were indistinguishable from the Pres-

[8] Smith, *Revivalism and Social Reform*, 32-33; Foster, *Evangelical United Front*, 251-52.

[9] For a different interpretation see Seymour Martin Lipset, "Religion and Politics in American History," Earl Raab, ed., *Religious Conflict in America* (New York, 1964), 64-65. T. Scott Miyakawa, *Protestants and Pioneers* (Chicago, 1964), offers a traditional interpretation, 198-209.

[10] "Records of the Presbyterian Church in Dearbornville," typed bound MS, BHC, 10-12, 38-40. Pp. 1-78 cover 1834-1860.

[11] "Histories of Churches in Washtenaw Presbytery," James Dunbar MSS, MHCol; these are contemporary histories written by ministers. See also "Diary of Peter Dougherty," I, 1838-1843, 8-9, MHCol (typed MS copy of original). Edwin O. Wood, *History of Genesee County, Michigan* (Indianapolis, 1916), I, 232.

byterians under their Plan of Union. In 1842 some broke away and formed a separate association. Schismatic and "ultraist" Congregationalists distressed Reverend Duffield. His diary frequently moans with complaints against the excessive zeal of the Congregationalists and their disrespect for church order. Duffield said that the "miserable spirit" of Congregationalism "disdained all watch and care of an eldership ordained to take the spiritual oversight, knows no obligation of governmental relations, and inflates each individual with the notion that they are judges and have as much right as anyone else to move in matters affecting the public social . . . interests."[12] However fair this remark, it brands the Congregationalists with the distinctive evangelical mark. Differences between Presbyterians and Congregationalists on this score, while important to Duffield, were largely of degree.

Michigan Baptists also shared the evangelical mood. They showed great interest in benevolence, missions, Sabbath-keeping, temperance, slavery, capital punishment, general immorality, and Popery. Stridently anti-Catholic, their state convention in 1850 declared that God had chosen this country for the genius of the Anglo-Saxon to develop, but America was threatened by "the tide of immigration which is setting from Europe and beating incessantly upon our shores," endangering "the religious institutions of mankind." Catholicism stalked abroad "with super abundant means to prosecute its work. It is grafting its ugly scions upon every branch, and growing with . . . the Tree of Liberty."[13] The Baptist *Michigan Christian Herald* also fought the Popish plague with great zeal. Its anti-Romanism waxed most intensely in the mid-forties, years of nativism's floodtide across the country. The *Herald* also believed that the poverty, crime, and intemperance it associated with immigrants inhered in the nature of Catholicism.[14] The state convention issued strong resolutions against liquor and criticized Sabbath desecration by traveling "or other unnecessary worldly employment." In 1842 it reprimanded the legislature for its "evil example" in setting the trains running on the Sabbath, and lending its high sanction "to a practice which is in gross violation of the laws of God and man."[15] Nor did the Baptists

[12] VanderVelde, ed., "Notes on the Diary of George Duffield," *Mississippi Valley Historical Review*, 24: 56. See also First Congregational Church, Jackson, *Church Manual or the Confession of Faith and Covenant of the First Congregational Church*, Jackson, Mich. (Detroit, 1846), 1-2, 8-9.

[13] *Minutes of the Michigan Baptist Association, 1850*, 19-21. Billington, "Anti-Catholic Propaganda and the Home Missionary Movement, 1800-1860," *Mississippi Valley Historical Review*, 22 (December 1935), 361-84.

[14] *Herald*, passim, 1842-1852; e.g., Dec. 18, 1843, Sept. 23, 1844, Jan. 6, 1845, Dec. 4, 1851.

[15] *Minutes of the Michigan Baptist Association, 1848*, 7; *ibid.*, 1850, 9; *Michigan Christian Herald*, Oct. 30, 1851: On the Sabbath: *Minutes Michigan Baptist Association, 1836*, 11; *Herald*, Dec. 1842, Feb. 9, 1846. See also on abolition, Ann Arbor, *Signal of Liberty*, July 21, 1841, Nov. 21, 1842.

equivocate on slavery. In 1840 the convention expressed its wish to "clear their skirts of this most accursed evil." The *Herald* opposed Texas annexation as a slaveholders' plot to "perpetuate the foul curse of Slavery, by giving the South the ascendancy in the National Councils." Not surprisingly, the Baptist leadership endorsed the Wilmot Proviso and denounced the Fugitive Slave Law.[16]

Townships across the state can be observed to test the hypothesis that to promote their values evangelicals voted anti-Democratic. Units can be compared as to their "evangelical preference," religiosity, party loyalty, and other variables. The evangelical preference of a town is any combination of Presbyterian, Congregationalist, or Baptist preferences. Table VIII.2 presents those units for which census and election data were available, and which had both evangelical preferences *and* religiosities of over 50 percent. Not only were three-fifths of the 26 towns on the Whig-Free Soil side, but they leaned disproportionately that way: all but one of them voted over 55 percent anti-Democratic, while 5 of the 8 Democratic towns voted less than 55 percent Democratic.

The first seven units in Table VIII.2 formed part of a cluster of townships, converging at the juncture of Wayne, Oakland, and Washtenaw counties, lying in a piety belt or "burned-over district." These units preeminently exhibited Yankee evangelical character and were nests of anti-Democratic votes—where even Democrats sometimes took on an evangelical coloring. Plymouth was perhaps the model of the species. Its two villages, crammed with skilled workers, did the most manufacturing of any township in Wayne, yet Plymouth surpassed all other units in occupied farms, improved acreage, and "industry, enterprise, and public spirit."[17] Western New Yorkers had settled the area and named it allegedly in tribute to Pilgrim ancestors. Church meetings appropriately began with civil organization: in 1833, 200 Presbyterians filled a barn. By 1850 seven churches stood containing more seats than the township had people. The community kept the Sabbath while Antimasonry, temperance, and abolition flourished: 84 percent of those voting in 1853 chose prohibition. Naturally Plymouth claimed a station on the Underground Railroad.[18]

[16] *Minutes Michigan Baptist Association, 1840*, 4; ibid., *1841*, 9; *Herald*, Nov. 6, 1843, May 6, 1844, March 7, 1845, Aug. 4, 1848, Feb. 28, 1850, Oct. 16, 1851; *Minutes Michigan Baptist Association, 1850*, 7.

[17] George C. Bates, *MHC*, 22: 311. *Advertiser*, Nov. 10, 1845.

[18] Daniel B. Riebel, "Founding a Pioneer Home in Plymouth, Michigan, 1825 to 1840 (unpublished M.A. thesis, Wayne State University, 1961), 1-32, 88-94, 98. Nettie L. Dibble, ed., "Historical Data of Plymouth Township, Wayne County, Michigan," typed MS, BHC (1930-31). Dibble, ed., "The Presbyterian Church in Plymouth," typed MS, BHC (1960). *MHC*, 1: 447. Burton, et al., eds., *Detroit*, I, 428. Jonathan Shearer to Levi Bishop, Sept. 23, 1871, Levi Bishop MSS, BHC. See also Starkweather MSS, BHC. Other comments on its political character:

TABLE VIII.2
Evangelical Townships, 1850: Party Percentage and Wealth[a]

		Party	Ev. Pref.	Relig.	Mean Value Farms	RLC
	Plymouth, Wayne County	79W	69	107		26
	Livonia, Wayne County	74W	70	73	$2,215	20
	Milford, Oakland County	66W	69	88	1,735	26
	Farmington, Oakland County	57W	60	68	2,292	
EAST	Augusta, Washtenaw County	61WFS[c]	48[b]	65		
	Saline, Washtenaw County	58WFS[c]	69	60		
	York, Washtenaw County	52D[c]	100	59	2,007	
	Salem, Washtenaw County	54WFS[c]	100	52	1,798	27
	Clinton, Macomb County	54D	58	111		
	Bruce, Macomb County	59W	56	58	2,341	
	Clyde, St. Clair County	68D[d]	57	51	2,575[e]	
	Adrian, Lenawee County	56W	59	57	2,155[e]	
	Tecumseh, Lenawee County	55D	54	105	2,451[e]	
	Medina, Lenawee County	56W	75	50	1,582	
	Hudson, Lenawee County	69W	100	65	1,459[e]	
	Tompkins, Jackson County	73W	57	56	994	
	Napoleon, Jackson County	60W	77	75	1,719	
CENTRAL	Grass Lake, Jackson County	55D	61	57	1,661	
	Battle Creek, Calhoun County	58W	64	113	1,871[e]	
	Vermontville, Eaton County	64W	77	100	1,135	47
	Coldwater, Branch County	55D	60	83	1,651[e]	
	Lockport, St. Joseph County	56W	53	75	1,937	33
WEST	Sturgis, St. Joseph County	66W	55	66	2,513[e]	34
	White Pigeon, St. Joseph County	69D	55	69	1,807	36
	Ontwa, Cass County	50	63	136	1,584[e]	
	LaGrange Cass County	58D	57	75	1,935[e]	

[a] Mean Value of Farms, and Rural Lower Classes when available
[b] Plus a Quaker preference of 19 percent
[c] 1850 returns not available; mean of other elections 1848-52
[d] 1852 election
[e] Misleading; majority of voters actually not farm-owners

Plymouth's sister unit in Wayne was Livonia, which shared its lifestyle and politics.[19] Canton Township, however, lay alongside the two burned-over units: though it rivaled them in prosperity it housed mostly strong Democrats. It differed also in religion with Presbyterian preference of 37 percent and a Methodist of 63 percent (religiosity 71 percent). And there are hints that Canton's New York-born, 55 percent of the potential voters, were predominantly of Yorker descent, an ethnocultural group that tended to be Democratic. The absence of evidence on one point is striking: both Plymouth and Livonia exuded signs of "Yankeeness," but not Canton.[20] Thus Plymouth and Livonia were mainly Yankee, Protestant, evangelical, prosperous, and Whig-Free Soil; Canton was chiefly Protestant, nonevangelical, prosperous, possibly Yorker, and Democratic.

In Oakland County, north of Livonia, lay Farmington. Quakers, Congregationalists, revival-prone Baptists, and Methodists gave it a super-heated religious climate in which the Democratic vote was very low. Nearby Milford resembled Plymouth with farms and thriving manufacturing villages; Presbyterians, Baptists, and Methodists from New York and New England favored temperance but not Democracy.[21] Of greatest interest in Oakland is Troy Township, excluded from Table VIII.2 by lack of census data. In this anti-Democratic and wheat, pork, wool, cattle, and livestock producing unit, marks of New England abounded. Not only Antimasonry but even Millerism and Morminism infected Troy residents. But the attributes of Troy's two leading citizens disclose at least two strains of social character. One man was a Whig, the other a Democrat. Both provided "headquarters for the early immigrants." Johnson Niles, born in New York and apprenticed there as a carpenter, came to Michigan in 1821, engaging in "mercantile enterprises." During the boom he platted a paper village, to be named after his friend Eurotas P. Hastings, the prominent Whig. Unlike Hastings, Niles was neither Whig nor Presbyterian but a Royal Arch Mason and Democratic leader. Post-

---

Mary Lyon to Laurinda Davis, Feb. 28, 1833, Starkweather Papers, BHC; E. J. Penniman, Plymouth, to William Woodbridge, Oct. 25, 1844, Woodbridge MSS, BHC.

[19] On Livonia: Farmer, *Detroit*, I, 1319; Burton, et al., *Detroit*, I, 426; Osband, *MHC*, 14: 434, 444, 447, 449; Plymouth Historical Society, "More About Toll Roads," 4-5; Domenic P. Paris, *The Heritage of Livonia* (1962).

[20] George B. Catlin, "Early Settlement in Eastern Michigan," *Michigan History*, 26 (Summer 1942), 334; Dibble, ed., "Historical Data," 15-17; Family Records, Osband Papers, 73, BHC.

[21] Samuel W. Durant, *History of Oakland County, Michigan* (Philadelphia, 1877), 166-74, 221-28; *Michigan Statistics, 1850*, 116-17, 120-21; *Michigan Christian Herald*, Feb. 17, 1845, Nov. 16, 1846; Lilian Drake Avery, ed., Oakland County Pioneer Papers, II, 18, typed bound MS, BHC; *Report of the Proceedings and Debates of the Constitutional Convention of 1850*, 199, 522.

master, state legislator, occupant of a string of offices, "no Democratic convention was complete" without him. Niles' "worthy compeer" and Whig counterpart was Stephen V. R. Trowbridge. Farmer, entrepreneur, county supervisor, territorial legislator, and state senator, Trowbridge fit Troy's dominant character. A founder and elder of the Presbyterian Church, he was "always a staunch friend of temperance, and an active Christian."[22]

West of Plymouth in Washtenaw County was Salem Township, stronghold of Whiggery, antislavery votes, and a record of "pure and simple progress, unmarked by crime or whiskey." Yankee Protestants gave it and nearby Webster names signaling New England—the latter after the illustrious Daniel. Webster's "moral and religious people" voted anti-Democratic. Temperance and Antimasonry had swept through, and in 1840 its Whigs braved a drenching downpour to campaign for Harrison shouting "any rain but the reign of Martin Van Buren."[23]

Other townships in the three county area, such as Commerce and Lyon in Oakland, Scio, Pittsfield, and Augusta in Washtenaw, also displayed evangelical traits and anti-Democratic politics.[24] They too formed part of eastern Michigan's piety belt. Appendix C presents similar data for townships throughout Michigan that had evangelical preferences of over 50 percent but religiosity of under 50 percent. Perhaps the best way of indicating what those tables show is to present their summaries here.

Distribution of Party Strength, by Towns

		Eastern		Central		Western	
		Anti-Dem.	Dem.	Anti-Dem.	Dem.	Anti-Dem.	Dem.
Total		12	7	3	2	8	3
Percentage	51–55	2	3	1		1	1
range	56–60	2	2	1	1	1	2
	61–65	3	1	1	1	4	
	66–70	2	1			1	
	70–80	3				1x	

x: 82

Prosperity and evangelical political character often went together in Michigan. Most evangelical anti-Democrats appeared generally more prosperous than the anti-Democratic group. "Improvement," moral and material, strongly compelled these farmers, skilled workers, rural entrepreneurs, and urban businessmen who sought to advance their values by voting Whig, Liberty, or Free Soil. Yet the anti-Democratic

[22] Durant, 285-95; *MHC*, 12: 395; *Michigan Biographies*, 491, 644-45.
[23] *History of Washtenaw County, Michigan* (Chicago, 1881), 668-81; Jeremiah J. Williams, "History of the Town of Webster," *MHC*, 12: 546-57.
[24] *History of Washtenaw*, ii, 751-66, 1242-59; Durant, *History of Oakland*, 158-64; *MHC*, 14: 421-30; *Report of Constitutional Convention, 1850*, 93.

nexus did not simply reflect a maturing Protestant ethic. Many Democratic opponents, including some anti-Democratic evangelicals, were poor. Socioeconomic influences appear to have had some relevance, but were less important than religious and cultural.

Data on Wayne County elites show similar tendencies and provide material for a more precise discussion of the relative weight of variables influencing political choice. Sabbath's study of Whig and Democratic leaders in Wayne in 1844 found evangelical denominations represented among the Whigs by slightly more than 2 to 1 over Democrats.[25]

	Democrats	Whigs
Presbyterian	12	21
Baptist	0	1
Congregationalist	0	3
	12	25

McCoy found an even stronger anti-Democratic trend among evangelical members of Wayne's 1844 economic elite. Only 2 elite members were Congregationalists: 1, Whig; 1, Liberty. One of 2 Baptists had no identifiable politics, the other was Whig. Presbyterians were the largest single religious group among the elite, 37 of 97 men. Only 16 percent were Democrats, 76 percent Whig, and 5 percent Liberty, for an anti-Democratic percentage of 81. Presbyterianism acted to subdivide the Yankees. Yankee Presbyterians tended also to be Whigs, only 1 Yankee Democrat was Presbyterian. Yankee Whig Presbyterians devoted themselves, more than the rest of the elite, to capitalist enterprise.[26]

Sabbath's data provides a rough sample of the urban middle class, or at least of its politically active sector. If McCoy's and Sabbath's data on Presbyterians are contrasted it appears that the combination of upper-class status and Presbyterianism tended to make for a stronger anti-Democratic trend among the elite than among the middle class. However, it is also possible that Presbyterians were overrepresented in the Democratic party leadership, that proportionately more Presbyterians could be found in leadership positions in the Democratic Party than in the party ranks. Groups that at large are strongly against a party are often disproportionately present in its organization, partly because of the latter's efforts to win greater support from the group generally. This inference finds support from evidence that one Detroit Democratic Presbyterian was regarded as a renegade by his fellow parishioners in the First Presbyterian Church. David Stuart's father had been a Whig stalwart, but in 1850 the son was campaigning for city prosecuting attorney

[25] Sabbath, "Political Leadership in Wayne County, 1844," 112.
[26] McCoy, "Wayne County Economic Elite, 1844, 1860," 131.

on the Democratic ticket. His mother thought he had astonishing success "in anything in a political way," and great influence in his party, but he was running against Whig Bethune Duffield, Reverend Duffield's son. "Dave told him a day or two since that those of the Pres. Church who do not vote out of love for him, would do it out of hate for Dave."[27]

Three minor denominations not represented among the economic elite, but evangelical or intensely pietist in disposition, were Free Will Baptists, Quakers, and Wesleyan Methodists. Free Will Baptists left no formal records but were, by general report, intensely pious and sectarian. Indirectly, they created a record of strong support of political anti-slavery. The 1850 census listed only 3 Free Will buildings; but 13 other societies could be found in county histories. The vote in these 16 mostly rural and poor towns for Liberty in 1844, and Free Soil in 1848 and 1852 clearly implies a connection between the Free Will spirit and anti-

TABLE VIII.3

Townships with Free Will Baptists,[a] Liberty Party Vote 1844,
Free Soil Vote 1848 and 1852, and Mean Value of Farms

	1844	1848	1852	Mean Value Farms
State Vote	7%	16%	9%	
Burlington, Calhoun County	31	49	38	$1,293
Leoni, Jackson "	26	53	31	1,382
Jackson, " "	12	20	10	2,095[b]
Bruce, Macomb "	3	14	23	2,341
Rives, Jackson "	34	66	45	1,209
Waverly, Van Buren "	46	20	19	703
Atlas, Genesee "	9	21	—NR	1,227[b]
Girard, Branch "	8	48	33	1,255
Duplain, Clinton "	0	7	11	568
Assyria, Barry "	10	30	31	822[c]
Salem, Washtenaw "	21	38	29	1,798
Wheatland, Hillsdale "	18	26	19	1,431
Commerce, Oakland "	9	43	21	1,896
Fenton, Genesee "	13	37	—NR	1,052[b]
Richfield, " "	0	32	—NR	749
Green Oak, Livingston "	21	38	29	1,663

[a] The ms census of social statistics listed Free Will Church Buildings for the first 3 towns; Free Will organizations were located in the next 13 by using county histories

[b] Majority of voters not farm owners, but figures for Fenton and Atlas probably not very misleading

[c] Mean value of real estate per number of families

[27] Sarah B. Stuart to Kate, Sept. 29, 1850, Marlatt, ed., *Stuart Letters*, I, 131. "The whole Church Dem. & Whig turned out against him, & worked with money and everything they could to beat him, but it was no go," John Stuart to Kate, Nov. 19, 1850, *ibid.*, I, 160.

slavery votes. In only 5 of the 44 cases in Table VIII.3 was the anti-slavery vote less than the statewide percentage. The last town in the table, Green Oak, the oldest in Livingston, produced many men influential in county and state affairs. The modestly prosperous rural town voted Democrat in off-year elections, but usually failed to give the Democrats a majority. In 1848 Free Soil won a plurality and in 1850 73 percent of the vote went to the Whig Congressional candidate. The Free Soil Baptists were the most significant religious group in town. Green Oak attracts special interest because it was the home of Kinsley Bingham, the Democrat of Free Soil tendencies who finally was read out of his party and wound up being elected "Fusion," or Republican, governor in 1854.[28]

Quakers, perhaps more than evangelicals, did not compartmentalize their lives into secular and religious sectors.[29] They did not share in revivalism but their temperament approached closely what Lenski described as devotional. Their intense pietism and desire for a moral society led them to vote overwhelmingly for Whig and antislavery parties.

Quaker association with antislavery is incontestable; they exerted influence far out of proportion to their numbers in abolition societies and the Liberty Party.[30] An early center of Quaker settlement was Lenawee County. Although Quakers put their gentle mark on the towns of Tecumseh and Adrian, by the mid-thirties population growth dwarfed the Quaker proportion of the electorate. They cannot provide the bases for credible generalizations about how Quakers voted.[31] In two smaller Lenawee towns Quakers were still a minority but represented much more of the electorate. In Rollin, Quakers amounted at best to one-third of the population. From 1835 Rollin was staunchly Whig, giving thumping majorities of 86 and 81 percent against the Democrats in 1837 and 1839. Raisin's Quaker settlement consisted of "a few families"; Congregationalists perhaps were as numerous as Quakers. Raisin delivered a Whig

[28] *History of Livingston County, Michigan* (Philadelphia, 1880), 332, 331-2.

[29] Robert Doherty, *Hicksite Separation*, 50.

[30] Kooker, "Anti-Slavery Movement in Michigan," 22, 108-09, 110, 113. John Cox, Jr., "The Quakers in Michigan," *Michigan History*, 29 (October-December 1945), 512-21. Gerald Sorin, "The Historical Theory of Political Radicalism: Michigan Abolitionist Leaders As a Test Case" (unpublished M.A. thesis, Wayne State University, 1964); of the 10 most important Liberty leaders 2 were Quakers, 54-72. Merton L. Dillon, "Elizabeth Chandler and the Spread of Anti-Slavery Sentiment to Michigan," *Michigan History*, 39 (December 1965), 494. Van Buren, "Michigan Pioneer Politics," *MHC*, 17: 255.

[31] Streeter was misled in this way into claiming a Quaker-Democratic association, *Political Parties*, 207, 213-14. Election returns: *Advertiser*, Dec. 5, 1837; *Free Press*, Nov. 16, 1839. Fuller, *Economic and Social Beginnings*, 236. W. A. Whitney and R. A. Bonner, *History of Lenawee County, Michigan* (Adrian, 1879), I, 40, 56, 57-58.

majority of 54 percent in 1837 and in 1839, with the vote total climbing from 54 to 93 it cast 65 percent for Whiggery.[32]

Farmington and Augusta townships, encountered earlier in the piety belt, also had Quaker settlements. Both were of evangelical and anti-Democratic character. In western Michigan Quakers formed part of the early immigration from the South. Calvin Township in Cass County grew famous for a colony of black farmers who gathered under the Quaker aegis. Ex-Southern Quakers also pioneered Penn township where religion and antislavery flourished in the 1840s and 1850s.[33] Calvin and Penn both followed a strong anti-Democratic path. In 1844 Calvin gave Polk 35 percent and Penn gave him 21 percent.

It is difficult to infer that Quakers voted Democratic to any extent. Rather, substantial credence should be given to a claim made by a Quaker requesting an appointment from Whig Governor William Wood-bridge in 1840. Henry Willis, a builder and former superintendent of the Michigan Central, wanted to be named to the Board of Internal Improvements: "It may not be amiss to state to thee for thy information that we know of but two individuals in all our Society in this State which is now becoming numerous—but what are Whigs and did exert themselves to the utmost to Secure thy Election and I am the only man out of the whole who will apply to thee for an office."[34]

An evangelical strain even existed within the vast array of Methodism. The Methodist Episcopal church avoided taking a stand on slavery and tried to muzzle antislavery dissidents within the church. This led to the Wesleyan schism, located mostly in western New York and Michigan. About 1,000 Michigan Methodists, mostly in Wayne and Washtenaw counties, seceded from their church in 1841. Not quite evangelicals, they easily outdid regular Methodists in piety, devotionalism, and moral reformism.[35]

The striking aspect of the Wesleyan secession was how few antislavery voters it produced. In Nankin Township in Wayne, Reverend Marcus Swift began antislavery agitation among Methodists around 1834. Opposed by the hierarchy and faced with lack of responsiveness from Methodists generally, Swift persuaded many piety-belt Methodists to join him

---

[32] Whitney and Bonner, *History of Lenawee*, I, 44-46; 51-52; Dillon, "Elizabeth Chandler and Anti-Slavery," *Michigan History*, 39, 481-94.

[33] Howard S. Rogers, *History of Cass County, from 1825 to 1875* (Cassopolis, Michigan, 1875), 208-09, 179, 185, 255-56. George K. Hesslink, *Black Neighbors: Negroes in a Northern Rural Community* (Indianapolis, New York, 1968), 31-40.

[34] H. Willis to Woodbridge, Feb. 9, 1840, Woodbridge MSS, BHC. Willis was described as an "ultra abolitionist," *Representative Men of Michigan* (Cincinnati, 1878), I, District 3, 103-04.

[35] William Warren Sweet, *Methodism in American History* (New York, 1933), 242. On Wesleyan piety see also "Address," Michigan Annual Conference, Ann Arbor, *Signal of Liberty*, Oct. 31, 1842.

in seceding. Most Nankin Methodists, including many of the town's first families, followed Swift, asserting that "slavery is the sum of all villanies: of that American slavery is the vilest that ever saw the sun." A pioneer remembered that the antislavery members constituted "the great majority" of Nankin's Methodists. In 1850 Nankin had: 2 Wesleyan churches, 53 percent preference; 1 Methodist, 26 percent preference; 1 Presbyterian, 21 percent preference; and 59 percent religiosity. Contrary to what might have been expected, Nankin usually went Democrat, though not by much. While it cast more antislavery ballots than any other of Wayne's Democratic towns, the number was not particularly impressive for a town where Wesleyans reputedly would lie awake at night "hating slavery." Then, too, Marcus Swift was a dynamic personality. A Whig until 1840, he dramatically turned his back on Harrison in 1840 and "gave his influence to the liberty party, and his vote to its candidate."[36] Yet that was the only vote given to the Liberty Party in Nankin in 1840. In 1842, after the secession, Liberty voters numbered 17, about 10 percent. In 1844 the total slipped to 13 (5 percent). In 1845 30 men gave Liberty its best showing (18 percent). Free Soil managed to gather 50 votes (17 percent) in 1848 and 39 votes (13 percent) in 1852. All or most of the antislavery votes did not necessarily come from Wesleyans, of course, but even if they did it does not appear that most of the voters in that church were political abolitionists. Two Wesleyan churches with a total of 500 seats certainly should have produced more votes for antislavery.

Pittsfield's Wesleyans also failed to deliver proportionate numbers of Liberty-Free Soil voters. The town's only church in 1850 was Wesleyan with 200 seats. In 1848 Van Buren and Free Soil garnered 63 votes (30 percent), but in 1844 James Birney had polled only 24 (10 percent), and in 1852 John Hale received only 25 (12 percent). The proper inference seems to be that more persons in Nankin and Pittsfield were willing to secede from the Methodist Church than from the Whig or Democratic parties, or to *vote* antislavery.

NONEVANGELICALS

The major nonevangelical Protestant groups were the Methodists, Episcopalians, Universalists, Dutch Reformed Christians, and German

---

[36] Melvin D. Osband, "History of the Pioneer Church of Nankin, Wayne County, Michigan," *MHC*, 28: 150-60. M. D. Osband, "My Recollections of Pioneers and Pioneer Life in Nankin," *MHC*, 14: 431-83. Reverend O. C. Thompson, "Observations and Experiences in Michigan Forty Years Ago," *MHC*, 1: 401. Bela Hubbard, "Memoir of Luther Harvey," *MHC*, 1: 407. Garden City [Nankin] Methodist Church, Petition for Withdrawal from Methodist Episcopal Church, 1841, MHCol.

Lutherans. The last two groups will be discussed in the next chapter. Universalists were few; if they resembled their brethren elsewhere, they were antievangelicals.

The nonevangelicals, as noted before, included many of pietist temper. Their split personalities may account for their not being consistently attached to either party. In any case it is difficult to give firm generalizations regarding their voting and loyalties.

The Methodists led all religious groups in size. The census data inadequately conveys the pervasiveness of Methodism. One must consult county histories and pioneer recollections to encounter the numberless Methodist circuit riders, classes, societies, and "organizations" never counted by census takers. The evangelical reputation of the Methodists rests on their frontier enterprise in bringing the gospel strenuously to people thinly spread over vast territories. They were thoroughly Arminian in their open attitude to converts: whomever would come could be saved. Methodists needed simply "to desire to flee from the wrath of God and to be saved from their sins." Michigan Methodists, according to one observer in 1838, were "very zealous in the cause of religion and seem to live in enjoyment of religion." During camp meetings "Excitement rose to fever heat and the shouts of the converted and those convicted of sin could be heard ringing through the woods." Methodist piety embraced those Christians who traveled through cycles of backsliding and getting religion, while the saints of the evangelical denominations perhaps more uniformly feared God and pursued good behavior.[37] Although a Methodist Antislavery Society existed as early as 1839 and piety-belt Methodists favored temperance, the group tended not to enroll in benevolent or moral reform movements. Before 1850 particularly they lacked social focus, taking no official stand criticizing slavery until 1854 and none on temperance until 1853. A suggestive lack

[37] Abel Stevens, *The Centenary of American Methodism* (New York, 1866), 110, 270-71. Margaret Burnham Macmillan, *The Methodist Church in Michigan: The Nineteenth Century* (Grand Rapids, 1967), describes emotionalism and "Winter Revivals," 124, 129-30, 134, 151, 177. Letter of John Fisher, March, 1838, in Tucker, ed., "Correspondence of John Fisher," *Michigan History*, 45: 234. William Ray Prescott, *The Fathers Still Speak: A History of Michigan Methodism* (Lansing, 1941), 76. Journal of Judson D. Collins, Aug. 7, 1845—May 5, 1849, MHCol, entries for Aug. 8, 9, 10, 1845. Mary E. Lunny, "History of the First Methodist Episcopal Church, Ann Arbor, Michigan," Seminar Paper, 1937, MHCol. Kinsley Bingham's wife ventured to a Methodist meeting in Marcellus and found that reports she had heard were not exaggerated: "At first I felt frightened. There was a woman . . . (she did not have the power) but she made such a screaming and slapping of hands I wondered that no one stirred or took any notice of her I began to see that it was nothing uncommon," Mary Bingham to K. S. Bingham, Jan. 16, 1848, Bingham MSS, MHCol; on "trances" during "protracted meetings," Palmer, ed., *Palmer Letters*, 85.

of evidence makes their attitudes on evangelical issues difficult to determine.[38]

Only a small minority took the Wesleyan stance. When Marcus Swift denounced the church for temporizing in 1835, "Not one of his fellow ministers stood by him." In 1837 the General Conference succeeded in "pretty thoroughly muzzling the abolitionist radicals." It declared slavery not a moral wrong and in 1840 adopted its version of a "gag rule" to immunize the church from controversy. The Conference censured the dissidents and abjured members from forming abolition societies or attending Methodist abolition conventions.[39] The Wesleyans departed in 1841 and in 1844 the General Conference itself split, ostensibly over slavery, into Northern and Southern wings. But Northern Methodists had not at all embraced abolition. As one Ohio abolitionist minister said of the Northerners: "They had no pity for the black man enslaved but when the Slave Lord sought to gag and manacle the Yankees that altered the case." Not constitutional issues, either, but Southern demands that the church accept slavery as a national institution prompted the split.[40] The Northerners did not thereafter change any of the existing provisions on slavery in their Discipline; they remained in 1860 as they had been in 1824. In abolition and other moral causes Methodists lagged far behind evangelicals.[41]

In the 5 Whig counties in 1850 there were 1,950 Methodist seats compared to 1,400 in the 5 Democratic counties. This finding is offset by local data which more often implies a Methodist Democratic leaning, as does impressionistic evidence. In Wayne County, for example, 4 towns with Methodist preferences and high religiosity all voted Democratic. Very alike in religion and politics the towns showed a greater range in

[38] Macmillan, *Methodist Church in Michigan*, 146; also Margaret B. Macmillan, *The Methodist Episcopal Church in Michigan During the Civil War* (Lansing, 1965), 1-17. Jackson, *Michigan Freeman*, Sept. 25, 1839. Rev. Paul M. Cargo, "The History of the Northville Methodist Church," MS (1959-60), MHCol. Methodists of the Genesee Conference early made favorable gestures to antislavery, *Signal of Liberty*, July 14, 1841.

[39] Macmillan, *Methodist Church During the Civil War*, 3-5; Sweet, *Methodism* 237-42; Kooker, "Anti-Slavery Movement in Michigan," 153-55, 280. Miyakawa, *Protestants and Pioneers*, 187. Wesley Norton, "The Methodist Episcopal Church in Michigan and the Politics of Slavery: 1850-1860," *Michigan History*, 48 (September 1964), 195-96.

[40] Quotation from Macmillan, *Methodist Church During the Civil War*, 3. This interpretation can be found in Donald G. Mathews, *Slavery and Methodism: A Chapter in American Morality, 1780-1845* (Princeton, 1965), 246-82, and corroborated by evidence in Robert D. Clark, *The Life of Matthew Simpson* (New York, 1956), 117-32, 139-47.

[41] Pilcher, *Protestantism in Michigan*, 129-30; *Advertiser*, Sept. 15, 1840; Prescott, *Fathers Still Speak*, 91.

	Democratic percentage 1848–52	Methodist percentage		
		Preference	Religion	Rural lower class
Monguagon	60	57	107	52
Canton	64	63	71	27
Nankin	56	79[a]	59	33
Redford	66	53	52	39

a: Includes 53 percent Wesleyan preference.

their rural lower class percentages. Sabbath also found more Methodists among Democrats at party leader levels in Wayne in 1844: 4 among the Democrats, 2 among Whigs.[42] Ethnocultural and other variables may have been related to the Methodist Democratic tendency. There may have been differences between intensely and marginally religious Methodists, but the data permit no inferences on this score. The Methodists probably had a Democratic tendency and undoubtedly favored the Democrats more than any other major native Protestant group.

Although many individual Methodists were prosperous, the denomination, in contrast to Presbyterianism or Episcopacy, had all the marks of a low-status religion. While Methodists were not uniformly poor or lower class, the startling absence of Methodists from Wayne County's economic elite is surely significant, given the large number of Methodists in the population. Their religious practices as well as status and class probably shaped Methodist identity as a religious subculture. Yet Methodists possessed little separate consciousness as a political group. In religion, they disputed warmly with the high-status Episcopalians and held aloof from the activist evangelicals.[43] Their relative lack of political presence must have stemmed in part from their indifference to larger social concerns, their general condition, and the sin-salvation cycle of their religion with its emphasis on individual choice. In the Methodist view of society, souls willed their fates one by one. In its origins as a religion of the dispossessed, Methodism did not expect much of the community, did not stress the organic relation of lower to upper social orders, and did not readily acquire the integrative outlook that accompanies the confidence of status. Methodism did not propel men to seek the moral society through government, not yet at least. To the extent that this impulse

[42] Sabbath, "Political Leadership in Wayne County, 1844," 112. Two other towns in Wayne, Brownstown and Van Buren, also had some Methodist activity. One was Democratic, the other Whig-Free Soil, both by about 60 percent. Farmer, *Detroit*, II, 1314, 1382-83; Samuel H. Robbe, *History of Van Buren Township, Wayne County, Michigan* (Van Buren, 1930), 36-40.

[43] When the Presbyterian, Baptist, and Methodist teachers of Detroit met to prepare students for participation in the July 4 celebration in 1843, the Methodists voted to exclude colored Sunday school children and were chastised by the *Signal of Liberty*, July 17, 1843; the low-status Methodists apparently felt more threatened by blacks.

existed within Methodism, it departed with the Wesleyans, a secession which did not itself produce the degree of moralism in politics common to the evangelicals.[44]

Although the Episcopal sect included individual pietists such as Whig Charles C. Trowbridge, the ecclesiastical leadership resisted involvement in evangelicalism. Episcopacy resided mainly in population centers making it difficult to determine its affiliates' voting using township data. The Wayne County studies found Episcopalians favoring the Whigs, perhaps by 60 percent. Yet Episcopalians also appear to have been an important religious group within the Democratic Party.

During the entire antebellum period church leaders ignored slavery. When the Democratic *Ann Arbor Argus* in 1850 denounced the crusade of a "portion of the Protestant Churches in the North" against Constitution and Laws, it exempted the "Episcopals" and praised their holding aloof from "higher law preaching."[45] Bishop McCroskey, in his 1850 address to the Diocese of Michigan, gave his rationale for noninvolvement in social or political affairs, using anti-Popery as a balance for anti-evangelicalism. Episcopalianism sought a middle course, he said, between her old enemy Popery, "that corrupt branch of the Church of Christ," and "the various sects who entertain no kind feelings for her." The Church would hold to her "conservative principles," serving God and brethren "scattered abroad separated by political and social interests." Thus would the Church "avoid all those irritating questions that so often separate brethren, and weaken the power and influence of the Church." The 1850 convention characteristically touched upon no "irritating questions." The parishes reported a humdrum record of non-benevolent activity.[46]

Streeter claimed that because Episcopalianism "represented the wealthy and conservative class, many of the voters" in that church were Whigs. Episcopalians did tend to be wealthy and conspicuous among the upper class. In 1850 there were 4 Episcopal churches in Wayne County compared to 6 Baptist and 15 Methodist. But in 1844 Episcopalians accounted for 29 percent of Wayne's economic elite compared to 2 Baptists and no Methodists. Of the 28 elite Episcopalians McCoy found 18 (64 percent) to be Whigs. Sabbath also found more Episcopalians, 15 or 58 percent, among Whig party leaders in Wayne in 1844 than among

---

[44] E. P. Thompson, *The Making of the English Working Class* (New York, 1963), has a very suggestive discussion of Methodism's relationship to English politics, 37-54, 355-400, esp. 45-46, 389-91.

[45] Streeter, *Political Parties, 1837-1860; Argus,* Nov. 27, 1850.

[46] *Journal of the Sixteenth Annual Convention of the Protestant Episcopal Church, Diocese of Michigan* (Detroit, 1850), 16-17, 23-28, 29-51. Episcopalians did not join other Protestants in the Detroit City Tract Association, *Michigan Christian Herald,* Jan. 24, 1850. Hudson, *American Protestantism,* 60.

Democratic, 11 or 42 percent. Thus urban upper and middle class Episcopalians had a strong Whig tendency. Yet Episcopalians constituted a significant group in the Democratic Party. For example, because of the smaller number of Democrats among the economic elite, Episcopalians actually constituted the largest of any religious group among elite Democrats, 36 percent.[47]

The 1850 census of social statistics listed 24 Episcopalian churches. Three were listed not by town but by county. In the remaining 21, 19 were in large towns with several other churches. In none of the 19 was the Episcopal preference over 30 percent; it was usually under 20 percent. In one of the "rural" towns the Episcopal church became defunct in the 1850s. The other rural town, Monguagon, had an Episcopal preference of 43 percent, Methodist 57 percent, and religiosity 107 percent. This strong nonevangelical preference may have been related to the town's Democratic strength of 60 percent. But Episcopalians could easily have split between the parties and in the Whigs' favor. At least one Episcopalian in Monguagon, however, was a Democrat. He was the richest man in town: Abraham Caleb Truax, friend of Lewis Cass and enterprising businessman. In the 1830s he developed Trenton village and directed the Huron Manufacturing Company. Truax had donated the lot and building of Trenton's Episcopal Church and before perishing in a steamboat explosion in 1844 was easily the most influential man in Monguagon.[48]

Evidence abounds of a vigorous antagonism between evangelicals, especially Presbyterians, and "fashionable" Episcopalians. "Fashionable," a favorite epithet of moralists, suggested decadence and immorality. Stevens T. Mason, Democratic governor from 1835 to 1839, possessed conspicuous social grace—the heritage of a proper Virginia breeding. He and his family were Episcopalians. When Harriet Martineau visited Detroit in 1836 the high point of her stay was "a charming evening party at General Mason's. . . . It was wholly unexpected to find ourselves in accomplished society on the far side of Lake Erie." According to Episcopalian Lucius Lyon his denomination shone brightest in "accomplished society." In 1838 he believed that Detroit had "a society which for intelligence, cultivation and refinement is equal to that of any town of similar size in the United States; and of the different religious societies there, the Episcopalian is decidedly the most respectable."[49]

---

[47] Streeter, *Political Parties*, 212. Blois, *Gazetteer, 1838*, 148-49. McCoy, "Wayne County Economic Elite, 1844, 1860," 129, 131, 134, 173-83. Sabbath, "Political Leadership in Wayne County, 1844," 112.

[48] Durant, *History of Oakland*, 285-95. Farmer, *Detroit*, ii, 1321. Fred Carlisle, ed., *Chronography of Notable Events in the Northwest Territory and Wayne County* (Detroit, 1890), 151-52.

[49] "Harriet Martineau's Travels In and Around Michigan," *Michigan History*,

Evangelicals disliked Episcopalianism because they associated it with worldliness, formalism, and Popery, and undoubtedly they resented the status of Episcopalians as leaders of "cultivated" society. Considerable public hostility materialized. In 1842 Duffield and McCroskey feuded over who represented the true church, trading personal insults. Evangelicals often baited Episcopalians by implying that Episcopacy was but one step removed from Romanism. Long ago puritan independents decided that "Association leads to Consociation; Consociation leads to Presbyterianism; Presbyterianism leads to Episcopacy; Episcopacy leads to Roman Catholicism." Indeed, *equating* Rome and Episcopacy seems to have been a cliché among evangelicals.[50]

In 1843 the Presbyterian Synod's pastoral letter condemned the "false theology and exclusive sectarianism, and jesuitical proselytism, together with opposition to temperance and revivals of religion, in the Episcopalian denomination." The Whig *Advertiser* and Presbyterian *Evangelical Observer* harassed Episcopacy by exposing its dirty laundry.[51] A member of Duffield's church who described herself as a "strong" Presbyterian lamented her son's decision to join Episcopalianism. She was not, she said, opposed to their beliefs: "their Doctrines are *literally* ours—that Chh. has turned out some of the brightest stars in the history of Chh." But "unless they have a godly Minister—Their beautiful *form*, their Elegantly *written* prayers, their perfect specimens of composition in Liturgy, all tend to make one 'at ease in Zion.' "[52] Reverend Duffield criticized the Episcopalians most for encouraging intemperance. At an 1849 dinner party he watched Bishop McCroskey join the rest of the group in strong spirits: "The Bishop drank freely and I could not help but thinking that it was no wonder the Episcopal church here stood in the way of temperance when the Bishop would sanction in this way the drinking of intoxicating liquor among his own folks as nearly all of them were. Oh what an obstacle in the way of true spiritual religion is that Episcopal church! I . . . mourn over its benumbing influence upon many members of my own church."[53] Alpheus Felch once received a complaint about a man who was causing trouble in all his group affiliations: "in the

---

7 (January-April 1923), 51; Lucius Lyon to Lucretia Lyon, May 5, 1838, "Lyon Letters," *MHC*, 37: 454. In New York City the Church was one of the mainstays of "high society," Douglas Miller, *Jacksonian Aristocracy*, 76, 166-67.

[50] *Advertiser*, Nov. 9, 11, and 12, 1842; Independent's quote from Hudson, *American Protestantism*, 53; *Advertiser*, Feb. 5 and 9, 1844. *Michigan Christian Herald*, passim.

[51] *Free Press*, Oct. 14, 1860; *Observer*, Oct. 21, 1845; Smith, *Revivalism and Social Reform*, 29; *Advertiser*, Oct. 3, 1843, Oct. 20, 1847.

[52] Elizabeth Sullivan Stuart, Detroit, April 4, 1853, Marlatt, ed., *Stuart Letters*, I, 505.

[53] VanderVelde, ed., "George Duffield Diary," *Mississippi Valley Historical Review*, 60-1.

Masonic Lodge, in the Episcopal Church, in the Democratic Party."[54] It was no accident for a man to belong to all three of those groups. While Episcopalians may have had an overall Whig tendency, they also had influential roles among the Democrats for the very reasons that Democracy, Masonry, and Episcopacy had something in common. Evangelical hell fire blasted all three and all tended to appeal to the secular and "doctrinally orthodox."

Perhaps the most obvious case of religious values shaping voting was provided by the Mormons of Big Beaver Island. The Latter Day Saint colony, a deviant religious group in a hostile environment, acted with virtual unanimity in politics.[55]

Jesse James Strang, one of the self-appointed successors to Joseph Smith, broke with Brigham Young and led a schismatic group of Saints to Wisconsin and then to Big Beaver Island in the 1840s. Big Beaver lay off Michigan's northwest coast and was part of Mackinac County. Possessing a good harbor and farm land, Beaver Island soon had 500 to 600 "industrious" inhabitants as well as a newspaper, the *Northern Islander*. By 1850 Prophet Strang's people crowned him King, then anticlimactically elected him to the state legislature as a Democrat in 1852— unanimously. Strang, a slightly built man, had charisma. His dramatic oratory flowed from behind a thick red beard, massive forehead, and Mephistophelean eyes. His intelligence won him grudging acceptance from many of his fellow state legislators, but his people remained almost in constant siege. Their neighbors constantly harassed them as pariahs or perverts; occasionally the Saints retaliated sharply. As Strang's phalanx of voters acquired Mackinac County's elective offices, politicians at Mackinac Island and St. Ignace counterattacked, encouraging vigilante raids and getting the United States Navy to bring Strang and his lieutenants to trial for obstructing the mails and other federal offenses. Hatred of the Mormons waxed deep throughout the north country. Internal dissension grew, Strang fell to assassin's bullets in 1856, and his murderers were feted at Mackinac; a Christian host then invaded and sacked the headless kingdom.[56]

In 1852 the Mormon clan voted for Democrat Pierce 164 to 1. Streeter attributed this to Strang's influence, but did not explain his "predilec-

[54] William S. Brown, Detroit, to Alpheus Felch, July 22, 1848, Felch MSS, MHCol.

[55] James S. Coleman, "Social Cleavage and Religious Conflict," Raab, ed., *Religious Conflict in America*, 96, 98.

[56] Quotation from Oswego, *Commercial Times* quoted in first issue of *Northern Islander*, Dec. 12, 1850, BHC. Very interesting accounts are in Edwin O. Wood, *Historic Mackinac* (New York, 1918), I, 364-70, and Milo M. Quaife, *The Kingdom of St. James* (New Haven, 1930), 116-36, passim.

tions." David Brion Davis has dealt with the Mormons as one of the groups which roamed as devils through the imaginations of nativists. Mormons merged into "a nearly common stereotype" with those other subversives of the American (Protestant) way, Masons and Catholics. Nativists imagined the polygamous Mormons to be wallowing in sexual immorality. Victims of delusion, to nativists Mormons were enemies outside the pale who could either be converted or exterminated.[57] Mormons could not have been hard put to associate this kind of mentality with Whiggery. The Whig *Advertiser* cheered the effort to jail Mormons and in 1852 deemed the Democratic vote of the Saints appropriate as Whigs did not want the votes of "Murderers, Polygamists, and Freebooters." In 1854 it warned that Mormonism would soon contaminate youth on the mainland unless "in all conscience" it were given a speedy end. As Strang lay murdered the *Christian Herald* pronounced him "tyrant, knave and hypocrite," and rejoiced that his death would "disorganize that band of robbers and pirates."[58] Strang no doubt knew his enemies. His anti-evangelicalism registered in a vigorous protest against a prohibitory liquor law in 1853. But the *Northern Islander* also explained that the 1852 Mormon vote did not imply great love for the Democrats but rather a recognition that Whigs persecuted Mormons "as a party measure."[59]

The Democrats did not embrace the Mormons, their newspapers often used epithets to describe them, and local Democrats joined in vigilantism against Big Beaver. Indeed, Strang's most passionate nemesis was former Democratic legislator Charles O'Malley, Irish born, trained to be a priest, but dispenser of dry goods and justice at Mackinac. Yet the only defenses of Mormon rights are to be found coming from Democratic editors. Even before Michigan's own "Mormon problem" arrived the Niles *Republican* established the basic line of argument. It condemned mob and vigilante action against Mormons, however deluded they were by false beliefs. "Anti-Mormon as we are, we are willing to see them enjoy their own opinion and the same rights and privileges that are extended to all." In 1851 on the acquittal of some Mormons for obstructing the mails the *Pontiac Jacksonian* berated a Whig editor for his untrue harangue against men now pronounced innocent. The *Adrian Watchtower* observed the growth of the colony without alarm, admired Strang, and condemned attacks on the island. The *Centreville Western Chronicle*

[57] Streeter, *Political Parties*, 226-27. Davis, *Mississippi Valley Historical Review*, 47, 208, 216, passim.

[58] *Northern Islander*, July 21, 1851; *Advertiser*, Nov. 15, 1852, Aug. 15, 1854; *Herald*, July 17, 1856.

[59] *Pontiac Jacksonian*, Feb. 6, 1853, film MSL; *Northern Islander*, Nov. 11, 1852; Quaife, *Kingdom of St. James*, 128, 135; for the Mormon sense of persecution, *Northern Islander*, July 3, 1852, April 3, 1851.

branded the anti-Mormon desperadoes as "guilty of acts which deserve the extreme penalty of the law."[60]

Perhaps more important to Mormons than occasional friendly puffs from Democratic editors, the Michigan Democrats had identified over the years with laissez faire ethics, and the Mormons probably believed that Democrats were less disposed to demand conformity to Christian ways. It is symbolic that in the year of the sack of Big Beaver the national Republican platform condemned that relic of barbarism, polygamy.

GENERAL ANTIEVANGELICALISM

Evangelicals by their very existence brought forth a chain of reactions from other groups of great importance to political alignments. Their drive for a moral society became at least vaguely identified with Whiggery. Subcultures with different values saw evangelical goals as threats and fell naturally into opposition to evangelicals and Whigs. The reaction of some groups on elite levels is well documented. The recoiling of "skeptical" frontier masses can only be inferred.[61]

Most evangelicals were New England Protestants who, as Dixon Ryan Fox once said, were "positive men," and therefore enlisted a strong response. The riposte to Yankee "cultural imperialism" was, in large measure, an antievangelical revolt against what Fox called the "holy enterprise of minding other people's business." The latter no doubt inspired Herman Melville to want to form a "Chinese Society for the Suppression of Meddling with Other People's Business." Evangelical philanthropy derived from the puritan strain which Ralph Barton Perry described as the "paternal sort."

It was a stern kindness, designed to repay the hurts of denial with the greater benefits which will accrue at some remoter time, in this world or the next. It was an inquisitive, because distrustful, kindness, which sought to regulate another's life, rather than to leave that life to the promptings of its own inward impulses and self-government. It was an arrogant kindness, expressing a conviction so free from doubt as to be untroubled by the protests of the beneficiary.[62]

For very different reasons Catholics, Unitarians, Campbellites, Universalists, and other religious liberals, freethinkers, atheists, and Mor-

[60] *Republican*, Oct. 11, 1845, MSL; *Pontiac Jacksonian*, July 16, 1851; *Watchtower*, Feb. 9, March 8, 1853; *Chronicle*, July 28, 1853. On O'Malley see Wood, *Historic Mackinac*, I, 366-67 and *Michigan Biographies*, 501.

[61] Richard L. Power once suggested that historians study the "earthy character of the opposition encountered in the West by the Yankee colonists . . . and their ideas and ways," "A Crusade to Extend Yankee Culture, 1820-1865," *New England Quarterly*, 12 (December 1940), 648, 649-51.

[62] Perry, *Puritanism and Democracy*, 326.

mons, were natural enemies of the evangelicals. Any call for a Christian Party threatened the laissez faire order which by design or neglect implicitly tolerated their life styles, however deviant.[63] It is not surprising that a vast, nebulous majority coalesced against the evangelicals. One Presbyterian minister believed the strength of the Christian Party overrated but strong enough to excite fear: "The mobocracy of the age hates us, because we are not liberal enough to suit their taste . . . and from every quarter there is a hideous outcry against us." Religious liberals feared union of church and state and many nonevangelicals simply resented anyone's trying to mind their business. Perhaps the classic expression of irritation with evangelical meddling came from a rural New Yorker who demanded of the *Temperance Recorder* in 1835 by what authority it continued to be sent to him. He warned that "if you do not like to have them returned to you with double postage, you had better wait till I subscribe before you send me another. We have Anti-Masonry, Anti-Rum, Anti-Gin, Anti-Brandy, and Anti-mind-their-own business people enough in this small town."[64] In Michigan, Presbyterianism acted as the lodestone of antievangelical complaints. Catherine Mason described an acquaintance in 1836 as "being a thoroughgoing Presbyterian" although she was "not as bigoted and illiberal as the generality of her brethren."[65] Such a stereotype does not seem to have been confined to Episcopalians turned Campbellite. A Congregational minister doing missionary work in Macomb County in 1835 believed that the "current of Infidelity" was strong in the territory: "Unwearied pains are taken to disseminate error. Infidel Publications are extensively circulated. . . . Universalism and Deism are the most common popular errors. *The majority of the community, however, do not care what they believe provided it is in opposition to the 'Orthodox' as they term the Presbyterians.*" (Italics mine)[66] When a Whig newspaper warned Catholics in 1835 against trying to wield political influence, it used the Presbyterians as an example of what not to do, a sect which had become "obnoxious to the jealousy of a large part of the people—and their power of usefulness—their *religious* influence, has been greatly weakened."[67]

[63] Blau, "Christian Party in Politics," *Review of Religion*, 11: 24-26. Bodo, *Protestant Clergy*, 23-25.

[64] Presbyterian quoted in Bodo, 47-8; New Yorker quoted in Krout, *The Origins of Prohibition*, 259n.

[65] Catherine Mason to Stevens T. Mason, Dec. 18, 1839, Mason MSS, BHC. A politician in Pontiac was described not only as a wildcat speculator but also as "a bigoted Presbyterian and cold water man," J. P. Richardson to L. Lyon, Nov. 8, 1839, Lyon MSS, Clements.

[66] Luther Shaw, Rome, to Rev. Levi Platt, Home Missionary Society, Aug. 22, 1835, William Warren Sweet, ed., *Religion on the American Frontier, 1783-1851,* III: *The Congregationalists: A Volume of Source Materials* (Chicago, 1939), 315.

[67] Ann Arbor, *Michigan Whig and Washtenaw Democrat*, April 16, 1835.

The temperance crusade of course aggravated many nonevangelicals and antievangelicals. A Democratic editor associated the cause with "New England puritans who scoff at 'Western morals,' " and the desire of many to drink and regulate themselves probably created Democratic voters. In 1836 Henry Schoolcraft, a Democrat, described how the "tendency to ultraism" of temperance men alienated moderates like himself. The movement, he wrote, had excited the community of Detroit: "Its importance is undeniable on all hands, but there is always a tendency in new measures of reform to make the method insisted on a sort of moral panacea, capable of doing all things, to the no little danger of setting up a standard higher than the Decalogue itself."[68] In an 1840 election of town officers in Farmington temperance men aroused such furor that a Justice was elected "rather in opposition to temperance principles." The victor proved such an enthusiastic drinker that even his anti-temperance backers joined some Whigs in requesting his removal.[69]

The case of Charles M. Bull, Detroit merchant in the 1830s, shows how resentment of Presbyterian moralists probably influenced politics. Bull, a Democrat, held several opinions more characteristic of Whigs. On such issues as the Bank of the United States, Jackson's removal of deposits, and submission to Congress on the Ohio boundary, Bull sustained potentially anti-Democratic postures. If he disliked "the Irish and French," as his younger brother Hampton did, there was additional reason for expecting him to be a Whig.[70] Yet one incident in 1834 points in an opposite direction. The Territorial Government had just raised the price of retail liquor licenses to $100—a tentative temperance move. This incensed tavern keepers as well as store keepers like Bull who kept a bar at one end of his counter. Merchants had submitted a petition of protest to the city council which included the names of "30 of the richest and most influential men in the place." Bull thought "we are safe now and have all on our side except the d----d presbyterians and them we do not care anything about we shall get about the best we can until we can get a new board."[71]

The evangelical demand for a quiet Sabbath irritated the unorthodox who wished to keep it as they pleased. The missionary in Macomb wrote of his encounter with "Universalists or Deists who wish to sell and go

[68] *Centreville Western Chronicle*, June 30, 1853. Schoolcraft, *Personal Memoirs*, 550-51.

[69] Seth A. L. Warner and Amos Mead to W. Woodbridge, Dec. 7, 1840, and related petitions in file, 1839-1841, Woodbridge MSS, BHC.

[70] Charles M. Bull to John Bull, Feb. 24, 1834; C. M. Bull to J. Bull, June 4, 1834; Charles wanted to have not "much to do with the Banks," C. M. Bull to J. Bull, Jan. 12, 1834; C. M. Bull to J. Bull, Feb. 13, 1837; C. M. Bull and Hampton Bull to J. Bull, Jan. 12, 1834, Bull MSS, BHC.

[71] C. M. Bull to J. Bull, Aug. 31, 1834, Bull MSS, BHC. Fitzgibbon, "King Alcohol," 2: 740-47.

farther into the woods—as one of them said . . . that he might be where he could hunt on the Sabbath and not disturb his neighbors."[72] Many local histories confirm that in the early days of many settlements a struggle was repeatedly enacted: the party of order and morality confronted the party of laissez faire and hedonism. Sometimes this contest elicited drama that only a Mark Twain could do justice to. In Jackson in 1839 the "decency folks" planned a Sabbath School celebration with accompanying temperance and abolition speeches, but "a Spirit showed itself undisguised." The antidecency folks put on their own show, beginning with the printing of a program "to ridicule ours full of low blackguard." The night before the celebration rowdies took the seats from the appointed grove and made a bonfire of them in the public square, waking many citizens with their drunken revelry. Then they disinterred "the corpse of a colored man who had been buried a few days before and then brought him into the session house and set him in the pulpit." The minister and his men quietly repaired the damage and went ahead with the celebration. It proceeded without incident until the assembly rose to sing a closing song. A "band of troublers" stole up behind them with a heavily loaded cannon and fired it off: "it gave the congregated schools a great shock and covered us all with smoke." When it cleared and the exercises properly closed, "All returned to their homes—more in favor of Sunday Schools and early religious instruction than ever."[73]

In his study of religion and politics in modern Detroit Lenski elaborated several concepts useful to understanding reactions to evangelicals and Whiggery in the 1830s and 1840s. They can be linked to Reverend Duffield's complaints of the "benumbing" influence of Episcopalianism over his congregation, and suggest why evangelical denominations did not wholly support piety or Whiggery. They indicate, too, why the uncommitted would be more likely to be attracted to the antievangelicals and Democracy.

Lenski found that "the degree to which individuals are involved in the churches greatly affects their attitudes on moral issues which the churches have chosen especially to champion." On issues of disagreement between churches he usually found "a neat progression in attitudes from the most involved members of one group to the most involved members of the other." For example, the Protestant churches condemn gambling and drinking but sanction birth control. The Catholic church tends to condone gambling and drinking but forbids birth control. Lenski

---

[72] Letter of Luther Shaw, Aug. 22, 1835, Sweet, ed., *The Congregationalists*, III, 315.

[73] Deland-Crary Family Papers, MS historical sketch of Jackson, June 6, 1866, MHCol. See also Angus, *What's Past Is Present*, regarding Brooklyn, Jackson Co., 16-32; *History of Livingston County*, 149-54, 167.

found that the most active white Protestants strenuously criticized gambling and drinking, while the most active Catholics accepted or defended these activities. Birth control, however, reversed the two groups. Of great interest here, those Catholics and Protestants who were not intensely involved in their churches:

> were closer to the activists supporting the *less demanding moral standard.* In other words, on the issues of gambling and drinking, the marginal members of the two groups were closer to the positions of the Catholic activists, the less demanding position. However, on the issue of birth control the marginal members of the two groups were closer to the Protestant activists. . . . These are examples of what might be called the *principle of social hedonism*: when two established and institutionalized religious groups support opposing moral norms, the less demanding norm tends to win the less committed members of *both* groups.[74]

Surely something like this influenced men's responses to social groups and political parties in the 1830s. Commitment to evangelical denominations usually accompanied opposition to the Democrats, yet not even Detroit's crusading First Presbyterian Church battled with complete unanimity for the Lord. Was it not likely that marginal Presbyterians, for example, would be less concerned about temperance and Sabbath-keeping and less likely than "strong" Presbyterians to vote anti-Democratic? The kind of data to test adequately such a hypothesis is not available.[75] Yet clearly the Whig Party supported more demanding moral standards than the Democratic Party. The "principle of social hedonism," in a heterogeneous society, would seem to have worked to help create the frequent Democratic majorities.

[74] Lenski, *Religious Factor*, 174-75.

[75] The cases of two Presbyterian Democrats encountered above, however, support this claim. Lewis Cass, the lone Presbyterian Democrat in Wayne's economic elite in 1844, was clearly a man of Jeffersonian and ritualist disposition in religious matters. His wife's pietism did not seem to infect him. Elizabeth Stuart, mother of the "renegade" Presbyterian David Stuart (see above), complained often of her son's failure to "see the light" and make a full commitment to religion. This motherly concern preceded and then accompanied her distaste for his political activity. (*Stuart Letters*, I, passim.)

Ethnocultural Groups and Parties: 1837–1852

That ethnicity powerfully shaped party loyalties is already clear. It is proper now to investigate systematically relations among ethnocultural groups as they affected political behavior, and to estimate the distribution of party preference within them. Politics in certain groups could be extraordinarily complex and dependent on many variables, yet overall patterns deeply imbedded in social cleavages may be discovered.

The old habit of positing a division between natives and immigrants is misleading. Party polarizations cut across and occurred within these broad categories. Although many contemporaries spoke often of the "foreigners" voting Democratic, most of them had certain groups implicitly in mind, not all immigrants. William Woodbridge once privately took care to differentiate explicitly among foreigners in asserting that the 1844 election had been decided by the " 'Foreign Vote'—the Irish and the Catholic Germans are very numerous in this state and no doubt is entertained that they almost universally voted the Loco Foco ticket"; he added that French imports from Canada augmented the Democratic vote.[1]

At first glance aggregate data do show an association between foreign presence and Democratic percentage. In only 1 of the 6 lowest Democratic counties in 1850 (Tuscola, Kalamazoo, Clinton, Genesee, Jackson, Hillsdale) did the foreign born exceed 16 percent of the population. On the other hand, in only 1 of the 8 most Democratic counties in 1850 were they under 10 percent; in 4, they exceeded 30 percent. Table III.3 showed a positive correlation between Democratic votes and foreigners in the eastern counties. Detroit, like Wayne County, yielded a strong positive correlation for Democratic percentage and foreign born in 1850—

[1] Dorr, ed., *Debates and Proceedings, 1835 Convention*, 184, 219-20. *Advertiser*, Nov. 15, 16, and 18, 1844; *Free Press*, Nov. 6, 1852; Marshall, *Democratic Expounder*, Sept. 28, Oct. 31, 1848: *Jackson Patriot*, Oct. 31, 1848. William Woodbridge, Springwells, Nov. 11, 1844, draft of a letter, Woodbridge MSS, BHC.

.530. Yet when such data may be compared with religious relationship to party, the Catholic-Democratic association appears stronger. In Detroit's wards the correlation between Catholic percentage in 1853 and Democratic mean 1848 to 1852 exceeded the foreign-Democratic correlation .673 to .457 (Table IX.1).

TABLE IX.1
Detroit Wards: Democratic Mean, 1848–1852, and Foreign and
Catholic Percentages, 1853

Ward	Democratic	Foreign	Catholic
8	75	75	47
4	65	82	57
1a	60	50	28
7	58	80	46
2	55	46	35
3	54	60	34
5	53	48	24
6	52	67	30

a In years of high turnout (1848, 1850, 1852) Ward 1 returned a much lower Democratic percentage than Wards 7 or 2.

This data joins other findings showing how highly influential religion was in politics, and warns that one must specify what one means by the "foreign vote." The foreign and native groups both included different, sometimes hostile political subcultures which need careful examination.

YANKEES, YORKERS, AND FRENCH CANADIANS

In 1844 Woodbridge described the native population as being "principally from New England and western New York . . . like that from which it is separated, it is industrious, intelligent and enterprising. Its interests," he believed, "are with the Whigs," and "its intercourse, political as well as social and commercial, ought to be—and is getting to be—with New England."[2] Yet the native born, including Yankees, gave votes to both parties. Yankees tended to be anti-Democratic, however, by at least 55 percent.

Many ex-New Yorkers were Yankees but a large number were "Yorkers" (Dutch, Old British, Old Germans, Huguenots). Since they were few, the Pennsylvania Dutch may be considered part of this group. In New York, Yorker-Yankee antagonism had flourished since the seventeenth century. Benson has shown this ancient feud's affect on party choice, with Yankees favoring the Whigs, and Yorkers (except Huguenots) favoring the Democrats by 60 percent. New York's Penn-Jersey-

[2] W. Woodbridge to [Jonathan Chapman], Boston, Sept. 14, 1844, Woodbridge MSS, BHC.

ites also voted Democratic by 55 percent.[3] In Michigan it was difficult to determine whether the omnipresent New York-born were of Yankee or non-Yankee descent. But some clues indicate a transfer of reference group patterns from New York to Michigan.

Antievangelicalism obviously included hostility to Yankees. On the positive side Yankees recognized their own. A Vermonter living in Schoolcraft, Kalamazoo County, tended to associate chiefly with ex-Vermonters: "He liked Yankees, and he disliked 'foreigners,' a general term by which he seems to have meant all those who were not of New England descent." Even for men not quite so ethnocentric, New England stood as a positive reference symbol, the model of the good society where one found the "original, operative and distinctly marked American character." One Whig politician wrote to another that a certain local office should be given to "some one whose character for intelligence and integrity is not below the New England standard."[4]

This sense of identity with Yankee culture was not without political meaning. The negative association of Yankees with Democratic voting in 6 counties in 1850 had a strength unmatched by several other variables in multiple regression analysis (Tables III.4 and III.5). The Sabbath and McCoy studies found elite Yankees decisively favoring anti-Democrats, though Yankees still were an important group in the Democratic Party. Sabbath identified 24 New England-born among Wayne County's Whig leaders in 1844 and only 15 Democratic leaders of New England birth; Yankees split between the parties 69 percent to 31 percent. McCoy's Yankee elite members chose the Whig and Liberty parties over the Democratic to an even greater degree. The 45 Yankees were the largest ethnic group among Wayne's economic elite in 1844: 33 Whigs (71 percent), 3 Libertyites (9 percent), and 9 Democrats (20 percent), for an anti-Democratic percentage of 80. The New England English were somewhat more anti-Democratic than the New York English:

	New England English		New York English	
Whigs	22	84%	11	58%
Democrats	4	16%	5	26%
Libertyites			3	16%
	—	—	—	—
	26	100%	19	100%

[3] Fox, *Yankees and Yorkers*, 1-26, 206-07. Benson, *Concept*, 177-85.

[4] Stanley Barney Smith, "Notes on the Village of Schoolcraft in the 1850s," *Michigan History*, 40 (June 1956), 151. *New Monthly Magazine* quoted in *Detroit Journal and Advertiser*, Jan. 30, 1835. George L. Gale, Paw Paw, to W. Woodbridge, Jan. 12, 1841, Woodbridge MSS, BHC. See also Austin Blair, Jackson, to A. T. McCall, Oct. 10, 1847, Blair MSS, BHC; MS dated April 12, 1847, relating to Michigan Education Society, Felch MSS, MHCol; Blois, *Gazetteer of Michigan*, 1838, 157-59; M. E. Van Buren to Woodbridge, April 14, 1846, Woodbridge MSS, BHC; Power, "Crusade to Extend Yankee Culture," 13: 639.

Yankees again constituted the largest single ethnocultural group in the Democracy (32 percent), and amounted to 54 percent of the Whigs.[5]

Thus at elite and mass levels Yankees voted strongly anti-Democratic. McCoy's elite probably held more anti-Democratic Yankees than the population at large because Presbyterians were so numerous among the economic elite; but among the mass electorate Presbyterians also voted strongly anti-Democratic.

Yorkers seem to have played a significant role in the Democratic Party. In 1831 Charles M. Bull described Jackson leader John Norvell as "a real Yorker." Bull, born in Columbia County, New York, may have been a Yorker, but Norvell was the son of a Virginian and born in Kentucky. This can be interpreted to mean that Bull associated nascent Democrats with Yorker characteristics.[6] Conrad "Coon" Ten Eyck, a Democratic leader of Dearborn, was a genuine Yorker. In the 1830s pioneers traveling through eastern Michigan stopped at his inn for refreshment and a dose of Democratic politics. For years Wayne County Democratic conventions assembled at "Ten Eyck's Tavern" and Conrad's neighbors often elected him to the state legislature. Two other Wayne County towns, Redford and Van Buren, had hints of Yorker strains present and both voted Democratic.[7] In 1850 Oakland County's banner Democratic unit was Addison, a moderately prosperous small farmer township. Addison presented strong signs of being almost entirely of Pennsylvania Dutch origins. Lenawee County's number two Democratic town in 1850 was Ridgeway, settled mostly by New Yorkers, some of whom built a Dutch Reformed Church. Macon in Lenawee also had a Dutch Reformed Church and usually voted Democratic.[8] In western Michigan the Pennsylvania Dutch figured prominently in the early settlement of Noble, Branch County, and Bertrand, Berrien County. Both voted Democratic in the 1840s but their early composition may have been unrelated to their later electorates after they grew. Less ambiguous is the case of Oronoko, Berrien County, a St. Joseph River valley township. Pennsylvanians with German or Dutch names dominated its civic

[5] Sabbath, "Political Leadership in Wayne County, 1844," 131. "Wayne County Economic Elite, 1844, 1860," McCoy, 160, 161; also, 166, 167, 175.

[6] Charles M. Bull to John Bull, July 1831, in Sidney Glaser, ed., "In Old Detroit (1831-1836)," *Michigan History*, 36 (Spring 1942), 204.

[7] Henry A. Haigh, "The Old Ten Eyck Tavern," *Michigan History*, 15 (Summer 1931), 441-45; Haigh, "Early Days in Dearborn," *Michigan History*, 5 (July-October 1921), 536-60. Benson, *Concept*, 184. Robbe, *History of Van Buren Township*, 32-40, 58-59.

[8] Durant, *History of Oakland County*, 123-29. Whitney and Bonner, *History of Lenawee*, I, 415-22. Henry S. Lucas, ed., *Dutch Immigrant Memoirs and Related Writings* (Assen, Netherlands, 1955), I, xix, 307. In Genesee County, two towns settled by families from "York state" were very likely Yorker areas. Wood, *Genesee County*, I, 234, 237-38, 240.

and social life. Oronoko alternated in being the first or second most Democratic unit in Berrien.[9]

It was inevitable that a community in Michigan which had transplanted the New England way rather intact should have had its early history recorded in rich detail. Vermontville, Eaton County, probably came closer to being a replica of an original New England town than any other in Michigan. Its behavior gives considerable insight into that of New Englanders in general. Vermontville tended strongly toward being the integrated Christian community in which schools, church, and local government served to reinforce the values, attitudes, and beliefs that gave them life.[10]

In 1835 and 1836 Vermont Congregationalists in the vicinity of East Poultney and Castleton held meetings to organize a "Union Colony" to carry their way of life West. Their constitution expressed a desire to spread the Gospel and help remove "the moral darkness which hangs over . . . the Mississippi valley." They believed "a removal to the west may be the means of promoting our temporal interest, and we trust be made subservient to the advancement of Christ's kingdom." The colonists pledged themselves "to carry with us the institutions of the Gospel," to perpetuate "literary privileges," to "rigidly observe the holy Sabbath," not to buy, sell, nor use strong spirits except for medicine ("and we will use all lawful means to keep it utterly out of the settlement"), and to practice good neighborliness. Their code of laws regulated land and other affairs, limiting the size of farm and village lots, insuring that the community would begin with no great inequalities in wealth based on land, and excluding nonresident land owners.[11]

Community and congregation were thriving in Eaton County by 1837. Their favorite eastern newspaper was the "religious weekly the New York Observer . . . as it was true-blue in its orthodoxy and its application of religion to politics, and more especially to the ominous slavery question."[12] This implied that Vermontville would be decidedly Whig. In 1837, 23 of 26 votes went to the Whig candidate for governor. There-

[9] Fuller, *Economic and Social Beginnings*, 303; *History of Berrien and Van Buren Counties, Michigan* (Philadelphia, 1880), 278, 279, 288-90.

[10] Works helpful here were: Perry, *Puritanism and Democracy*, 321-62; Fox, *Yankees and Yorkers*, 1-3; Morris C. Taber, "New England Influences in South Central Michigan," *Michigan History*, 35 (December 1961), 305-36; Lois Kimbal Mathews, "Some Activities of the Congregational Church West of the Mississippi," in Guy Stanton Ford, ed., in *Essays in American History Dedicated to Frederick Jackson Turner* (New York, 1940; reprinted, New York, 1951), 3-34. See also Page Smith, *As a City Upon a Hill: The Town in American History* (New York, 1966), 17.

[11] Edward W. Barber, "The Vermontville Colony: Its Genesis and History," *MHC*, 28: 204, 205.

[12] *Ibid.*, 237. Barber wrote with the bitterness of a Liberty man, Free Soiler, and early Republican.

after, the record shows a less spectacular but uniformly anti-Democratic vote.

	Total vote	Democratic percentage	Whig percentage	Liberty-Free Soil percentage
1837	26	12	88	
1839	36	44	56	
1840	50	40	60	
1843	39	23	59	18
1844	56	36	55	9
1846	46	30	48	22
1847	59	30	63	7
1848	56	30	41	29
1850	55	36	64	
1851	42	38	62	
1852	84	35	57	8

Not more than 10 men (22 percent) ever voted for the Liberty Party and Free Soil support peaked in 1848 with 16 votes (29 percent). The Congregational Church became agitated when one member withdrew to the Wesleyan Methodists over inaction on slavery. Stung, the brethren resolved on May 2, 1847, that slavery was "a system of unrighteousness, alike opposed to the law of God and to the Gospel of his Son, decidedly detrimental to the true interests of humanity; and that we do sincerely desire its speedy abandonment in every land under heaven." This careful last phrase avoided the fire brand of "abolition" and implied voluntary action on the part of the slaveholder.[13] Here in microcosm breathed the essentially cautious spirit of most of the Yankee Protestant North. Vermontville was above average in religion and antislavery, yet that translated into relatively few abolition votes. The town's historian described its politics as mostly "conservative Whig"; voters divided according to their Vermont county of origin. Most men from Rutland and Addison voted Whig while Bennington men were "rock rooted Democrats." Most Vermontvillers preferred the party of their fathers.[14] Party loyalty certainly proved stronger than political antislavery.

In 1850 Vermontville probably contained a greater percentage of potential voters born in New England, almost 60 percent, than any other township in Michigan; many of the 27 percent New York-born no doubt were also Yankees. While supporting the claim that Yankees, especially evangelical Yankees, voted anti-Democratic, Vermontville also displays the complexity of Yankee behavior. Other conditions than party loyalty must also have affected party choice. Vermontville's historian remembered clearly that *"a majority of settlers on land outside the colony purchase were staunch Democrats."*[15] (Italics mine) This sug-

[13] *Ibid.*, 259.   [14] *Ibid.*, 236-37.   [15] *Ibid.*, 237.

gests that later arrival, lack of acceptance by the in-group, rejection in whole or in part of accepted norms, lack of integration, perhaps alienation or anomie, all could have contributed to making patterns of political behavior. Such cleavages within many townships may have been similarly conditioned by an outsider-insider axis related to the dominant community ethos.

Many towns in Michigan could provide an instructive counterpoint to Vermontville, but perhaps the best unit to contrast with it was the far northern county of Houghton on the Keewenaw Peninsula jutting into Lake Superior. This boom mining camp was not "a land of steady habits." By 1850 it had gathered in a rush a potpourri of natives and foreigners to mine its copper beds. Most of the natives came from the upper Great Lakes region; the foreign born were English, German, Irish, and Scots. This raw, lawless crew of miners, laborers, fishermen and their suppliers, held irregular elections and sent out returns haphazardly.[16] One surviving record registered a 93 percent Democratic majority in 1850.

Vermontville's moral cohesion contrasted sharply with the atomistic hedonism of the Keewenaw. The north countrymen were much further removed from the moral center of the New England ethos than those Vermontvillers on land "outside the colony purchase." Indeed, they virtually inhabited a different moral universe, reflected not so much in the many miles between Vermontville and Copper Harbor, as in their political polarization.

Another ethos characterized the French Canadians of Michigan, too, most of whom inhabited the southeastern shore counties. Although a force to be reckoned with in territorial politics, by 1837 the French even in the southeast constituted a majority of voters only in a few townships. French traders had opened southwestern Michigan too, but their presence had "left little but tradition and a few geographical names." As late as 1850 a newspaper addressed the "French voters" of Mendon, St. Joseph County, but they amounted to only 5 to 10 percent of the potential voters there. In 1837 statewide the French could not have amounted to more than 7 percent of the population or 10 percent of the electorate. Even in Detroit by 1834 they numbered not much more than 15 percent of the population.[17]

[16] Ruth Robbins Montieth, ed., "Census of 1850 for Michigan Counties of Houghton, Marquette, Michillimackinac, Schoolcraft and Ontonogan," typed copy of 1850 MS of federal population census schedule (partial: value of property owned omitted), BHC.
[17] Blois, *Gazetteer, 1838,* 156-67. Fuller, *Economic and Social Beginnings,* 258, 502. *History of the Upper Peninsula of Michigan* (Chicago, 1883), 363-67. *Centreville Western Chronicle,* Nov. 2, 1850, MHCol. Trowbridge, *History of Michigan Baptists,* 45.

In New York the "Old French" voted about 90 percent Democratic, and French Canadians recently arrived voted about 95 percent Democratic.[18] Neither old nor new French in Michigan seemed to have voted as heavily Democratic as the New Yorkers. One old pioneer recalled ambiguously that all "Canada Frenchmen" never failed to " 'Cast a vote for Gen. Jackson.' No insult was more keenly felt than to be charged with lack of fealty to the 'old party,' although it was well understood that the last man to give him a ballot and the longest plug of tobacco secured his vote." Nevertheless, a strong French attachment to the Democratic Party seems to have been clearly established by the mid-thirties.[19] The French often tantalized Whig leaders by appearing ready to switch, but usually gave the Whigs frustration instead of votes. A Monroe Whig leader in 1844 became convinced that the French would go for Clay, but later lamented "that the Sabbath previous to the Election, their Clergy here and at the Bay urged on them the duty of voting the Polk ticket as the Clay Party, should they succeed, would burn their Churches, and otherwise act hostilely to all Catholic Interests."[20]

In Detroit French voting influence is difficult to measure even by the late 1830s, but French Catholics in the Third, Fourth, and Sixth wards probably added to Democratic majorities in the period 1837 to 1844. In 1851 some "Old French" organized the French Democratic Association, proposing to undertake the political education of half the French Canadian population which, "not understanding the English" needed to learn "what is done around them and for their benefit." The Association said it intended to act only to increase Democratic majorities. It probably also sought to regain French influence in the party. Although French Canadians had been increasing by immigration, their numbers could not compare with the masses of Germans and Irish. French status in the city, if not in the party, had been falling. From 1824 to 1836, of 51 Common Council members, at least 11 and probably 14 were French; from 1836 to 1856, of 99 Councilmen, only 7 names of certain French origin could be counted and only one of these appeared after 1846.[21] The Association's action also indicated that some French were either voting Whig, or not voting at all.

[18] Benson, *Concept*, 175-76, 185.

[19] E. S. Smith, "Pioneer Days in Kalamazoo and Van Buren Counties," *MHC*, 14: 279. *Detroit Courier*, July 10, 1833. Caleb M. Ormsby, Detroit, to John Allen, March 11, 1833, Allen MSS, BHC. *Free Press*, Oct. 23 and 25, 1838. Evidence that the French possessed early a political consciousness as a group, and a friendship for Democrats-to-be, can be found in Mast, *Always the Priest*, 207, 260-64.

[20] Oliver Johnson, Monroe, to W. Woodbridge, Nov. 20, 1844, Woodbridge MSS, BHC.

[21] *Free Press*, Oct. 31, 1851. Leigh G. Cooper, "Influence of the French Inhabitants of Detroit Upon Its Early Political Life," *Michigan History*, 4 (January 1920), 301-02. An 1825 poll list for Detroit noted "242 [Voters] in all of these 66 are French," Samuel Zug MSS, BHC. The *Advertiser*, Oct. 29, 1851, mocked the association and French Canadians.

The most Democratic French probably were the woodsmen and fishermen of Mackinac County. From the 1820s this child of the American Fur Company had been an organizational stalwart, first Republican, then Democratic. It frequently won the Democratic banner after 1837; its 89 percent Democratic vote in 1850 was representative. In 1844 "mixed" Holmes Township gave Polk 58 percent of its vote while French Ignace and Moran townships gave him 81 percent and 100 percent.

In southeastern Michigan most French lived a more sedentary life as farmers or farm laborers. Most voted Democratic. A poll list of voters in Hamtramck in 1840 held 336 names, 185 or 55 percent of which appeared to be French. Hamtramck voted 70 percent Democratic in 1840 and it is unlikely that all or most of the 104 Whig votes came from Frenchmen. In 1844 a group of 75 Hamtramck Democrats met to announce support of Lewis Cass and 80 to 90 percent were French.[22] In Monroe County, Frenchtown was probably more homogeneously French in 1840 than Hamtramck. Across the Raisin River from Monroe, Americans had originally chosen it as the county seat but French natives refused to sell their land to developers. This enclave voted 79 percent Democratic in 1837, 72 percent in 1840, and 76 percent in 1844.[23]

Not all French communities had a Democratic attachment. Ira Township, St. Clair County, usually cast a strong Whig vote. Its potential electorate even in 1850 was well over 50 percent French (mostly Old French).[24] The county history yielded no clues as to why these largely poor farmers preferred Whiggery. Another "deviant" French town, Ecorse, Wayne County, did not consistently favor either party. Ecorse's French were both old and new. The old settlement nestled in southern Wayne County on the Ecorse and Detroit rivers. Yankees settled the western half but broke off in 1846 as the separate town of Taylor, which then became the county's banner Whig unit. Both before and after the division Ecorse vacillated between parties and produced a 51 percent Whig mean from 1848 to 1852. In 1850, 54 percent of its potential voters were Michigan-born French, and about 25 percent were new French. Ecorse's French, like those elsewhere, never cast a vote for Liberty or Free Soil. Similarly, in 1850, 60 voters decided against nonwhite suffrage and none for it. This typical Democratic and French behavior makes Ecorse's lack of Democratic tendency more striking.

Ecorse offers no support for the traditional class interpretation accord-

[22] *Free Press*, Oct. 19, 1837, Feb. 24, 1844, May 26, 1840. The Hamtramck poll list is in the John R. Williams MSS, BHC. An 1839 or 1840 census of Hamtramck is in the Woodbridge MSS, BHC. It lists 133 male household heads, including 35 resident farm owners, 16 tenant farmers, 3 unidentifiable, and 9 nonresidents. Of the residents 40 to 45 percent of the names are French.

[23] Edgar E. Brandon, "A French Colony in Michigan," *Modern Language Notes,* 13 (April 1898), 1-3.

[24] Ruth Robbins Montieth, "Census of 1850, St. Clair Co.," 76-87, BHC.

ing to which it (like Ira) should have voted Democratic. Over 60 percent of its potential voters were in the rural lower classes. Mean values of farms and tools were the lowest in Wayne; only 12 farmers owned farms worth $1,000 to $3,000; none owned farms worth over $3,000. In contrast to other small farmer towns in Wayne it had a relatively large number of tenants (12 percent) and farm laborers (21 percent). Its mostly French-speaking, uneducated, and illiterate farmers did not build a Catholic church until 1847, though it was an old settlement. All of this suggests apathy or isolation. Perhaps cleavages between old and new French assumed importance. Ecorse received few immigrants other than French Canadians, unlike Hamtramck, Grosse Pointe, and Greenfield. Those towns bordered one another in Wayne's northeast corner, presenting a belt of Democratic strength resting on French, German and Irish Catholics, and German Lutherans. The 3 towns contained many poor, uneducated persons, yet some of the flower of the Democratic leadership also lived there; they had a spirit that was lacking in Ecorse.[25]

If Ira and Ecorse resist satisfactory comprehension, McCoy's findings for French members of Wayne County's economic elite, rich and "urban," perhaps provide additional analytical tools. Of 11 native French elite members, McCoy identified 5 (45 percent) as Democrats, 3 as Whigs (27 percent), 2 were of no identifiable party, and 1 probably was a Whig. McCoy assumed (correctly) that most Wayne County French voted Democratic and thus decided that the French elite were less Democratic than the French masses. Since Wayne County's elite was predominantly Whig McCoy thought it possible that "class identification" helped account for the greater Whiggery among the rich French. Of at least equal significance, however, was McCoy's discovery that the "most puritan" of the French elite were those attracted to Whiggery. The Catholics among the French elite numbered 7. Three of these were the 3 positively identifiable Whigs and 4 were Democrats.[26] Thus 7 of 8 with strong party affiliations also had religious commitments, and 3 men with uncertain or no party identification had no discernible religious connection. These data, as well as that for Ira and Ecorse, suggest that strong political loyalty tended to accompany religious involvement. It is certain, finally, that French Whigs could be found among the poorest and richest strata of society.

FRENCHMAN AND YANKEE

The Yankee Protestant and French Catholic cleavage in Michigan resembled in several ways the Yankee-Yorker rift in New York. The

[25] All data from Wayne County sources given above.
[26] McCoy, "Wayne County Economic Elite, 1844, 1860," 169-70, 180.

French, *anciens habitans* of the lake country, regarded the Yankees as interlopers, much as Yorkers had looked upon New Englanders busily intruding on New York for over a century. The Yankees, even when freshly arrived, treated the French as "foreigners." Little tension, however, existed during territorial days. As Detroit and Michigan grew and as native Protestants began to try to shape communities to their models of the good society, conflict ensued.

In 1856 a novel appeared, *Shoepac Recollections: A Wayside Glimpse of American Life*, by "Walter March," in which Detroit's Yankee-French cultural clash provided the setting. Walter March was the pseudonym of Orlando B. Wilcox, a young native Detroiter and an army officer. Wilcox had fought Mexicans and Arapahoe Indians in the 1840s, kept peace in Boston during the Burns riot of 1854, then covered himself with glory in the Civil War. After the war Brigadier General Wilcox returned to chasing Indians in the Far West.[27] His survival through all this suggests that he was a far better soldier than novelist. *Shoepac*'s turgid prose, rambling construction, cardboard characters, and unexciting melodrama have consigned it to literary oblivion. Yet it holds great interest for the social historian. The author thought he was probing an essential of American life through Detroit's cultural conflicts. The narrator, March, was an Episcopalian of English descent whose sympathies rested with the French. Significantly, the novel had strong streaks of antievangelicalism.

Shoepac were "old fashioned Canadian shoes," representing early French culture. March told of how Frenchmen contemporary with him laughed at the outmoded footwear, but in earlier days they had laughed at their cousins who donned shoes. Changing styles of footwear symbolized the succession of cultures in the Northwest. "The moccasin must make room for the Shoepac, and the Shoepac, in its turn, for the iron heel of the British, and all together exclaim—'Room! Room! for the American.' "[28]

Shoepac opened with a description of the time "when Indian, French, Briton and American commingled harmoniously." (This was no melting pot, but more than peaceful coexistence.) The easygoing French set the pace; immigrants had not begun to pour in; the "spirit of speculation" slumbered. "There was no touchiness about position in the social scale and consequently neither stiffness or affectation." The "mercurial" Frenchman would ride "in his two-wheeled cart to market with white fish and onions . . . screaming a rascally *patois*" or drive his bride "at full

[27] Walter March [Orlando Bolivar Wilcox], *Shoepac Recollections: A Way Side Glimpse of American Life* (New York, 1856) (Hereafter referred to as *Shoepac*); *Summary of History and Services of Orlando B. Wilcox, Colonel 12th U.S. Infantry, Brevet Major General, USA, BHC. Farmer, Detroit, II, 1105-06.*

[28] *Shoepac*, v-vi.

speed to church, two and two, in little antique catechés; the bride . . .
dressed in white but wearing a veil that sweeps the ground"; or *correurs
du bois* would come down by pirogue from Mackinac, pulling red oars
and keeping "joyous quick time."[29] The Yankee invasion, however,
dispelled ease, insouciance, and sociability. Before the Yankees, the narrator recalled:

Our community was not yet divided on the question of Bibles in the schools,
or wine on the side-boards. Slavery was little talked of, and as far as disunion—the mere word was considered by the veriest Kanuck as a profanation of the human language.
   But as settlers from New England began to thicken among us—Bostonians
they were indiscriminately denominated—it gradually came to light that our
lively little community were scarce a grain better than the wicked, nay than
the very heathen; witness the fiddling and dancing on Sunday evenings.
   There were the prettiest and most mischievous-eyed French girls dancing
away for dear life with the good-looking, frank-mannered voyageurs . . . in
their red, yellow, or green sashes, long black hair, and blue calico shirts.
Such abominations attracted the "growing attention" of the strict sober sides
from the land of Jonathan Edwards, as he passed these dens of Apollyon, on
his way to the place where prayer was wont to be made. Then was there not
racing to church the year round, and racing home again? And were there not
regular trotting matches on the afternoons of the great days of the church? . . .
   Then on Easter morning, was not the church-yard of St. Ann's fairly riot-
ous with boys cracking painted eggs? Nay . . . were not idolatries frequently
committed? Was not the Host brought in procession by chanting Jesuits and
nuns, to a high mound called Calvary? . . . Doubt not that these abominations smelt in the nostrils of the sons of the Puritans.[30]

   In earlier days Catholic and Protestant boys went to school and played
together. "Father Robert"—a thinly disguised Father Gabriel Richard—
was loved by even "*unco good* Protestants." He died before "men came
who would have known him not" and before "another element of happy
discord considered now indispensable in every well organized city" had
developed: "the foreigner question. . . . The Frenchman would have
been astonished to have been branded as a foreigner."[31]
   March's narrative sheds no light on the process of social change which
he laments. The villain is Magroy, a Scot with Yankee ways and wife.
On the death of March's father, Magroy, his former friend and business
associate, persecutes the March family. He opposes the marriage of his
son (an un-Magroy like person) to the March girl. Enter Monsieur
Latrobe, a good Frenchman, who aids the widow March and unselfishly
protects her daughter and sons. In the denouement, Magroy is thwarted
by the March boys and repents as he dies, revealing that his antagonism

[29] *Shoepac*, 11, 15.
[30] *Shoepac*, 17-19. Also, Frederick Marryat, *Diary in America*, Jules Zanger, ed.
(Bloomington, 1960), 120-21.
[31] *Shoepac*, 22-23.

grew from a frustrated love for Mrs. March. Returning abruptly to social commentary the author closes with a discussion of the sad, ludicrous plight of the once proud French in Yankified Detroit.[32]

March rightly emphasized religion as a vital wedge between Yankees and Frenchmen. When the evangelicals were not denouncing French Catholics as "pariahs" deprived by their "priestly oppressors" of liberty and reason, they were likely to be trying to convert them.[33] Yet the Frenchmen's Catholicism did not mean, contrary to the impression given by some writers, that they were "religious" or "pious." The French were more hedonist than Catholic. Observers uniformly noted their love of merrymaking, but often added that "yet" the French were "pious." French piety probably waxed most intensely among women. Even then it seemed largely ritual. It did not promote an uncompartmentalized view of life. The French, as Bela Hubbard said, were "not bigoted. Their religion was simple as their tastes." No one ever accused them of religious zeal; their hostility for what they regarded as fanaticism is reflected in their lack of sympathy for antislavery and temperance. Monsieur Latrobe of *Shoepac* was, significantly, neither Protestant nor Catholic, and casual about religion. March said "he had a strange opinion that there was but one God and one Savior for both churches."[34]

"The social virtues," said Hubbard, "never shone more brightly among any people." Desire for sociable living as much as protection dictated the arrangement of French settlements in long narrow ribbon farms with houses in a row at one end. On Sundays the French redoubled their efforts to enjoy life, while the puritan condemned unnecessary visits let alone "social intercourse." Reverend Elijah Pilcher, in his history of Methodism, not surprisingly described the French as having "little or no regard for the Sabbath."[35]

Bishop Lefevre of Detroit tried to promote temperance among the French in the 1840s. Whatever superficial assurance he received from

[32] *Shoepac*, 359, 302-15 summarizes most of the plot. For a fascinating suggestion that Magroy was modeled on William Woodbridge, see O. B. Wilcox to Woodbridge, Dec. 24, 1841, and O. B. Wilcox to Woodbridge, Jan. 16, 1841, Woodbridge MSS, BHC.

[33] *Michigan Christian Herald*, Oct. 3, 1851: an article by a Frenchman and former Catholic with the imprimatur of Rev. Duffield.

[34] Bela Hubbard, *Memorials of a Half Century* (New York, 1887), 146. Hoffman's 1833 description was very similar, *Winter in the West*, 121. *Shoepac*, 65. French laxity in religion and indulgence "in all manner of vices and excesses" in the Grand River Valley were described by Catholic missionary Andrew Viszosky, July 25, 1844, letter in John W. McGee, *The Catholic Church in the Grand River Valley, 1833-1950* (Grand Rapids, 1950), 111; also, Frank A. O'Brien, "Le Pere Juste," *MHC*, 30: 264.

[35] Fuller, *Economic and Social Beginnings*, 103. Hubbard, *Memorials*, 139-41. Richard Clyde Ford, "The French Canadians in Michigan," *Michigan History*, 27 (Spring 1943), 49-50. Pilcher, *Protestantism in Michigan*, 43.

the flock, French voters did not favor the cause. In the 1853 referendum on a liquor law no area of French concentration gave significant support to prohibition but rather strongly opposed it. French reaction to moral reform probably helped defeat the Democratic candidate for mayor in 1839. Jonathan Kearsley, though a Democrat, was a Presbyterian, promoter of benevolence, and recently identified as an "uncompromising foe of intemperance." He made one of the poorest showings ever by a Democratic candidate for mayor, losing by 886 to 373 votes to Whig DeGarmo Jones. Democratic entries before and after him received 744 and 644 votes. Kearsley received few votes in the Fourth Ward, usually a strong Democratic ward. The Fourth, with many French voters, gave 82 percent of its vote to Jones but simultaneously elected two Democratic aldermen: both were prominent French Democratic politicians.[36]

In the eyes of Yankee observers the French violated the work ethic by not being (to put it mildly) diligent, thrifty, hard working, and productive. William Woodbridge, not pious by evangelical standards, wondered to his wife in 1815 whether "the lives of this people consist in one constant succession of amusements—dances, rides, dinners, and parties, and all the *et cetera* of dissipation, following in one long train, treading each upon the heels of the other." Yankees regarded the French as lazy farmers, ignorant of "modern" methods and not interested in learning them.[37] Their critics failed to see that for the Frenchman to change farming methods meant changing a way of life. French farming did not compulsively follow a productive ethic. There were exceptions, of course, but most Frenchmen did not farm as a business. They left much acreage deliberately unimproved as a source of timber for fuel and other domestic uses. The restless Yankee rather tended to view the farm as an investment, not as a "folk heritage of land and lore . . . but as a speculative commodity in the wagon of a roving entrepreneur—a rational symbol to be manipulated by other rational symbols like maps and mortgages."[38]

These different values led to some painful disagreements in Detroit. One of the most notorious centered on the refusal of the French in the

[36] Paré, *Catholic Church in Detroit*, 440. *Free Press*, Feb. 17, 1844, April 13, 14, and 18, 1839; *Advertiser*, April 24, 1839.

[37] W. Woodbridge, Detroit, to Juliana Woodbridge, March 5, 1815, quoted in Charles Lanman, *Life of William Woodbridge* (Washington, 1867), 15. Rev. W. Fitch, *MHC*, 5: 539. Hubbard contrasted the "practical, hard-working money-getting Yankee" with the "careless, laughter-loving French man," *Memorials*, 154; see also Hubbard, *Memorials*, 118-20; Fuller, *Economic and Social Beginnings*, 104-13.

[38] Frank N. Kramer, *Voices in the Valley* (Madison, 1964), 63-64. On Yankee restlessness, Harold Fisher Wilson, *The Hill Country of Northern New England: Its Social and Economic History, 1790-1930* (New York, 1936), 57; Levi Beardsley, *Reminiscences*, 232-33.

1830s to allow the city or developers to extend Jefferson Avenue across their ribbon farms although, as Hoffman said in 1833, "large sums are continually offered for the merest slice in the world off their long tailed patrimonies." Yankees interpreted French reluctance as due to stubbornness and ignorance. The French were insulted by Yankee lack of tact and distrustful of Yankee bargains.[39] The French also opposed public improvements because they feared taxes. Opposition to a school tax movement in Detroit in 1841-42 reportedly came from "large landowners," some of whom probably were French. French names were conspicuously absent from the bipartisan endorsers of the tax.[40]

The antagonism between Yankee and Frenchman, then, was cultural, religious, and to some extent economic. The French Catholic culture tended to be traditional, land-rooted, and hedonist; the Yankee Protestant to be ascetic, rationalist, and "improvement" oriented.

IRISH CATHOLICS

The strongest Democratic group in Michigan, as in other parts of the United States, were the Irish Catholics. As in New York the Irish voted 95 percent Democratic "whether they were day laborers or freehold farmers."[41] Class and status factors reinforced the deep cultural antipathies that did most to shape their tenacious Democratic partisanship. Yet even in this group of nearly monolithic party loyalty, instructive short-run and individual variations may be observed.

Irish Catholics first arrived in force around 1833. Many worked on railroads and canals during the boom days, lived in camps along construction routes, then returned to Detroit and other towns to find work. One Whig recalled spending hours in 1837 at a camp in Wayne County haranguing laborers, but to no avail. Such maneuvering for the votes of Irish workers continued into the 1840s, with Whigs continuing to be largely unsuccessful.[42]

In Detroit during the 1840s the Irish moved preponderantly to the western side of town where, in 1848, a new ward was created encom-

[39] Hoffman, *Winter in the West*, 120-21. Fitch, "Reminiscences of Detroit," *MHC*, 5: 537. Fuller, *Economic and Social Beginnings*, 131-32. John Bell Moran, *The Moran Family* (Detroit, 1949), 54-55.

[40] Dorr, "Origins of the 1835 Michigan Constitution," 125, 126; Fuller, *Economic and Social Beginnings*, 131. Arthur B. Moehlman, *Public Education in Detroit* (Bloomington, Ill., 1925), 77.

[41] Benson, *Concept*, 172.

[42] George C. Bates, "By Gones of Detroit," *MHC*, 22: 34-50. Catlin, "Early Settlement in Eastern Michigan," *Michigan History*, 26: 340. *Advertiser*, Aug. 22, 23, Sept. 15, 18, Nov. 20, 1837; *Adrian Michigan Whig*, Nov. 7 and 14, 1838; *Coldwater Sentinel*, Nov. 1, 1850.

passing most of "Corktown." There the Irish built Holy Trinity Church, "the headquarters of Irishmen in Detroit."[43] According to Johnston's 1853 census, 44 percent of the Eighth Ward's population was Irish Catholic, probably too low a figure. In 1849 it cast a 74 percent Democratic vote, and thereafter consistently won the Democratic banner. The percentage of Irish Catholics in each ward in 1853 correlated with Democratic percentage strength in 1852 at a very high +.704.

Elsewhere in Wayne County pioneers recalled that Dearborn's Irish Catholics voted Democratic.[44] A "New Ireland" had been planted in Washtenaw County's Northfield Township as early as 1831 and a church built soon after. By 1840 some 90 Catholic families were present, and Franklin Sawyer, Whig editor in Ann Arbor, told William Woodbridge that "Most of the Catholics in this place and vicinity, particularly in Northfield, have hitherto been our warmest opponents." Though Sawyer hoped to change their voting habits, he had no lasting success, if any. Returns for 1840 are not available, but in 1844 Northfield voted 69 percent Democratic. Irish Catholic farmers also settled Emmet Township, the banner Democratic unit in St. Clair County in 1852 when it cast 98 percent of its ballots for Pierce. In western Michigan Irish Catholics and natives pioneered rural Grattan Township in Kent County in the mid-1840s. Grattan voted 64 percent Democratic in 1846. Irish farmers flooded the township of Orange in Macomb from 1837 to 1842 and in the latter year changed its name to Erin. First available returns show a 91 percent majority for the Democrats in 1843, 84 percent in 1844, 85 percent in 1848.[45]

As the bête noire of evangelicals, the Irish embodied all the evils of Popery. Evangelicals blamed the Irish for obstructing temperance, Sabbath-keeping, antislavery, and moral and political reform generally. They linked Irish drinking with poverty and crime. On election days the Irish drank and brawled, disrupting the democratic process and intimidating native citizens. By voting en masse for the Democrats the Irish

[43] John A. Russell, *The Early Irish of Detroit* (1930), 1-5, BHC. [Richard R. Elliot], "Roman Catholics in Detroit," *MHC*, 13: 435, 545-55.

[44] Col. Joshua Howard Chapter, Daughters of the American Revolution, ed., "History of the Churches in West Dearborn, Michigan" (bound typed MS, BHC; Dearborn, 1939), 20. F. A. Gulley, "Old Dearborn Families: Historical and Genealogical Sketches," MS, BHC. Farmer, *Detroit*, II, 1828.

[45] *History of Washtenaw County*, II, 636-37. F. Sawyer to W. Woodbridge, Sept. 19, 1840, Woodbridge MSS, BHC. William Lee Jenks, *St. Clair County, Michigan: Its History and Its People* (Chicago, 1912), I, 239. *History of St. Clair County, Michigan* (Chicago, 1883), 760-62. *History of Kent County*, 755-76. Catholic Irish farmers scattered through Oakfield, Vergennes, and Walker townships in Kent, and Tallmadge, Ottawa County, may have contributed to the frequent Democratic majorities in most of those towns, McGee, *Catholic Church, Grand River Valley*, 120, 123. Earlier election returns for St. Clair are not available.

gave the evangelicals' enemies a seemingly unbeatable trump card, and made a mockery of the independent, reasoning voter. They obeyed party dogma as blindly as they followed Papal and priestly dictates.

In the evangelicals, the Irish recognized their natural enemies: Protestants, generally of hated English descent, who vilified their religion and insulted their manhood. From their experience with oppression they brought clannishness, talent for extralegal politics, and a tradition of personal loyalty to leaders. Irish Catholics hated Protestant Scotch Irish; the few Orangemen in Detroit's Corktown were "looked upon with a bad eye" and given "bad scran." When a Catholic newspaper came into being in 1853 it began to return the knocks Irish Catholics had taken from evangelical and Whig journals for years. The Protestants to whom the paper gave the most "bad scran" were "Doct. Duffield" and the Presbyterians.[46]

The Irish and Presbyterians dealt with one another on more prosaic levels. The Irish constituted the majority of the servant labor supply in Detroit, while Presbyterians were numerous among the wealthy, so naturally many Irish women (and some men) served as domestics in the households of Presbyterians. Though servants are usually inarticulate in historical records, masters sometimes discussed their employees at length. The letters of Elizabeth E. Stuart, Presbyterian widow of businessman and prominent Whig Robert Stuart, provide enough such material that some servant attitudes may be inferred. Indeed, Mrs. Stuart was preoccupied with the "servant problem" and believed that "the whole happiness of a family is in the power of Servants." She, her family, and friends experienced constant trouble in finding reliable help. Most domestics appear to have disliked their work; they changed jobs often and abruptly. Mrs. Stuart complained of her "great talent in *elevating* and rendering servants utterly useless for myself." The smart ones who learned quickly either moved on or up enough to become "Uppish." She frankly recognized that "if they have brain enough to be such as *we* would wish, they have too much brain to be servants."[47]

Mrs. Stuart discussed most the Irish Catholics in her employ. She distrusted and disliked them and used them no doubt because of the cheapness of their labor. She vastly preferred "a good Protestant German girl" to a "headlong Irish, heedless animal." There was, however, a desirable "Class of Irish," who, with the right combination of affection and discipline, would *"identify herself with you."* (Italics mine) Although Mrs.

---

[46] Robert Ernst, *Immigrant Life in New York City, 1825-1863* (New York, 1949), 105, 106, 165. Russell, *Early Detroit Irish*, 4. Detroit, *Catholic Vindicator*, June 4, Aug. 13 and 20, 1853, microfilm, University of Detroit Library. And see below notes 80-83.

[47] E. E. Stuart to Kate, July 7, 1852; E. E. Stuart to Kate, April 28, 1851; E. E. Stuart to Kate, May 4, 1853, *Stuart Letters*, I, 177-78, 523-24.

Stuart regarded "these 'cattle' " with deep contempt, she comforted herself with two ideas. One was simple realism: "were they not just what they are we should be obliged to be our own Hewers of Wood and Drawers of Water." But more often she invoked the idea of *civilizing mission*. "Protes. is no better than Cath., [but] let us endeavor to instill in them 'Thou God seeist me,' and then we shall have done them some good." When two of her daughter-in-law's helpers left suddenly, Mrs. Stuart hoped that the third would stay, but warned "time may identify her with you but I feel as you do, their *heathenism*, not religion, puts an effective barrier between us."[48]

The separation between Presbyterian mistresses and Irish servants was thus one of class *and* culture. The daily experiences of a small part of the Irish labor force may or may not have affected the political perceptions of Irish artisans, grocers, farmers, and others all across the state. They had reason enough already to resent persons such as wealthy evangelical Presbyterians. Relations between Presbyterian and Irish had many abrasive edges. Even when an exploitive economic relationship or class differences did not exist, religion and culture would cause hostility.

GERMANS, DUTCH, AND NEW BRITISH

German immigration began in the late 1820s, and by 1833 was quite evident in eastern Michigan. During the 1840s German colonists settled throughout the state. Both Catholic and Protestant Germans favored the Democrats, with Catholics, as in New York, being the more Democratic of the two groups. "Rationalist" Germans also leaned to the Democrats.[49]

In 1845 Detroit's two most German wards, Four and Seven, voted strongly Democratic. The *Free Press* attributed the Fourth's being the banner Democratic ward (72 percent) to the work of German Democrats.[50] Both wards were middle and lower class. Neither contained commercial or manufacturing establishments of great size. They had roughly the same proportion of foreigners (55 percent and 57 percent) and Ger-

---

[48] E. E. Stuart to Kate, July 6, 1852; E. E. Stuart to Kate, July 7, 1852; E. E. Stuart to Kate, May 4, 1851; E. E. Stuart to Kate, April 28, 1851; E. E. Stuart to Kate, April 6, 1852, *ibid.*, I, 186, 177-78, 304. "Dr. Dodridge says, 'Christian Masters and Mistresses should never omit carrying their domestics in the Arms of Faith to their Heavenly Father, that he would grant them all needful blessings, for we are hardly sensible how much the happiness of ours and our families depends on them.' " E. E. Stuart to Kate, Nov. 29, 1851, *ibid.*, I, 235-36.

[49] John A. Russell, *Germanic Influence in the Making of Michigan*, 54-71. Benson, *Concept*, 173-74. On Germans voting Democratic see e.g., *Detroit Journal and Courier*, April 15, 1835; *Advertiser*, Sept. 10, 15, 1836, Nov. 2, 1846; *Free Press*, Oct. 21 and 25, Nov. 2, 1837.

[50] *Free Press*, Nov. 4, 1847.

mans (49 percent and 52 percent) in 1853, the Seventh having slightly more in both cases. Yet the Seventh's Democratic mean from 1848 to 1852 was 58 percent compared to 65 percent for the Fourth. Both had similar percentages of French Catholics and British Protestants. The Fourth, however, had more German Catholics (31 percent) than Protestants (over 18 percent) while the Seventh had about the same proportion of German Catholics and Protestants (26 percent and 27 percent). The Fourth also contained twice as many Irish Catholics (12 percent to 5 percent). The Irish and German Catholics probably provided the extra margin of Democratic strength in the Fourth.

Rural Germans in Wayne County also voted Democratic. An old pioneer remembered that both Catholic and Protestant Germans in Dearborn had voted Democratic.[51] Wayne towns with the largest proportions of German-born among their potential voters were, with one exception, strongly Democratic. All across the state, German farming settlements of Catholics and Lutherans voted strongly Democratic (Table IX.2). None of these places was particularly prosperous, but most of

TABLE IX.2

Michigan German Settlements, 1850:[a] Democratic and Religious Percentages

Unit	Democrat	German	German Catholic	German Protestant
Warren, Macomb County	72	75[b]	40[b]	40[b]
Freedom, Washtenaw County	69	64	73	27
Riga, Lenawee County	77	50–75[b]	—	50–75[b]
Bainbridge, Berrien County	63	40[b]	20[b]	20[b]
Westphalia, Clinton County	94	100	100	—
Saginaw County	61 (1852)	50[b]	—	50[b]

[a] Freedom: *Ann Arbor State Journal*, Nov. 6, 1839, *Advertiser*, Nov. 27, 1839. Warren: *History of Macomb County*, 852-57, 360-61; Warren's Democratic vote in other years: 1840—69 percent; 1844—61 percent; 1848—61 percent; 1849—72 percent; 1852—67 percent. Riga: Bonner, *Lenawee Memoirs*, I, 423-26. Saginaw County: William L. Jenks, "Michigan Immigration," *Michigan History*, XXVIII, 73-74. *Free Press*, Aug. 20, 1847, reported that 500 Germans had recently arrived in Saginaw; the 1850 Constitutional Convention noted the Saginaw colonies, *Report*, 279. *History of Saginaw County, Michigan* (Chicago, 1881), 226. Robert Arthur Dengler, "The German Settlement at Frankenmuth, Michigan, in its First Century" (unpublished M.A. thesis, Michigan State College, 1953), 26.

[b] Estimated.

them were already displaying industry, efficiency, and accumulative habits that would make some "exceedingly prosperous." That was the case with Westphalia, a thoroughly German Catholic colony from the time its pioneers arrived in 1836. Few Michigan towns exceeded West-

---

[51] Gulley, "Old Dearborn Families." In the countryside Protestant Germans were predominantly Lutheran.

phalia in Democratic loyalty. It exemplified the conditions under which rural ethnoreligious groups produced virtual unanimity of political behavior. Its homogeneous people were isolated by space and language on the frontier north of Lansing. The county historian described its people as sharing a common Fatherland, religion, and sympathy so that "they are banded together by a fraternal bond that makes them more like members of one family than of a community."[52]

Urban Germans who in many ways were the polar opposites of the Westphalians also voted Democratic. The German Workingmen's Association of Detroit enjoyed the public condemnation of evangelicals and Catholics. The Association was anticlerical, rationalist, and socialist. Its "bible," according to opponents, was the New York *Workingmen's Republic*, a fomenter of class warfare and godless red terror. The "German Mechanics" of the Association rejected Jesuit priests who led Germans around "by the nose" but their antipathies for evangelicals and Whigs seem to have led them to prefer the Democrats. One of the Association's officers also acted as a Democratic ward leader.[53]

Most Germans in the period from 1835 to 1852 voted heavily Democratic. Although a "good Whig German"[54] was more likely to be Protestant than Catholic, Protestant Germans voted mostly Democratic. Largely Lutheran, they disliked American evangelicalism and revivals. Pious in a practical way they viewed native evangelicalism as a threat.[55] To a great extent Protestant and Catholic Germans responded to the evangelicals' nativism as Germans. The greater Democratic loyalty of the Catholics can be attributed to their reactions being reinforced by both ethnic and religious considerations.

The German "sense of peoplehood" should not be exaggerated. Germans came from a "Germany" which was, as Metternich said of Italy, a "geographic expression." They came from many little states and subcultures and brought many parochialisms with them. Antagonism was hardly as intense, however, as the kind which drove apart Catholic and Protestant Irish. In the 1830s two Detroit congregations of Germans,

[52] *History of Shiawasee and Clinton Counties*, 533-34. Democratic votes: 1840: 91 percent; 1844: 93 percent; 1848: 63 percent; 1852: 69 percent. Free Soil in 1848 and 1852 won 31 percent and 17 percent of Westphalia's vote. In 1850 it voted 92 percent against colored suffrage.

[53] *Advertiser*, Feb. 15, 1851; Caspar Butz was the Democrat, *Free Press*, March 1, 1852. *Michigan Christian Herald*, Oct. 16, Nov. 27, 1851.

[54] William Woodbridge wanted his family to get one to saw wood, W. W. to Julia Woodbridge, Dec. 14, 1844, Woodbridge MSS, BHC.

[55] Smith, *Revivalism and Social Reform*, 57. Eugene Poppen, *A Century of Lutheranism in Michigan* (Toledo, 1934), 5-28. Robert E. Erickson, *History of the Evangelical Lutheran Church of Wayne, Plymouth, Livonia, Pontiac, Farmington, Northville, Rochester, and Redford* (Detroit, 1922), passim, and Robert E. Erickson, *A Short Historical Sketch of the Activity of the Evangelical Lutheran Church of Michigan from 1833 to 1863* (Detroit, n.d.), passim.

Catholic and Protestant, lived harmoniously: "At marriages and baptisms they are never concerned about which preacher they should choose, but that they should have a good time in German fashion."[56] As the number and variety of Germans grew their relations became less harmonious; yet the sense of ethnocultural solidarity remained strong, as did the desire that *Gemütlichkeit* should prevail. "Good times" (*Gemütlichkeit*) and *Lebensgemuss* (joys of life) also had much to do with Democratic majorities among the Germans. Lutheran and Catholic churches tended to tolerate drinking and recreation on the Sabbath. The native evangelical churches condemned practices which Germans did not regard as immoral but rather as "normal." Whig nativism and evangelicalism determined German party preferences to a significant degree, as did the Democrats' laissez faire ethics and willingness to tolerate, indeed enjoy, the pleasures of life.[57]

In 1847 the famous Holland immigration to western Michigan began, concentrating in Ottawa County and the Grand Rapids area. These people came for a mixture of spiritual and mundane motives which can be called solely "religious" only if one ignores the subtle ways in which temporal aspirations for status, comfort, and prestige blend with sublime but more easily articulated values. In the 1830s in reaction to enlightenment rationalism and the statism of the government, a "Réveil" swept part of the Dutch Reformed Church. Economic hardship joined with religious persecution a decade later and prepared the middle and lower class members of this lay sectarian movement for a leap across the ocean to a new life. Refusing to accept a state church, the pietists also needed the push of potato famines and bold leaders. Reverend Albertus Christian Van Raalte traveled all the way to Lake Michigan to survey land, then return to Holland to gather the vanguard and lead them back to this chosen land.[58]

With help from prominent citizens in Detroit, Grand Rapids, and elsewhere, 1,200 Dutch landed in Ottawa County by 1847. The main group settled with Van Raalte in a township they called Holland. Shortly after a second group founded nearby Zeeland. A visitor in 1848 found them to be "industrious, persevering, and intelligent . . . every man owning and

---

[56] Catholic missionary quoted in Russell, *Germanic Influence*, 54.

[57] Suggestive here are Thomas, *Nativism*, 211-12; Mark O. Kistler, "The German Language Press in Michigan: A Survey and Bibliography," *Michigan History*, 44 (September 1960), 304.

[58] Lucas, ed., *Dutch Immigrant Memoirs*, I, 1-3, 42, 45, 50-53, 53-68; for pioneer accounts stressing religious and economic motives, 90-91, 132, 185-86, 471-78. Also pertinent: Gerrit Van Schelven, "Michigan and the Holland Immigration of 1845," *Michigan History*, 1 (October 1917), 97-100; Paul Honigsheim, "Religion and Assimilation of the Dutch," *Michigan History*, 26 (Winter 1942), 56; Marvin Lindeman, "A Non-Hollander Looks at Holland," *Michigan History*, 31 (December 1947), 408, 409.

cultivating his own land, and living in his own home—subject to no rent or church tithes." Very devout, their farming was not "after the improved Yankee style, but this they will soon acquire. They are very generally a reading and writing people, considerably wedded to a set custom, but they desire to change their own customs, and adopt those of our own people."[59]

The "Kolonie" suffered much in the early winters and outsiders marveled at its stoicism. By 1850 the Dutch began asking government aid for harbor improvements at the outlet of Black Lake and for a plank road from Kalamazoo. Though still in a barter economy they had built several mills, a boatyard, "eight places of worship and six schools, two of which are taught by Americans; also several dry goods stores; and a temperance hotel; but *not one grog shop.*" Although "utterly unable to speak a word" of English they were allegedly "anxious to become Americanized." This observer also found them "remarkable" for piety and morality, and "perhaps their strict observance of the Sabbath, is unparalleled by Protestant Christians. Sabbath breaking and profane swearing are seldom known, and the assiduous care of the church for its poor, its widows and orphans, affords a worthy example for American Churches."[60] Religion pervaded the Hollanders' lives. Sectarian puritanism, self-denial, the Protestant ethic, inner direction, community integration and consensus on ascetic values characterized these moral societies in the wilderness.[61]

With an overriding compulsion to establish a moral society the Dutch seemed "naturals" for the Whigs, and the latter lavishly encouraged them to give them their votes.[62] Why, then, did the Dutch cast their first votes so preponderantly for the Democrats and align themselves, in effect, with leaders and groups with whom they had so little in common? Even in the 1850 Constitutional Convention some Democratic politicians had expressed fears that Van Raalte was a Whig. The first occasion on which Hollanders made "a fair show of their political opinions" in 1851, they voted 88.5 percent Democratic (31 to 4). The Zeelanders kept pace

[59] Quote from Grand Rapids, *Grand River Eagle,* Nov. 17, 1848; see also *ibid.,* July 28, 1847, Nov. 24, 1848, MHCol. *History of Ottawa County, Michigan* (Chicago, 1882), 88, 93.

[60] *Marshall Statesman* quoted in *Grand River Eagle,* Sept. 18, 1850. Lucas, ed., *Dutch Immigrant Memoirs,* I, 478, 493.

[61] Lucas, ed., *Dutch Immigrant Memoirs,* I, 97-398, passim. Gerrit J. Diekma, "Holland Emigration to Michigan: Its Causes and Results," *Michigan History,* 1 (October 1917), 106-07. Honigsheim, "Religion and Assimilation," *Michigan History,* 26: 59. Albert Hyma, *Albertus C. Van Raalte and His Dutch Settlements in the United States* (Grand Rapids, 1947), 239-45, 247-48. Aleida J. Pieters, *A Dutch Settlement in Michigan* (Grand Rapids, 1923), 103, 129.

[62] In addition to issues above see *Grand River Eagle,* July 28, 1847, Nov. 17, 1847, Sept. 18, 1850.

with a 57 to 8 vote for the Democrats (87.5 percent).[63] In 1852 Holland voted 96 percent Democratic (123 to 5) and Zeeland 90.7 percent (128 to 11 to 2). The first newspaper read in the Kolonie was Dutch, from Wisconsin, and Democratic. (*De Hollander*, their own paper, began operating in 1850.) In 1852 Holland and Zeeland both sent Dutch delegates along with natives to the Ottawa Democratic convention—which showed itself quite sensitive to Dutch demands. But these are more effects than causes.[64]

Like the puritans of Massachusetts, to whom they were often compared, the Dutch did not want to practice religious freedom, but sought freedom to practice their own religion. In 1846 America struck Van Raalte with the "degree of freedom felt and enjoyed by the average citizen who does what he wants to, without being hampered by the government, the only exception being that one may not harm another or his property. . . . If a few families settle in the wilderness . . . they choose their own justice of the peace, who manages everything and settles disputes."[65] As the puritans had, Van Raalte conceived of the Kolonie almost as a religious state within a state. The Dutch pietists' goal could be realized within the laissez faire American framework with its emphasis on localism. Therefore it is probable that the positive approach to government of the Whigs helped alienate the Dutch. If Whiggery should have attracted them as the party of the moral society, it must also have repelled them as the party threatening most (however remotely) that very union of church and state from which they had escaped. This pioneer Dutch reaction resembled, ironically, that of Mormons and Catholics.

The Dutch leaders were shrewd and capable men and it is unlikely that Democratic propaganda or the habits of other Dutch determined their actions. The Whigs, in fact, had ample opportunity to win them, and quite possibly the evangelicals themselves drove the Dutch into the arms of the Democrats; conceivably the Whigs and their allies suffered from overexposure. Before the immigration Van Raalte told his people that he had found great public sympathy in America and met with kind cooperation especially in "influential, God-fearing circles." Among the American leaders assisting the Dutch, Whigs and Presbyterians were

[63] Grand Haven, *Grand River Times* (Dem.), claimed the Dutch associated the Whigs with the "kings, tyrants and aristocracy of Europe," Nov. 12, 1851. John S. Bagg chided Democrats in the Constitutional Convention whose imaginations were "chased by the ghost of the priest of the Dutch colony," *Report, 1850*, 496-97.

[64] *Grand River Times*, Oct. 20, 1852. A. S. Kenzie, "Newspapers in Ottawa County," *MHC*, 9: 296. Lucas, ed., *Dutch Immigrant Memoirs*, I, 530-32. See also Governor Ransom's praise of the Dutch in his message of Jan. 3, 1848, Fuller, ed., *Messages of Michigan Governors*, II, 109. The reasons given in Lucas, *Dutch Immigrant Memoirs*, I, 542-43, are inadequate.

[65] Quoted in Pieters, *Dutch Settlement*, 169.

conspicuous. Presbyterians, including Reverend Duffield, were so much in evidence that the Dutch nicknamed their most solicitous attendants the "Presbyterian Coterie." Whigs and antislavery men such as Robert Stuart, E. P. Hastings, Shubael Conant, Flavius Littlejohn, and C. C. Trowbridge were among the influential and concerned people.[66] That this relationship soured is implied by what Van Raalte wrote later in "strict secrecy" to a fellow Dutchman:

> The Americans despise the Dutch in general, and we Hollanders are embittered by their cold egotism. They try to get our money and our influence by bold compliments, but in reality they despise us as uncivilized, dull and slow people and boast of their greater knowledge. You will never be able to go about them as a friend among friends, in hearty confidence and openheartedness. I cannot bear that contempt and thank God I live in the midst of my own people, although subjected to many troubles.[67]

Perhaps the Dutch and Presbyterians were too much alike to get along. At any rate it seems probable that the assumption of superiority on the part of "Americans" identified with evangelicalism and Whiggery, plus the Whigs' reputation for nativism, and the church-state threat implicit in Whig political moralism, all combined to make Democrats of the early Michigan Dutch.

In New York the New British were the strongest Whigs of any immigrant or native group except blacks.[68] The data, impressionistic and systematic, does not permit such a firm conclusion for New British in Michigan. New British did generally prefer the Whigs, though most of those arriving from Canada in the 1840s tended rather to be Democrats.

"Scotch Settlements" in both Dearborn, Wayne County, and Bruce, Macomb County, allegedly voted mostly Whig and Free Soil.[69] An early Scots township in Genesee County, Montrose, cast all 12 of its votes for Whiggery in 1848. Although Sabbath found no New British disposition among the leadership of either party in Wayne County in 1844, I have been impressed with the number of English born among secondary Whig

---

[66] Van Schelven, "Holland Immigration," *Michigan History*, 1: 75, 81, 87-96. Lucas, *Dutch Immigrant Memoirs*, I, 73, 74, 75, 80-81. Whig evangelicalism seems to have been evident in Ottawa County, too, where in 1849 Whigs ran a former Methodist clergyman for state representative, *Grand River Eagle*, Oct. 26, 1849.

[67] Quoted in Lindeman, "Non-Hollander," *Michigan History*, 31: 413. This bitterness acquires poignancy when it is added that Van Raalte earned a reputation as a "liberal" on assimilation, "seeking always larger connections, adopting as rapidly as possible the language and customs of his new fatherland in himself and in his family," *History of Ottawa County*, 75-76. On varying Dutch reactions to assimilation see Martin Ten Hoor, "Dutch Colonists and American Democracy," *Michigan History*, 31 (December 1947), 353-66.

[68] Benson, *Concept*, 166.

[69] Gulley, "Old Dearborn Families"; Streeter, *Political Parties*, 174. Wood, *Genesee County*, I, 259.

party leaders throughout the state; however, a systematic study is obviously needed. Although dealing with very few individuals McCoy found British immigrants to be the largest foreign group among Wayne County's economic elite in 1844. They had an anti-Democratic distribution of 64 percent.[70]

The Canadian Rebellions of 1837-38 illustrated how Britain and her subjects functioned as a reference group in Michigan politics; the Canadian troubles also sent many Democratic voters to Michigan among New British immigrants. Whatever the goals of the anti-British revolts in Upper and Lower Canada, Catholic French and Irish, chafing under British rule, ardently supported them. The rebels hated Protestants and things Anglo-Saxon in general. All along the United States border the uprisings provoked the formation of Hunters' or Patriots' Lodges, which aided the rebels. Anglophobes and adventurers rallied to the Patriots' side. As in Canada, Anglophobia waxed intensely among French and Irish Catholics, but was not limited to them. Some authors have noted the surge of frontier rabble into the Patriot cause and interpreted it as a conscious class movement. However, many Patriot leaders and sympathizers were men of respectability or wealth. While American compassion for republicans and underdogs was present, "hatred of all things British" provided the most combustible motive, especially among the Irish Catholics.[71] Perhaps the best example of the latter in Detroit was Edward Theller, businessman, editor-publisher, adventurer. Captured by the British in Patriot action, Theller escaped and returned to Detroit to publish a thrilling story of his experiences. His hatred for Protestant England, British aristocrats, "Orangemen," and American Tories had easily pushed him to join those fighting for autonomy.[72]

President Van Buren directed Michigan authorities to maintain neutrality. The Brady Guards, local militia, tried to enforce this but could not prevent Patriots in the Detroit area from launching several attacks across the Detroit River.[73] Van Buren's position may have cost him votes in 1840 among French Canadians and other Patriot partisans

[70] McCoy, "Wayne County Economic Elite, 1844, 1860," 171.

[71] Edwin C. Guillet, *The Lives and Times of the Patriots* (Toronto, 1938), 178, 187. Alfred D. Decelles, *The Patriots of '37* (Toronto and Glasgow, 1916), 1-6. On the classes involved, Schoolcraft, *Personal Memoirs*, 581-82, which stresses the "lowers," while the John Anderson MSS, MHCol show the participation of "influentials": Eliza A. Wing to Alexander Anderson, Jan. 5, 1838. On ethnic and religious groups: Orin Edward Tiffany, "Relations of the United States to the Canadian Rebellion of 1837-1838," *Publications of the Buffalo Historical Society*, 8 (1905), 14. Robert R. Ross, "The Patriot War," *MHC*, 21: 513-14 (one of the best accounts); Tucker, ed., "John Fisher Correspondence," *Michigan History*, 35: 233. Hemans, *Mason*, 337, 343, 352.

[72] Edward A. Theller, *Canada in 1837-38* (Philadelphia and New York, 1841), I, 115, 207-15; II, 37, 302; on French participation, I, 29, 108-09.

[73] Hemans, *Mason*, 349; Ross, "Patriot War," *MHC*, 21: 552.

in New York state. The Michigan Democrats, however, became identified with the Patriot cause. Whigs and evangelicals denounced Patriot
fellow travelers and activists in the Democratic state administration, including Governor Mason. The Lodges seem to have operated secretly as
a pressure group as late as 1841, and while they may not have automatically delivered their votes to the Democrats, there is no indication
that they ever gave the Democrats significant opposition.[74] The "Patriot
Wars" reinforced the Democratic loyalty of Anglophobic Irish and
French Canadians. The widespread sympathy for the Patriots showed
the potency of the negative symbol of "British Whiggery" used by Democrats all through this period. While a content analysis of this theme
would be useful, Democratic campaigners used it conspicuously in 1840
and 1844.[75] Seemingly fantastic charges that Whig leaders were in the
pay of "British Gold" may have linked Whigs with Federalism and
stimulated Anglophobia among ethnic groups and classes of Americans
vulnerable to this appeal. To what extent anti-Whig reaction to this was
fed by the presence of New British voters in the Whig party cannot be
determined. The dispersal and rapid assimilation of the New British in
the native population probably worked against it. Moreover, New British
from Canada in the 1840s preferred the Democrats. Many Irish, Scotch
Irish, English, and French, with some New Englanders, settled Sanilac
County in the late forties, a frontier area just under the tip of Michigan's "thumb" on Lake Huron.[76] Sanilac's pioneers allegedly came as
refugees from Canadian turmoil; the county voted heavily Democratic
in its first elections from 1850 to 1854: 70 percent in 1852. Lexington,
the first center of settlement, voted 72 percent Democratic.

The demographic character of Whig-Free Soil towns in the 6 sample
counties suggests that the *non-Canadian* New British voted anti-Democratic. All the extreme anti-Democratic towns in those counties had relatively few foreign born, and those present tended to be disproportion-

[74] Democratic sympathy: *Detroit Morning Post*, Dec. 27, 28, 1837; Hemans,
Mason, 245-47, 337; Ross, "Patriot War," *MHC*, 21: 526-28, 576-77; *Free
Press*, Jan. 11, 16, April 17, 1838; Theller, *Canada in 1837-38*, I, 127, 188, 194;
Tiffany, *Publications. Buffalo Historical Society*, 8: 89-92; Bates, "By Gones of
Detroit," *MHC*, 22: 417-18. Patriot opponents: Ross, 527-28, 603-04; *Free
Press*, Jan. 13, 1838. Patriot politics: Lucius Lyon to E. Ransom, July 13, 1839,
"Lyon Letters," *MHC*, 27: 524; Lyon to T. C. Sheldon, Jan. 3, 1839, *ibid.*, 512;
same to same, Jan. 3, 1839, *ibid.*, 513; Joshua Howard to W. Woodbridge, May 12,
1841, and George C. Bates to Woodbridge, May 28, 1841, Woodbridge MSS, BHC.
Hemans claimed that in 1839 Elijah J. Roberts won appointment as clerk of the
Michigan House of Representatives because he was a "Patriot" leader, *Mason*, 454.
[75] For 1840 see e.g., *Free Press*, Sept. 10, 11, 1840, and *Kalamazoo Gazette*,
Oct. 30, 1840.
[76] *Portrait and Biographical Album of Sanilac County, Michigan* (Chicago,
1884), 453; Ruth Robbins Montieth, ed., "1850 Census of Michigan Counties
of Saginaw, Sanilac, Tuscolo, Huron, Midland, Mason, Newaygo, and Oceana,"
typed copy of MS schedule of federal census, 1957, BHC.

ately New British. This was particularly striking in Wayne County because it otherwise had such a large foreign population of non-British. Not so with the anti-Democratic towns:

	Percent Foreign	*Percent New British*
Taylor	17	13
Plymouth	7	5
Livonia	8	5
Brownstown	32	21
Sumpter	13	11

This same pattern appeared in 13 of 15 anti-Democratic towns in the other 5 counties. This suggests that the type of town that would attract New British immigrants and few non-New British would be likely to vote anti-Democratic. In this chicken-egg situation, cause and effect blur into one another. The New British certainly were assimilated more easily by those groups that tended to be the core Whig groups. The remark of an English immigrant in 1832 that he was "proud to be received as a citicen [sic]" was less likely to be made by a non-New British immigrant. In 1833 Hoffman noted that the English immigrants in St. Joseph County were "quite popular with the American settlers." And several decades later a county historian expressed the opinion that of all foreigners who came to America "there are none who make better citizens or who are more gladly welcomed than the hardy, honest sons of Old England."[77] The ramifications of these deep, persistent attitudes, affected the party loyalties acquired by most immigrant groups.

ESTIMATES AND ONE MAN

Relative estimates can be made of the voting distribution of ethnic and religious groups discussed above (see next page for estimates). It is obvious, though usually ignored, that understanding of why the majority of a group voted for a party is considerably more developed than why the minority did not. Why did 5 percent of the Irish Catholics deviate? Political scientists call this phenomenon a "breakage effect" or the "law of the imperfect mobilization of interests." Multiple and conflicting individual interests "guarantee that every group will have a minority in the 'other' political camp."[78] Those legions of individual interests,

[77] Tucker, ed., "John Fisher Correspondence," *Michigan History*, 35: 224-25. Hoffman, *Winter in the West*, 219. John S. Schenck, *History of Ionia and Montcalm Counties, Michigan* (Philadelphia, 1881), 425. See also William Candler to Homer C., July 20, 1849, and same to same, July 30, 1849, printed in Henry E. Candler, *A Century and One: Life Story of William Robert Candler* (New York and London, 1933), 146, 151-52, 161-62.

[78] Robert Lane, *Political Life*, 264.

	Percent Democratic	*Percent Anti-Democratic*
Catholic Irish	95	5
New Dutch	90	10
Catholic Germans	80	20
Protestant Germans	65	35
French Canadians	65	35
New British	40	60
Yankees	35	65
Yorkers	65	35
Pennsylvania Dutch	65	35
Churched Protestants	40	60
Evangelical Protestants	20	80
Quakers	5	95

shifting like sand over the short run, for the most part elude the historian of mass political movements.

Every group dealt with here contained, of course, many unique and complex individuals. No historian should fail to recall often Marc Bloch's question: "Is not man himself the greatest variable in nature?"[79] A consideration at this point of the complexities of one individual should be chastening. It can also, however, better illuminate some central themes developed above.

Edward A. Theller, the Patriot of 1837-38, began publishing his own newspaper in 1839, the *Spirit of '76*. Theller devoted himself to the rights and status of naturalized citizens, by which he usually meant Irish Catholics. Wanting "to extinguish all invidious distinctions," he traced anti-Irish feeling to "an European aristocratic origin" and especially to "British hatred." One might have expected Theller to have been a Democrat, but while he claimed friends in both parties he admitted to being "more opposed" to the Democrats than the Whigs.[80] Indeed, the force of his antipathies did do most to set his political compass. Theller also seemed genuinely imbued with antipartyism.[81]

Theller disliked the Democrats for their treatment of naturalized citizens. He complained particularly about special political appeals to "foreign voters," "Irish" or "German voters," or even to "Adopted Citizens." He, and many others like him, asked to be treated and addressed no differently from other citizens. Theller's attitude resembled that of Bishop Hughes in New York who advised his Irish flock not to put themselves so completely in the Democrats' pocket. This only earned the contempt of friends and enemies. More could be gained in the long run by inde-

[79] Marc Bloch, *The Historian's Craft* (New York, 1953), 197.
[80] [Detroit] *Spirit of '76*, Aug. 14, 30, 1839, MSL.
[81] *Spirit of '76*, Aug. 26, Nov. 2, 4, 5, 1839, MSL. Theller's antipartyism: *Spirit of '76*, Sept. 5, 18, 21, Nov. 1, 2, 1839, MSL.

pendently voting for men, measures, and principles.[82] Theller denied that foreigners owed the Democrats anything, certainly not for the liberal suffrage provision in the 1835 Constitution. He pointed rather to the insulting denial of office to foreigners who could nevertheless vote. "Native Americans," he knew, dwelled in both parties.[83]

In March 1840, Theller wrote an unusually candid analysis of ethnic political behavior and nativism. When men spoke of foreigners, he said, they usually meant Irish and Germans. Both groups voted heavily Democratic, although often against their interests. Theller attributed this to two "reasons." The first was "political." The Irish and Germans came from oppression and were told "and in fact they see, that the Whig party, far from being friendly to them, are in the daily habit of abusing them." Thus they vote for those who are for "equal rights and equal laws" in contrast to the Whigs "who, they are told, go for monopolies and privileges to the few, that they will not allow to the many." Secondly, most Irish and Germans were Catholic and were taught that the Whigs believed as did those who oppressed them in Europe, and would oppress them here; though false, these teachings were believed. The natives of England and Scotland, he added, had not been oppressed and thus lacked reason to fear the Whigs and vote Democratic.

When Theller made this analysis he was becoming disenchanted with Whiggery but still ostensibly on its side and not yet embittered by disappointment over patronage. His criticism is not easily discounted as exaggerated partisan attack. Theller understood the variance between social reality and its images, and recognized the power of stereotypes in governing voting and party loyalty. His juxtaposition of "equal rights" and "daily abuse" of foreigners gives deeper understanding of how groups who felt themselves outsiders responded to Democratic anti-aristocratic rhetoric. Of course this rhetoric served many purposes and there is no intention here to divest it of meaning in the realm of political economy. But it also absorbed traditional ethnic group antagonisms and reflected cleavages generated by different status and class positions of ethnoreligious groups. A hallmark of an aristocracy—or bourgeois upper class—is its exclusiveness and contempt for those below. The Yankee Protestant middle class certainly radiated this aura. The Democratic denunciation of "aristocracy" or "aristocratic Whigs" fed poor Irish hostility toward the nativist evangelical in-group they associated with Whig-

[82] Benson, *Concept*, 187-91.
[83] *Spirit of '76*, Aug. 30, Sept. 25, 1839, MSL. V. O. Key, Jr., observed that people still "resent the imputation that they belong to a voting bloc. They may vote for every union-endorsed candidate on the ticket or for every Catholic on the ballot and simultaneously declare that they make up their own minds how to vote," *Public Opinion and Democracy*, 519.

gery and British Protestant oppression. For other minority out-groups it probably performed similar functions.

Significantly, as Theller broke decisively with the Whigs he exploded into antievangelicalism. Theller's pen waxed livid over ultraist moral reform, piety, Antimasonry, Sabbatarianism, abolition, "and every hypocritical association." He believed that abolitionism connected church and state.[84] By April 1840, loss of the Senate printing contract enraged him to absolute hostility and the Whigs cast him out—perhaps with relief. By October the ticket of Van Buren and Johnson unblushingly adorned the masthead of the *Spirit of '76*. While explaining his support for Van Buren, whom he said he disliked, Theller again demonstrated that his strongest antipathies charted his course. "The anti-Masonic, Abolitionist, union of Church and State" elements interlaced the Whig party, and should Harrison win the country might witness a revival of the alien and sedition repression.[85]

Theller's migration makes manifest again the impact of Whig evangelicalism on party choice. Patterns of negative reaction between evangelicals and other groups explain much voting behavior in Michigan from 1835 to 1852. But they do not explain all of it. These patterns put in context some observable central tendencies. They do not usually account for short-run influences, and are most relevant for those persons closely tied to the norms of salient groups. A maverick such as Theller, for example, educated, traveled, possessed of insight and knowledge about politics, moving among a variety of social groups, had a cosmopolitan mentality removed from the limited perspectives of most Irish Catholics. His reaction to parties was understandably complex. He obviously experienced intense crosspressures, of which his antipartyism may have been a manifestation.

[84] *Spirit of '76*, March 17, 30, 1840, and March 12, April 11, 1840, MSL.
[85] *Spirit of '76*, April 12, 13, 14, 22, Sept. 17, Oct. 17, 1840, MSL.

X

Preparation for Change: 1844–1852

While the field of forces maintaining Democratic dominance seemed well entrenched, some of the props of that hegemony carried the seeds of its own destruction. Evangelicalism and nativism among the Whigs caused Whiggery to adapt poorly as a political structure in a society that was becoming more heterogeneous. Yet even as immigration added more votes to the sources of Democratic majorities, cultural shock grew among the native Protestants. It would feed a renewed, expanded, and pragmatic evangelicalism that would create a new political majority in the 1850s. Similarly, antislavery politics had worked resoundingly to the Democrats' advantage by drawing off votes from Whiggery. Both major parties kept political antislavery in a minority by practicing the politics of anti-Southernism and antiabolitionism. The long-run result was that they nurtured anti-Southernism around them and in their own ranks. This volcanic material slipped into apparently ever-deeper slumber after the compromise of 1850, but chance as well as the logic of earlier choices activated it just as the nativist evangelical reaction gathered momentum, and the two hurtled through the convulsive 1850s. But the preparation for all of this often wore a misleading guise.

CULTURAL POLITICS AND NATIVE AMERICANISM

American politicians played "ethnic politics" before the 1830s, but the advent of mass parties probably caused the game to become more deliberate than it had been. Michigan politicians "balanced" tickets by giving nominations to ethnic leaders, distributed patronage to group members, legislated aid to immigrant colonies, made speeches at ethnic clubs or celebrations, and generally worked with men recognized by the groups as their representatives. At least two of the variables affecting such transactions were the receptivity of the group and their voting strength.[1] The Democrats brought a better will to these chores and

[1] The Irish Catholics, besides being numerous, possessed notorious sensitivity for such matters. In the 1840s the state legislature changed the names of several

accordingly performed them with greater effectiveness. Whig instincts at their crudest perhaps appeared in the anxiety of Henry Powers of Monguagon, Wayne County, who asked in 1835 if he had been mistaken to have "believed all my life long, that our grand source of danger was from the sea of aliens constantly flooding upon us? Mistaken have I indeed been, if the profligate Irish, the mercenary border Dutch and German, and mindless Canadians, the hired Britains, and [illegible] foreigners, may all be put in the hands of heartless politicians . . . to be used at will, and yet without danger to the property of the individual or the quietude of the state." He could not imagine any magic in the atmosphere which would heal "the moral turpitude of the refuse foreigners the moment they inhaled it." Such extreme xenophobia and stereotyping were not common among Whigs, but a party with tendencies leading in Powers' direction would not be flexible. Apropos of magic in the atmosphere, Democrats of Detroit's Third Ward in 1840 resolved that "the moment a foreigner presses the soil of freedom and inhales the first breath of liberty" he was as well qualified as any to discharge the duties of a citizen: therefore Congress should "ameliorate" the naturalization law's 5-year waiting period.[2] These metaphysics no more represented all Democrats than Powers represented all Whigs, but they did suggest that the party which produced them would study well the formal and informal ways of ethnic politics.

When Whigs did move themselves to such stratagems, usually with reluctance, they were often not only clumsy but also risked a counterreaction in their own ranks. In 1838 Detroit Whigs, on the eve of a city election, distributed bread and pork to the city poor. A visitor described French Canadian and Irish women and children, as well as "well fed farmers" crowding up again and again to fill their baskets: "Most of the Whigs were sufficiently disgusted before the farce was ended." In 1850 Democrat David Stuart, son of Whig stalwart Robert Stuart, was "scouring the Country and of course spending money to secure his election" to Congress. His mother thought this "humbling," and was horrified at how her dead husband would have reacted to Dave and his wife attending the Irish Emigrants Ball: "Sainted father, if he could come back, how soon would he do it."[3]

---

projected counties from indigenous Indian nomenclature to those of places or men of the Emerald Isle; Hemans, *Mason*, 479; Edwin O. Wood, *Historic Mackinac* (New York, 1918), I, 367.

[2] *Free Press*, Oct. 17, 1840. For evidence of the Third Ward's strong belief in pluralism, *ibid*., Oct. 15, 1841. Henry P. Powers to Woodbridge, Oct. 5, 1835, Woodbridge MSS, BHC.

[3] Quoted in Hemans, *Mason*, 446-47. See also *Advertiser*, March 17, 19, 23, 31, 1838, and *Free Press*, Oct. 25, 1838. Elizabeth E. Stuart to Kate Stuart Baker, Nov. 1, 1850, *Stuart Letters*, I, 149.

The potential for a revulsion to ethnic politics within Whig ranks seems to have been fairly constant over the years. The safest Whig tactic was to charge Democrats with hypocrisy and to try to exploit potential sources of discord in the heterogeneous Democratic coalition. Whigs often charged the Democrats with cheating the Irish out of "prominent places" on their tickets; and Democratic nativists, they said, would secretly not vote for those foreigners who did not receive Democratic nominations.[4]

On balance the Democrats managed nominations well and distributed jobs to ethnics with a deliberate eye to elections. According to Robert Lane, "Ethnic politics breeds a kind of group patronage in which awarding jobs, contracts, or privileges to a member of the group, rather than to the individual becomes important." Systematic studies at the local level are needed of the relationship between party constituencies and patronage before one can generalize with any confidence. But that a relation existed there can be no doubt. In 1842 A. H. Stowell of Detroit, who described himself as a self-made man well-tutored by experience, wrote Governor John S. Barry regarding ethnic politics and patronage. His letter is a rare specimen and worth quoting at length. Stowell recommended that Barry take account of

the different floting class of our population we have probably 1000 voters in this County that cannot read the tickett they put into the Ballot Box [.] among them are a few men in Each Division that they Look to as Leaders and if those Leaders get some little Emoluments all the rest are satisfied if not all of them go with the Leaders for instance in 1840 one man an Irishman got dissatisfied in this county and after he went through this he went to wastanaw and from there to Monro. I followed him myself but could accomplish little or nothing in counteracting his moves [.] in the first place he was there native Countryman he was of the same religion againe he was acquainted with the leading men and now [knew] how to excite their passions [.] again we have the Dutchman in this place humble men in the Eyes of most men but with their own Countrymen they have the power and this and McComb and other Counties to Controle more political influence than 20 of what we terme Greate men and the same with a few men among the french population. and then among the English and Scotch [.] now all these men ask is that a few men leading men and honest industrious men maybe Employed in an[d] about the railroad.[5]

Negotiations like this usually occur informally, not to say *sub rosa*, but politicians also court ethnic votes by openly cultivating organizations with which particular groups identify. In the 1840s the Irish Repeal Association briefly achieved prominence as such a formal pressure group.

---

[4] See, e.g., *Advertiser*, Oct. 12, 22, 23, 25, 26, Nov. 2, 3, and esp. Nov. 11, 1842, and *Detroit Constitutional Democrat*, March 30, 1844.

[5] A. H. Stowell to Gov. John S. Barry, Feb. 7, 1842, Executive Records, Elections, MHCom. Lane, *Political Life*, 239-40.

Its ostensible purpose was to promote Home Rule for Ireland. It served also as an outlet for Anglophobia and stumping ground for campaigners. In 1843 the Repeal Association became the means by which a Whig was elected mayor of Detroit with the help of Catholic Irish votes. Whig Zina Pitcher, physician and scholar, sometime Democrat, and President of the Repeal Association, won the mayoralty in an election which otherwise went Democratic. Pitcher's popularity and Irish pique over nominations, according to the *Free Press*, led to this astonishing result which had the Whig *Advertiser* cooing over "our warm-hearted Irish friends."[6]

Irish defection at this point probably resulted also from a factional fight in the party between the ascendant group which had put John Barry in the governor's chair and the "old faction" associated with John Norvell and Isaac Crary. Robert McClelland and Lucius Lyon also orbited in the new Democratic constellation and it is pertinent to recall that they and Barry in 1835 had opposed Norvell on alien voting preferring a basic requirement of citizen voting. The ethnic minorities in the Democratic party seem to have been associated with the Norvell faction and their relations with the Barry group were cool.[7] At any rate, in the summer of 1843 political wonders continued to explode like Fourth of July rockets. The Whigs began finding nominees for office among Repeal Associations and nominated Pitcher for governor. The *Free Press* said that the Whigs believed that Pitcher would draw "two thousand Irish democrats" to the Whig ticket. The *Advertiser* insisted that "adopted citizens" be regarded as "American citizens" now that they were becoming "undeceived" of the Locos, announced that Pitcher's qualifications for office included a full blooded Irish maternal grandfather, apologized for printing an anti-Catholic squib by mistake, and denounced American Republicanism or "any crusade against Catholics" as "anti-Republican and anti-Christian." Although Pitcher was badly defeated, he ran better in Detroit than the Whig gubernatorial candidates of 1841 and 1845, and did particularly well on the west side of town where most of the Irish lived. If the Irish did cast a sizable vote for the Whigs, it was a phenomenon not often repeated, and probably confined to Detroit.[8]

Some Whigs, of course, despised the Irish courtship. William Wood-

---

[6] *Free Press*, March 7, 1843; *Advertiser*, March 7, 1843; Ann Arbor, *Signal of Liberty*, March 13, 1843. The I.R.A.'s organizing officers included prominent Whigs and Democrats, *Advertiser*, Sept. 13, 1841.

[7] *Free Press*, Feb. 28, March 18, 1842. Robert McClelland to John S. Bagg, Sept. 1, 1849, Bagg MSS, Huntington Library. *Advertiser*, Nov. 12, 1842.

[8] *Free Press*, Aug. 26, 1843; *Advertiser*, July 22, Oct. 4, 5, 19, Nov. 2, 7, 1843. In August 1843, one other I.R.A. existed in the state in Ann Arbor. Its president was Whig editor Franklin Sawyer, *Signal of Liberty*, Aug. 14, 1843. After the 1843 election the *Michigan Argus* congratulated the Irish farmers of Northfield for supporting the Democrats, Oct. 18, Nov. 18, 1843. Township returns for that year are not available.

bridge referred contemptuously to the Whig "Irish Repealers" as a "new sect among us" and his son William reviled the politicians who were "making a great handle of this 'Irish Repeal' concern. There are a great many about Detroit who expect to get boosted up over the shoulders of others, to attain party ends and get hold of the reins of power, men who are themselves the dung of the earth, who do not know who their grand-fathers were, the very impersonations of putridity who rise into high places by the very men to whom they would not extend the hand of charity to, after they had got into power."[9] Whig reactions bore deeply, of course, because Irish Catholics were involved. When ethnic politics involved Germans, Whigs usually did not become apoplectic. Indeed, they seemed to deal with the Germans with relative ease, if not with success. The Germans did not vote as strongly Democratic as the Irish and, best of all, many were Protestant. A Washtenaw County Whig described the German population there in 1844 as "truth-loving and reliable" and capable of being "brought into the right political path."[10]

Wayne County Whigs frequently ran candidates of German descent for city offices and state representative. On one occasion the Democrats circulated tickets including the German Whig nominee for state representative, for the purpose, the *Advertiser* said, "of getting the German vote for the balance of their ticket." In 1848 Detroit Whigs nominated Frederick Buhl, a merchant-manufacturer for mayor, and it was the first time "that a descendant of Germans has been designated to so important a post." Although Buhl won—in neither of the most German wards, Four and Seven, did the vote surge for the Whigs. In the next city election the Whigs ran better in both wards. While strong shifts in the electorate may have been concealed in the aggregate data, Buhl's candidacy did not seem to stir greatly the "German vote." Perhaps this should not have been expected. Buhl was of German descent but was not a poor immigrant. Born in Pennsylvania, wealthy, and Presbyterian, he qualified as a member of McCoy's economic elite of Wayne County. German voters had less reason for identifying him with the "Fatherland" and more for linking him with the Yankee Presbyterian elite group so prominent in Whiggery.[11]

Whigs also maneuvered to make allies of the French. In 1839 Whig

[9] W. Woodbridge to Hon. Willie P. Mangum, Aug. 25, 1843; W. L. Woodbridge to Dudley Woodbridge, July 8, 1843, Woodbridge MSS, BHC.

[10] M. Howard, Ann Arbor, to W. Woodbridge, July 8, 1844. Howard said that the circulation of Whig campaign tracts in German were "deemed by our German Whig friends here most excellent." P. B. Thurston, Mt. Clemens, to Woodbridge, Aug. 27, 1844, Woodbridge MSS, BHC.

[11] Quotes from *Advertiser*, Nov. 2, 1846 and March 6, 1848. McCoy, "Wayne County Economic Elites, 1844, 1860," 40, described Buhl as a merchant-manufacturer.

leaders in Monroe and Macomb counties expected William Woodbridge to do very well among the old French population because of his long residence in Michigan, his ability to speak French, and his alleged friendship for the French *Citoyens*. Woodbridge's ability to speak French placed him on demand through the 1840s with Whig leaders in Macomb and Monroe. Whigs negotiated with local spokesmen, their rivals, or dissident minorities within French communities.[12] When the Whigs lost Macomb County in 1840, however, it seemed characteristic for a Whig leader to complain that there was "not one man" on the Whig ticket "calculated to call out any portion of the French population to our support, who number about one hundred fifty voters in the lower part of the county."[13]

More Whigs than Democrats shared the sentiments of Whig Thomas Rowland, Detroit Postmaster in 1842. He declined an invitation to officiate at a St. Patrick's Temperance dinner because he could not persuade himself that he liked "the idea even indirectly of countenancing the absurd custom of keeping saints day" and did not want to foster "a foreign feeling of separate nationality amongst those who profess to be American citizens. . . . The mawkish efforts which are so much in use by demagogues through repeal societies and other means to flatter that class of citizens is exciting pretensions and claims on their part entirely inimical to the public good." Rowland well realized that his was "an act of temerity which would doubtless be pronounced unwise by any modern politician of the school democratic."[14]

And so it would be. The inflexibility of the Rowlands lessened Whig effectiveness and worked to Democratic advantage. Some Democrats no doubt shared Rowland's sentiments, but practical considerations seem to have governed most of them. Even Robert McClelland, a conservative on alien suffrage, illustrated this pragmatism as he worried about how the Irish would vote in 1843: "Will the Irish vote be cast for Barry and if not, will this affect me [?]. . . . You must not rely on your county and Washtenaw on mere reports. They ought to be seen and those who have influence with them. And seeing them often will do no harm. . . . Let us not act on the principle that one can do without the aid of such men. This

[12] Circular, "Attention! Aux Citoyens Français, et Anciens Habitans du Michigan"; William Dusell, Macomb, to Woodbridge, July 8, 1839; Daniel S. Bacon, Monroe, to Woodbridge, Sept. 1, 1839; Henry D. Terry, Mt. Clemens, to Woodbridge, Sept. 27, 1844; Oliver Johnson, Monroe, to Woodbridge, Oct. 22, 1844; William W. Studdifud, Monroe, to Woodbridge, Sept. 16, 1848; George Laurian, et al., Monroe, to Woodbridge, Oct. 12, 1848, Woodbridge MSS, BHC.

[13] Richard Butler, Mt. Clemens, to Woodbridge, Nov. 6, 1840, Woodbridge MSS, BHC.

[14] Thomas Rowland to Woodbridge, March 17, 1842, Woodbridge MSS, BHC.

is the course of the Whig party and it has occasioned them many a disaster. Let us be firm to our principles, but conciliatory in our conduct towards men."[15]

Ethnic politics overlapped to some extent with denominational politics, which here means primarily the politics generated by rivalries between the major native Protestant denominations. A broader religious politics also functioned in the chasm opened by the Catholic-Protestant cleavage. An example of the latter appeared in 1835 as the first party contest gathered headway. John R. Williams, Detroit Democrat and Catholic, wrote to Michigan's Territorial Delegate, Lucius Lyon on the subject of Indian missions—and religious politics. Williams's spiritual father, Bishop Résé, had persuaded him that Catholics were being discriminated against by the federal government. One Protestant mission received $2,000 in aid while six Catholic missions, serving many more Indians, received a total of $1,000. This "partiality" rewarded Catholics poorly for their immense service in "civilizing those unfortunate beings." The deserving Bishop enjoyed great popularity for his talent and "liberal principles." In case Lyon had missed the point Williams abruptly switched to discussing the prospects of the Democracy in Michigan: "Our party is thriving fast . . . and the Catholics are generally warm supporters of the democratic cause and principles. The Rev. Bishop is a decided friend of the present administration. The Catholics hold it to be their duty, to support the government under which they live.—hundreds of Germans and Irish emigrants are every day taking incipient measures to become naturalized Citizens—democracy is increasing daily in strength, and Michigan, I trust, will take her stand in the Union, as a decidedly democratic state."[16]

Religious and ethnic politics obviously blended together. As the different "nations" of Catholics grew after 1835, ethnic politics *within* the Catholic group became increasingly important. French, German, Irish, and native Catholic rivalries created problems for church administrators —and Democratic party managers. Denominational rivalries, on the other hand, had their origins in the intense competition among Protestant

[15] Robert McClelland, Sept. 5, 1843, and Robert McClelland, May 30, 1843, Bagg MSS, Huntington Library. Gov. Alpheus Felch admitted to not giving enough care to "sectional considerations" in his appointments. He may also have neglected other considerations such as his unwillingness to attend a St. Patrick's Day celebration indicated. A. Felch to Lucretia Felch, March 18, 1846, Felch MSS, MHCol. Also, same to same, Jan. 26, 1846.

[16] John R. Williams to Lyon, Feb. 6, 1835; another Democratic leader also pressured Lyon on this point, John McDonell to Lyon, Feb. 14, 1835, Lyon MSS, Clements. Religious politics and Indian missions constituted a source of trouble between Gabriel Richard and Lewis Cass much earlier, Mast, *Always the Priest*, 282-83, 312-14.

sects for converts and public status. The contest between "free, absolutist groups in the vast free market of souls"[17] extended into politics as sects sought testimony to their worth by getting government bestowed patronage or some other kind of official recognition, as illustrated by the maneuvering accompanying appointments to Michigan's Board of University Regents. Until the twelve regents' offices became elective in 1851 they were appointed by the governor with the advice and consent of the Senate. Denominations competed for representation on the Board and bellowed with alarm at the threat of any rival controlling it. In 1841 as Governor Woodbridge made his appointments to the Board, the Senate recoiled at growing Presbyterian and Episcopalian domination of the Board of Regents, "and a majority seemed to think, that a more equal distribution among the different denominations would be right and proper and give a more general satisfaction." The Democrats criticized the Whigs precisely on this ground and claimed that only because of the efforts of their gubernatorial candidate, John Barry, "Methodists, Baptists and some other denominations have now (though not to the fullest extent which their relative numbers would seem to deserve) a representation in the Regency."[18] After three Woodbridge appointments were rejected, the *Free Press* admonished the Whigs that in the university, as in government, all interests should be equally represented: "This representation of different interests is what is meant by checks and balances in government, and the politician who disregards them is either ignorant of the nature of our free institutions . . . or wants . . . character to overcome his personal prejudices."[19] A study of patronage distribution would be necessary before Democratic claims regarding patronage policy could be accepted, although the composition of the Democratic Party argues in favor of its being more attuned to society's heterogeneity. Practical politics, and perhaps some "melting pot" idealism, made the Democrats more responsive to the aspirations of groups feeling frustrated or excluded and needing recognition. A number of out-groups seem to have been persuaded that promotion of their "welfare and fame,"[20] that is, of their interests and status, was more likely to occur under Democratic auspices.

[17] Sidney Mead, "Denominationalism," *Church History*, 23: 316. A good discussion of how denominational politics and patronage affected Indiana parties in the 1840s can be found in Robert D. Clark, *The Life of Matthew Simpson* (New York, 1956), 99-111.

[18] James M. Edmunds to Woodbridge, Feb. 27, 1841, Woodbridge MSS, BHC. *Free Press*, Oct. 20, 1841.

[19] *Free Press*, Sept. 12, 1841. The Regents themselves in appointing a faculty tried to balance appointments among leading denominations, Willis F. Dunbar, *Michigan Record in Higher Education,* 69.

[20] *Advertiser*, Oct. 23, 1848, used this phrase in arguing the opposite point of view.

In the 1844 campaign some Whigs tried to break the hold of the Democrats on Irish, French, and German voters, and to spread the idea that more nativism and anti-Catholicism existed among Democrats. But church burnings in Philadelphia, agitation to change the naturalization law, and the Whig origins of most nativists caused the election to testify to the impact of history and existing fears and hopes.[21] After Polk's victory, Whig frustration found a scapegoat in foreigners. Although Whigs recognized the damage done by the Liberty Party, their attitudes to foreigners became reckless. They conducted a semi-public debate as to whether a new party and an explicit appeal to nativism were necessary.

The *Oakland Gazette* claimed that "the filth of Europe" had browbeaten and murdered Americans on their way to the polls. Scores of illegal alien votes went to the Democrats while "gangs of drunken Irishmen" clubbed legal voters away. Since the present immigration rate would create a foreign majority of voters by 1848, the *Gazette* found nativist doctrines attractive: "Why not change the naturalization laws, why not let the foreign born wait twenty-one years to vote as did the native born, and who else but Americans should rule America?"[22] From Mackinac County a Whig "Protest" signer of 1835 regretted to learn that "the foreners have *elected Polk*. I do hope this will Rouse Our American Citisens to a Sense of there Duty [sic]." George W. Wisner, leading Pontiac Whig, asked William Woodbridge if foreigners would not always oppose Whig principles and sound doctrines and urged "a bold appeal to native Americanism, get up a storm of passion and sweep the country. . . . The contest will be a bitter one I know, but what will it be in 20 years or so when our children will be called upon to fight." Wisner firmly believed that "the catholic religion, united with lawless democracy, will seise [sic] this country . . . unless it is put down immediately. . . . All the whigs of the north and part of the democrats are squinting towards native Americanism. *What shall we do?*"[23] A Monroe Whig leader also reported many Whigs to be talking of adopting Americanism, while in Washtenaw County Whigs decided that "Native Americanism must not be agitated in the country to the extent it is carried in the cities."[24]

[21] *Advertiser*, March 12, 1844; *Free Press*, June 7, 10, July 27, Aug. 3, 14, Sept. 17, Oct. 1, 14, 16, 18, 19, 22, 24, 25, 28, Nov. 2, 5, 1844; *Michigan Argus*, Oct. and Nov., 1844 passim; *Niles Republican*, Aug. 10, 31, Nov. 2, 1844; Howell, *Livingston Courier*, July 3, 1844, Resolutions of Democratic Convention, Livingston County, June 29, 1844.

[22] Nov. 6, 13, 1844. The Irish bore the brunt of the *Gazette*'s indignation Nov. 13, 27, 1844. The Ann Arbor, *State Journal* (W.) took up the same line, *Gazette*, Dec. 4, 1844.

[23] Michael Dousman, Mackinac, to Woodbridge, Jan. 7, 1845; George W. Wisner to Woodbridge, Nov. 14, 1844; also Wisner to Woodbridge, Jan. 13, 1845, Woodbridge MSS, BHC, also *Oakland Gazette*, Nov. 13, 1844.

[24] Oliver Johnson, Monroe, to Woodbridge, Nov. 20, 1844; H. G. Crittenden, Saline, to Woodbridge, Dec. 26, 1844, Woodbridge MSS, BHC.

The nativist feelings running through the Whig party were no secret and Democrats began predicting Whiggery's demise. The Detroit *Advertiser* opposed any bolt to Americanism as impractical, and its explanation was revealing. The Whig Party, it said, was already the most effective agent of native American principles and could be known by its enemies: "Abolitionists, foreign influence, foreign money and foreign votes."[25]

In early 1845 a native American newspaper appeared in Detroit, and a native American ticket entered the city election. Of 1,644 votes the "Natives" got only 32, but it probably was a phony ticket. Considering the nativist hue of Detroit Whiggery, and that the native mayoral candidate, merchant Orus Field, had been a regular Democrat, the vote hardly measured nativist sentiment adequately.[26] Another American newspaper surfaced briefly during 1846 in Ann Arbor, but the nativist spasm was fairly well spent by then.[27]

In the late 1840s the parties returned to image-making routines developed earlier and to working out techniques for dealing with the slavery extension controversy. With the subsidence of the latter in 1850, Michigan Whigs vigorously renewed courtship of the foreign and Catholic vote. In 1851 a fresh Whig leader emerged as Zachariah Chandler won an upset victory to become mayor of Detroit. Chandler plunged heartily into ethnic politics. At St. Patrick's Day celebrations he joked that he was Yankee by birth, English by name, and one-half Irish by blood. He endorsed the Irish Emigrant Society and St. Patrick's celebrations because they promoted assimilation and Americanism. Breaking the ice of "national" feelings, they prompted neighbors to forget whether they were native or foreign, Protestant or Catholic. Chandler flattered the Irish with references to their sacrifices in the American Revolution and no doubt paid similar compliments to the Germans when he joined a fund raising drive for German liberty.[28]

The Whigs nominated the newcomer Chandler for governor in 1852, and by all accounts never tried harder to woo Irish and German votes.

[25] *Advertiser*, Nov. 15, 18, 20, 1844; also *Free Press*, Nov. 14, 1844, and *Michigan Argus*, Nov. 20, 27, Dec. 4, 1844.

[26] Three issues of the *Detroit American Vineyard* are in BHC; Oct. 23, 1846, April 23 and Dec. 17, 1847. A copy of the *Vineyard*, Nov. 22, 1844, II, 4, its probable predecessor, is in the MHCol. *Detroit Directory, 1845*, 121, said that Edward D. Ellis printed the Detroit *American Citizen*. For city election: *Free Press*, March 3, 8, 1845; *Advertiser*, Feb. 27, 1845. Field was a delegate to a Democratic county convention, *Free Press*, May 29, 1843.

[27] The Ann Arbor *American* appeared due to the efforts of Whig editor E. L. Fuller, according to the Ann Arbor, *News and Advertiser*, Dec. 22, 1857, special edition, MHCol.

[28] *Advertiser*, March 19, 1851. Warren W. Florer, "The Liberty Meeting in Detroit, December 1851," *Michigan History*, 16 (Autumn 1932), 100.

All through the Northwest the 1852 Whig campaign for Winfield Scott sought to win foreigners and Catholics. The Democrats responded by escalating attention to ethnic and religious themes, frequently becoming hysterical. Judging by postelection analyses and voting returns, Whig ethnic politics failed again. Foreign Catholics, as well as German Lutherans, French Canadians, and Dutch Reformed Christians remained strongly in the Democratic camp.[29]

As in 1844-45 the humiliation of defeat sharpened the resentment of Whig nativists against foreigners and Catholics, and perhaps more than usual because the latter had spurned Whig offerings. This frustration merged with a nativist mania developing on other fronts. Several dramas of cultural confrontation flowed together in 1852-53 leading to a party-shattering upheaval.

ANTIABOLITION AND ANTI-SOUTHERNISM

Though they often drained away crucial votes from the Whigs, the Liberty and Free Soil parties failed to *convert* many voters to political antislavery. Political antislavery after 1844 also affected the parties deeply in other ways. The major parties met it by undercutting it with tactical and symbolic moves of an antislavery nature, and by "niggering," that is, by stigmatizing abolitionists as deviants and charging them with favoring the general social integration of blacks. However, it became crucial for both parties simultaneously to convey their independence of Southern domination. From 1844 to 1850 Southern aggressiveness joined with political antislavery to make anti-Southernism a pervasive element in campaigns. After 1850 the controversy over territorial expansion quieted, and anti-Southernism retreated to those minorities engaged in a declining Free Soil movement. But among the leaders of the major parties who had practiced it, and among many of their followers, a budding resentment and matured rhetoric had accumulated which could be activated by renewal of sectional conflict.

Abolitionists had begun in the 1830s with a hatred of an institution and some compassion for the slaveholder as a partial victim of an evil system. They also had seen slaveholders as men to be converted to emancipation by moral suasion. Their anti-Southernism increased as slaveholders in Congress sought to stamp out abolition everywhere and as more abolitionists felt slavery's political power. Abolitionists were the first to resent keenly and to complain publicly of the slave-

---

[29] *Advertiser* and *Free Press*, 1852, passim; *Coldwater Sentinel* (Branch Co.), Aug. 20, Oct. 15, 22, 1852; *Marshall Statesman*, Oct. 13, 20, Nov. 10, 1852; *Adrian Watchtower*, Oct. 5, 19, 26, Nov. 2, 1852; *Pontiac Jacksonian*, Sept. 29, 1852; Thomas, *Nativism*, 63-78; Lucas, ed. *Dutch Immigrant Memoirs*, I, 532, 542-43, for Whig gestures toward the Dutch.

holders' influence in the national government and of the subservience of Northern politicians which made it possible. By 1841 it was common for an abolitionist to protest that "the people feel very much disposed . . . to charge our Northern members with bowing at the beck of the South. We truly feel that the Southern influence, Slavocracy, bears too great a sway." Although abolitionist concern for the brutalized slave had earned them ridicule and repression, many men now looked forward "to the time when we can send men . . . with Northern principles men who will stand upon their legs and do the business of the North in such a manner as is for their interest instead of crouching to the South."[30] Although the Liberty Party fervently pursued its one-idea from 1840 to 1847, it helped awaken Northern consciousness on a wide range of issues. The abolitionist campaign against Congress's "Gag Rule," for example, educated Northerners in the basics of anti-Southernism.

While the direct impact of abolitionism was not negligible, its indirect impact on Whiggery was more important. Because the Whig constituency was most vulnerable to the Liberty appeal, the Whigs moved furthest along the anti-Southern spectrum. Conviction, too, joined political expediency here, because many Whigs genuinely resented what they saw as disproportionate Southern influence in national affairs. Opposition to the use of the federal government's power, while not confined to Southerners, seemed to Whigs a peculiar product of "Virginia arrogance and presumption." Tyler's veto of the Bank Bill caused a Whig to declare that custom, court decisions, and popular consent did not weigh "a feather" in Southern estimation "when one of their favorite [states rights] abstractions are put into the scale."[31] Whig state platforms from 1843 to 1852 emitted almost as much anti-Southernism as did Liberty declarations.[32] Yet Whig hostility to the South cohabited quite cozily with anti-abolition. Whig bitterness against the Liberty Party waxed especially strong after Henry Clay's narrow defeat in 1844. Rage directed at abolitionists and the South appeared in neat tandem in the remark of an anti-slavery Whig that the slaveholders owed abolitionists a debt of gratitude "for it is alone their *inverted* influence, that keeps back the mass from strong expression of deep abhorrence, at their [Southern] doings"; because of divisions created by abolitionists "we are ruled by a minority and the spirit of freedom and personal independence is crushed by the haughty, domineering insolence of Southern *chivalry*, and prostrated by

---

[30] Erastus Ingersoll, Farmington, to Woodbridge, Dec. 9, 1841, Woodbridge MSS, BHC. For similar attitudes see James Birney to Lewis Tappan, Saginaw, Jan. 14, 1842, and Birney to *Albany Evening Journal*, May 19, 1845, in Dumond, ed., *Birney*, II, 659, 938; also *Signal of Liberty*, July 28, 1841.

[31] Thomas Rowland to Woodbridge, Aug. 24, 1841, Woodbridge MSS, BHC.

[32] Randall, "Gubernatorial Platforms, 1834-1864," 43, 53, 54, 59, 60, 62.

the servile hopes of a slaveholding patronage."[33] When the *Detroit Advertiser* told the South that it should stop encroaching on Northern rights, it found itself criticized by Democrats and abolitionists: "The one because it is the ready parasite of the south; and the other because it wishes to engross for itself all northern feeling."[34]

During 1844 the Democrats' promotion of Texas annexation and the Liberty presence forced Whigs in many areas to lash out at the South and its peculiar institution.[35] As the actual annexation of Texas appeared imminent in early 1845 one Whig declared he would rather see the Union dissolved than "see the perpetual exercise of Southern domination. . . . what . . . has the North gained by the Union in forty years? What but the derision and contumely of our Southern masters (who have in fact ruled the Nation) and the privilege of footing the Bills of Southern prodigality."[36]

Whigs who favored Congressional appropriations for rivers and harbors improvements and saw them defeated by the Democrats because of the "fierce opposition" of "slave-holding politicians" had additional reasons for disliking the "chivalry" and "doughfaces." When Polk vetoed a harbors bill in 1846, he loosed a flood of Whig anti-Southernism and made both Whigs and Democrats more receptive to the Wilmot Proviso preventing the extension of slavery into territories acquired in the Mexican War. In 1846 Wayne County Whigs condemned the "Southern Policy" of the administration and its Congressional majority. After mentioning the harbor bill veto and the Polk administration's lowering of the tariff, the Whigs resolved to "wage an endless war against the Southern Policy and against the further extension of Slave Territory."[37] Anti-Southernism and opposition to the extension of slavery did not cloak economic motives, rather, for Whigs vetoed internal improvements appropriations and lower tariffs flowed from the same complex of power and arrogance which again and again made the primacy of its "interests" the price of Union. By 1847 the Whig party was committed to the

[33] Quote from Henry W. Taylor, Marshall, to Woodbridge, Feb. 16, 1846, Woodbridge MSS, BHC; also Fladeland, *Birney*, 246, 247; *Niles Republican*, Nov. 23, 1844; *Advertiser*, Nov. 12, 13, 15, 25, 26, 1844.

[34] *Advertiser*, Nov. 19, 1842.

[35] E.g., *Address of George W. Wisner* (1844), Jenison Collection, MSL. Anti-Southernism was also manifest in a speech of Woodbridge's, MS dated 1844, Woodbridge MSS, BHC.

[36] "The country must awake and send more *businessmen*, men that will do something beside make everlasting speeches," J. J. Deming to Woodbridge, Feb. 17, 1845, Woodbridge MSS, BHC; also, *Advertiser*, March 11, 1845.

[37] Letters of Woodbridge reprinted in Lanman, *Life of William Woodbridge*, 92-93, 93-94; Oliver Johnson, Monroe, to Woodbridge, July 1, 1845, Woodbridge MSS, BHC; *Advertiser*, Feb. 24, 1844, Sept. 22, 1846. Streeter *Political Parties*, 234-35, 237, 238-40.

Wilmot Proviso. While its state platform rejected slavery extension at length (but treated Southerners gently) Whig newspapers and local conventions and speakers roasted the South in a heated effort to show that the Liberty Party was quite unnecessary.[38]

Anti-Southernism in the Democratic Party gained ground much more slowly. Some Democrats thought it reprehensible to be a "most Southern Northern man,"[39] and at one point the legislative party apparently endorsed the Wilmot Proviso, but Democrats handled the slavery extension nettle ultimately as professional politicians who placed party unity above all. Yet even the tactical anti-Southernism of the Democrats must have contributed to a sectional consciousness. The Southern demand for a witchhunt of abolitionists in the North had made some Democrats uncomfortable, but the defeat of Martin Van Buren for the 1844 Presidential nomination probably created resentment among some Michigan Democrats. Southerners and their allies used Texas annexation and slavery extension to defeat Van Buren and to nominate Polk. The Michigan organization swallowed Polk and Democratic legislators passed resolutions in January 1845, cheering on the quick annexation of Texas. But as one student of Democratic reactions to Texas concluded, "rather than being converted by a passion for manifest destiny, Michigan Democrats chose to support annexation because it was a political necessity."[40] An undercurrent of discontent with Southern imperiousness accompanied acceptance of such necessities, and it grew stronger as the Mexican War intensified the controversy over the extension of slavery.

In January 1847 the Democratic-led legislature endorsed the Polk administration's conduct of the war, but Proviso sentiment grew. The Senate defeated but the House recommended extending the Ordinance of 1787 over any new national territory, an implicit though tactful endorsement of the Proviso. In January 1848, the House passed an explicit antislavery extension resolution with only three negative votes, but in March the Senate defeated a similar measure. During 1848 Democrats swung away from the Proviso, rallying around Lewis Cass, the probable nominee of the national convention for President, a Texas annexationist and advocate of popular sovereignty opposed to the Proviso. Democratic leaders wheeled behind Michigan's favorite son. Party unity no doubt promised much by way of patronage, prestige, and power. As Whigs

[38] *Advertiser*, Sept. 18, 1847, also Sept. 28, 29, 30, Oct. 6; the Grand Rapids, *Grand River Eagle* made an especially intense attack on Southerners, e.g., Sept. 11, 1847.

[39] James B. Hunt, Pontiac, to Alpheus Felch, Jan. 24, 1848, Felch MSS, MHCol.

[40] On Democratic factions, James C. N. Paul, *Rift in the Democracy* (Philadelphia, 1951); H. O. Mann, Monroe, to A. Ten Eyck, Nov. 18, 1843, Bagg MSS, Huntington Library; quotation from Stephen Maizlish, "Michigan Democratic Party Politics and the Annexation of Texas," 2, University of Michigan History 866 Paper, 1968, MS, MHCol.

sounded more anti-Southern than ever, and in some districts coalesced with Free Soil, Democrats responded with a pragmatism that led one newspaper, for example, to support Cass and attack the Proviso, but also to declare that "territories now free must FOREVER REMAIN FREE."[41]

Although Van Buren and Free Soil attracted more Democratic voters than Liberty ever did (or Free Soil and Hale in 1852), not many normally Democratic areas defected in 1848 and Free Soil drew most heavily from the Whigs. Most rank and file Democratic voters followed their leaders. If the new strength of Free Soil did not boost anti-Southernism, certainly the continuing acrimony between North and South in Congress caused more wrestling in the Michigan parties over slavery extension.

Meanwhile, Democrat Alpheus Felch, a moderate on slavery-related issues, left the governor's chair to be replaced by Epaphroditas Ransom, a Proviso Democrat and member of a Western faction feeling injured over nominations, patronage, and the cavalier treatment of rivers and harbors improvements by Cass and the national Democrats. On January 1, 1849, Ransom asserted Congress's power to regulate slavery. The legislature added, by large votes in both houses, that Congress also had the duty to prohibit slavery in new territories. Yet this same legislature then reelected Lewis Cass—Proviso opponent and champion of popular sovereignty—as United States Senator. A bloc of Western Democrats tried to elect Ransom and failed, narrowly in the Senate and lopsidedly in the House. The large majorities confirming Cass's nomination meant that some men who voted for the Proviso also cast ballots for a Senator who was a known opponent of the Proviso.

Cass's reinstatement signaled the start of a great consolidation movement within the Democratic Party as it drew together for 1849 and worked out strategies for compromising internal differences and squeezing antislavery out of the political arena. Fears of a split and defections to Free Soil prompted "some mutual concession and a spirit of forebearance."[42] The party chose the hardy wheel horse John Barry to run for governor. He soon announced that he favored "excluding slavery from the territories now free" and opposed making the subject a test of political faith.[43] Similarly, Macomb County Democrats admitted "a dif-

---

[41] Streeter, *Political Parties*, 99-103; Phineas Homan, Detroit, to A. Felch, Washington, D.C., Jan. 24, 1848; James B. Hunt, Pontiac, to Felch, Jan. 24, 1848; George B. Cooper to Felch, Jan. 28, 1848; M. Hawks, Allegan, to Felch, July 12, 1848; Phineas Homan to Felch, July 20, 1848; William S. Brown to Felch, July 22, 1848, Felch MSS, MHCol. *Coldwater Sentinel*, Oct. 26, 1848.

[42] David A. Noble to A. Felch, Jan. 22, 1849; Thomas Fitzgerald, Niles, to A. Felch, June 26, 1849, Felch MSS, MHCol.

[43] On Barry's conservatism on slavery see Thomas "John Stewart Barry, 1831-1851," 101-03; Robert McClelland to A. Felch, May 18, 1845, Felch MSS,

ference of opinion" on Congress's legislating on "the domestic affairs of states or territories" but they did not consider it "a test of democracy or as affording the slightest ground why the Democracy . . . should be divided and defeated."[44]

The Whig-Free Soil coalition decried the Barry nomination as the triumph of pro-Southern "Hunkerism" in the Democracy,[45] but the Democratic state convention went beyond any previously in opposing the extension of slavery to New Mexico and California. Some county and district conventions, meanwhile, lashed the South verbally.[46] In 1850 the legislature endorsed a free California and would not approve eulogies by Cass and Clay on the 1850 Compromise, yet it did rescind the 1849 legislature's instructions to support the Proviso. This vacillation accompanied an embracing of the Compromise by the Democracy. Lewis Cass and Alexander Buel, an incumbent Congressman who had voted for the Fugitive Slave Law, campaigned hard for justification. Buel lost to a Whig-Free Soil coalition candidate as the Democrats went under in two of three Congressional districts in 1850, but this was only the tail lash of the dying sectional storm. Simultaneously, Democrats carried a large majority of elections for state representatives and in the legislature thereafter enshrined and monumentalized the Compromise as the Union's Salvation. In 1851 Democrats brusquely dismissed petitions asking for a repeal of the Fugitive Slave Law and incanted the virtues of the Compromise formula as the guarantor of moderation.[47]

Robert McClelland, an opponent of Texas annexation and identified with Proviso Democrats, had been too "provisoish" for the Democracy in 1849. But they ran him for governor in 1851 and masterfully undercut their opponents and consolidated the reaction against "agitation." McClelland's nomination defused state politics, killed chances of a Whig-Free Soil coalition, and thus resulted in the lowest turnout (in percent)

MHCol; Grand Rapids *Grand River Eagle*, Sept. 28, 1848.

[44] *Free Press*, Sept. 7, 1849.

[45] Streeter, *Political Parties*, 111; *Advertiser*, Sept. 6, 21, 1849; and esp. *Grand River Eagle*, Sept. 28, 1849.

[46] *Free Press*, Sept. 21, 1849; reports on the Wayne County and First Senatorial District conventions are in the newspapers of Oct. 15 and 18, 1849. Meanwhile Barnburner Democrats became persona non grata in patronage, John C. Ball, Ionia, to Felch, Dec. 12, 1849, Felch MSS, MHCol.

[47] This account is based in part on information in Streeter, *Political Parties*, 91-137, though the interpretation here is different. On the 1850 campaign, Ann Arbor, *Washtenaw Whig*, Oct. 16, 23, 30, 1850; *Grand River Eagle*, Oct.-Nov. 12, 1850; *Advertiser*, Oct. 14, Nov. 1, 1850; Jackson *American Citizen*, Oct. 16, 1850; the *Hillsdale Gazette* (D.), Nov. 14, 1850; *Free Press*, Nov. 11, 1850. Elizabeth Stuart had a different view of the reaction to the Fugitive Slave Law: "*Taxes and spending money* occupy much more of my thoughts than these indignation slave meetings," E. E. Stuart to Kate, Nov. 1, 1850, *Stuart Letters*, I, 148-49.

in a gubernatorial election since 1835. The total number of voters was only 1,200 more than the 1845 total and 42,000 less than the total turn-out in 1852. Most of those Free Soilers who voted probably favored McClelland.[48]

McClelland's reputation as a "radical" Democrat is undeserved, and even the quality of his anti-Southernism was quite pragmatic. His sup-port of the Proviso was not antislavery but anti-Southern, he opposed slavery extension because it injured Northern sectional interests. In 1849 although McClelland worked hard privately to get the Democratic con-vention to adopt some resolution opposing slavery extension, he made it clear that he valued party unity and that pragmatism required some kind of antiextension plank to undercut the blossoming Whig-Free Soil marriage.[49] McClelland was also aware that the Proviso was a tool of intraparty factions seeking greater recognition in patronage and prestige, including the dispensation of state printing contracts to party news-papers. Assessing the Democrats' situation in late 1850 McClelland ad-mitted that excitement over the Compromise and Fugitive Slave Law was hurting the Democrats, but it would be a disaster to retreat by having Cass resign from the Senate. He traced recent defeats to "that portion of the party, which favored the proviso, [which] is not fully satisfied with the manner they have been treated." Previously they fought for the party and even "for those who were nominated on grounds directly antagonist to them, yet they have been looked upon with suspicion." McClelland and his friends had done everything to elect Buel but "we could not con-trol those we influenced before, because they were determined on revenge. I have conversed with several . . . that voted against him, *and they care no more about the fugitive slave law than we do.*" (Italics mine) Therefore, urged the man whose nomination for governor paralyzed Free Soilers the next year, simply avoid "excitement" over the Compromise or Fugitive Slave Law.[50]

Thus, Democratic anti-Southernism, in addition to being a weapon between rival factions in the party, also resulted from the necessity of

[48] Streeter, *Political Parties*, 139. The *Marshall Statesman* charged that McClel-land sold out to the Hunkers, Oct. 1, 1851, but later said that he received "very large support" from Free Soilers, Nov. 12, 1851. The *Advertiser* stressed Free Soil support for McClelland, Nov. 7, 10, 1851, but returns for Wayne County do not support this. The *Pontiac Jacksonian* touted McClelland as a "Unionist" and "Compromiser," Oct. 29, 1851. Free Soil leaders in 1849 feared McClelland's nomination because he was "known personally to be free soil," Isaac P. Chris-tiancy, Adrian, to Austin Blair, Jackson, Sept. 13, 1849, Blair MSS, BHC.
[49] R. McClelland to A. Felch, Aug. 25, 1849, Felch MSS, MHCol; R. McClelland to J. S. Bagg, Oct. 13, 1849, Bagg MSS, Huntington Library.
[50] *Free Press*, Jan. 1, 1849; R. McClelland to Felch, Aug. 25, 1849, Felch MSS, R. McClelland to Felch, Dec. 23, 1850, Felch MSS, MHCol. For a fine analysis of the general political background, Chaplain W. Morrison, *Democratic Politics and Sectionalism: The Wilmot Proviso Controversy* (Chapel Hill, 1967).

tactical moves to protect Democratic power. The Proviso Democrats, however, were not merely opportunists. McClelland had opposed Texas annexation and supported the Proviso openly. He and men like Alpheus Felch were more responsive to those sincerely opposed to the spread of slavery and to Southern arrogance.[51] But McClelland's nomination in 1851 was precisely the move designed to discomfit Democratic opponents and to take the wind out of anti-Southernism. The Democrats knew well how to use men like McClelland to thwart opponents and internal dissenters by symbolic accommodation. The danger of such a game lay in the chance of sectional controversy reviving and forcing these men occupying bridging positions to choose between the party and the position to which they allegedly pointed it.

Free Soil's weakness in the Democratic Party manifested itself in 1848 as Democrats defected in far fewer numbers than Whigs to back Van Buren. If one looked only at Van Buren's 16 percent of the vote one could still overestimate political antislavery in Michigan. Free Soil was a complex phenomenon, containing contradictions and ambiguities. The Free Soil and Liberty parties differed in many ways, perhaps most conspicuously in their leaders. Old Liberty men fell into the background, as did ministers, while lawyers, professionals, and officeholders came to the fore. Even Democratic politicians embarked on Free Soil. This transformation led to a flexibility that immediately resulted in Whig-Free Soil coalitions.[52]

Although a systematic study of Free Soil leaders is needed, a common type was the ex-Whig who later became a Republican, such as Austin Blair, elected governor by the Republican party in 1860. Blair came from western New York in 1841 to practice law in Jackson. A freethinking Unitarian with a social conscience, Blair avoided politics at first, then gradually threw himself behind Henry Clay whose approach to political economy he strongly approved. After Van Buren lost the 1844 Democratic nomination Blair concluded that "Calhoun went into Tyler's cabinet . . . only to destroy Van Buren and compel the whole party to bow down at the foot stool of the dark spirit of slavery, and it seems Mr. Polk is the chosen instrument to be employed in the business of . . . war and disunion and all for the purpose of establishing more securely the right of one man to enslave another." Blair enthusiastically backed Clay, convinced that Whig doctrines were "thoroughly republican" and that his business was doing well under the "Whig tariff." As the returns showing Clay's narrow defeat came in, Blair exploded in anger: "we are

[51] On the persistence of anti-Southernism in the Democratic Party, even in 1852 and 1853, e.g., N. Mosher, Dexter, to Felch, May, 1852; John Galloway, Rose, to Felch, Dec. 27, 1853, Felch MSS, MHCol.

[52] Smith, *Liberty and Free Soil Parties*, 155, 158, 159.

beaten by the Birneyites. . . . A more dishonest and corrupt set of rascals never lived." If Blair hated the "dark spirit of slavery" he hated abolitionists no less. In March 1845 he confessed that he "could have cried like a child" over the election: "it seemed so humiliating to me that such a creature as Polk should beat Clay that I refrain from despising the country and its institutions ever since. . . . I hate a Birneyite worse than a massasauga and want to throw eggs at them in the streets." The "crowning iniquity," Texas annexation, humbled the free North as Northern men in Congress sold Northern liberty for loaves and fishes.[53]

Blair's disillusionment with politics continued but gradually made room for a belief that Whiggery would sweep the North in the next two years and that " 'Freedom to the slave' will be the watchword and the Whig party will raise that banner." After Polk's veto of rivers and harbors improvements and the introduction of the Wilmot Proviso, Blair concluded that "Northern politicians must cut loose from the slave car or the North will cut loose from them. There must be no more *slave* territory and no more favour to that already existing."[54] "Southern Polkery" clearly was leading Blair to Free Soil. His anti-Southernism ran to bold ground. Blair was one of the rare major party politicians who advocated the cause of Michigan's oppressed black citizens. As a legislator in 1846 he gained notoriety by proposing nonwhite suffrage as a first step in breaking the circle of discrimination, degradation, and prejudice to which blacks were subjected. His eloquent and rational report on the issue leapt far ahead of its time. Whether or not this contributed to Blair's failure to be reelected, it took courage to call for black suffrage in a Northwestern state whose laws and customs kept blacks in a lower caste.[55] While compassion and social justice motivated Blair, his call for black voting also stemmed from his general posture which he described succinctly in May 1848: "it is a cardinal point with me now to oppose Southern institutions in every way possible." Blair admitted then the Free Soil movement aimed to act as a spoiler, preferably to beat Cass. "I am both upon principle and for vengence sake a Free Soil man."[56]

[53] A. Blair, Eaton Rapids, to A. T. McCall, Bath, N.Y., Feb. 19, 1843; Blair, Jackson, to McCall, Aug. 30, 1844, Blair MSS; Blair to McCall, Mar. 16, 1845, Blair MSS, BHC. McCall was a Democrat.

[54] Blair to McCall, April 5, 1846; Blair to McCall, Sept. 8, 1846, Blair MSS, BHC.

[55] The report was reprinted and discussed in the *Advertiser*, May 6, 1846. State of Michigan, *Documents Accompanying the Senate Journal, 1846* (Detroit, 1846), Doc. No. 12.

[56] Blair to McCall, May 29, 1848; same to same, Dec. 1, 1848, Blair MSS, BHC. Battle Creek Free Soilers told William Woodbridge that "the degree of difference between Cass and Taylor and the old feeling against Democrats and abolitionists and even the old hatred of Mr. Van Buren are of but little consequence . . . if he betrays us we will break his sword over his head and choose another Leader and

Free Soil's acceptance of Van Buren in 1848, the long time "Northern man with Southern principles," was one of the greater ironies of American politics. It indicated both the weakness and pragmatism of Free Soil. A Michigan leader could later say of the Hunker-Barnburner split among New York's Democrats that this was the first great opportunity "which promised a hope of success in our efforts against slavery and its extension." Van Buren's candidacy especially heartened Isaac P. Christiancy not because it promised success but because it had "given us access to the democratic party to make converts to our principles, which was the most we could then hope."[57]

After 1848, Free Soil leaders began arranging "union" or "fusion" with Whiggery. These managers hoped to avoid mistakes of the abolitionists who had too often rejected "sound policy" because of principle. Christiancy, an ex-Democrat, urged that the Free Soilers hold a convention after the Whig and Democratic conventions met, then work for a coalition with whichever one took Free Soil ground, which he expected would be the Whigs. This strategy would improve their organization and "get up a little enthusiasm and spirit in our ranks which we much need at present." Morality, pragmatism, and antagonism for "Cass men, hunkers, and intriguers" dictated this strategy: "Let us teach the servile tools of slavery and the slave power among us that when they abandon the cause of freedom and the rights of the North they *shall not triumph* —Let us show them that their *bread and butter* depends upon their doing right. . . . I for one should be much better satisfied to see a Whig triumph in the state this fall than to see a Cass triumph."[58] Christiancy's realistic assessment of options indicated that no overwhelming tide of Free Soilism engulfed the electorate. Although a majority perhaps favored "proviso principles" Christiancy warned that "We cannot again arouse our free soil enthusiasm without some hope of success."[59]

The 1849 Whig-Free Soil union, as seen earlier, failed miserably. Before the election Whigs hoped that the approximately 23,000 Whig votes of 1848 could be combined with the 10,000 Free Soil to dwarf the Democrats' 30,000 of that year. But while the Democratic total fell to 27,837, the coalition did not do as well as the Whigs alone had the previous year or even in 1844, polling only 23,540 votes. The coalition candidate, Flavius Littlejohn, a Free Soiler and ex-Democrat, reportedly repelled many Whigs. Some Whigs thought the coalition tended to "*dena-*

Still prosecute the War." John L. Bolkcom, Elias C. Manchester to Woodbridge, Aug. 3, 1848, Woodbridge MSS, BHC.

[57] Quoted in Van Buren, *MHC*, 17: 259-60.

[58] Isaac P. Christiancy to Austin Blair, Sept. 8, 1849, Blair MSS, BHC. This letter is eleven and a half pages long and is a full description of Free Soil strategy as a minority party.

[59] I. P. Christiancy to Blair, Sept. 13, 1849, Blair MSS, BHC.

tionalize the Whig party" and resented the choice nominations going to the minority partners.[60]

Former Libertyites probably found Littlejohn repulsive, too, as he had been no friend of theirs nor of the black man's. Eric Foner has argued persuasively that in New York the transition from Liberty to Free Soil and to a broad popular base for political antislavery made a casualty of concern for the amelioration of the black man's condition. When Van Buren and the Barnburners entered the Free Soil coalition, demands for black rights fell out of the white-oriented Free Soil platform. The nomination of Littlejohn gives symbolic meaning to Foner's thesis in Michigan, as the flamboyant ex-Democrat had authored a demagogic House report in 1843 denying the justice of extending the suffrage to black people and raising the bogy of "amalgamation."[61]

While a Cass Democrat prematurely asserted in January 1850 that the last election "put a veto on free soilism," the consolidation movement did gradually deflate Free Soil and anti-Southernism over the next three years. Isaac Christiancy later recalled that the period "from 1850 to 1854, was to all outward appearances, the most discouraging period for the free-soil cause."[62] One sure indication of the decline of agitation could be found in the Presbyterian Synod's postponement in 1851 of any statement on the Fugitive Slave Law. The unfavorable climate fostered uncertainty and backbiting in Free Soil ranks. In November 1852 the *Detroit Advertiser* agreed with the *New York Times* that "there has been no time within the last ten years, when the Anti-Slavery party *as such*, had less hold upon the public favor than it has now." The *Times* judged, prophetically, that "until some new aggressions of pro-slavery ambition shall arouse new jealousies, and awaken new resistance, ultra Abolitionism [sic] will cease to be felt as a disturbing element in our national politics." In late 1853 a Free Soil lecturer reported a disheartening tour through Michigan as he had little success "in obtaining either audiences or funds," although the cause sparkled briefly in Oakland County's piety belt.[63] Even in Yankee Congregationalist Vermontville, when a new doc-

[60] *Advertiser*, Nov. 13, 1849. Also, *Advertiser* and *Free Press*, Sept.-Nov. 1849, passim; Streeter, *Political Parties*, 153-54.

[61] Eric Foner, "Racial Attitudes of the New York Free Soilers," *New York History*, 46 (October 1965), 311-29. State of Michigan, *Documents Accompanying the House Journal, 1843* (Detroit, 1843), Doc. No. 3.

[62] William Anderson, Ann Arbor, to John Barry, Jan. 25, 1850, Executive Records, MHCom. Van Buren, *MHC*, 17, 262.

[63] Vandervelde, "Synod," 22; *Marshall Statesman*, July 6, 1853; State of Michigan, *Documents Accompanying the Journal of the Senate and House of Representatives, 1851* (Lansing, 1851), House Doc. No. 16; on antagonism among Free Soilers, Fred Porter, Detroit, to John S. Porter, Sept. 2, 1853, and J. S. Porter to F. Porter, Nov. 1, 1852, John S. Porter, MSS; for reports of Free Soil lecturing, J. S. Porter to Fred B. Porter, Nov. 12, 1853, George A. Porter, Bloomfield, to F. B. Porter, Nov. 24 and Nov. 25, 1853, G. A. Porter, Detroit, to Charles Porter,

tor in town voted for John P. Hale, "a good deal of feeling manifested" at this arrival of a "firebrand." The village's indignation and curiosity seems to have climaxed when a leading Whig asked Dr. Kedzie: "Doc, do you believe that a nigger is as good as a white man?"[64] The question suggests again that in addition to conservative Unionism, indifference to slavery, and dislike of abolitionist ultras and their moralism, antiblack phobias helped inhibit antislavery parties.

To these inhibitions must be added the tactics Democrats and Whigs used to divide, buy off, or absorb antislavery or anti-Southern independency. Even in township elections Democrats and Whigs nominated Free Soilers, divided the antislavery vote or blunted its impact.[65] Abolitionists early in the game recognized how the rhetoric and politics of accommodation dulled their moral appeal. "We find," Guy Beckley and Theodore Foster wrote to Birney, "that a large share of the leading clergy are ready enough to concede that slavery in general, or in the abstract is a bad thing—very bad—but in certain circumstances, practiced with good intentions it is justifiable, or excusable. In this way their hearers are kept easy, and the edge of antislavery truth is taken off."[66]

Another reason that abolition, antislavery, and anti-Southernism declined in 1852-53 was that evangelicals were absorbed in a cultural conflict other than that between the North and South; their energies were flowing into moral fights immediately within Northern society.

Dec. 2, 1853, John S. Porter MSS, BHC; *New York Times* quoted in *Advertiser* Nov. 9, 1852; also *Pontiac Gazette,* Oct. 29, 1853.

[64] Barber, "Vermontville Colony," *MHC*, 28: 239-41.

[65] Letter in John S. Porter MSS, BHC, April 13, 1851, Richland.

[66] John Beckley and Theodore Foster to Birney, Dec. 19, 1843, in Dumond, ed., *Birney Letters,* II, 764. An excellent example of a Democratic newspaper's temporary adoption of Free Soil rhetoric can be traced in the files of the *Kalamazoo Gazette,* 1847-1849; esp., Nov. 6, 1849.

XI

The Old Party Structure Shakes: 1853

> I think Sectarianism in Europe is fast being driven into
> *Protestantism*—I read much in the Scotch Papers, & looks
> much to me as if the Battle has begun & the Trumpet sounded,
> which is to bring Christians in one solid body, that "we may
> all be one"—that *they* may know Christ the sent, is reconcil-
> ing the world to Himself—We are living in a wonderful
> day—Elizabeth E. Stuart, April 22, 1852

> I rejoice to tell you that Politics seem to be lost sight of,
> in the simple word Protestant—Elizabeth E. Stuart,
> January 26, 1853[1]

The established view of Michigan politics in the 1850s holds that the Kansas-Nebraska Bill loosed a political revolution. Opposition to slavery extension into territory declared free by the Missouri Compromise created the Republican Party in 1854 and propelled it to victory in elections through 1860. Tradition recognizes that long-standing reform movements such as temperance also flowed into the new party, and native Americanism is granted a brief impact, but the moral force of antislavery more than anything else receives credit for making a new party system. The Compromise of 1850, the story goes, satisfied no one. Many Whigs and Democrats agreed with Free Soilers that the Fugitive Slave Law was an abomination. The Nebraska Bill flung one outrage too many on al- ready sensitive Northern consciences. After defeat in 1852 many Whigs looked about for a new party. Some found it in Know Nothingism, but this was a temporary and abnormal stop on the way to Republicanism.[2]

---

[1] *Stuart Letters*, I, 323-24 and 460. Perry Miller observed that religious groups throughout the period 1800 to 1860 lamented the divisiveness of party spirit in the church. Miller also sensed similar connections between religion and politics, anti-Catholicism, antiparty, and romantic patriotism. *The Life of the Mind in America: From the Revolution to the Civil War* (New York, 1965), 46, 55-57.

[2] Streeter's account is the most complete and that on which all others in some way depend, e.g., M. M. Quaife and Sidney Glazer, *Michigan, from Primitive Wilderness to Industrial Commonwealth* (New York, 1948), 203-07; Burton, et al., *Detroit*, I, 463-64; J. Elaine Thompson, "The Formative Period of the Republican Party in Michigan, 1854-1860" (unpublished M.A. thesis, Wayne State University, 1949), 2, 39; Farmer, *Detroit*, I, 346-47; Dunbar, *Michigan*, 418-20, is most aware of Republicanism's complexity, but relies too much on Streeter, deemphasizing some of his own findings in work cited below.

This interpretation, while it could in fairness be further elaborated, would still need revision in its basic propositions and sequence of events.

The period from 1850 to 1854 was a time of repression of antislavery agitation. Discontented minorities remained tense but isolated. The Whig Party retained its viability through 1852. Scott's defeat did not scatter Whig loyalists to the four corners of the political compass, and the long-run causes of Whiggery's refashioning after 1852 must be sought in social cleavages of the preceding two decades. The immediate causes erupted in 1853 when previously contained conflicts became uncontrollable in traditional political channels. Catholic-Protestant antagonism cut through the party system in 1853, operating within local politics with statewide repercussions. In early 1854 a mobilizing evangelicalism, springing from many sources but most of all from hope of a temperance millennium, joined a driving anti-Catholicism. Then Kansas-Nebraska unleashed anti-Southernism among Whig and Democratic leaders and provided them an organizing focus for a variety of discontents and aspirations. Antislavery men and abolitionists rallied to the new standard, bringing zeal, moral rhetoric, and compassion for the oppressed. But anti-Southernism best describes the common linchpin holding together various groups in a "great white coalition" of opposition to the Democracy.

During genesis and infancy the coalition called itself the "Fusion" or "Independent" movement as often as it called itself "Republican." The frequent use of these "other" names through 1854-55 has been ignored, but it told much about the new organization's character. It testified, firstly, to its intense anti-Catholicism and evangelicalism. Anti-Southern and antislavery attitudes certainly were common among the leaders of "Fusion," but these managers also seized their opportunity from upheavals preceding the electorate's awareness of Stephen Douglas's Frankenstein. Much of Fusion's success in 1854 depended on Know Nothing cooperation all over the state, from "cities," to hamlets, to farms. Since Floyd Streeter it has been recognized that the Americans carried several large towns on their own in 1855. But then, the conventional version has it, Know Nothingism was swallowed up by the antislavery spirit and its own shame at being un-American. Actually, Americanism continued to operate semi-autonomously in many localities through 1856 and after. Further, it shaped a major part of the Fusion legislative program of 1855-56, through which it gained symbolic gratification and played at status politics with anti-Popery.

INDEPENDENCY

In 1827 Detroit's Common Council bought some lots from Antoine Beaubein for a City Cemetery. A committee divided the grounds into two equal parts, Catholic and Protestant. The dividing line had to be run through family lots. This potential source of trouble, said Detroit historian Silas Farmer, proved convenient for families with both Protestant and Catholic members: "Thus the sanctity of the ground was preserved, while in the same lot, and yet in two different cemeteries, those of opposite faiths reposed in peace."[3] Such ingenuity often failed to keep peace among the living.

It was seen above how antagonism between evangelical Protestants and Catholics affected the formation of party loyalties. Evangelicals remained sporadically on the offensive through the 1840s, a minority, but perhaps expressing the latent attitudes of a majority of Protestants. Reverend Duffield and the Presbyterian *Evangelical Observer* did not allow preoccupation with temperance to exclude occasional jousts with Popery. The Baptist *Michigan Christian Herald* claimed to be the boldest in dragging forth "the enormities of Romanism to the hated light of heaven." Anti-Popery also had less respectable or at least less learned allies than Dr. Duffield and the *Herald*, such as Reverend McDowall who published a barely literate sheet called the *Daily Vine* and took himself to street corners to call the masses to holy war on intemperance and Popery. Meanwhile, "in the countryside," according to one observer, "the Protestant clergy . . . are constantly stirring up feeling against Catholicism." And Michigan received its share of renegade monks and other itinerant salesmen of Popish horror stories who canvassed the nation during this period.[4]

In the 1840s the American Catholic hierarchy sought to consolidate the Church's internal affairs. Bishops moved to secure control over their laity, particularly to regain authority over church property which in many areas had been granted to lay trustees. Trustee resistance elicited Protestant sympathy and stimulated hatred of Roman authoritarianism. So it was in Detroit. Bishop Lefevre swung most parishes easily into line but St. Mary's of Detroit, mostly German, rocked with rebellion. A group of trustees, inspired according to their pastor by "Protestant ideas," insisted on a voice in church matters and control over property. Disruptions at mass brought suspension of worship at the church and the Bishop's excommunication of the rebels. The *Michigan Christian Herald* inevitably saw the "spirit of manly independency" which was in harmony with "American principles" being crushed by the old hierarchical despotism.[5]

---

[3] Farmer, *Detroit*, I, 55.

[4] *Michigan Christian Herald*, Aug. 22, Dec. 18, 1843, Dec. 4, 1851; quote from Jan. 6, 1845; *Advertiser*, Feb. 1, 5, 1844; *Evangelical Observer*, Feb. 11, May 20, July 1, 29, Oct. 21, 1845, extant copies, BHC; *Daily Vine*, Aug. 11, July 11, 1845, extant copies, BHC; *Detroit Daily News*, July 22, 1845; G. W. Wisner, Pontiac, to Woodbridge, Jan. 13, 1845, Woodbridge MSS, BHC; Andrew Viszosky, Grand River, letter of July 25, 1844, in McGee, *Catholic Church in Grand Rapids*, 111.

[5] The "Journal" of St. Mary's said that laymen formed a "corporation" to take

Such incidents touched the mass of citizens only indirectly. But one confrontation in Detroit during the 1840s revealed the chasm of discord which could open in the community. The tremors of the "Bible War" of 1843-45 foreshadowed the quakes of 1853-54. This conflict involved the public schools, the institution which during the rest of the century became a historic focus of Protestant-Catholic disputation. This controversy not only touched many citizens directly but was extremely emotional. It touched them through their children and raised basic questions of identity: each group felt its children threatened by values it abhorred. Each wanted to defend its own model of how its children should grow to adulthood.

Public schools in the United States were not often hospitable places for Catholics, at least not as judged by the ordinary schoolbooks. In a comprehensive study of "the books most widely read in nineteenth-century America" apart from the Bible, Professor Ruth Miller Elson discovered that "No theme in these schoolbooks before 1870 is more universal than anti-Catholicism." While no study of Michigan books has been made, there are many reasons for assuming that the type of schoolbook analyzed by Elson was commonplace in Michigan schools. Indeed, the evangelical view of Catholicism as it appears in these pages is identical to that described in the schoolbooks. The rhetoric of Michigan Protestants provides eloquent testimony to the educative power of the books which, according to Elson, were authored mainly by persons steeped in New England puritan traditions and who identified Americanism with Protestantism.[6]

Fear of Protestant and Catholic disagreement had delayed, in fact, establishment of a free school system in Detroit as authorized by constitution and law since 1837. A School Board Report of 1843 tactfully blamed the "heterogeneity of the Detroit population." Meanwhile, it said, destitute immigrants providing for their own children's education grew in number with the result that "hundreds were growing wholly ignorant and greatly vicious."[7] In 1841 a bipartisan movement elected

---

care of revenues, MS, St. Mary's Rectory, Detroit. This story has been constructed from clues in the "Journal" and a conversation with the pastor in 1964. Paré, *Catholic Church in Detroit,* 439-40, 443-47. John Gilmary Shea, *A History of the Catholic Church within the Limits of the United States, 1808-1843* (New York, 1890), 518-20, 538-43. Ellis, *American Catholicism,* 44-46. *Michigan Christian Herald,* Feb. 25, 1848.

[6] Ruth Miller Elson, *Guardians of Tradition: American Schoolbooks of the Nineteenth Century* (Lincoln, 1964), vii, 57, 49-53, 62; "Catholicism is depicted not only as a false religion, but as a positive danger to the state; it subverts good government, sound morals, and education," 47.

[7] Moehlman, *Public Education in Detroit,* 72, 77-78; *Free Press,* Feb. 26, 1842; *Advertiser,* Sept. 8, 1841; "Report of the Board of Education of the City of De-

Dr. Douglas Houghton mayor on a school tax platform and the schools were under way. In 1843 Protestants began to agitate for Bible instruction in the schools, and the school board unanimously decided to exclude the Bible. While revering it as "the text book of all moral obligations" the board feared it as "the source of all the bitterness of sectarian animosity." Some Protestants accused the board of succumbing to Popish influence. One pointed out to the *Christian Herald* that Protestants paid far more of the school tax than Catholics and asked if "our Protestant and New England population" would submit to the censorship of priests.[8] But even most evangelicals do not seem to have been aroused at this stage.

On May 2, 1844, John Hulbert, a Whig school inspector, proposed that either the Protestant or Catholic version of the Bible be used in the schools without comment or coercion. The Board defeated this resolution 7 to 4. Now the *Herald* rang out with war cries against the "domineering genius of Papacy" and "Protestant" politicians who truckled to fear of Catholic votes. Protestants of many denominations circulated a protest petition and presented it on June 13. According to the Board "many taxable inhabitants" signed it, expressing the discontent of "a large portion of the Protestant population of this city." Still, Hulbert and the Bible lost again in December, 6 to 4. The Board then printed opposing reports.[9]

A secular majority explained that it saw its choice reluctantly as between the Bible and the school system. Catholics and Protestants both maintained the system. Catholics objected to use of the Bible (most school teachers, the Board omitted to say, were Protestants), school taxes were involuntary, and it would be unjust to tax "the old and numerous Catholic population" for a system that they might then be compelled from a sense of religious duty not to use. The minority report read like an evangelical tract, laced with italics, quotations from Scripture and other religious sources. It held that the Protestant Bible should be used without comment; children whose parents desired it could be excused from study. All history showed that Bible reading and liberty went

---

troit," *Documents Accompanying the Journal of the House of Representatives, 1843* (Detroit, 1843), Doc. No. 10, 48-49. The percentage of native whites 5 to 15 years of age in school was 99.5, compared to 66.8 percent of foreign whites of that group, DeBow, *Compendium*, 150.

⁸ "Report of the Board of Education," 51; *Herald*, Jan. 1, 15, 1844. In 1837 the Presbyterians advocated Bible usage in schools, Comin and Fredsell, *History of the Presbyterian Church*, 77.

⁹ *Reports of the Committee of the Board of Education of the City of Detroit on the Petition for the Admission of the Bible into the Public Schools of the City* (Detroit, 1844), 3-4, 4-7; *Free Press*, May 15, 1844; *Christian Herald*, June 3, 17, 1844.

together, as did Catholicism, illiberality, and moral disability. The minority asserted, in effect, that Bible reading was the American way of life.[10]

The dispute ended in February 1845 when the Board reached a compromise close to the Protestant position. New members and changed votes produced a 7 to 1 majority for reading of the Protestant or Catholic Bibles without note or comment.[11] This controversy probably did not become more serious because from the start the Board had not split along party lines, and the controversy was not perceived as a party issue. This is not to say that Catholic self-consciousness was not intensified and that such an episode had no relation to their overwhelming support of the Democrats in 1844. But the underlying social cleavage did not find formal political expression as it did in 1853 and after.

The American Catholic hierarchy went on the offensive by 1852-53, pursuing its "rights" in the political arena. It followed strategies already marked out in the 1840s by the aggressive Bishop John Hughes of New York. Echoes of Hughes's battles sounded as Bishop Lefevre led his supporters into pressure group politics in 1853.[12] Detroit's growing pains as a city provided the issues for the opening confrontation. On January 3 members of the Common Council proposed several amendments to the city charter for public improvements: for street paving in the city's center to be financed by property taxes on adjoining land; to establish a city workhouse and almshouse; and to establish a Public Water Works and Board of Water Commissioners with power to borrow up to $400,000 to replace the inefficient system which operated at a loss. All but two aldermen, Riopelle and Doyle, favored the amendments.[13]

Bishop Lefevre made no secret of his opposition. It stemmed, according to his critics, from his church's ownership of large property, now exempt from taxation, which would be taxed; he wanted a general tax if any. He allegedly feared too that the proposed alms workhouse would divert city revenue from his charity hospital. His critics attributed his opposition to the water works to fear of taxation and a reactionary spirit typical of "ecclesiastic property-holders." The Bishop and his allies allegedly argued that the new measures would oppress the poor and were

[10] *Reports of the Committee of the Board of Education*, 6-10, 11-32. The Bible bloc consisted of two Whigs and two Democrats: *Advertiser*, May 12, 1844; *Free Press*, May 15, 1844; *Herald*, June 3, 1844.

[11] *Advertiser*, Feb. 6, 1845; *Free Press*, Feb. 7, 1845; *Herald*, Feb. 17, 24, 1845.

[12] Ray Allen Billington, *Protestant Crusade*, 289-314; Shea, *History of the Catholic Church*, 526-32; Glyndon G. VanDeusen, "Seward and the School Question Reconsidered," *Journal of American History*, 52 (September 1965), 313-19. In 1840 Catholics petitioned the legislature for a share of the common school fund and received a polite answer but no action, Paré, 460-63. In the spring of 1852 a Catholic "revival" apparently stirred up "a very bitter, rancorous feeling . . . against the Protestants—the Tract and Bible—," Elizabeth E. Stuart to Kate Stuart Baker, April 6, 1852, *Stuart Letters*, I, 305.

[13] *Free Press*, Jan. 5, March 5, 1853.

antirepublican.[14] Be that as it may, the Bishop's position can be understood somewhat in terms of his institution's having provided social services no public agencies could or would undertake. Now that the nascent city moved to assume municipal responsibilities, the Bishop must have felt threatened by more than loss of revenue and taxes.

The issues rapidly became obscured in the uproar following the Bishop's plunge into politics. He first denounced the improvements from his pulpit. Then he, his priests, and vocal partisans descended in force on a public meeting on January 5, 1853, intimidating all opponents. Every contemporary report said that the Bishop's brigade allowed only him and his allies to speak without interruption. Even had the meeting taken place with decorum, evangelical Protestants would not have reacted calmly. This provocation threw the Whig *Advertiser* and especially *Tribune* into livid tirades against foreign Catholics. The rage of the *Christian Herald* passed all bounds. Its "eyewitness" account, "The Spirit and Manners of the Beast," claimed that the Bishop, Father Shaw, and a drunken Irish layman decided who could speak or who would be "assaulted with the most abusive and indecent epithets, and bellowed down." The latter included John Ladue, Democrat and former mayor, and Whig lawyer Jacob M. Howard. But the Bishop and his priests, "German, French and Saxon," could command attention instantly from their "army of excited foreigners."[15] Even the new editor of the Democratic *Free Press*, Wilbur F. Storey, while straddling the improvements issue, criticized the clergy for going into the political arena. Storey especially regretted the allegations that only Catholics could speak freely. The rumors regarding the suppression of free discussion were "calculated to do great injury to our Catholic brethren."[16]

The furor over this meeting rapidly dovetailed into a revived controversy over the schools. In late 1852 the Bishop renewed a long-standing Catholic demand for a share of public school money.[17] By mid-January

---

[14] Advocates of the new works believed that "water rents would pay the interest on the whole cost, and provide a sinking fund to pay off the principal," *Free Press*, March 5, 1853. Among the Bishop's allies were rich Catholics such as John R. Williams.

[15] *Herald*, Jan. 13, 1853. Criticism of the Bishop from several other papers was quoted in this issue. Elizabeth Stuart believed that "Our Citizens, Dem. & Whigg, have come out nobly, and altho Bishop, Priest & People went in such a body as to pack the City Hall, meaning to choke down our common Council, & *twice compelled* them to adjourn! Yet, last night, they met, & most nobly, to a man, voted AYE! (except one Irish Roman Catholic & Bagg, who ever lives on Office) that the charter should be Ammended [sic]," Letter to her son, Jan. 12, 1853, *Stuart Letters*, I, 450-51.

[16] *Free Press*, Jan. 11, 12, 1853. Walsh, *To Print the News and Raise Hell*, discusses *Free Press* positions, 81-85.

[17] *Herald*, Dec. 16, 1852; *Free Press*, Jan. 5, 10, 12, 13, Feb. 11, 1853; *Detroit Tribune*, March 12, 1853.

the Bishop and his entourage were "in daily attendance" lobbying in Lansing, according to the *Herald*, "with all the blandness of the most practiced courtesans." Thus the "Jesuitical Hierarchy" with every Catholic vote at their beck "seem determined to carry the war 'to the knife.' We propose to give them 'the knife to the hilt.' " The First Presbyterian Church of Detroit remonstrated against this attempt to subvert "the very citadel of Republican strength in the free education of youth and the consequent independence of mind." Meanwhile, Catholics all over the state bombarded the legislature with petitions backing Lefevre and objecting to being forced to support a school system which discriminated in the recruiting and hiring of teachers. They asked that the "business" of teaching be "placed on the same legal footing as the other learned professions" and opened to talent and ability. Opening teaching to Catholics probably was a major secondary goal of this Catholic drive.[18]

The schools issue split the Democratic Party in two. After the regular party machinery made nominations for city offices a large group of "Independents" presented their own ticket. The Whigs lined up behind the Independents who charged that Catholics had controlled the regular nominations, especially those for school inspector, nominating men hostile to "free schools." The Bishop's activities disgusted them, and they could not tolerate Irish Catholics from the Eighth Ward carpetbagging in other wards to control Democratic caucuses. Some Independents saw a plot. Some explained that while the Democrats had never proscribed men on national or religious grounds, "when a Catholic Bishop . . . undertakes to seize the machinery of the democratic party . . . it is time to protest, and, if necessary, for *rebellion* . . . especially if the Bishop is a *whig*." In nonpolitical quarters, Protestant analyses were probably less subtle than even these conspiracy oriented views. Elizabeth Stuart, although fairly well informed, wrote her son that "the Bshp & Cath. Priests having made a *full nomination of Men, pledged to them*, to carry out their crusade against our Public Schools . . . the cry now is Protestantism against Popery."[19]

"Regulars" answered Independents by calling conspiracy talk nonsense and by warning that while some men honestly doubted the Bishop's wisdom, others, moved by hatred for Catholics and Democrats, were just

[18] *Herald*, Jan. 27, 1853. Paré, *Catholic Church in Detroit*, 464-66. In 1841 New York city's Catholics failed to get a share of the school fund but succeeded in getting the schools out of the control of a private Protestant corporation and onto a public basis.

[19] *Free Press*, March 5, 1853. Elizabeth E. Stuart to her son, Feb. 26, 1853, *Stuart Letters*, I, 481. "How true, 'God works in a mysterious way'—he allowed these Cath. to aid the Democracy, to so fully identify themselves with the most inveterate Anti-democratic body on Earth. . . . Then confounded their council, by giving them up, to work destruction (we believe on themselves)."

trying to divide the Democrats. In going to Lansing the Bishop had done what "other Christians" have done. Only 3 to 9 inspectors nominated were Catholics, and even they were "staunch adherents to the common schools." But whether or not Catholics were guilty of the charges against them, many Independents believed they were. Some probably wanted to disassociate themselves from any taint of Catholic control. One hundred and twenty Independents issued a public letter explaining that concern for essential improvements and free schools prompted their actions. Their ticket was "purely democratic"; they made no personal war on regulars, who had a right to their own views.[20]

Though it conceded that the party was divided, the *Free Press* still tried to bridge the rift. While favoring improvements and existing schools, Storey was an organization man and thus supported the regulars. He probably relieved his frustration somewhat by answering the constant anti-Catholic tirades of the *Advertiser* and *Tribune*.[21] The apocalyptic rhetoric of these papers and the *Herald* no doubt stimulated visions of Armageddon among Protestant pietists: "Popery in her *Man* Wisdom, & arm of flesh, Goliath like, [comes] armed for the conquest—Next week will show the power of the Sling and Stone . . . much prayer is put up for that terrible struggle." Elizabeth Stuart believed that "Every Christian has to buckle on his Armour—& keep it Bright—The Battle of the Lord of Hosts has begun."[22]

No doubt both Independents and regulars believed God on their side on election day, March 7. Both at least nominated John Harmon for mayor, but thereafter their tickets diverged, and the contest for the second highest city post, recorder, focused their combat. The Independents won a sweeping victory, best measured by comparing the 1852 mayoral vote with that for recorder in 1853. The year before the Democrats had carried all eight wards; seldom had they run poorly in any ward in city elections. In 1853 the "Regular" candidate for recorder carried only reliable Eight, the Irish Catholic fortress, and even there the Democratic majority plummeted from its normal landslide proportions.

Voting largely, though not exclusively, followed religious lines. It cut across native-immigrant groups. The *Advertiser*'s observer at the polls claimed he saw Germans, mostly Catholic "Old Frenchmen," "the

---

[20] "Justice," *Free Press*, March 4, 1853; *Free Press*, Feb. 24, 1853.

[21] Letter of J. Riggs, *Free Press*, Feb. 25, 1853; *ibid.*, Feb. 23, 24, 25, Jan. 12, Feb. 11, March 1, 1853; also, Feb. 11, March 3.

[22] E. E. Stuart to her son, Feb. 26, 1853, and E. E. Stuart to Kate Stuart Baker, March 12, 1853, *Stuart Letters*, I, 418, 496. There were rumors of firearms being collected, *Free Press,* March 7, 1853, and reports of Irish threats to burn the homes of *Tribune* editors, E. E. Stuart to her son, March 3, 1853, *Stuart Letters*, I, 482. Bishop Lefevre was urging his flock to keep calm and not to resort to force; something of a Catholic boycott of schools may also have been going on, E. E. Stuart to her son, Feb. 26, 1853, *Stuart Letters*, I, 482.

TABLE XI.1

Detroit Wards: Party Percentages for Mayor 1852 and Recorder 1853

| | 1852 (Mayor) | | 1853 (Recorder) | |
	Democrat	Whig-Independent	Democrat	Whig-Independent
Ward 1	54	46	30	70
Ward 2	56	44	24	76
Ward 3	51	49	28	72
Ward 4	65	35	30	70
Ward 5	53	47	23	77
Ward 6	51	49	20	80
Ward 7	52	48	33	67
Ward 8	73	27	54	46

'Canny Scot,' " and the Protestant Irish going almost to a man for Independency. Although the great body of Irish went for the Priest's ticket, even a handsome number of them voted "*right.*" The *Christian Herald* claimed that the Bishop had alienated "many of his own flock," especially Germans and French. Mrs. Stuart believed that the "Germ. & French Cath. behaved nobly," but "the Irish and Belgians were his Satanic Majesty's Standard Bearers." From the regulars signs of anti-Yankee feeling suggested that Yankee Protestants played a conspicuous role in Independency.[23] A correlation of the distribution of Independent percentage strength with party, ethnocultural, and religious percentages yielded some unsurprising results. The strongest positive association found among the variables tested and Independency was with the Republican vote in Detroit's wards in the 1854 state election ($+.588$); the weakest was with the Democratic vote in the 1852 presidential poll ($-.812$). Protestants were almost as strongly associated ($+.547$) with Independency as was Republicanism in 1854, while the typical regular probably was (as suggested by the correlations) a hard core Democratic voter, a group that naturally included many foreign Catholics, especially Irish. (Independency's correlation with Irish Catholics: $-.699$; with foreigners: $-.474$.) Whigs, Free Soilers, and swing voters probably supported the Independent ticket overwhelmingly. Regulars also charged that Democrats who bolted to Independency were of questionable party loyalty anyway because of their free soil tendencies, which included being "against the annexation of Texas, a barnburner, and abolitionist," and striving "to have the colored gentlemen vote . . . on a par with the white man."[24] While the Independent-regular rift may have

[23] *Advertiser*, March 9, 1853; *Herald*, March 10, 1853. A bitter Regular charged that "the codfish aristocracy of the democratic party" had united with the Whigs; but America "was not made exclusively for the emigrants from the New England States," *Free Press*, Feb. 26, 1853. E. E. Stuart to her son, March 12, 1853, and to Kate Stuart Baker, March 12, 1853, *Stuart Letters*, I, 491, 496.

[24] *Herald*, March 8, 1853; *Advertiser*, March 9, 1853; *Free Press*, Feb. 26, 1853.

overlapped somewhat with existing factional disputes, clearly the free soil issue had nothing to do with the immediate causes.

Independency culminated in 1853 with Levi Bishop's election as president of the school board. Bishop, a leading Independent, began by speaking out for free schools, "but deprecated arousing hard feelings." The latter, however, did not subside. The evangelicals had been claiming that the fight against the "Pope's ticket" was but one battle in a far-flung war. Mrs. Stuart had rejoiced after the charter election that "Our Free Schools & City Improvements, & Americanism are yet ours," but she also believed that "The Battle" had just begun. Even the *Free Press* admitted the existence of a Catholic push for a pro rata division of school funds nationwide.[25] Protestant fears would not let the "Catholic question" leave politics as quickly as it had entered.

Nor did Catholics remain passive. On April 30, 1853, the Detroit *Catholic Vindicator* appeared. Richard Elliott, a leading Irish Catholic closely identified with the paper, told three decades later of how "the war against the Catholic Church, and Irish Catholics more especially," made it necessary to have a paper to refute falsehood and to vindicate "Catholic rights in regard to Public Schools." The *Chicago Western Tablet* printed it "ostensibly as a Detroit paper and the organ of the Rt. Rev. Bishop."[26] The *Vindicator* defined the school question as one of life or death. Catholics had come to America to pursue their faith and fortune, and had earlier done so quietly. But now that Catholics were numerous "Protestantism thinks it high time 'to put us down.' That creed, or no creed, which boasts its sincere and sole reliance to be reason, whips up a majority, by the thong of every prejudice, overpowers us at the polls with mere numbers, prowls about the cradles of our children, kidnaps and binds with its own Chinese bandages their infant minds, seeking but one end through all—to make them unlike their fathers and mothers." Contrary to *Free Press* dogma, "anti-Christian common schools were not 'an essential element of government.' Catholics possessed their own ideal of a 'true education for Christian children.' "[27]

Even the Catholic counterattack betrayed the injury done to Catholic, especially Irish, self-esteem. "They have," said Mrs. Stuart, "lost caste monstrously among us." Throughout 1853 Catholics exhibited deep disenchantment with the Democrats and a strong sense of isolation and

[25] *Free Press*, March 7, 21, 24; *Herald*, March 10, 1853; *Tribune*, March 12, 1853. Letters of E. E. Stuart in notes above. Michael B. Katz, *The Irony of Early School Reform: Educational Innovation in Mid-Nineteenth Century Massachusetts* (Cambridge, 1968), discusses Know Nothingism and schools in Lawrence, 102-05,
[26] Manuscript introduction to the files of the Detroit *Catholic Vindicator*, 1853-55, by Richard Elliott, microfilm, University of Detroit Library. *Vindicator*, April 30, May 28, June 4, 1853; also, May 7.
[27] *Vindicator*, May 7, 4, 1853.

persecution. The *Vindicator* feared that many in both parties were ready for a "Protestant party." One Irish layman suggested that Catholics join in a "union of inaction," aloof from both parties and bid for by both, a strategy reminiscent of that favored by Edward Theller over a decade before, but now hatched by desperation. A Catholic Fourth of July orator in Monroe told his fellow citizens they had a bounden duty to see that Catholic interests in the legislature were represented. He claimed that Catholics constituted half the population but in the last legislature of 104 members only 3 were Catholics: "101 against us, besides the Governor and all the State Officers." Apathy and "want of Catholic principles in our political matters, is the reason we are now so cramped in our most vital interests."[28] Accordingly, Monroe Catholics organized a "Conservative Association" pledged to battle in defense of Catholic rights, "and to oppose and expose those political demagogues, who before election approach us with the smile of a Judas . . . but who afterwards, when in power, endeavor to rivet on us the chains of slavery." At year's end Detroit's *Vindicator* asked "Are We Persecuted?" and answered that "in no other city of the west has the same degree of illiberality and bigotry towards Catholics so generally prevailed."[29]

During 1853 strong emotions in Detroit unsettled old loyalties. If the Democratic Party was not quite in disarray, the bases were being laid to prepare some Democrats to shake free of the party and fuse with the anti-Democratic coalition of 1854. And Independency's impact was not limited to Detroit.

Voters in many parts of the state must have heard of events in Detroit. Others read about them. Both Democratic and Whig newspapers discussed the school issue in ways suggesting that they assumed their readers knew about it, the Bishop's lobbying, and Independency. Democratic papers would have preferred to avoid the problem and some did. Others reported crisply on Detroit's election, favored free schools, and rebuked "priestly dictation" but not Catholics. Whig papers such as the *Marshall Statesman* and *Jackson American Citizen* rejoiced at the victory in Detroit of good over evil, while the *Pontiac Gazette*, always on the qui vive to the latest footprint of the cloven Catholic hoof, sprang to the task of lambasting Jesuits and Democrats.[30]

[28] *Vindicator*, April 30, July 16, letter of John Fitzgerald, July 23, 1853. The *Monroe Commercial* and *Detroit Tribune* were named as foes. For an example of the *Tribune's* anti-Popery, see the "sermon" of a Protestant street preacher in the *Free Press*, May 3, 1853.

[29] *Vindicator*, July 16, James Sheeran's Address, July 23; quote from Dec. 17, 1853.

[30] *Coldwater Sentinel*, Dec. 24, 1852, Jan. 7, March 13, 1853; *Adrian Watchtower* (D.), March 15, 29, 1853; *Statesman*, Jan. 26, Feb. 3, March 9, 1853; *American Citizen*, March 16, 1853; Baxter, *History of Grand Rapids*, 195-96; *Centreville Western Chronicle* (D.), contained nothing; *Hillsdale Standard*, March 29, 1853; *Pontiac Jacksonian*, Feb. 6, 1853; *Pontiac Gazette*, March 5, 12, April 9, 1853.

Independency or some form of Know Nothingism may have existed in various parts of Michigan in the spring of 1853. The signs of this must be seen in relation to what came afterwards. In Oakland County's township elections "Independents" carried 5 of 15 towns, while Whigs and Democrats broke even. Some Independents were Free Soilers, some were prohibitionists, some had no other identification. In Adrian's city election voters ignored party lines to an extent remarkable even for a local election, electing a Whig mayor by 448 to 301 and a Democratic recorder 528 to 250. The Democratic *Watchtower* cryptically refused to go into the causes of this outcome. In Marshall two tickets entered the charter contest, a "People's" and Democratic, and parts of both were elected. Kalamazoo held a quiet election but "strong hostility was manifested by some democrats towards a portion of our ticket" and some regulars were defeated. From Coldwater came word that officers representing "Young America" gained election without opposition; references were made there also to "knowing ones." In Branch County, Whigs and Democrats split county offices, in part because of dissension within the Democracy over prohibitionism.[31] If Independency or Know Nothingism were not afoot one thing seems clear: strong currents were affecting voters in both parties to act independently of party loyalty.

PROHIBITION

Before 1853 political managers kept the temperance issue pratically out of politics. During 1853 traditional controls stopped working. Temperance zeal surged out of neutral channels and joined other influences disrupting voter loyalties so that by early 1854 it was having an unprecedented political impact.

As the 1850 Constitutional Convention met, nationally prominent temperance crusader John B. Gough lectured to full houses at the Presbyterian Church in Detroit. The convention received twice as many petitions relating to temperance than any other subject (at least 32 of more than 80). Yet a straight prohibition article could muster only 13 votes to 70 against. The delegates voted 64 to 26 not to submit a prohibition referendum to the people, and also refused 57 to 29, to disfranchise drunkards.[32] With many delegates protesting to be "temperance men" they approved an ambiguous article forbidding the legisture to authorize

[31] *Pontiac Gazette*, April 9, 1853; *Jacksonian*, April 6, 13, 1853; *Watchtower*, April 12, 1853; *Statesman*, April 13, 1853; *Kalamazoo Gazette*, April 8, 1853; *Sentinel*, March 8, April 1, 8, 1853.

[32] Farmer, *Detroit*, I, 840; *1850 Report of Debates and Proceedings Constitutional Convention*, 933-34, 93, 159, 326, 341, 358, 428, 483, 465, 510, 522, 558, 590, 698, 682, 604, 621, for petitions; debates and votes, 397-411, 413, 467-73, 478. Among the 13 prohibitionists were both Whigs and Democrats; few Whigs were present, so a high percentage of them supported it.

the granting of licenses for selling liquor. This smoke screen obfuscated the temperance drive for the next three years. Many temperance men asked its repeal while a Senate committee could not determine its significance and left it to the Michigan Supreme Court. Meanwhile, however, the 1851 legislature passed a version of the "Wisconsin Law" abolishing the license system but requiring any liquor dealer to give bond to the state guaranteeing payment of damages resulting from his trade. Detroit refused to give up the income it derived from granting licenses, but in 1852 the state Attorney General and Supreme Court ordered Detroit to stop licensing. This removed all restraints on liquor selling in Detroit and victimized the poor as license fees had gone into the poor fund.[33] By early 1853 temperance fever reached such a pitch that even Democratic Governor McClelland cautiously endorsed a law "adapted to the condition of the state." Petitions streamed into the legislature. By January 20 petitions asking for a "Maine Law" bearing some 70,000 names had arrived from every part of the state, especially from "burned-over" towns.[34] The House and Senate in early February passed by votes of 57 to 12 and 23 to 9 a Maine Law prohibition, allowing only one controlled dealership. Two Whigs and 10 Democrats in the House, and 9 Democrats in the Senate opposed it. The law had to be submitted, however, to a popular referendum in June.[35] With voter approval it would take effect in December. Temperance preachers and exhorters then launched a campaign which no doubt would have talked every drunkard into sobriety if they had heard only a small part of the torrent of words. Newspapers, whether hostile or sympathetic, Democrat or Whig, discussed little else that spring.[36]

As the legislature's vote indicated, Democrats gave the cause far less sympathy than Whigs. Thus the new sympathy for the reform displayed by Democratic newspapers revealed the growth of temperance strength. While the *Detroit Free Press* still anathematized liquor laws, this did not typify out-state papers. Through either silence, ambivalence, qualified or full support of prohibition, Democratic papers in Pontiac, Kalamazoo, Grand Haven, Coldwater, and Adrian, paid a careful *deference* to tem-

[33] Farmer, *Detroit*, I, 840; Streeter, "Prohibition Legislation," *Michigan History*, 2: 293-95; Clark F. Norton, "Early Michigan Supreme Court Decisions on the Liquor Question," *Michigan History*, 28 (Jan.-March 1944), 42-45; *Michigan Christian Herald*, Jan. 31, 1850; *Advertiser*, Feb. 15, 1851.

[34] Streeter, *Political Parties*, 294-95; Fuller, ed., *Messages of the Governors*, II, 253; *Journal of the House of Representatives, 1853* (Lansing, 1853), 496-513, for an index of petitions; *Journal of the Senate, 1853* (Lansing, 1853), 395-400. The Grand Division of the Sons of Temperance also lent a hand, *ibid.*, 478.

[35] Streeter, *Michigan History*, 2: 295; the law said that no person should manufacture or sell "any spiritous liquor or intoxicating liquors."

[36] E.g., activity in Oakland County, *Pontiac Gazette*, April 16, 23, 1853.

perance not characteristic of Democratic postures one or two years earlier. The Democratic *Centreville Western Chronicle* dramatically reversed itself between December 1852 and June 1853, castigating the *Free Press* for its stubbornness and praising the Democratic "country presses" for their "independent spirit."[37]

Temperance won a stunning victory at the polls. Of 36 counties for which returns are available only 2 voted against the law by small majorities. Sixteen favored the law by margins ranging from 55 percent to 64 percent, 9 voted between 65 percent to 74 percent for it, and 5, 75 percent for prohibition. Turnout in this special election was low compared to a presidential election but the fall-off was not much more than that for a state election. Counties all over the state and in all stages of economic and population growth heavily backed the law. Party loyalty acted as one substantial influence on voters, particularly in certain eastern and central counties. In Detroit and Wayne County the correlations between the percentage "no" and the Democratic mean (1848-52) in wards and townships were .602 and .516. In 18 of 19 counties (for which data was available) the correlations between the percentage of "Yes" votes and the percentage of Whig-Free Soil strength in 1852 were positive; in 8 the correlations were over .400. Table XI.2 shows the positive relationship between anti-Democratic voting in 1852 and support of prohibition in 1853. More importantly, it points ahead to the dynamics of the anti-Democratic Fusion coalition of 1854. The relationship between Republican voting in 1854 and temperance in 1853 was also strong. Again, in only 1 county was there a negative correlation. But in 13 of the 19 counties the correlation between prohibition support and Republican voting was stronger than between prohibition and anti-Democracy in 1852.

Prohibition's landslide signaled not an end but a beginning. In Detroit temperance men organized the Carson League, a "Mutual Protective Association," to test and enforce the law. Antiprohibitionists counterattacked, boosted by B. Rush Bagg, a Democratic police justice, who refused to enforce the law and on December 9 published a long argument attacking its constitutionality. Liquor dealers, with Germans and Irish conspicuous among them, then met at City Hall to organize to overthrow the law, condemning the Carsonians as illegal and dangerous to peace. Many continued, of course, to sell liquor. Compliance with the law probably was greater outside of Detroit, and enforcement seems to have de-

---

[37] *Jacksonian,* Oct. 24, 1851, Oct. 6, 1852; *Kalamazoo Gazette,* March 11, 1853; *Sentinel,* Oct. 29, 1852, Jan. 21, April 22, 1853; *Grand River Times,* Feb. 16, 1853; *Western Chronicle,* Dec. 9, 23, 1852, Feb. 24, June 9, 1853; Norton, *Michigan History,* 28: 47; also, *Marshall Statesman* (W.), May 18, 25, 1853.

TABLE XI.2

1853 Percent YES on Prohibition by Townships in 19 Counties
Correlated with: 1852 Whig-Free Soil Percentages,
and 1854 Republican Percentages

Counties	1852 Whig-Free Soil	1854 Republican
Washtenaw	.735	.687
Monroe	.157	.172
Macomb	.735	.743
Lenawee	.355	.284
Hillsdale	.433	.534
St. Clair	.268	.177
Lapeer	.338	−.012
Clinton	.552	.570
Eaton	.605	.710
Jackson	.384	.650
Branch	.177	.260
Calhoun	.534	.605
Cass	.414	.638
Kalamazoo	.295	.621
Barry	.281	.318
Allegan	.414	.157
Berrien	.322	.314
Kent	−.202	.505
Van Buren	.274	.377

pended on local community sentiment. Yet Detroit remained the center stage of the drama.[38]

On February 1, 1854, three Supreme Court decisions staggered temperance forces. In the most important, *People v. Collins*, the court split 4 to 4 on the law's constitutionality. Opponents generally agreed that the June referendum had been a delegation of legislative power to the people and hence unconstitutional. Supporters argued that legislative power had not been delegated any more than it might be in submitting a bank law or a constitution to popular vote; in none of these cases did the people act on substance in any way. Justice Abner Pratt delivered an opposition opinion crackling with antievangelical energy and scorn for moralists. Allowing the people to vote on statutes, he said, would lead to perversion of government and a *"collective democracy,* the most uncertain and dangerous of all governments." The forfeiture and destruction of all domestic liquor he called an unlawful seizure of private property, "disgraceful, unjust. . . . It outrages humanity."

The doctrine itself is the mere thunder of canting hypocrites and political demagogues; the most detestable of all beings that ever infested a civil government. The world has never . . . been reformed by oppressive penal laws,

[38] Farmer, *Detroit,* I, 840-41; *Advertiser,* Dec. 20, 1853. The *Coldwater Sentinel* and *Kalamazoo Gazette* criticized Bagg, while the *Free Press* supported him, Norton, *Michigan History,* 28: 48.

which are destructive of liberty and the right of property. And a legislative body might as well undertake, by a despotic penal enactment, to chain down the winds of heaven to prevent their blowing, as to compel the American people, by such enactments, to be sober, moral, or religious.[39]

In two other decisions, decided by votes of 4 to 3, the court seemed to approve the law. In *People v. Hawley* the court held that the act prohibited the manufacture and sale of strong beer and ale. *People v. Hoffman* sanctioned the defendant's paying jury fees in cases of liquor law violations. But the judges spoke on constitutionality only in *Collins*. This case was referred back to Justice Douglas of Wayne Circuit Court who on April 10 followed his own course and the court's: in *Collins* he had held the law unconstitutional and in *Hawley* he had decided against the defendant.[40] Many persons must have joined the *Coldwater Sentinel* in judging all this to be neither law nor justice. The *Adrian Watchtower,* no Maine Law zealot, called it a *"studied fizzle decision."* The *Kalamazoo Gazette* observed that "the whole moral force of the law was lost." Even the *Free Press* was unsatisfied. A student of the Michigan court has estimated that the liquor law decisions caused "more controversy than any other case disposed of" before the Civil War.[41]

Thus a temperance enthusiasm enduring maddening frustration came together with other impulses in early 1854, namely nativism and anti-Catholicism. Such a merger was hardly unnatural. Temperance everywhere tended to be nativist and anti-Popish as reformers frequently associated immigrants, especially Irish Catholics, with drunkenness. And in case evangelicals with common cause needed confirmation of the enemy's identity, the Detroit *Catholic Vindicator* denounced Michigan's Maine Law as a tyrannical puritan blue law.[42]

[39] Norton, *Michigan History*, 28: 49, 50, 51, 52, 54. In Kalamazoo a protest meeting said the law rested on the principle that people "are not capable of controlling . . . their own appetites, and that guardians are to be appointed for them by their servants, to deal out in measured quantities, those luxuries heretofore permitted by Divine authority." But Col. Johnson's Sunday Mail Report had established that officials should "represent the people's political, not their religious nor their moral views." *Kalamazoo Gazette*, Feb. 17, 1854; also *Grand River Times*, Feb. 15, 1854. A Carson League was organized in Branch County, *Coldwater Sentinel*, Jan. 13, 1854.

[40] Norton, *Michigan History*, 55-59; Justice Warner Wing wrote the majority opinion in *Hawley* even though he held the law unconstitutional in *Collins*.

[41] Norton, *Michigan History*, 48, 57-60, for opinion of *Washtenaw Whig*, 60; *Watchtower*, Feb. 7, 1854; *Gazette*, April 21, 1854; also *Pontiac Jacksonian*, Feb. 15, passim. On the continuing bitterness among lawyers and judges, Frederick B. Porter, "Journal," entry of March 25, 1854, MS Diary, MHCol. William Woodruff, "Diary" entries April 4, 7, 1854, MS MHCol described torch light processions celebrating anti-Maine Law decisions.

[42] Billington, *Protestant Crusade*, 323; Thomas, *Nativism*, 123-26; the only issues of the *Detroit Vineyard* known to me are Aug. 9, Oct. 11, 1844, July 11, 1845, BHC; *Vindicator*, June 18, 1853.

In the winter of 1853-54 nativism and anti-Popery hardly needed the indirect stimulus they received from temperance zeal. These impulses were rising all over the country, stimulated in part by the kinds of conflicts evident in Michigan. This was the season of trustee conflicts within the Roman church, and struggles over the Bible and school funds. During 1853 the Papal Nuncio Bedini visited America and a series of riots, including one of the worst in nearby Cincinnati, trailed in his wake. The ex-priests Gavazzi and Achilli and other vendors of titillating and sensational anti-Popery brought their wares to thousands in packed halls, parks, and streets. The Madiai affair (involving alleged Italian atrocities against Protestants) prompted Michigan's own Lewis Cass to denounce in the Senate the Duke of Tuscany for committing "one of the most flagrant violations of the rights of conscience recorded in the long chapter of religious intolerance."[43]

While Michigan papers reported these events only sporadically, one wonders how much these stories traveled via rumor, fantasy, and fear. Two reactions to "Father Gavazzi" by Democratic newspapers are revealing. Gavazzi was a rabble-rouser who preached a ferocious blend of anti-Popery and nihilism. After his performance in Montreal was mobbed, the *Coldwater Sentinel* complained of the suppression of free speech. The *Centreville Western Chronicle* agreed and found his published *Lectures* "not overrated" and "exceedingly pungent." Riots in Cincinnati over Bedini's visit in December 1853, and January 1854, stimulated discussion in Michigan of the Roman question.[44]

On February 28 in Detroit Jacob M. Howard, Whig politician and crusader for temperance, lectured on Jesuitism to an enraptured throng at the Young Men's Hall. The *Advertiser* reported that Howard traced Jesuitism from its birth in Loyola's bosom "till it came under the fostering care of the Romish church, where it assumed its perfection of mental and moral hideousness." Although most of the lecture was historical, Howard concluded with an "application . . . which elicited the unanimous applause of the audience." An eyewitness privately told his diary that Howard described Jesuits murdering, bribing courts, and taking bribes, and gave examples "of the causistry by which any crime was rendered excusable. . . . He spoke about an hour and three quarters to a

[43] Billington, *Protestant Crusade*, 262-399, passim; Sexon E. Humphreys, "Lewis Cass, Jr., and Pope Pius IX, 1850-1858," *Michigan History*, 41 (1957), 145-49; also Samuel H. Hall, Marshall, to A. Felch, April 12, 1852, Felch MSS, MHCol.

[44] Billington, *Protestant Crusade*, 301-04; *Sentinel*, June 17, 1853; *Chronicle*, July 21, 1853. Thomas, *Nativism*, 123; *Free Press*, Feb. 9, 1854; *Pontiac Gazette*, Feb. 4, 1854; also Jackson, *American Citizen*, March 9, 1853, Feb. 15, 1854; *Washtenaw Whig*, Feb. 1, June 28, 1854.

crowded house, and hardly one of his audience left . . . before he had finished."[45]

Some Democrats charged that Howard was trying to stir up religious strife to affect the coming charter election. Whether he was or not, Whig newspapers certainly exploited the Independent-regular split of a year ago and the Catholic threat to free schools. Although a meeting protesting the pending Kansas-Nebraska Bill in Congress had been held in Detroit as early as February 18, the schools, Catholics, and temperance dominated the political scene. The Whigs would have been happy to rerun the past election, and continued to make capital use of Bishop Lefevre and the Catholic clergy, although new manifestations of their misanthropy did not seem to be available.[46]

The prohibition battle also rolled into the city election, helping to lay waste party lines. After the court's decisions the *Free Press* observed more liquor being bought and sold in the city than ever before, the traffic being as open as that in potatoes, and pronounced the Maine Law "an utterly dead letter upon the statute books." The following day, appropriately, the Friends of Temperance organized for the city election, resolving to cut party ties and support only temperance men of either party.[47] The election yielded some confusing returns on prohibition. Oliver Hyde, the anti-Democratic candidate for mayor, pronounced "right" on temperance by his Whig and Free Soil supporters, easily carried the city. Yet B. Rush Bagg won reelection as police justice over a challenge from "the attorney of the Carson League," 2,421 votes to 2,058. (The year before the city had voted for the Maine Law, 2,042 to 1,744.) Of course local elections are seldom governed wholly or mostly by issues. But this was no normal election. The counting of votes was unusually slow because of "the multitude of splits." The voters reportedly "paid little attention to party lines, each voter cutting and carving to his own taste." The Whigs carried the top of their ticket, but a good many Democrats were also elected.[48]

Whatever weight is given to temperance, the disruption of party lines cannot be attributed to antislavery or anti-Southern sentiment. The Kansas-Nebraska Bill was conspicuous by its absence from most of the campaign. Whig leaders, notably the editors of the *Advertiser* and

[45] *Advertiser*, March 2, 1854; Frederick B. Porter, "Diary, 1854-5," entry Feb. 28, 1854, p. 10, MS MHCol. Two months later Porter saw at a rebuttal lecture by a Catholic "a tolerable turnout, but there were very [few] members of Protestant churches who condescended to be present." Entry, May 3, 1854.

[46] *Free Press*, March 3, 5, 1854; *Advertiser*, Feb. 24, 28, and esp. March 4, 5, 1854.

[47] *Detroit Daily Democrat*, Feb. 21, 1854; *Free Press*, Feb. 25, 1854.

[48] *Free Press*, Feb. 28, March 5, 7, 8, 1854; *Advertiser*, March 10, 1854; *Daily Democrat*, March 7, 1854; *Herald*, March 9, 1854.

Tribune, circulated a last minute letter committing Hyde to an anti-Nebraska stand. Their purpose clearly was to prepare his expected victory for use as a popular verdict on Douglas's bill.[49] The *Democrat*, Detroit's only Free Soil paper, ignored slavery extension. Its preoccupation was "temperance and reform" and it lined up behind Hyde only after local temperance committees endorsed the Whig ticket. In explaining its position it said it did not oppose the Democrats on grounds relating to national politics [!] but because the Democratic ticket was "an out and out rum ticket." Secondly, it was "an Anti-Missouri Compromise ticket." And thirdly, "It is a 'Belgian ticket.' Every man who ran on the 'school ticket' last spring has been ostracized by the party this spring." In its analysis of the Democratic defeat it returned to these three points, charging that Democratic caucuses and the *Free Press* had made slavery extension an issue. In fact, the *Free Press* had proclaimed Nebraska's irrelevance. The *Christian Herald* also viewed the election in terms of "temperance and free schools," and *afterwards* observed that Hyde was an opponent of slavery extension.[50]

The Whigs carried the election primarily because the Democratic rift had not subsided. The Whigs egged on regulars and Independents against one another, but the warring Democrats needed little coaxing from Whig cheerleaders. The *Free Press* tried to reconcile the factions while some Independents charged that they were being proscribed and shut out of nominations as punishment for their "necessary stand" on free schools and city improvements the year before. Much of the controversy centered, significantly, around Levi Bishop, president of the school board. After the election the *Free Press* "pretty plainly" assessed Democratic troubles and said that "the division in the democratic party . . . *which occurred last spring*, was not yet cured." (Italics mine) Editor Storey said that if ward meetings were better attended there would be fewer complaints over nominations. Recently "the democratic ward meetings were not attended by the businessmen and commercial men and professional men of the party."[51] This comment raises interesting questions about the social sources of the Independent-regular split, suggesting at a minimum that the Independents tended to be amateurs or marginal politicians, not pros or organization men. Earlier a strong positive correlation was noted between Independency and Protestantism; it is pertinent to add here that in Detroit there also tended to be a relationship between white collar, business occupations, and Protestantism.[52]

[49] *Advertiser*, March 7, 10; *Free Press*, Feb. 19, March 7, 8, 9, 10.

[50] *Free Press*, March 8, 1854; *Democrat*, Feb. 24, March 3, 7, 1854; *Herald*, March 2, 9, 1854.

[51] *Advertiser*, March 3, 4, 9, 1854; *Free Press*, March 4, 2, 3, 9, 1854.

[52] Based on assessment of data here and in Chapter XII.

The new failure of the Democrats to gain their normal vote in 1854 testified to the persistence of the party split. Table XI.3 shows that not until 1855 did they rebound from the debacle of 1853. While in most

TABLE XI.3
Detroit Wards: Democratic Percentages for Mayor,
1850, 1852, 1853,[a] 1854, 1855

Wards	1850	1852	1853[a]	1854	1855
1	51	54	30	38	50
2	47	56	24	31	40
3	44	51	28	32	48
4	60	65	30	49	80
5	52	53	23	37	48
6	44	51	20	35	48
7	57	52	33	30	65
8	61	73	54	52	70

[a] Recorder.

wards through 1853 the total number of voters had usually risen from year to year, from 1853 to 1854 the total vote in 6 of the 8 wards dropped (though in 1 ward this amounted to only 1 vote). Increases came only in the Fourth, heavily German, and the Eighth, heavily Irish Catholic, both growing wards. The drop in turnout might very well have been due to the Democrats' factional warfare inducing cross-pressures and withdrawal or deliberate rejection and nonvoting. The origins of these impulses, assuming they existed, had little or nothing to do with slavery extension or Kansas-Nebraska. To repeat, regulars may have tended to be "Hunkers" and Independents may have tended to be Free Soilers,[53] but such differences served as reinforcements to other burning cleavages.

In early April out-state county and township elections repeated, in a variety of combinations, the jumbled politics of Detroit. The Maine Law, according to the *Michigan Argus*, was the issue in many places. In Ann Arbor itself most of the city offices went to a ticket of "Fusionists," a mysterious coalition of "all the factions and isms against the democracy." Fusionists elected 10 to 21 supervisors in Washtenaw County. The *Washtenaw Whig* backed the coalition, calling it a "People's ticket" of *"friends and supporters of our educational system in all its phases."* (Italics mine)[54]

In Calhoun County, Democratic, Whig, and Anti-Nebraska tickets took the field, but Democrats won a majority of the supervisors. No more information is available, but Nebraska apparently failed to make much

[53] *Advertiser*, March 9, 1854.
[54] *Argus*, April 13, April 6, 1854; *Washtenaw Whig*, March 29, April 5, 1854.

impact in Calhoun by April 3. Berrien County also saw a "people's ticket" riding to success over party lines. The *Niles Republican* witnessed a new feature: "Old party lines were forgotten, and whigs warred against whigs, and democrats against democrats." This phenomenon began weeks before when "a few ultra hot heads" decided new men should rule the village council and concocted secret plans "to crush every man who did [not] believe exactly as they did in relation to the enforcement of the Maine Law." In Constantine, St. Joseph County, an "independent ticket" headed by a Democrat won the township elections. Several townships also elected Whigs as temperance and probably "schools" played major roles in voter action. In Coldwater, Branch County, Democrats won 14 of 16 township supervisor posts. The briefly reported Coldwater city election raises interesting questions because considerable interest accompanied the election though only one ticket entered the field. In Jackson County the *American Citizen* claimed that Nebraska was "a test" in some towns. Some units "went it on the old whig and loco systems" but most anti-Democrats ran on platforms "generally anti-Nebraska, Liquor Law and anti-corruption." In few towns were "strict party tickets run by old parties" and several of the new coalitions called themselves "Independent."[55]

All this *independent* and *secret* activity may have had no relation at all to a Know-Nothing or native-American movement gestating all over the North. But possibly it did. That estimate becomes a probability when the strength and effectiveness of Know Nothingism in Michigan in the fall of 1854 is observed below. For now, it cannot be overemphasized that the major disruptive influences that spring in county, township, and charter elections throughout Michigan, as in Detroit, involved social cleavages and value conflicts generated from within local communities, and reaction to the pending Kansas-Nebraska legislation played at best a very minor role.

[55] *Marshall Statesman*, April 5, 1854; *Niles Republican*, April 8, 1854; *Centreville Western Chronicle*, April 6, 13, 1854; *Coldwater Sentinel*, March 19, April 7, 1854; at least one of the Supervisors elected had been a Free Democrat, *ibid.*, April 15; *American Citizen*, April 5, 1854.

XII

Rise of the Anti-Democratic Coalition: 1854–1855

Our Triumph has been glorious—it must not be called
Protestant but Independent *Republican* ticket—Or
Education Ticket—Elizabeth E. Stuart, March 12, 1853

The movement that removed the Democrats from state office in 1854 fell well short of being a developed party. "Fusion," the name most often used at the time, best describes the coalition of anti-Democratic leaders, organizations, pressure groups, and publics whose very being as a party emerged slowly.

After the 1854 spring elections, Whig and Free Soil managers began deliberately organizing the armies of the aroused into a united front against Kansas-Nebraska. Opposition to the extension of slavery and Southern power became the most common denominator of the anti-Democratic coalition. Popular concern for the slave, however, was negligible. Genuine compassion for black slaves and black neighbors moved some Fusionists, but expediency kept such motives muted or repressed. Hostility to slavery as an institution grew with recognition of *slaveholders'* "oppression" of Northern whites. The perception of Southern dominance of the national government usually preceded cognizance on a wide scale of slavery as an economic threat to free labor and free farms.

While each reform movement had independent stimuli, they shared some common ground, particularly in the minds of evangelicals. Abolitionists, temperance men, anti-Catholic nativists, and moral reformers generally had often been the same men, or had thought about reform in a similar fashion. Consonance among these impulses before 1853 naturally facilitated the fusion of 1854.[1] It was wholly appropriate, for

[1] Louis Filler, *The Crusade Against Slavery, 1830-1860* (New York, 1960), 78-79, 148-49; Fladeland, *Birney*, 220-21, 238; Alice Felt Tyler, *Freedom's Ferment: Phases of American Social History to 1860* (Minneapolis, 1944), 317, 319-20, 322-25, 327-29, 365-66; Dumond, ed., *Birney Letters*, II, 816-17; *Detroit Daily Vine*, July 11, Aug. 11, 1845, temperance and anti-Popery; *Detroit Daily Democrat*, Sept. 3, 1854, anti-Irish Free Soil paper; Marshall, *Michigan Temperance Advocate*; the *Signal of Liberty*, 1841-47, embraced many causes besides abolition, especially temperance, and also displayed nativist impulses, Nov. 18, Dec. 16, 1844, Jan. 16, 1843.

example, that the Free Soil Party had declared in 1852 that the "vice, suffering and curse, which flows from the unrestricted sale of intoxicating liquors" was the most important question confronting the state legislature.[2]

The Mechanics of Fusion

In the 1854 spring elections temperance claimed the lion's share of attention. But Floyd Streeter's account of the 1850s described a period of "violent" protest against the Nebraska Bill beginning on January 14 that persisted thereafter through June to the organization of Republicanism-Fusion-Independency in July. Streeter telescoped the period from January to June, indiscriminately mixing events at the beginning and end of that period.[3] One must differentiate more carefully the stages of Fusion's growth. True, protesters against the Nebraska Bill in February and March met in several large towns (notably Albion, Detroit, Pontiac, and Dexter), but more meetings had been held in 1853 to call for a Railroad Law, and popular interest in the Bill in March hardly equaled that in temperance or free schools. If the Pontiac affair is a good example, the anti-Nebraska meetings were vigorously anti-Southern and antislavery. Pontiac anti-Nebraskaites denounced Northerners such as Lewis Cass who voted for the Bill as representatives of "slave-breeders," viewed slavery as "an unmitigated curse," and pledged to wage "unceasing war against slavery, in all climes, in all forms, without respect to the color of its victims."[4] Seen in the general political context, however, these meetings did not constitute a mass movement. Indeed, anger at Kansas-Nebraska was burning primarily among informed elites, political leaders, and editors.

Free Democrats (Free Soilers)[5] and Whigs discussed coalition possibilities as early as December 1853. A caucus of Whig editors camped alongside a Free Democratic convention in February and sent two liaison men to them who by their affiliations embodied the mixture of political currents then abroad. One was Halmer H. Emmons, a leading temperance orator who in 1850 had been provoked by the Fugitive Slave Law to lend his voice to political antislavery. With him went Henry Barnes, whose *Detroit Tribune* had championed anti-Popery, prohibition, native resistance to alien influence, and Northern interests.[6]

---

[2] *Advertiser*, Sept. 6, 1852; *Daily Democrat*, Feb. 2, 1854. Also: *Advertiser*, March 2, 4, 1846; *Free Press*, Nov. 14, 1850; *Pontiac Jacksonian*, Sept. 8, 1852; *Coldwater Sentinel*, Nov. 12, 1852; Farmer, *Detroit*, I, 840.

[3] Streeter, *Political Parties*, 184-85.

[4] *Pontiac Gazette*, Feb. 25, March 3, 11, 1854.

[5] Free Soilers now had the formal name of Free Democrats.

[6] Charles V. DeLand, *DeLand's History of Jackson County, Michigan* (Jackson, 1903), 166-88. The meeting was in Jackson. DeLand, editor of the *American*

The Free Democrats showed a receptivity to broader political action. Their platform opposed repeal of the Missouri Compromise, decried immense executive patronage, advocated cheap postage, free land to actual settlers, rivers and harbors improvements, and government land to a transcontinental railroad. In state affairs it called for a new and constitutional liquor prohibition, general banking laws, "free schools," and opposed lending public money at 1 percent interest.[7]

Yet distrust still kept the Free Democrats and Whigs apart. The Free Democrats kept their own ticket in the field until they were assured their principles would be fully incorporated in any new movement. A rare record exists of a secret planning meeting of Fusionists in Detroit on March 22. A diarist termed it a "Whig Democratic Free Soil Caucus," and referred to the group as "conspirators." This surely indicates something about the state of anti-Nebraska feeling in March, namely that leaders were plotting behind the scenes to capitalize on a sentiment that had not quite emerged as an irresistible force. Yet the Free Soilers reportedly drove a hard bargain, pledging support only to a man who had been "a consistent opponent of slavery." Also, in February or March a meeting of editors had gathered in the office of the *Detroit Tribune* and broken up in apathy and disagreement.[8] It was probably not at all apparent at this stage that anti-Nebraskaism held the key to successful fusion. Fusionist George A. Fitch of the *Kalamazoo Telegraph* recommended an "Independent" convention to discuss nothing more specific than "the leading questions which now agitate the masses of the people."[9] Whig papers denounced the pending Nebraska Bill, applauded cooperation, and simultaneously wondered if cooperation between Free Soilers and Whigs was possible. As the hated bill passed in late May, protesters gathered spontaneously in the streets of Detroit. Two weeks later, in bad weather, anti-Nebraskaites assembled at City Hall only to find that "The Democracy had carried off the key and turned off the gas." The crowd broke the lock, turned on the gas, and listened to Jacob Howard and Kinsley Bingham. Yet a Free Soil observer still listened to Howard with skepticism, distrusting his Whiggery. That same day, June 8, the *Washtenaw Whig* predicted that three parties would again take the field in the fall. The *Christian Herald* observed that although indignation over

Citizen, and fusion organizer, wrote an informative account of the negotiations of 1854. William L. Stocking, "Michigan Press Influence on Party Formation," *Michigan History*, 11 (April 1927), 208-13; Wood, *Genesee*, I, 327.

[7] DeLand, *Jackson County*, 168-69.

[8] Fred B. Porter, "Journal," entry March 23, 1854, Porter MSS, BHC. Joseph Warren of the *Tribune* later received credit for continuing to promote harmony among potential coalitionists, William Stocking, "Little Journeys in Journalism: Joseph Warren," *Michigan History*, 22 (Autumn 1938), 404. Van Buren, *MHC*, 17: 264.

[9] Stocking, *Michigan History*, 11, 211.

Nebraska was not manifesting itself "in loud and rapid demonstrations . . . it is nevertheless deep, determined, and will be none the less effective *because it is now a little smothered or restrained*."[10] (Italics mine)

The turning point came on June 21 when the Free Democrats in "mass" convention of 150 to 200 persons at Kalamazoo agreed to withdraw their ticket and submerge themselves in a fusion movement. They would join the mass "independent" convention of all anti-Democratic elements planned for July 6 at Jackson. With the Free Democrats' organization dissolved it was less easy for resentment to develop against their getting too much recognition in the coalition—as in 1849. Jackson came to symbolize a merger dependent on all disavowing "the pride of party association," partly so that Whig (and Democratic) fusionists would not "lay themselves open to the charge of having gone over to the free-soilers, or 'wooly heads.' " Fusionists then and later also claimed that a prerequisite of fusion was an agreement that party offices and nominations be distributed according to the relative strength of the parties at the polls, and that leading Free Soilers "should remain in the background and not be pressed for prominent positions."[11]

THE NATURE OF FUSION

What then was the nature of the coalition formed "Under the Oaks"? The platform began with the most thoroughgoing denunciation of slavery ever delivered by any party in Michigan. Its rhetoric was more militantly antislavery than the Free Democratic addresses earlier that year. It asserted Congress's power and duty to control slavery in the territories, detailed the injury to Northern interests wrought by repeal of the Missouri Compromise, and demanded repeal of the Nebraska Bill and prohibition of slavery in those territories. Perhaps the height of antislavery sentiment was expressed in two belligerent, almost self-consciously reckless resolutions:

That after this gross breach of faith and wanton affront to us as Northern men, we hold ourselves absolved from all 'compromises,' except those expressed in the Constitution, for the protection of slavery and slave-owners, and we now demand protection and immunity for ourselves; and among them we demand the *Repeal of the Fugitive Slave Law*, and an Act to abolish slavery in the District of Columbia.

. . . That we notice without dismay certain popular indications by slave-

[10] DeLand, *Jackson County*, 173; Henry E. Candler, *A Century and One*, 197-98; Fred B. Porter, "Journal," entry June 8, 1854; Streeter, *Political Parties*, 189-90; the *Washtenaw Whig* became optimistic on June 27; on May 24 the *Marshall Statesman* was still uncertain.

[11] Letter of Isaac P. Christiancy, April 11, 1884, printed in Van Buren, *MHC*, 17: 263; also, letter of June 27, 1890, *ibid.*, 262; *Detroit Tribune*, Aug. 2, 1854.

holders on the frontier of said Territories of a purpose on their part to prevent by violence the settlement of the country by non-slaveholding men. To the latter we say: Be of good cheer, persevere in the right, remember the Republican motto: 'The North will defend you.'[12]

The platform closed with vague calls for "economical administration" in state affairs, debt paying, less taxation, support of a general railroad law, and a desire to be known as Republicans until the contest ended. The opposition to slavery extension manifested genuine hostility to the institution, but was obviously generated in large measure by resentment of "aggressions of the slave power." The persuasive appeal aimed at "Northern Feeling."

Remarkably, the platform omitted a liquor law plank, yet Fusionists everywhere were identified as the "Maine Law Party." The State Temperance Convention had met at Jackson two weeks before and demanded a new prohibitory law free of constitutional objections. They appointed a political committee to organize the temperance vote for November. Among its members were former Libertyites, Whigs, anti-Nebraska men, and Silas M. Holmes, whom the Fusionists then nominated for state treasurer.[13]

Fusion candidates individually and collectively appealed to several "reform" elements. Jacob M. Howard's name (candidate for attorney general) suggested not only temperance, but also benevolence, evangelicalism, and anti-Jesuitism. At the head of the ticket stood Kinsley S. Bingham, Free Soiler and ex-Democrat. His dual antecedents provided his supporters with flexibility in shaping his image. His Free Soil past gives more insight into the alleged antislavery character of Fusion.

As a Democratic Congressman representing the Third District—one of the two districts which elected a Whig-Free Soil coalitionist in 1850—Bingham voted for the Wilmot Proviso in 1847-48. He explained his position to James Birney in 1848: "Let us do what we are sure we have a right to do, *Keep Slavery* out of the *Territories*, and it will certainly be settled by a population who will be as anxious to preserve their State Constitution from the Stain of Slavery as we are."[14] In 1849-50 Bingham further upset orthodox Democrats by insisting on presenting antislavery petitions from his constituents who requested it. But contrary to the disapproving *Free Press*, Bingham was not antislavery but pro-Northern

---

[12] DeLand, *Jackson County*, 177-80; Randall, "Gubernatorial Platforms," 107-14.

[13] *American Citizen*, June 26, 1854.

[14] Elizabeth Agren, "Kinsley Scott Bingham, and the Slavery Controversy," University of Michigan Seminar Paper, 1958, MHCol, 5-7; Bingham to Birney, Sept. 24, 1848, Dumond, ed., *Birney Letters*, II, 1112.

white. He opposed most of the Compromise of 1850 and the Democratic organization denied him renomination in 1850, anathematizing him out of the party. More than dislike of slavery per se, Bingham's resentment of the dominance in national affairs of "the 'chivalry' " led him eventually to Fusion.[15]

It has been too little appreciated how deep was the resentment of Fusionists of the domineering arrogance of "our southern masters." Whatever else the destructive "influence" of slavery might imply, the impact of the "overbearing nature these nabobs have acquired in their custom of giving commands to their miserable serfs" directly pricked the pride and self-esteem of Northern men of influence. Slaveholders' arrogance offended Northern elites more than any reaction to shifts in a theoretical balance of power, or the economic competition of slaves in a remote territory at some remote time, or the direct effects of Southern opposition to rivers and harbors and other politicoeconomic legislation of intended benefit to the Northwest. "They are intolerant," said the *Christian Herald*, "not occasionally, nor by accident,—but habitually, and on principle. . . . It is the slave driver's lash, differing a little in shape, and applied to Northern white men, instead of Southern slaves, but wielded for the same end, the enforcement of their will, and by essentially the same means,—brute force instead of reason and justice."[16] Appeals for "bleeding bondsmen" were heard in 1854, but even in the most habitually compassionate of quarters these emotions were enmeshed in hard resentment of "our Southern masters." Even an old abolitionist like Seymour B. Treadwell, in calling upon the Free Democrats to join the fusion movement, although he dropped a phrase or two showing concern for the "freedom of the enslaved," developed far more assiduously his concern for the freedom of white Northerners. A Whig State Convention which met in October made no nominations but aspired to new heights of anti-Southern grandiloquence: its only product was an address devoted almost entirely to castigating "the undying efforts of the Slave power for political supremacy."[17] The rhetoric of a man such as Treadwell may have been a pragmatic tactic designed to capitalize on the moment, but that is precisely the point: the audience's disposition and the situation itself called for emphasis on the arrogance of the Slave Power in its dealings with the free, white North.

Allied to the Slave Power theme in Fusionist rhetoric was the Demo-

[15] *Free Press*, June 13, 1850; K. S. Bingham to J. S. Bagg, Dec. 24, 1849, Bagg MSS, Huntington Library.

[16] *Herald*, March 26, 1854; the *Pontiac Gazette* contained fine examples of anti-Southernism, quotations are from June 10, Aug. 4, Sept. 23, 1854.

[17] *Detroit Daily Democrat*, July 5, 1854, for Treadwell letter to Kalamazoo Free Democratic Convention; J. S. Smart, *The Political Duties of Christian Men* (Jackson, 1854), 6; *Pontiac Gazette*, Oct. 14, 1854.

cratic "doughface" strain. Judging by the reaction of the Democratic press, this was a profitable line of attack. With at least one exception Democratic papers generally defended, ignored, or obfuscated on the Nebraska issue in the early months of 1854. They grasped at innocuous formulas such as "Congressional noninterference," or claimed that "popular sovereignty" or "self-government" were truly antislavery concepts. The *Centreville Western Chronicle* wished that all "new party tests" and "isms" might disappear. It submitted perhaps the leading irrelevancy of the day by proposing that the Democrats stand on a platform of "Opposition to Monopolies and Monarchies; the Sub-treasury system and the Monroe doctrine." The *Kalamazoo Gazette* called the Nebraska act a legislative achievement "more important . . . perhaps, than any which has preceded it in our history" because it referred slavery to the people, thereby settling the issue and making the United States "an undivided nation." Wilbur F. Storey's *Free Press* defended Nebraska as vehemently as it labored to tar Fusion with the stigma of abolitionism, making one of the most frenzied appeals in the North to Negrophobia and racism.[18] But most Democrats, with an amazing show of calm, battened down the hatches and prepared to ride out the storm. The men who had played politics by the book and picked up most of the winnings for years, met in state convention in September, listened to Lewis Cass defend popular sovereignty, nominated for governor the sure winner of the past, John S. Barry, and handed the voters a short platform which endorsed a general railroad law, affirmed the 1852 Baltimore platform, and said that "the doctrine of Congressional non-intervention . . . is the only platform upon which the democratic party of the Union can maintain its nationality and its ascendancy, and preserve the Union."[19]

Fusionists passionately denounced "the timid, weak-minded, servile, fawning, venal spirit" of Northern Democratic doughfaces. Yet Fusionists also recognized that "a deep feeling of dissatisfaction" pervaded the Democratic Party and needed "but wise and energetic action to overthrow the ruling dynasty." Consequently, coalitionists combined castigation of doughface leaders with steady appeals to enlightened Democrats among the rank and file.[20]

[18] *Kalamazoo Gazette*, Feb. 24, May 26, 1854; *Adrian Watchtower*, Feb.-June, 1854; *Grand River Times*, Feb. 22, May 31, 1854; Streeter, *Political Parties*, 197; *Free Press*, Jan. 15, 1854; *Niles Republican*, Feb. 18, March 4, 1854; *Grand Rapids Enquirer*, May 21, 1854; *Pontiac Jacksonian*, Feb. 16, 24, May 25, June 1, 1854; *Centreville Western Chronicle*, March 23, April 30; differences of opinion occasionally were admitted, *Grand River Times*, Oct. 25, 1854.

[19] *Free Press*, Sept. 15, 1854; *Pontiac Gazette*, Sept. 23, 1854; F. B. Porter, "Journal," entry Sept. 14, 1854.

[20] *Pontiac Gazette*, Feb. 11, 1854; *Herald*, June 8, 1854; J. M. Edmunds to W. Woodbridge, May 25, 1854, Woodbridge MSS, BHC; *New York Baptist Register*, 31, July 6, 1854, letter of Ten Brook, June 30, 1854, MHCol; also,

Fusionist antidoughface tirades often contained strong dashes of antiparty. Most believed that the lash of "party drill" had joined the slaveholders in consummating the act of perfidy. In the 1840s Whigs had often linked pro-Southern or pro-slavery measures with the "despotism of party." In 1848 the *Advertiser* said that the Northern accomplices of Southern rule were "slaves of party" without an "Independent Soul." In 1854 *Pontiac Gazette* editor Zephaniah B. Knight's antiparty ran deeper than outrage over Nebraska. Knight believed that a man who did the bidding of party without question "gives up his own conscience . . . casts his reason away . . . leaving others to think for him, to dictate his conclusions, and to be his keepers." No true Whig, however, had ever submitted to leaders as thoughtlessly as Democrats did by habit. In cheering on Fusion, Knight recommended "independent" nominations "without consulting party or caucus. . . . This is the true Republican way." Like the *Gazette*, the *Jackson American Citizen* tended to be one of the most evangelical, anti-Popish, and anti-Southern of Whig papers. It also believed that party spirit caused political contests to be "fought over a dry and barren platform and a sounding and tinkling name instead of over men and principles." As the *Christian Herald* urged Christians to take an interest in political issues in 1854, it strongly opposed "becoming the slaves or appendages of party." After July 6 the *Gazette* predicted that now that the "Independent people" had adopted a platform and ticket the Whigs could be relied on to act as individuals as they always had. Whiggery "has never been a party, at all, in the real sense of the term. There was an aggregation of independent thinkers."[21] Thus the evangelical roots of antiparty still lived and Fusion naturally inherited Whiggery's antipartyism.

The *Gazette* was not alone among Fusionists in cultivating the notion that their movement was not a "real" party. Again and again they stressed the irrelevance of former party associations, the necessity of burying past loyalties, that no old party's banner would fly over the coalition, and that the new organization was not really a party. The very strength of former party loyalties and hatred required these techniques, but their rhetoric usually breathed genuine hostility to party per se.[22]

---

address of Ionia County Fusionists, *Pontiac Gazette*, Oct. 21, 1854, and *ibid.*, Oct. 28, Nov. 4, 1854.

[21] W. Woodbridge to S. C. Phillips, Charles Allen, and C. F. Adams, Sept. 18, 1845; Woodbridge to E. Robinson, Nov. 1846, Woodbridge MSS, BHC; *Advertiser*, Jan. 19, 1848; *Gazette*, April 15, 1854; first quotation from March 18; also April 2, 1853, Feb. 25, 1854; *Citizen*, March 29, 1854; *Herald*, July 22, 1854; *Advertiser*, Aug. 3, 1854.

[22] E.g., editors Rufus Hosmer and Theodore Williams of the *Detroit Weekly Inquirer*, May 2, 16, June 6, 13, 1854; *Daily Democrat*, June 7, July 5, 1854; DeLand, *Jackson County*, 173-74. Platform of Whig county committee printed in *Weekly Inquirer*, Aug. 22, 1854.

In late summer and early fall, Fusion (or Independent, or anti-Nebraska, or Republican) and Whig conventions began meeting on the same day; or Whig conventions met shortly after to ratify Fusion choices. The Whig shadow conventions served in part to undercut the non-Fusion *Advertiser*. The interlocking conventions also meant that more persons could participate. With the Free Democrats disbanded, the ritual of joint Whig conventions provided insurance against the claim that the Whigs had been betrayed because their leaders sold out to Free Soil.[23]

INDEPENDENCY, 1854

In Jackson County Fusionists met in an explicitly "Republican" convention. Oakland County Fusionists called theirs a "Mass Convention." The latter typified widespread avoidance of any party name at all in 1854. Fusion names varied over time and place but almost all anti-Nebraska fusionists at some point described themselves as "Independent."[24]

What did invocation of Independency signify? The answer in part is obvious, in part it can be deduced. It had several symbolic meanings: independence of Southern slaveholders in national affairs; of party; of the Democratic party, notoriously given to party usages; of liquor and rum sellers; of foreign influences; and independence of Popery, which threatened subversion of common schools and thus the republic— Popery which sanctioned slavery, and whose voting herds aided the Democrats, party, and Slavocracy. Independency in this sense bore close kinship to evangelicalism. Of the evangelical nature of Fusion there can be little doubt.

Willis F. Dunbar, in an excellent article in 1955, observed that a variety of reform movements created the Republican Party and that "antislavery forces" alone probably could not have won the state.[25] Dun-

[23] The *Pontiac Gazette* printed, Aug. 12, 19, Sept. 2, proceedings of the Whig State Convention and James A. Van Dyke's address which urged Whigs to act "not as a party man, but as a free northern man," Oct. 14. The mechanics of Whig conventions: Martha M. Bigelow, "The Political Services of William Alanson Howard," *Michigan History*, 42 (March 1958), 8; Holderreid, "Jacob M. Howard," 80-81. Oakland County Whig and "Mass Convention" proceedings, *Gazette*, Sept. 16, 1854.

[24] *Gazette*, July 1, 15, 1854; *Detroit Tribune*, Oct. 18, 1854; *Portrait and Biographical Album of Sanilac County*, 460; the *Advertiser* referred to the "Independent" and "Republican" ticket in the same paragraph, Nov. 7, 1854; *Weekly Inquirer*, Sept. 26, Oct. 10, 1854. In 1844 a Catholic priest used the word "Independents" synonymously with "Protestant zealots," Andrew Viszoszy, letter of July 25, 1844, Grand River, in McGee, *Catholic Church in Grand Rapids*, 111.

[25] Willis F. Dunbar, "Public Versus Private Control of Higher Education in Michigan, 1817-1855," *Mississippi Valley Historical Review*, 22 (December 1935), 401; Streeter, *Political Parties*, 206. Also, Willis F. Dunbar, "Year of Decision on Michigan's Education Policy: 1855," *Michigan History*, 39 (December 1955), 455-60.

bar's thesis can be elaborated. In 1854 evangelicals came politically into their own after a long spell in the cold. The Independent cause, temperance battles, and the Nebraska Bill politicized them. The breezes of the gathering coalition wafted to them the scent of power and "recognition." Hence they renewed pursuit of goals which had been sought for decades, such as degree-granting powers for church related schools. Evangelicals had never accepted the state's commitment to centralized, secular education. They again pressed their criticism of the state university, demanded denominational schools, an agricultural college, and asked for women's rights in education and other areas.[26]

It was no secret that large numbers of Protestant clergymen plunged into politics in 1854. The Democrats complained incessantly of religious interference, and the fusion-evangelical presses shot back with complaints of "Interference of Politics with Religion." There existed much local food for controversy, but national incidents also fed this source of antagonism, particularly the New England ministers' remonstrance against the Nebraska Bill, and Douglas's counterattack.[27] Perhaps never before did so many so unabashedly "assume to be the correctors of public morals."[28] The cultural-religious conflicts of the past two years had recast on a wider scale than ever before the old struggle of evangelicals versus antievangelicals, and had given new strength to the former.

The best example of Fusion evangelicalism was a sermon delivered by a Methodist minister at Jackson, which was not easily distinguishable from a campaign speech. J. S. Smart's *The Political Duties of Christian Men* echoed the political evangelicalism of the 1820s in contending that the two "most agitated" public questions, slavery and intemperance "are just as much moral as political questions, and consequently just as appropriate for pulpit discussion as legislative debate." He also wanted more "representation" of religious interests in government and better Sabbath-keeping. Even now the popular will was being betrayed and he blamed Democrats. Party names meant nothing, he said, but men who opposed the Maine Law where a 20,000 majority favored it, and men who favored slavery where 99 out of 100 opposed it, such men should not be called "Democrats." A more appropriate name was "Slavocratic

[26] Dunbar, *Michigan History*, 41: 451-52, and *Mississippi Valley Historical Review*, 22: 402. The University's situation in the 1850s was quite complex and it was under attack from a number of sides, Charles M. Perry, "The Newspaper Attack on Dr. Tappan," *Michigan History*, 10 (October 1926), 495-514.

[27] *Free Press*, March 17, 24, 27, passim, 1854; *Christian Herald*, April 6, 1854; *Kalamazoo Gazette*, Feb. 24, 1854; *Jackson Patriot*, April 26, 1854; *American Citizen*, April 19, 1854; *Pontiac Gazette*, April 22, 1854; Philip P. Mason, ed., "Apologia of a Republican Office Seeker," *Michigan History*, 41 (March 1957), 85-87.

[28] *Jackson Patriot*, July 11, 1855.

Rumocracy."[29] Implicitly, Smart argued that parties elected vicious men. Ministers should teach that "conscience extends to the ballot box, and that conscience should cast the vote instead of party prejudice." Smart did not concern himself with dilemmas of choosing between two evils. Nothing he said suggested withdrawal: "It is just as much a moral act to vote as to pray. Indeed, every vote which we deposit is the invocation of a curse or a blessing upon the land."[30]

The engaged evangelicalism of 1854 ran parallel to a grassroots Know-Nothing movement whose driving force was anti-Catholicism. "Independent" often seems to have been a euphemism or code word for Know Nothing. The *Advertiser* explained in September that conditions encouraging Know-Nothing growth had been "flourishing" in Michigan with Catholic lobbying in Lansing and the Bishop's politicking. And Catholics and foreigners had offended natives for a long time by their "aloofness" and their acting "as a unit in political matters" with scarcely any exceptions.[31]

The Know Nothing or American Republican Party probably organized primarily against Catholic influence in politics, and less against foreigners. The *Catholic Vindicator* claimed that nativism was only incidentally antiforeign and pointed to the prominence of foreign Irish Orangemen in the Order. Analysis of the movement is complicated because of its secrecy, which in Michigan was well kept. But too many traces and tracks of the Order have been overlooked, and its extent and significance severely underrated. Streeter understandably found it difficult to estimate American strength "since it placed few if any candidates in the field."[32] To my knowledge, Know Nothings placed no candidates openly in the field in 1854. Rather, they caucused secretly and independently and supported Fusionists or Democrats to their liking. For the most part they chose Fusionists.

"Independency" to Know Nothings meant invocation of the struggle against Popish influence and a shout of freedom from "party." Know Nothings were vigorously antiparty, from necessity and character. Article VII of the 1855 American Party platform declared hostility to "leaders of party" and their methods, and promised imitation of "practices of the purer days of the Republic." In Detroit's 1855 city election an "Independent" opposition to the Democrats, dominated by Know Nothings, recommended its nominees as men "who will know no party in the administration of city affairs." This resolution symbolized the antiparty-

---

[29] Smart, *Political Duties of Christian Men*, 8, 13-14.

[30] *Ibid.*, 4-5, 12, "a christian . . . should free himself from all party prejudice, and always vote for the best men," 14-15.

[31] *Advertiser*, Sept. 6, 1854.

[32] *Detroit Catholic Vindicator*, July 29, 1854. Streeter, *Political Parties*, 180, exaggerated the influence of the *Advertiser*.

ism of Fusion-Republicanism, Independency, and Know Nothingism, since it was offered, according to the *Free Press*, by I. S. Sprague, the man who as secretary of the Know Nothings' Grand Council recommended that Americans support Fusion candidates in 1854. In Berrien County a perceptive Democratic editor realized that the appeal of Know Nothings came from more than "forms and ceremonies." A potent attraction was the promise by former Whigs "to have dropped all former party prejudices" and that "they would cut aloof from all old 'office seekers,' 'party hacks,' as they termed them and stand forth with new men and new leaders."[33]

The Know Nothings allegedly organized on a state basis on June 2, 1854. The earliest clue found of their organizing appeared May 18 in the Ann Arbor, *Michigan Argus*. During the campaign, references to the existence of Know Nothings came from all quarters of the press. All must be treated with caution. But so many of the comments on Know Nothingism, reliable or not, were so obviously tactical that they make an argument for its presence. The still nonfusing *Advertiser* apparently thought the Americans would be strong enough to justify the paper's "independent" course. The Democratic press in Wayne, Washtenaw, Oakland, Lenawee, Kalamazoo, and Berrien counties accused the Fusionists of being allied with or identical to Know Nothings. Led by the *Free Press*, Democratic editors circulated in October a sensational exposé of the conspiracy between Fusion and Know Nothingism.[34] Storey's *Free Press* also stirred up Negrophobia, thus making explicit the group hatreds he expected to mobilize Democratic loyalties. "Is a White Man as Good as a Negro?" Wilbur Storey asked on November 4, and answered that the fusion "abolitionists" were crusading to "confer upon negroes the highest civil and political privileges, [while] they would degrade foreigners, and Catholics, and Protestants having Catholic wives to a secondary status"; freedom shriekers "*love* a negro, but they hate a German, an Irishman, or a Scotchman, or a Catholic of whatever nativity." Despite Storey's vehemence, which suggested total war between Democrats and Know Nothings, it was possible that Know Nothings in some localities worked through the Democrats.[35] The Fusion press gave comparatively little at-

[33] Know Nothings resembled Antimasons in antipartyism and other ways. Thomas, *Nativism*, 134; Richard Hofstadter, *Paranoid Style in American Politics*, 19-23. In 1844 the Order of United Americans declared "We disdain all association with party politics; we hold no connection with party men," quoted in Billington, *Protestant Crusade*, 336; *Christian Herald*, June 15, 1854. *Free Press*, Feb. 25, 28, March 3, 1855 on Detroit; *Niles Republican*, June 16, 1855, on Berrien.

[34] *Michigan Argus*, Oct. 20, 27, 1854; *Kalamazoo Gazette*, Oct. 27, 1854; *Niles Republican*, Oct. 28, 1854; Streeter, *Political Parties*, 180; *Adrian Watchtower*, Oct. 31, 1854.

[35] The *Advertiser* claimed that at the Wayne County Democratic convention

tention to the Know Nothings. Most of it was cautious, euphemistic, indirect.[36] Considering the Democratic outpouring, the argument from this general silence for a Fusion-Know Nothing alliance is quite strong.

Know Nothingism's presence and disposition in Detroit may be judged by audience reaction to an election eve speech at City Hall by Democratic champion Lewis Cass. Cass spoke for two and a quarter hours, Fred Porter wrote in his diary, and "He had a very large and attentive audience, but though there were present a good number of Irishmen, and from twenty-five to fifty persons applauded the general at every convenient opportunity, I strongly suspect that a majority of the crowd were not Nebraska Democrats." Cass showed his anti-Southernism by lambasting the *Richmond Enquirer*, and defended popular sovereignty as not legislating slavery into the territories: *"When Cass made his first allusion to the Know Nothings which he did by saying that there was a body of that name there were double the number of cheers that greeted any other portion of his speech, and when he went on to denounce them, it was very evident that he met with very little sympathy from any except Irishmen."*[37] (Italics mine)

The election resulted in an impressive although not a stunning victory for Fusion. Bingham received 43,652 votes, or 52.1 percent to Barry's 38,675, or 47.1 percent. Most impressive was the level of voter interest in a nonpresidential context. Every state election since 1841 had seen voter turnouts sag far below preceding presidential turnouts. In 1849, for example, some 13,000 fewer voters went to the polls than the year before. In 1854 only 612 fewer voters, 82,327, turned out than in 1852. If one assumes that virtually the same electorate voted in 1854 as in 1852 then it is clear that the hope of uniting the anti-Democratic vote had finally been realized. (See Table II.1) One cannot assume that the same electorate did turn out, but the data make it clear that the Fusionists managed to unite the greater part of Whig and antislavery voters for the first time since 1840. Democratic defections, while probably small, were significant in giving the Fusionists a victory. The Democratic

---

"Some of the country delegates complained that about 20 of the 24 city delegates were . . . foreign born citizens, indicating that the 'Know Nothings' are 'going it' in the out-towns," Sept. 11, 1854. For a full discussion of Storey's racism, Walsh, *To Print the News and Raise Hell*, 50-64.

[36] *Pontiac Gazette*, Oct. 28, 1854; *Marshall Statesman*, Oct. 11, 1854, claimed that a Know-Nothing paper, the *Western Sentinel*, had been established in Detroit; *Washtenaw Whig*, Aug. 2, Sept. 13, 1854. Detroit had a "Crime in the Streets" problem in 1854 which the anti-Democrats linked with "Irishmen," *Daily Democrat*, Sept. 12, 1854, *Advertiser*, Sept. 11, 26, Oct. 31, Nov. 24, 1854; the Republican city administration in 1856 showed great interest in a professional police force, Walsh, *To Print the News and Raise Hell*, 101-02.

[37] F. B. Porter, "Journal," entry Nov. 6, 1854, MS, MHCol. Fusionists the night of Nov. 6 "had an immense crowd at City Hall," entry Nov. 7.

numerical vote declined by 3,167, a drop of 2.6 percentage points. Some Democrats probably stayed home while new voters were added. Yet Democratic defections, particularly through the channel of Know Nothingism, played a role in the Fusion victory. At this point it bears recalling that the "Independent" vote in Detroit's wards in 1853 had a +.588 correlation with Fusion percentages in 1854. The Fusion vote in Detroit's wards in 1854 also had these correlations, based on ward data for 1853: Protestants +.907; Irish Catholics —.629; foreigners —.842.

All over the state the Democratic press emphasized not Nebraska but Know Nothingism as the cause of Democratic defeat. The *Free Press* predictably bemoaned "A complete fusion, know-nothing victory." This "new element of opposition" was diffused throughout the State . . . a *secret* agent . . . its very existence denied by those who directed it." The *Grand Rapids Enquirer* echoed that "the black flag of Abolition, Religious Intolerance and Political Proscription waves in triumph." Although it took no notice of Know Nothingism before the election the *Centreville Western Chronicle* claimed that Know Nothings elected all but two men on the Fusion ticket. When "reliable Democratic towns . . . give a majority of 70 to 112 against our regular nominees, it will require no great degree of shrewdness to perceive a secret influence unusual in the annals of elections." The *Ann Arbor Michigan Argus* said it knew a Know Nothing vote existed in Ann Arbor, but could not say how large.[38] The *Niles Republican* announced Democratic defeat in Berrien County with a few lines of jumbled type to symbolize a "NO NOTHING TRIUMPH" by a "secret, silent vote" behind a "People's ticket." The *Republican* confronted squarely the question of the relative significance of anti-Nebraskaism and Know Nothingism and judged that the Nebraska issue "of itself . . . could not have overthrown the democracy of the north so effectually." The *Catholic Vindicator* agreed that the election ended "most triumphantly for the anti-Catholic Know Nothing party."[39]

On the anti-Democratic side the *Advertiser* of course led with kudos for the Know Nothings. The result was not "a party victory. . . . The mysterious order undoubtedly held the balance of power." On the other hand the *Marshall Statesman* denied that in Calhoun County "our Dragon fell by a secret hand." Yet it simultaneously printed a eulogy of the Know Nothing Party with a statement of its "fundamental doctrines," the foremost being "An exclusion of foreigners from office, by these

[38] *Free Press*, Nov. 8, 1854; *Kalamazoo Gazette*, Nov. 9, also Nov. 10, 11, 1854; Baxter, *Grand Rapids*, 196; *Western Chronicle*, Nov. 9, 1854; *Argus*, Nov. 10, 1854.

[39] *Republican*, Nov. 18, 1854; first quote is from Nov. 11; also, Nov. 18, Dec. 9, 1854; *Western Chronicle*, Nov. 23, 1854; *Kalamazoo Gazette*, Nov. 17, 1854; *Vindicator*, Nov. 11, 18, 1854.

meaning Catholics." The paper also reported that in Eaton County a Nebraska Democrat ran 200 votes ahead of his ticket because of Know Nothing support. The *Washtenaw Whig* candidly admitted that "the mysterious organization . . . exists to some extent in this state," but credited it only with increasing the majorities of the victory-bound "independent ticket." Although the order had chosen men of both parties in Washtenaw County, "at least nine-tenths of their number are Whigs, or else the Democratic Know-Nothings cheated like sin." In Jackson County the great issue, according to the *American Citizen*, was "Shall the Government of this free and enlightened christian nation become a great propagandist of human slavery?" Yet Republican leader Austin Blair could also write from Jackson on December 10 that Fusionists were "tormented with these infernal 'Know Nothings' whom may Heaven confound. What is going to be done with the scoundrels? let them run as the boy did the molasses till they all run out."[40]

PROGRAM AND PARTY-MAKING

The ambiguities of Fusion in 1854 suggest a political organization which did not yet have the cohesiveness, stability of leadership, and integration of a functioning political party, an organization still timid to call itself a party.[41] Its supporters vested in it a wide range of idealistic and mundane expectations. An applicant for state librarian believed that "a great moral principle . . . has triumphed and may the Ball keep rolling until Slavery shall be swept from the land." Isaac P. Christiancy, on the other hand, warned the new governor that the last legislature had incurred great unpopularity because it was too much influenced by "R.R. Companies and neglected matters of general interest." He hoped the new legislature would "not pay the least regard to a set of lobbies hired for a consideration to get special favors for these corporations at the public expense."[42]

On January 4, 1855, Governor Bingham's long inaugural message set forth many of the new coalition's goals. Historians have emphasized the

[40] *Advertiser*, Nov. 8, 1854; *Statesman*, Nov. 21, 1854, also Nov. 29, Dec. 20, 1854, Jan. 17, 1855; Ann Arbor, *Washtenaw Whig*, Nov. 15, Sept. 20, 1854; *Citizen*, Oct. 4, 1854, resolutions of Jackson County convention; Austin Blair to A. T. McCall, Dec. 10, 1854, Blair MSS, BHC.

[41] The factional nature of the party is evident in H. Barnes to Gov. K. S. Bingham, Dec. 10, 1854, Executive Records, Elections, MHCom; Stocking, "Joseph Warren," *Michigan History*, 22, 404; *Jackson Patriot*, May 23, 1855, film, MSL. The *Congressional Globe* listed Michigan's three fusionist Congressmen as "Americans" while the *Tribune Almanac* listed them as "Republicans," Thomas, *Nativism*, 181. *Advertiser*, Dec. 8, 1854.

[42] R. B. Hall, Saginaw City, to K. S. Bingham, Nov. 9, 1854; I. P. Christiancy to Gov. Bingham, Jan. 26, 1855, Executive Records, Elections, MHCom; also George A. Coe to K. S. Bingham, Dec. 4, 1854.

economic interests that formed Northwestern Republicanism, interests that some commentators have suggested caused the "moral" concern over slavery expansion. Southern power, this argument runs, had to be contained to liberate industrial expansion. New slave states had to be aborted to protect the economic interests of farmers and workers who wanted free land, of laborers and mechanics who wanted no competition or loss of status from black slave labor, or businessmen who wanted tariffs and government aid. Bingham's message gives some credence to this view, but passages on economic issues must also be seen in historical context. Underlying Bingham's recommendations was an activist attitude toward the role of government that had been the soul of Whiggery. Activism embraced both economic development and moral improvement. His rhetoric of "enterprise" married itself to a concern for the general welfare and a hostility to the narrow interests of the capitalist favor seeker. Bingham observed that "Our past experience teaches us that the same economy and foresight which directs private enterprise cannot be expected of the agents of the State in their management of public improvements." Thus, Bingham would have the purchaser of state swamp lands and not the state drain the lands, and he urged that lands be sold in limited quantities to actual settlers. The pioneer could then get land at a moderate rate "instead of enriching the capitalist and speculator by an indiscriminate sale." Any surplus from land sales should go into an education fund.[43]

Bingham talked most about slavery. Beginning with a long history of how the Northwest had become attached to the Wilmot Proviso, he argued that slavery recently had made "great strides." Slaveholders had been given a permanent position of dominance in national affairs through the Nebraska act, a "stupendous scheme . . . to nationalize slavery . . . and to sectionalize freedom." Bingham saw the union endangered not by Northerners defying Southerners but by "unmanly concession." He proposed specific methods "to restrict and denationalize slavery." "There should be no slavery in the District of Columbia—none in national Territories—no slave catching under national law—no slave trade in American vessels, allowed or regulated by acts of Congress—no slave auction under process, out of the Federal courts."[44]

Surely this gladdened evangelicals—and for them there was more. Bingham rehearsed the evils caused by intemperance and the need for a new prohibition law. He also proposed "seminaries" to educate young ladies. His remarks on common schools must be seen in the context of Independency: "We rely," he said, "for the permanency of free institutions upon the universal diffusion of knowledge through their instru-

---

[43] Fuller, ed., *Messages of the Governors*, II, 287.
[44] *Ibid.*, 292-99.

mentality, and every effort made to improve their character, and make them free, furnishes an additional guaranty against pauperism, and crime, and taxation." If one can construe anti-Popery from this, one cannot infer nativism from the message otherwise. Rather, Bingham eulogized the most recent immigrants to Michigan (mostly Germans and Dutch).[45]

In the realm of political economy Bingham endorsed a general railroad law that would protect the public interest and encourage investment, an agricultural school, a general banking law which would avoid the evils of wildcat days, a national homestead law, and Congressional aid for improvement of the Sault Sainte Marie Canal. One can see in these recommendations a concern for business enterprise, also for the more businesslike conduct of state affairs; and one can see hostility to special interest groups fattening themselves at public expense. In concluding Bingham urged the legislature—as Christiancy had—to remove suspicion from the public mind regarding the "malign and corrupting influences . . . brought to bear directly upon the members" by lobbies.[46]

Advice to the legislature came from other quarters, too. Evangelicals sent numerous petitions praying for a variety of objects, including: a prohibition law, an agricultural school, a college and voting rights for women, laws to protect fugitive slaves, voting rights for black men, and a voter registration law.[47] The antislavery actions of the legislature have attracted the most attention from later observers. It passed a joint resolution against further extension of slavery, condemned the Michigan Congressman who had voted for Kansas-Nebraska, and asserted Congress's power and duty to abolish slavery and the slave trade in all territories and the District of Columbia. To Michigan's Congressional delegation it sent instructions to oppose slavery extension and work for repeal of the Fugitive Slave Law. The legislators further expressed anti-Southern sentiment by passing a law obstructing the Fugitive Slave Law—thus symbolically defying slave power *over them*. Erastus Hussey of Calhoun County, a former abolitionist, introduced this "Personal Liberty Law" in the Senate. It gave accused fugitives defense by county prosecuting attorneys, habeas corpus, and trial by jury, and denied the use of public buildings to imprison fugitives.[48]

Antislaveryism and anti-Southernism, however, occupied a relatively small part of the legislature's time. Evangelicals won their general college law permitting denominational schools to grant degrees. A college

[45] *Ibid.*, 283-84, 288-89.
[46] *Ibid.*, 283, 285-86, 289-92, 300-01.
[47] *Michigan House Journal, 1855*, 658-73; *Michigan Senate Journal*, passim.
[48] Streeter, *Political Parties*, 201-03; *Acts of the Michigan Legislature, 1855*, 463-65, 413-15, 415-16; *Christian Herald*, Feb. 1, 1855; *House Journal, 1855*, 408-09, 243-44, 606-07; *Free Press*, Nov. 6, 1855.

for women was not obtained, but some women's rights were secured. The legislature made the property of married women not liable for a husband's debts and permitted married women to sue, be sued, and contract and sell. And at last evangelicals could rejoice at the passage of an iron-clad Maine Law. The old law was repealed and the new one not referred to popular vote. Prohibition rolled quickly through the House and Senate by votes of 51 to 21 and 23 to 0; all the House opponents were Democrats.[49] Reformers may have welcomed an agricultural college more than farmers, but the General Railroad Law was widely popular. Prosperity and rising expectations created great faith in the benefits it would bestow, but significant increases in capital investment in railroads did not immediately follow.[50] As with many of these measures, its psychic import far exceeded its economic.

Other activities of the 1855 legislature, wholly missed by historians, reveal Know-Nothing influence. Anti-Catholic and related legislation indicate that debts to Know Nothings were paid. The origins of the anti-Democratic coalition did indeed reach back to the Independent movement of 1853. "An Act Concerning Churches and Religious Societies" established the legal position of lay trustees and undermined the Catholic hierarchy in its disputes with trustees over nonecclesiastical affairs. It laid down "uniform rules for the acquisition, tenure, control and disposition of property conveyed or dedicated for religious purposes." Trustees could "take into their possession . . . all the temporalities of such church, congregation or society, whether the same shall consist of real or personal estate." Trustees could sue and be sued and acquire property no matter who held it. The act affirmed the precedence of state law over any common or canon law in governing relations between trustees, congregations, and clergy. It even voided any legacies made to churches in last wills made "during the last sickness." Thus Michigan Know Nothings joined their brethren in other states (Connecticut, Maryland, Massachusetts, Indiana, Pennsylvania, Arkansas, New Jersey) who were attacking Popery by giving legal weapons to trustees. New York's legislature went so far as to make all clerical ownership illegal.[51]

Michigan's church property bill passed the House February 7, 5 days before the Personal Liberty Law, and 6 days after the Senate passed the

---

[49] Dunbar, *Michigan History*, 39: 458; Dunbar, *Mississippi Valley Historical Review*, 22: 404; *Acts of Michigan, 1855*, 51-55, 420; Streeter, "History of Prohibition Legislation," *Michigan History*, 2: 298.

[50] Dunbar, *Michigan History*, 39: 459; *Acts of Michigan, 1855*, 153-79, 279-82; Dunbar, *Mississippi Valley Historical Review*, 22: 403-05; *House Journal, 1855*, 509-10; Edmund A. Calkins, "Railroads of Michigan Since 1850," *Michigan History*, 13 (Winter 1929), 7-8.

[51] *Acts of Michigan, 1855*, 313-21, esp. 315, 318, 319, 320; Billington, *Protestant Crusade*, 295-300.

Maine Law. The legislators meanwhile considered other measures to contain Popery. Ever since the Maria Monk type of sensational exposés of Catholic convents had become popular in the 1830s, nativists had tried various approaches to "purifying" convents and seminaries. The 1855 legislature thus considered a bill "for the regulation of Roman Catholic nunneries and schools" and for their visitation by state authorities. The Know Nothing tide ran farther, though the entire legislature did not go all the way with it. Henry C. Ashmun, a half-Indian first-term representative from upstate Midland County, wanted the House to revise the naturalization laws. But an internal fight blocked any action. Detroit representative Asa P. Moorman, chairman of the Elections Committee, and sponsor of the "nunneries" bill, did issue a report promising to petitioners for a voter registration bill that at the next session "some measure will be adopted by which the ballot box may be protected from the polluting touch and assaults of individuals who, in sentiment and birth, are inimical to the free institutions of our own country; and who, as aliens, without the right of citizenship, or the possession of those moral virtues that marks American character, readily become the instruments of designing demagogues . . . sapping the life blood of the nation."[52]

Perhaps the relative strength of Know Nothingism in the legislature can be estimated by this crude indicator: the House passed the anti-slavery resolution 48 to 23, the Personal Liberty Law 40 to 28, Prohibition 51 to 21, and the "Act Concerning Churches" 50 to 9. But most newspapers ignored the "American" activities of the new legislature. Even the *Catholic Vindicator*, which noted that "Rum, religion and runaway negroes seem to have engaged much of the time of the State Legislature," only briefly denounced the bills for "the secularization of Church property" and "for violating the privacy of Convents."[53] Perhaps the most significant clue amidst the silence came from Berrien County, where the Democrats had been riddled by Know Nothingism. The *Niles Republican*, former critic of "No Nothings," printed the church act and described it as a law "that will commend itself to every true lover of his country" and which "pretty effectively puts a stopper on the rapacity of the Romish Church."[54]

[52] *House Journal, 1855*, 284, 396, 492-93; *ibid.*, 285; *Michigan Biographies*, 49; *Documents Accompanying the Journal of the House of Representatives, 1855*, House Doc. No. 32; Billington, *Protestant Crusade*, 68-76, 85-90, 413-14. Other evidence of Know-Nothing influence appeared in discussion of the General College Law, Dunbar, *Mississippi Valley Historical Review*, 41: 404.

[53] *House Journal, 1855*, 440-41; *Pontiac Gazette*, Nov. 18, 1854 described the new legislature as about two-thirds anti-Nebraska; *Vindicator*, Feb. 17, 1855.

[54] *Republican*, Feb. 24, 1855. An ex-Democrat later wrote to the paper: "Catholic efforts . . . have been made to get hold of a portion of our school monies in various States. That they wish to banish the Bible from our common schools. You are aware that many of our citizens are under the control of Catholics and

Some critics charged the legislature with incompetence due to "inexperience." Its defenders thought inexperience an advantage. It is suggestive that the men who could be identified with Know-Nothing legislation were all first-term legislators. A complete and comparative study probably would show that most nativist legislators were relative amateurs in politics. Political nonprofessionalism characterized, as Oscar Handlin has shown, Massachusetts' Know-Nothing legislature of 1855 which also passed a variety of moral and secular reforms.[55] In both cases Know-Nothing amateurs took bold actions which they believed "politicians" and "party" had frustrated for years.

As this orgy of reform drew to a close, local politics began thawing out for the spring elections. On the basis of these contests Streeter concluded that the Know Nothing Party was "strongest in the cities." In Detroit, he observed, an Independent ticket was backed by Republicans and Know Nothings. The American party won in Marshall, Battle Creek, Pontiac, Mt. Clemens, and in Kalamazoo with Republican help; it also elected a majority of supervisors in Cass County.[56] Whether this shows Know Nothingism strong in cities or not depends in part on one's definition of a city. Detroit had a population of 42,000 in 1855, but the Democrats won there. The other rural metropoli named by Streeter had populations of 2,000 or less, which usually included some farmers. In Cass County not even a large village could be found. The Know-Nothing phenomenon, in short, was quite as rural as "urban."

Although "Independents" lost in Detroit the receding but still strong Know-Nothing movement there bears close analysis. Fusionists again tried the successful formula of 1853 and 1854: an anti-Democratic, nonpartisan coalition appealing primarily to anti-Popery and nativism. Slavery stayed in the background. The *Advertiser* and *Tribune* again brought out for campaign work the schools and the Bishop and the Pope, brazenly parading Know-Nothing influence in the Independent forces. The *Advertiser* charged that "Seventeen of the twenty-four delegates to the [Democratic] city convention were Catholics" and that their mayoral nominee, Henry Ledyard, was anti-Know Nothing, pro-Catholic, and pro-Nebraska. The *Free Press* meanwhile discerned a split between Know Nothings and Republicans.[57]

---

that they are continually grasping after civil power. You are aware that politicians are always bidding for the foreign vote. Now do you approve of these things?" June 23, 1855.

[55] *Branch County Journal* quoted in *Marshall Statesman*, March 21, 1855; Moorman, Ashmun, and Samuel G. Ives were all first-termers, *Michigan Biographies*, 473-49, 373-74; Oscar Handlin, *Boston's Immigrants* (Cambridge, 1959), 200-03.

[56] Streeter, *Political Parties*, 180, 181.

[57] *Vindicator*, March 3, 1855; *Advertiser*, Feb. 27, March 3, 1855; *ibid.*, Feb. 24, March 1, 2, 5, 1855; *Free Press*, Feb. 25, 26, 27, 28, March 1, 3, 4, 1855.

Ticket splitting gave both sides some lower offices but Ledyard won a decisive victory, 2,798 to 2,026, suggesting that the Democratic split had been somewhat repaired. Ledyard had been a leading Independent in 1853 and, as Lewis Cass's son-in-law, must have had some appeal to the more orthodox, Hunkerish Democrats. Another factor in the result, according to the *Advertiser*, was Know Nothingism's frightening many foreign Protestants away from the Independents while foreign Catholics voted Democratic "as *foreign Catholic voters*." But "hundreds of . . . Scotch, English, and German Protestants" voted Democratic so that almost every Independent vote "was that of a native born American." Ledyard's opponent allegedly carried "every ward where foreign citizens did not have an overwhelming majority."[58] In fact, large majorities in the Fourth, Seventh, and Eighth wards, 80, 65, and 70 percent respectively, did contribute substantially to the Democrats' victory, though they also carried the populous First by 50.4 percent.

Before the election the *Advertiser* had meticulously identified the foreigners and Catholics on the Democratic and Independent tickets. It was no surprise that 11 of 19 candidates on the Democratic ticket were foreign or Catholic (as were 26 of 41 ward nominees), but the *Advertiser* also singled out 8 foreigners and 2 Catholics on the Independent ticket.[59] Perhaps this was done to let Know Nothings know who not to vote for on the Independent side, and such maneuvers in this election certainly could have driven many foreign Protestants to the Democrats. And the presence of even a small number of foreigners and Catholics on the Independent ticket could have suggested to ardent nativists that the new fusion party was becoming as decadent as the old parties, causing defection from that quarter as well.

Reckless abandon among nativists may very well have aided the result. Throughout the country Know Nothings committed excesses that made them appear ludicrous or dangerous.[60] So it was in Detroit. Shortly before the charter election one Alderman Craig took advantage of a routine petition of Bishop LeFevre to denounce the Bishop as a devil. The petition involved an exchange of land between Bishop and city, and Craig rejected the request because "Peter Paul LeFevre" already had too much land which really belonged to many of our fellow citizens:

. . . inasmuch as said Lefevre is a subject and emissary of a foreign Potentate, who, like the locusts of Egypt, not only devours the substance and productions

[58] *Free Press*, March 6, 7, 1855.
[59] *Advertiser*, March 5, 1855.
[60] Billington, *Protestant Crusade*, 413-18, exaggerates the "incompetence" of Know-Nothing legislatures; Handlin, *Boston's Immigrants*, 200-06, offers a balanced picture of accomplishments and excesses; also, William G. Bean, "Puritan Versus Celt, 1850-1860," *New England Quarterly*, 7 (1934), 70-80.

of the soil, but stultifies and withers the intelligence of his subjects and fills the land with beggary and crime.

Encouragement to such a Potentate would be reprehensible in a half-civilized people and positively criminal in a body of American citizens. The conduct of said LeFevre has satisfied your committee *that clothing him in the similitude of a man is a monstrosity—that he is a fit companion only for dragons and devils.* Your Committee recommend that he do not ask for the usual amount of ground allotted to man, viz.—*two feet by six*—but that he take his body back whence it came and there let it remain and enrich the soil it has impoverished.[61]

The *Catholic Vindicator* called Craig a blackguard and bigot, and denounced the other members of the council who accepted the report *"by their silence and sanction it by their acceptance* and thus spit contemptuously on the whole Catholic community." After the election, with Craig "home sick," the council expunged the report from its record and approved the Bishop's petition for land exchange. Soon after, Henry Ledyard gave his inaugural address to the council and implicitly scolded the Know Nothings: "Let us extend equal justice and equal rights to all our citizens, of whatever country and religion—for *here* they are all Americans."[62]

The rebuke to Craig did not signify the sudden eclipse of nativism in Detroit. Rather, the entire episode testified to the continuing salience of religious cleavages. Further, the conspicuous lack of attention to slavery extension must be noted, and too much emphasis cannot be given to the fact that the Detroit Democracy reconciled its warring factions sufficiently to produce, however incompletely, victory for the first time in two years by nominating *an Independent of 1853 who was a Nebraska Democrat and son-in-law of Mr. Popular Sovereignty himself, Lewis Cass.*

From across the state in March, April, and May 1855, came reports of a political patchwork of competition between Americans, Republicans, and Democrats in local elections, with the former two often mixed under a Fusion, Independent, or Citizen's label. In Pontiac, for example, an independent, "no party, Citizen's ticket" won the village election while anti-Nebraska supervisors allegedly were elected in half the towns in Oakland County.[63] Know Nothings carried Adrian, however, on their own and by large majorities, and did the same in Ypsilanti. In Monroe old party lines dissolved as "the issue has been Catholic and Protestant" with victory going to the latter.[64] Know Nothings also played important or dominant roles in anti-Democratic victories in the western towns of

[61] *Vindicator*, Feb. 24, 1855.

[62] *Ibid.*, March 10, 17, 1855; *Free Press*, March 14, 1855; *Vindicator*, March 17, 1855.

[63] *Pontiac Gazette*, May 12, 1855; *Free Press*, April 5, 1855; *Kalamazoo Gazette*, April 18, 1855.

[64] *American Citizen*, April 4, 1855.

Kalamazoo, Marshall, and Grand Rapids. In Berrien County, in a Judge of Probate election a Know Nothing confronted a Democrat in an open contest and carried off 654 votes of 1,245.[65]

In some areas Know Nothings worked on the Democratic side. In Ingham and Jackson counties Know Nothings worked either independently of Fusionists or with Democrats in county elections. The *Jackson American Citizen* included "the know nothing clique" as among Fusion's enemies while Austin Blair continued to be "astounded at the villainy of . . . a gigantic secret society based upon political and religious bigotry carried on by lying and fraud."[66]

Reports of Know-Nothing activity in at least two counties found their way into county histories—rare and probably accidental events. The county histories of the late nineteenth century were mostly chronicles or compendia of local data. Yet in the annals of Hillsdale and Branch counties in southern Michigan the Know Nothings impressed themselves strongly in local traditions. Hillsdale's Camden and Wright townships, rural and moderately prosperous, had voted Democratic in the 1840s and in 1854 returned Democratic percentages of 65 and 61. But thereafter the Democrats "became hopelessly in the minority." In causing this "the 'United Americans' or 'Know Nothing' societies took a somewhat prominent part." Both towns voted Republican in 1856, Wright 60 percent, Camden 59 percent.[67]

In Branch County the "mysterious order" operated in 3 towns, 2 of which had been strongly Democratic. In Gilead, which had been anti-Democratic, Know Nothings "carried" the fall 1854 election, then reorganized under the Republican banner to win the spring 1855 election. By 1856 the Democratic vote plummeted to 24 percent and in 1859 and 1860 dropped still lower. Batavia, named after a town in western New York, had usually voted about 70 percent Democratic. In 1854-55 a Know-Nothing club organized and swept town meetings and elections. In 1856 "a sort of reaction set in" and the Democrats returned to power. "But now the Republican party sprang into existence, and received large accessions from the Know-Nothings. It at once assumed political control of the town." In Bethel Township, just south of Batavia, Know Nothings also organized secretly in the winter of 1854-55 and drove the Democrats out of power. The two organizers of the Order were elected super-

[65] *Grand River Eagle* quoted in *Marshall Statesman*, May 9, 1855; *Kalamazoo Gazette*, March 9, June 15, 1855; Streeter, *Political Parties*, 181; *Niles Republican*, May 12, 26, June 9, 1855.

[66] *American Citizen*, March 21, 28, April 4, 11, 18, 1855. "*Is it not wonderful that such a number of men* have been found to join in this movement, men who have been supposed to have a 'conscience.' " Austin Blair to A. T. McCall, April 14, 1855, Blair MSS, BHC; *Lansing Republican*, April 28, 1855.

[67] *History of Hillsdale County, Michigan* (Philadelphia, 1879), 306, 206, 204, 209.

visors for 1855 and 1856. "Internal strife" broke it up and Republicanism emerged to dominate the town, winning 66 percent of the vote in 1856.[68]

Voters in these towns were predominantly native Protestants, many from New York. Their behavior suggests that native Protestant Democrats found Know Nothingism a convenient way of opposing the party to which they had been loyal before going over to nascent Republicanism. The relative formlessness of the latter probably helped their transition. "Americanism" in the countryside, like Independency in Detroit and elsewhere, constituted a half-way house for Democrats and Whigs who found it hard to disavow suddenly their traditional loyalties and hatreds. Inspection of changes in percentage strength of the Democratic vote in townships all over the state between 1852 and 1854, and 1852 and 1856, shows that both strong Democratic and anti-Democratic towns shifted markedly away from the Democracy by 1856. The clues from Hillsdale and Branch suggest that Know Nothingism probably provided the vehicle of change in many towns of both types.

In the fall of 1854 and spring of 1855 "the Republican Party" meant a variety of rallying symbols, movements, and men. Know Nothings still operated independently in many localities and the Republican organization lacked stability of leadership, goals, symbols, and cadre workers. Fusion-Republican-Independent leaders in the spring of 1855 still showed reluctance to speak of "the Republican Party." Even an applicant for patronage, James Dale Johnston, publisher of the Detroit city directories in the 1850s, explained to Governor Bingham that while his *Directory* was unconnected with politics "I myself am indeed with Party, being purely independent of the *hitherto* recognized political codes or 'platforms' but thoroughly 'American,' thoroughly 'Republican.' "[69] Johnston's suggestion that his politics consisted of Americanism and Republicanism together in a setting that allowed him to be "with Party" but "purely independent" reflected the fluidity of the political arena and the new movement.

Americanism and Republicanism did not always coexist so harmoniously. In Jackson County, as noted above, a virtual state of war existed between them. In Detroit the Know-Nothing *Advertiser* continued in March 1855 to wish for the speedy demise of Republicanism and for an American Party to take its place. Most Fusion papers ignored the *Advertiser*'s assaults and maintained a friendly or neutral attitude to the

[68] Johnson, *History of Branch County*, 252, 258, 261, 262, 265-76, 281-83, 288-91.

[69] James Dale Johnston to Gov. Kinsley S. Bingham, Jan. 24, 1855, Executive Records, Miscellaneous Claims, 1855-1860, MHCom.

Americans. The *Pontiac Gazette* is a good example of a Fusion paper, intensely anti-Southern, which wanted Fusion victories to be regarded as a rebuke of doughfaceism on slavery extension and national economic policy. Meanwhile, it encouraged the Know Nothings to merge silently with the Republican Party under the auspices of the 1854 Jackson platform.[70]

Most Fusionists wanted to retain a firm commitment to anti-Southernism and antislavery extension. A development within the national Know Nothing Party enormously helped them. The "discords of the Sam and Sambo branches" of Americanism split that movement, led to its decline, and gave the Republicans confidence as the dominant element in the anti-Democratic coalition—and as a party.

The national convention of Americans met in Philadelphia in June 1855. Militant Southerners and a group of antislavery extension Northerners combined to defeat a proposal that would have avoided slavery extension completely and allowed the party to transcend sectionalism. Then the majority of Southerners, with the help of Northern votes, adopted a resolution favoring the South, saying that "Congress ought not to legislate on the subject of Slavery within the Territories . . . and that any interference by Congress with Slavery as it exists in the District of Columbia would be . . . a breach of the National Faith."[71]

The Northern Americans, who opposed slavery extension and had voted against noncommitalism, now withdrew from the convention denouncing Southern dictation and Northern doughfaceism. Leaders of these bolting Americans were really free soilers in disguise who had planned on such a contingency from the beginning. While sharing many American attitudes some had been using Know Nothingism for their own ends, some had to cooperate with or join Americanism to keep or get power. Now they called themselves Know Somethings. These men tended to be both anti-Popish and anti-Southern, but they had no more intention of being ruled by slaveholders than by Jesuits. The Fusion-Republican press and leadership in Michigan welcomed the appearance of the Know Somethings. In May and early June they had already begun predicting that Northern Know Nothings were moving to strong antislavery ground, that the national American Party could not avoid the slavery extension

[70] *Advertiser*, Feb. 27, March 3, 7, 1855; *Free Press*, March 4, 1855; *Gazette*, March 31, April 7, 14, 1855; *Christian Herald*, Dec. 28, 1855.

[71] *Jackson Patriot*, July 4, 1855. The American platform is reprinted in the *Pontiac Gazette*, June 30, 1855. The resolution is quoted and described as "pro-slavery" in Billington, *Protestant Crusade*, 426. It is described as "noncommittal" in J. G. Randall and David Donald, *The Civil War and Reconstruction*, 2nd edn. (Boston, 1961), 102. Textbooks often fail even to mention the American Convention of 1855.

issue, and that a neutral or pro-Southern position by the Americans would cause their disruption.[72]

In late June Fusion-Republicans excitedly circulated the news of the Know Something group and published copies of its platform written by the Northern bolters in Cleveland, June 14. The Know Somethings declared that the issue between freedom and slavery had been forced by the aggressions of the slave power, and that freemen would invade the right of no state but would resist the admission of any more slave soil. The Know Somethings juxtaposed a friendly hand to foreigners with an implicit warning to Jesuits: "the friends of Freedom in this Republic should make Principles and Character, not Birth-place, the test of admission to citizenship and its constitutional rights"; but freemen would sustain freedom of conscience and "repel every politico ecclesiastical interference in political affairs, by potentate, pontiff, or priest, or their abettors." The Know Somethings also promised support for temperance, free schools, free labor, improvement of rivers and harbors, and would unite with all who favored these goals.[73] This articulation of Know-Something principles, welcomed and disseminated by Fusion-Republicans, was an essential step in the emergence of the Republican Party.

Republicans cautiously moved during 1855 to prepare to campaign in 1856 as a Republican Party organization. As late as July 1855 Republicans could convey a still tentative attitude toward organization as a party. As the *Pontiac Gazette* urged fusionists to maintain the movement because the slave power was still aggressive and the Kansas-Nebraska outrage was unpunished, it advised that "there must be organization and concert of action. . . . Not in the sense of party organization heretofore existing, maybe," but in some undefined way that would insure success and an open future. Hence the paper favored "a meeting of the friends of what is known as the Republican movement" during the fall "to discuss matters, and take such steps as may be found best, to promote the cause of Aggressive Freedom."[74] In retrospect, only a political innocent would believe that Republican editors and leaders held views as tentative as this in private, but the egg-treading adroitness of their public rhetoric

[72] *Pontiac Gazette,* May 12, 26, June 16, 1855; *Marshall Statesman,* June 6, 1855; the brand new *Lansing Republican,* with Henry Barnes, Rufus Hosmer, and George A. Fitch as editors, emphasized opposition to slavery extension, prohibition, and local economic policies, mostly ignoring the Americans, April 28, May 15, June 10, 19, 26, July 3, 17, 1855. Its prospectus, *Pontiac Gazette,* May 5, 1855. The editors were leading Fusionists and influential men and their editorial policy reflected the image characterized in the text. The *American Citizen* took a similar line, May 16, 1855.

[73] E.g., *Lansing Republican,* June 26, July 10, 1855; *Marshall Statesman,* June 20, 27, 1855; *Christian Herald,* June 21, 1855; *Pontiac Gazette,* June 30, 1855.

[74] *Gazette,* July 28, 1855. On May 18, 1856, the *Lansing Republican* wrote: "We do not desire that blind devotion to party . . . characteristic of the Democrats."

suggested a climate among their "independent" constituents highly hostile to party and authority.

On August 21 a group with the temerity to call itself the Republican State Central Committee issued a message "To the Republicans of Michigan." It implied, however, that its action was not that of a party, but rather that of the continuing "alliance" of all friends of freedom who had cast behind all previous party ties to oppose the repeal of the Missouri Compromise. Taking up the Republican name and organization meant throwing "aside the vain trappings of mock warfare and stand[ing] upon the arena . . . for a death struggle with a living issue." The committee called for a September 12 mass meeting at Kalamazoo to prepare for the Presidential campaign. On that date Michigan Know Nothings transformed themselves formally into Know Somethings. Rejecting the national party's platform, the Americans declared that "the question of slavery should not be introduced into the platform of the American party . . . [and] that we believe in, and shall ever defend, the right of freedom of opinion and discussion on that and every subject not intended to be embraced within the designs of the organization." While this ground was not as strong as that of the Know-Somethings' Cleveland platform, the Michigan Americans approved of their delegates' withdrawing from the Philadelphia convention and said they would elect delegates to the bolters' meeting to be held November 21.[75] They were not yet Republicans, but their language suggested the rationale of a working alliance.

Thus, by the fall of 1855 the stage was set for the emergence of a full-fledged party organization. The task of Fusion-Republican party builders became much easier after the split in the national American Party in June 1855. The 1854 Jackson platform's anti-Southernism could continue to be the rallying cry.

[75] *Pontiac Gazette*, Aug. 26, 1855; *Free Press*, Oct. 21, 1855; *Vindicator*, Sept. 15, 1855. A voice for Know Somethingism was the *Hillsdale Standard*, a former Whig paper, unavailable from Sept. 1853 to Oct. 1855. On Oct. 28, 1855, however, it supported Know-Nothing and Republican principles.

XIII

The Crusade for White Freedom

John Brown was no Republican.—Abraham Lincoln

From 1856 to 1860 Republicanism became a party. The organization acquired a life of its own and a survival-urge that dictated pragmatism and eclecticism in acquiring votes. The movement of 1853-55 sharply defined its goals, but the party pulled back these issues, blunting some entirely. Traces of antiparty rhetoric and behavior lingered, but Republican leaders confidently asserted the indispensability of their organization "in the cause of human freedom."[1] Despite extravagant claims, however, the Republican crusade in its essential being did not pursue the broad interests of humanity. Its passion flowed from the desire of most Northern white Protestants to assert their rights and manhood against the threat of domination by white slavocrats, and to protect their values and status from the threat of disintegration from aliens and Catholics. Meanwhile, Republican freedom-seekers found it necessary, some with reluctance, to repress the aspirations of free and unequal black neighbors, whose hopes Republican rhetoric stimulated but deluded.

During 1855-56 events in Kansas and Washington increasingly attracted attention. "Border Ruffianism" and "Bleeding Kansas" became symbols closely allied in the Republican lexicon to "Doughface" and "Slavery." In March 1855, pro-slavery men in Kansas elected their own legislature with the aid of armed gangs from Missouri. In 1856 free-state men separately held a constitutional convention at Topeka and prohibited slavery. Blustering, bullying, and fraud had been the order of the day in 1855, with the "Wakarusa War" a bloodless farce. Republicans had exaggerated the violence in their reporting, but reality in Kansas soon caught up with Republican propaganda. In May 1856, acts of violence and madness seemed to intersect. In Kansas, a pro-slavery mob sacked the free town of Lawrence, John Brown and his sons murdered and mutilated five pro-slavery men at Pottawatomie, then fought an inconclusive

---

[1] John McKinney, Lansing, to George Willard, May 20, 1857, Department of Treasury MSS, Letters Sent and Received, 1857-1882, MHCom.

battle with a large pro-slavery force at Osawatomie. In Congress, Representative Preston Brooks of South Carolina walked into the Senate and caned Charles Sumner of Massachusetts into a bloody wreck for insulting one of Brooks's kinsmen in his recent speech "The Crime Against Kansas."[2]

Such dramatic events could not fail to upstage domestic conflicts in Michigan, to accelerate anti-Southernism, and to influence Republican factional struggles. Republicans and Know Somethings no doubt welcomed the news from Kansas. Anti-Popery and nativism could be tacitly merged in the rhetoric of anti-Southernism and anti-Doughfaceism. The lowest common denominators cutting through the Republican coalition and Northern society could be the explicit bonds of party union. The cause of free speech, free territories, and free men could not be rivaled in nobility. Yet domestic cleavages were hardly repressed or forgotten, but were very much present in social and political consciousness.

KANSAS AND ANTI-SOUTHERNISM

In December 1855, the *Free Press* viewed the fruits of Fusion government in Lansing and Detroit: "the nullification of the federal constitution and of a law of Congress; the increase of salaries and of extravagant appropriations; the creation of new offices . . . the passage of the Maine liquor law, by which an article of merchandise recognized as an article of property since the beginning of the world was declared a nuisance, and the personal liberty of the citizens abridged and circumscribed." The Democratic editor looked forward to the rejection of this political aberration in Detroit's city election in early 1856. But in February Detroit voters elected the Republican mayoral nominee, Oliver M. Hyde, whose victory appears to have been won with Know-Nothing support. Republican leaders tried to portray the election as a test on Kansas and as an expression of anti-Southernism. For the first time, in fact, the slavery extension question probably played a role in a local Detroit election. Hyde, an unceremonious commoner, was sufficiently "antislavery" in sentiment to have signed a petition in 1855 asking the legislature for black rights. However, even as he won, the Democrats elected 7 of 8 aldermen, every one of whom was a "popular sovereignty—Kansas Nebraska democrat . . . notoriously such." Heavy ticket splitting showed that flux and change still ruled in local elections and that Know Nothings were still cutting and carving to their taste.[3]

[2] For an excellent discussion of reactions to the Brooks-Sumner incident, David Donald, *Charles Sumner and the Coming of the Civil War* (New York, 1960), 288-311.

[3] *Free Press*, Jan. 26, 27, 29, 31, Feb. 6, 7, 9, 12, 1856; *Advertiser,* Jan. 14, 26,

In April, township and village elections, usually sleepy, one-sided affairs, waxed hot and crowded. Party alignments bowed to ticket splitting, and the opposition to the Democrats presented throughout the state a variety of anti-Democratic coalitions. Know Nothings, "Citizens' Tickets," pro-Nebraska Democrats, and prohibitionists all showed strength along with Republicans.[4] As the latter prepared for presidential campaigning in 1856 Know Nothingism continued to be a subterranean engine of the party. One leader, although conceding that the Republican organization consisted of two "wings," believed that "the genuine anti-Nebraska sentiment" was very strong in Michigan, especially compared to many eastern districts represented by Congressmen who voted with the Republicans but avoided any connection with the party ". . . as they would a plague. Pure and unadulterated Republicanism has no strength in their districts and if they cut loose from Americanism, they drop like a stone—In those sections the public sentiment has not yet come up to the right standard to sustain such a man as the voters of Michigan would."[5]

However, the legislature's activities in 1855 and the pattern of local elections in 1856 suggest that Michigan Republicans were not entirely free to "cut loose from Americanism." In fact, all the evidence points to a continuing alliance between Republicans and Americans—that is, the Know Somethings or Northern Americans. In April Schuyler Colfax, Indiana Republican Congressman, wrote to Michigan Republican editor Charles S. May that an "Anti Neb. American Whig" ought to be on the ticket with "F. [Fremont] for Vice" so that "both wings of this movement of the People" would be represented on the national ticket. Colfax trusted that Michigan would be represented in the June 12 convention of North Americans by "a Delegation that will go in cordially for that hearty union of the opposition which alone can carry the country, and which the Phil[da] call unites without naming any party specially, Republican, American or Free Soil. You are in a position where you can see to this important matter, the only breaker but fear is in our way." In May the Michigan Americans' Grand Council met in Detroit and chose delegates to Philadelphia, approving the Know-Something actions of the year before, upholding "local autonomy" for American lodges, and pledging opposition to slavery extension.[6]

29, Feb. 1, 4, 5, 6, 1856; *Michigan House Journal, 1855,* 197; quotation from *Free Press,* Feb. 7, 1856.

[4] *Lansing Republican,* April 15, 22, 1856; *Kalamazoo Gazette,* April 11, 18, also March 21, 28, 1856; *Jackson American Citizen,* April 10, 1856; Henry Waldron, Washington, D.C., to C. S. May, April 12, 1856, C. S. May MSS, BHC.

[5] Henry Waldron, April 26, 1856, to C. S. May, "Private," May MSS, BHC.

[6] S. Colfax, April 29, 1856, to F. R. Stebbins, Stebbins MSS, MHCol; Thomas, *Nativism,* 223.

Kansas allowed anti-Southernism to dominate the Republicans' 1856 campaign, and drove the Democrats to preoccupation with state issues. Their platform endorsed the Union, the constitution, and James Buchanan; their solicitude for their Southern brethren extended even to using "the confederacy" as a synonym for "the Union." Half of the Democrats' platform, though, discussed state issues, while the Republican was full of blood, bayonets, and civil war in Kansas.[7] Democratic warnings notwithstanding, the Republicans were not abolitionists, although old Free Soilers and even old Libertyites decorated their state and local tickets. The great issue "whether Liberty or Slavery shall be nationalized" continued to be a question of whether slaveholders could play the master with Northern white freemen. Which section would define what was "national" or "American"?[8]

Concern for the black slave was a subject Republicans avoided or translated into slavery's oppression of Northern whites. Undoubtedly many viewed slavery as wicked. The impulse that brought most to active outrage, however, and which could be shared by far more white men than had ever been tempted by the Liberty Party, was the sense that the fruits of slavery, whatever their source, were now being borne by white Northerners in Kansas and Congress. To whatever extent a man saw free-state Kansans or Senator Sumner as representative of himself, to that degree did he resent Southern rule. William Seward came to Detroit on October 2 to tell of how the slave-holding class occupied every major seat of power in the national government, from their "apologist" in the presidency, through committees of the House and Senate, to the Cabinet officers and their flunkeys. And Seward courageously made the kind of call for Northern unity that indicated why the Americans continued to despise him through the national Republican nominating convention of 1860. Whether slaveholders would govern America, he said, "concerns all persons equally whether they are Protestants or Catholics, native-born or exotic citizens. And, therefore . . . this is no time for trials of strength between the native-born and adopted freemen, or between any two branches of one common Christian brotherhood." Two days later, in Jackson, Seward went further: "if the great mass of men are ever to exercise control in the affairs of government, they must be willing to take the

[7] *Free Press*, Aug. 8, 1856; *Advertiser*, July 20, 1856; Henry Waldron to C. S. May, May 27, 1856, May MSS, BHC.

[8] *Lansing Republican*, Aug. 19, 1856. Democratic newspapers are the best sources in which to find Republican candidates identified as former abolitionists, e.g., *Niles Republican*, Oct. 18, 1856. For anti-Southernism and related themes: *Marshall Statesman*, 1856, passim; *Advertiser*, Aug. 13, 1856, on a meeting of Republican editors in Oakland County; and [H. H. Covert] A Young Democrat, *The Freeman's Pamphlet; or Republicanism and Locofocoism, Their Measures and Policy* (Detroit, 1856).

votes of Irishmen, Scotchmen, Frenchmen, Germans, Catholics, Protestants,—*negroes*."[9]

While Seward appealed to the best in his party, neither the distant slaves of the South nor the close but distant black freemen of the North fired the usual Republican leap to great moral abstractions so much as a sense of grievance for their own manhood. The Republicans talked ever of "backbone." Democrats and doughfaces lacked it; Republicans had it and would face up to the "chivalry" with its insulting hauteur and arrogance, which had culminated in the whipping of Sumner with a riding stick. Seward's speeches expressed anti-Southernism, but his comments on Catholics and blacks did not reflect Michigan Republicans' views. Republican policies of the later 1850s would show that Know Nothings continued to wield influence, Catholics would continue to be polarized away from Republicanism, and blacks would continue to be excluded from the political arena. Renewed demands for black suffrage met with considerable support among Republican legislators, but not enough to overcome Democratic demagogy, heightened Negrophobia, opposition in their own ranks, and expediency.

Meanwhile Republicans wholeheartedly embraced the white settlers of Kansas. Their 1856 platform heard the blood of two Michigan men slain in Kansas calling "to us from the soil . . . where they have fallen victims of Border Ruffianism, and to all who are opposed to the conspiracy against freedom in the territory, to revenge their murder . . . at the ballot box." Most Republicans sincerely wanted Kansas to come into the Union free, however useful the issue was as a campaign weapon. Usually they made it clear whose freedom they were talking about whenever slogans such as "Free Men" were invoked.[10] Freedom also meant not having Democratic doughface presidents kill rivers and harbors bills for the white Northwest, which Pierce did with a pocket veto in 1855. Even Democratic newspapers joined in the chorus of criticism, and when Pierce again vetoed the bills in 1856 the Democratic state convention rebuked him. The improvements finally passed over his vetoes with Democratic support, but this kind of slavocratic oppression of white Northerners even the most "hunkerish" Northern Democrats were hard put to ignore.[11]

---

[9] *Advertiser*, Oct. 4, 1856; slaveholding rule in Michigan would even mean "no free CHRISTIAN RELIGION," *ibid.*, Oct. 8, 1856.

[10] H. Waldron to C. S. May, Aug. 2, 1856, May MSS, BHC; S. B. Treadwell, Jackson, to Gov. Bingham, June 2, 1856, Executive Records, Elections, MHCom; and [Covert] *Freeman's Pamphlet*, show the intense interest in Kansas. For talk of backbone, George, "Zachariah Chandler," 58; *Lansing Republican*, Sept. 9, 1856; and an earlier but excellent example of this metaphor, J. W. Rood to Reuben E. Bird, May 15, 1852, Reuben E. Bird MSS, MHCol.

[11] This account is based on Streeter, *Political Parties*, who devoted an entire

Republican "freedom" also owed something to its "Independent" heritage. In July Republicans welcomed the appearance of a new book, *Outlooks of Freedom*. It dealt not with Kansas, however, but rather "traces the growth of the Republican idea and its relation to Romanism, recalling history and the past with a view to its present application. The direct purpose . . . is to demonstrate the antagonism of Romanism to Freedom and true Progress." The book would "do a good mission in the cause of Free Thought, Free Speech, and Free Church."[12] This is a rare explicit example of the evangelical Republican view of the tie between oppression in Kansas and Popish despotism. This view included the perception that Catholic voting support for the Democrats helped perpetuate slavocratic oppression. By 1856 the *Catholic Vindicator* mightily reinforced this perception. Shaking off its ambivalence to the Democrats, the *Vindicator* slowly moved to support James Buchanan because of Republican anti-Catholicism, though it was the last of 17 Catholic newspapers in the United States to do so. But the Know Nothing-Republican alliance had to be opposed as they constituted "two dangerous factions, of which one openly proscribes Catholics, while the second is opposed to the Union." The *Vindicator* increasingly denounced "abolitionist atrocities" in Kansas as it decried black Republican fanaticism at home which everywhere denied "free exercise of our religion, the freedom of our convents and schools, and the standing among our fellow citizens guaranteed to us by the charter of our common country."[13] The "Black Republican Know-nothing party" had disgraced Michigan's statute books with anti-Catholic laws, led by Attorney General Jacob Howard, "the most bitter and inveterate public defamer of Catholic Bishops and Priests" in the state, "the great wire worker and operator of the combined elements of wickedness . . . and any Catholic who would willingly vote for the party he represents and guides deserves to go back and live in the old blue law days in New England." Thus, Catholics must vote for Democrats, and observing this, Republicans would note that while slavery was not a part of the Catholic creed "we see the large majority of those professing the Roman Catholic belief . . . generally . . . sustaining the pro-slavery candidates."[14] Thus the Republican and Catholic

---

chapter to the issue, esp. 245-48; *Argus* quoted on 248; also *Advertiser*, July 10, 1856.

[12] *Advertiser*, July 11, 1856.

[13] *Catholic Vindicator*, Feb. 2, 1856, printed the Democratic city ticket without endorsing it; Feb. 9, June 14, July 12, Aug. 9, 23, Oct. 11, Nov. 1; vital to understanding the *Vindicator's* course is the account of R. R. Elliott, owner-editor, introducing his MS index to the paper, on microfilm with the *Vindicator*, University of Detroit Library. The paper eventually split with the Bishop over its political course, Oct. 18, 1856. On Catholic antievangelicalism and antiabolitionism, Walsh, *To Print the News and Raise Hell*, 84-85.

[14] *Vindicator*, Oct. 18, 1856; *Advertiser*, Oct. 23, 27, 30, Nov. 13, 1856.

cleavage deepened even though all Know Nothings were probably not in anti-Democratic ranks.[15] After the election the *Vindicator* described the victorious Republican party as a "Cauldron" of "Macbeth's witches . . . Free Love, Lager Beer, No Sunday, Robespierre, Rifle Beechers, and Freedom Shriekers, all mixed up and well peppered with Irish Orange-ism. All that is needed to cement and consolidate this union, is the enforcement of the Maine Liquor Law."[16]

The liquor law was not being well enforced, at least not in Detroit. After its passage high hopes had stirred for a dry millennium. In Detroit all leading saloons stood wondrously silent—for a time. Then the mayor found it necessary to "appeal" for obedience and soon "nearly all" the bars resumed their trade. Arrests, arraignments, indictments, appeals, and courtroom conflict and confusion followed; the *Free Press* soon proclaimed that the law was "stone dead and stinks in the popular nostrils."[17] The Democratic state convention, though it did so in timid and dissembling language, grew bold enough to ask for the law's repeal, its worst offense being failure. Less cautiously they charged Republicans with a sudden suspension of all efforts to enforce the temperance law with an election approaching.[18] Temperance and antitemperance forces lined up mostly as before, with "whiskey" going against the Republicans and the Maine Law men for them.[19] Yet Republicans, holding fast to the low common denominator of anti-Southernism, grew increasingly silent about the whole matter, content to rest on early victories and symbolism.

THE SURGE OF 1856

Election day 1856 brought a smashing victory to the Republicans and established the once amorphous movement as a party, wiping away lingering doubts as to its viability. Fremont won 57.2 percent of the vote to the Democrats' 41.5 percent and the national Americans' 1.3 percent. The Democrats took their worst beating ever, going 5.7 percentage points below their previous low. The Democratic vote increased from 1852, 41,842 to 52,139, but the Republican avalanche accumulated 71,762 votes, an increase of 30,000 over the combined Whig and Free Soil vote totals of 1852.

[15] *Advertiser*, Oct. 26, 28, 1858; *Citizen*, Oct. 16, 1856; also *Republican*, Oct. 7, 28, 1858, *Advertiser*, Oct. 28, 1856.

[16] *Vindicator*, Nov. 8, 1856.

[17] *Free Press*, Nov. 3, 1855; Farmer, *Detroit*, I, 841; also *Jackson Patriot*, May 9, 1855.

[18] *Free Press*, Aug. 8, 1856; also *Niles Republican*, Sept. 20, 1856; Streeter, *Michigan History*, II, 298-99; *Advertiser*, Sept. 25, 1856.

[19] *Advertiser*, Sept. 13, 17, Nov. 10, 1856; *Jackson Patriot*, Aug. 1, 2, 15, 1856; also *Pontiac Gazette*, Aug. 18, 1855, description of state temperance conventions 1854 and 1855.

The election clearly possessed all the features of a "surge," that is, a contest in which the electorate is unusually stimulated and short-term generators of interest such as issues or candidates motivate "peripheral voters" to come to the polls. Peripheral voters are those with low political interest and involvement who usually do not vote. But in surge elections, they join "core voters" in trooping to the polls in large numbers. Surge turnouts, furthermore, tend to favor one party heavily. Angus Campbell, in fact, considers the latter characteristic to be the distinctive feature of a surge election. Both independent voters, who may have voted for the disadvantaged party previously, and peripheral voters tend to move toward the party being favored in a kind of snowball movement.[20]

In matching election returns with census data all the available indicators point to 1856 as a year of high turnout comparable to 1840. Michigan's 1856 turnout reached, as in 1840, about 85 percent. The percentage increase in the whole number of votes in 1856 exceeded that of any other election from 1840 to 1860, and the increase again strikingly resembled that which had occurred between 1837 and 1840: in both cases some 52 percent (1837 is used rather than 1836 because the latter was not a party election in Michigan).

TABLE XIII.1

Increase in Total Vote and Turnout, Major Michigan Elections, 1837–1860[a]

	Total Vote	Numerical Increase	Percent Increase	Turnout
1837	29,901			
1840	44,350	15,449	51.7	84.9
1844	55,751	11,401	25.7	81.2
1848	65,000	9,249	16.6	74.5
1852	82,939	17,939	27.6	74.9
1856	125,561	43,234	52.5	85.4
1860	154,747	29,186	23.2	80.0

[a] Turnout percentages are based on estimates of the total electorate using data from the U.S. Census 1840, 1850, and 1860, see Erik Austin, "Turnout in Michigan, 1836–1960," University of Michigan 601 Paper, 1969, Michigan Historical Collection. McCormick, "New Perspectives on Jacksonian Politics," *American Historical Review*, LXV, 288-301.

The 1854 gubernatorial election, seen in a similar perspective, generated tremendous interest and participation for an off-year election. In nonpresidential years Michigan turnout fell off sharply, ranging as high as 37.3 percent fewer votes than delivered in the previous presidential

[20] Angus Campbell, "Surge and Decline: A Study of Electoral Change," *Public Opinion Quarterly*, 24 (Fall 1960), 397-408; "The conditions which give rise to a sharp increase in turnout invariably greatly favor one party over the other," 408.

election (Table XIII.2). In 1854 less than 1 percent of the number that voted in 1852 failed to cast a ballot. And the strikingly low drop of 3.4 percent from 1856 to 1858 also testifies to the continuing high political stimulation. It even suggests, in retrospect, the superheated climate that made men ready to take up arms in civil war. Turnouts in 1854 and 1858

TABLE XIII.2

Decrease in Vote in Gubernatorial Elections from Total Turnout in Previous Presidential Election, 1841–1858

	Total Vote	Numerical Decrease	Percent Decrease
1841	37,665	− 6,685	−15.1
1843	39,067	− 5,283	−11.9
1845	39,462	−16,289	−29.2
1847	46,214	− 9,537	−17.1
1849	51,377	−13,623	−21.0
1851	40,728	−24,272	−37.3
1854	82,939	− 612	− .7
1858	121,269	− 4,292	− 3.4

were relatively high, 67.5 percent and 60.5 percent, compared, for example, to the 1850 Congressional election, in which political leaders showed great interest but less than 55 percent of those eligible voted.

The Republican victory seems to have been more of a *party* victory than 1854 even though more changes in party loyalty appear to have registered between 1854/56 than between 1852/54. In 1854 Governor Bingham had run 3,168 votes ahead of the bottom of the Republican state ticket, Seymour Treadwell, candidate for Commissioner of the State Land Office. In 1856, however, the margin separating the two was only 182, in a much larger vote, and it was in Treadwell's favor. If Fremont's vote is taken as the top of the ticket, 178 votes separated his 71,762 votes from Treadwell's 71,584. This suggests, as well as aggregate data can, that less ticket splitting occurred in 1856 than 1854 and that it was a strong party election, a *maintaining* election. One observer in Plymouth in 1856 reported "556 straight tickets in a poll of 626"—or 89 percent straight ticket voting.[21] That sort of thing all over the state, reflected in the vote totals of the tops and bottoms of township returns, made for the closeness of the totals of Fremont, Bingham, and Treadwell.

Republicans, especially in Democratic strongholds such as Wayne County, gave great publicity during the campaign to Democratic crossovers. The Democratic state convention of March 12, 1856, referred to "the many right-minded and conservative men who were deluded and

[21] *Advertiser*, Nov. 10, 1856.

seduced from their democratic allegiance during the last campaign."[22] Whig defection and conversion to the Democrats also occurred, but the dynamics of a surge election and other evidence suggest that the Democratic bridge to Fusion-Republicanism was more heavily traveled among the mass of voters. This may not have been the case among political leaders and cadre workers. A study of party allegiance among political leaders in Wayne County found a different pattern. Of 133 men identified as Democrats in 1848, 97 remained Democratic in 1856, only 5 (3.7 percent) switched to the Whigs, and the rest could not be located. But of 109 Whigs in 1848, 68 became Republicans and a surprising 22, or 20.1 percent, became Democrats.[23] These trends were unrepresentative of what happened overall, even in Wayne. The Democrats barely carried Wayne in 1856, dropping 3.9 percentage points between 1852 and 1856 and running worse than they did in 1848. Yet the whole number of voters rose sharply, and large Republican gains among new voters or peripheral voters may have offset an unfavorable "balance of trade" among core voters. It should also be noted that the proportion of each party represented in the sample of leaders in the study above did not conform to the distribution of the vote among the mass electorate. Both Whigs and Republicans in 1856 were overrepresented among the political leaders studied.[24]

In a comparison of the party affiliations of the economic elite in Wayne County in 1844 and 1860 McCoy found that significantly more Whigs switched to the Democrats than Democrats changed to Republicans.[25] These men possessed in general above average political interest and some were party activists. Thus, among political and economic elites in Wayne County changes in party loyalty on balance ran against the trends moving the mass of voters. Further evidence is thus provided for the inference that independent and peripheral voters did indeed surge to the anti-Democratic party in 1854 and particularly in 1856.

Interyear correlations of Democratic percentage strength by counties and by townships within selected counties show that 1854 and 1856 tended to be the years of greatest change. While individual counties fol-

[22] *Advertiser*, July 1, 1856; also July 9, 11, 12, 15, 18, 22, 28, 29, Aug. 7, 13, 16, Sept. 2, 12, 29; on Sept. 20 the *Advertiser* published a list of 250 former Democrats and on Sept. 24 gave many of their occupations. *Free Press*, March 13, 1857.

[23] Dorothy Fischer, "Personnel of Political Parties in Wayne County," 1-15; of 6 Free Soilers, 3 became Republican and 2 Democratic.

[24] In 1848 Whigs constituted 47 percent of Fischer's sample, but 40.5 percent of the aggregate return.

[25] McCoy, "Wayne County Economic Elite, 1844, 1860," Chap. VI. For a systematic analysis which distinguishes between elite and mass trends in changing party loyalties in the 1850s in one city, see the excellent study by Michael Fitzgibbon Holt, *Forging a Majority: The Formation of the Republican Party in Pittsburgh, 1848-1860* (Yale, 1969), 184-218.

lowed slightly different patterns the year to year correlations of Democratic percentage strength in 36 counties from 1840 to 1860 in presidential elections and the 1854 state election show the overall tendency.

TABLE XIII.3

Interyear Correlations of Democratic Percentage in 36 Counties, Presidential Elections, 1840–1860, and Gubernatorial Election, 1854

	1844	1848	1852	1854	1856	1860
1840	.622	.385	.345	.079	.242	.106
1844		.786	.810	.611	.280	.603
1848			.858	.562	.389	.551
1852				.827	.389	.551
1852				.827	.063	.589
1854					.228	.066
1856						.482

To probe further the partisan and social sources of Republican gains and Democratic losses, election returns were compared for all units for which continuous returns were available for at least 1852, 1854, and 1856. In 81 townships in all parts of the state Democratic percentage strength dropped 10 points or more between 1852 and 1854. Democrats tended to lose most where they had more to lose, in habitually Democratic towns (Table XIII.4). They also lost fairly heavily in towns with Free Soil tendencies. With the 1848 returns available for 64 of the 81

TABLE XIII.4

1852 Democratic Vote of 81 Townships in Which Democratic Percentage Fell 10 Points or More from 1852 to 1854

	Democratic	Anti-Democratic
50% plus	55	26
60% plus	21	13
65% plus	14	5

townships, 29 of 64 were found to have voted equal to or more than the state Free Soil percentages of 16 in 1848. But the tendency of formerly strong Democratic units to decline (1852-54) was more impressive than that of those with Free Soil proclivities.

Thirty-nine townships could be identified as losing 20 Democratic percentage points between 1852 and 1856: 27 of 39 had been 55 percent or more Democratic in 1852; 16 had been 60 percent Democratic or more. The Free Soil urge had been again not as strong. Of 31 of the 39 for which 1848 returns were available, only 11 had voted 16 percent or more Free Soil in 1848.

The 39 units declining drastically in Democratic strength presented a variety of rural, farming townships, very much like any group of 39 units which did not suffer large Democratic losses. Their mean values of farms in 1860 ranged from the poor to prosperous, although most could be found among the less prosperous units in their counties. For 21 no useful religious data was available. In the other 18 a variety of denominations were present in 1860, although Methodists and Baptists were most numerous; 8 had evangelical preferences, most with low religiosities.

Thus, Democratic defections occurred on a substantial scale and in units that were "pools" of potential or actual Democratic voters. All kinds of rural units in different stages of economic development and socioeconomic condition shifted away from the Democrats, particularly average and less prosperous farmers. Native Protestants, especially Methodists and Baptists, moved even more decisively to the anti-Democratic side. The already strongly anti-Democratic Presbyterian and Congregationalist groups became still more anti-Democratic.

THE IRONIES OF DEFINING FREEDOM

After 1856 Republicans became less issue oriented and more winning oriented. Within the party strains developed with Know Nothings growing restless, and to satisfy them the organization launched an offensive to "purify" elections from alien contamination. In the past, the Democrats' opponents had taunted them with their inconsistency in giving aliens the vote but denying the same rights to black citizens. Now, as the Republicans challenged the slave oligarchy and gathered their strength by moving against illegal alien voting, they found it necessary to deny black petitions for enfranchisement.

In 1857-58 news from Kansas continued to stimulate Republican propagandists and campaigners. Intermittent violence accompanied the efforts of the pro-slavery forces with the aid of the Buchanan administration to enter the Union under the auspices of their Lecompton constitution, a creation of a rump convention. Over this issue the North's leading Democrat, Stephen A. Douglas, broke with Buchanan and his coterie of fire eaters. By summer, 1858, however, the Congressional compromise of William H. English had been arranged and in August Kansas voted overwhelmingly to come into the Union without slavery: "The role of Kansas in the sectionalization of the country had been played."[26]

Meanwhile anti-Southernism received fuel from other sources. After the 1856 election the Democratic *Kalamazoo Gazette* admitted that the masses of the North did not trust the Democrats. The Pierce administration had furnished a "seeming basis" to charges that the Democratic platform favored "ultra Southern dogmas." It warned that the Buchanan

---

[26] Randall and Donald, *Civil War and Reconstruction*, 117.

administration must let popular sovereignty work and that Southerners must stop outraging Northerners. The *Gazette's* warning became prophecy all too quickly. The Dred Scott decision in early 1857 confirmed the Republican belief that no national Democratic administration could be trusted. And it provided Republican legislators with an introduction to their campaign "Address" in preparation for a Supreme Court Justice election: "Slavery is National and Liberty is NOWHERE!" The Republican Party must persist, and practical matters, too, must be attended to, such as swamp lands, railroad grants, a general banking law, and a $10,000 appropriation to free-state Kansans. The legislators praised their choice for United States Senator, Zachariah Chandler, as a "MAN . . . not affected by spinal weakness."[27]

Democrats prepared for the Supreme Court Justice election by accusing the Republicans of fanaticism, corruption, and plunder. In Congress, Republican shrieks for freedom merely cloaked freebooting for "corrupt money corporations." Thus "philanthropy and religion, under the garb of '*freedom*,' and morality, under the garb of temperance or 'Mainelawism,' are basely prostituted." The *Free Press* described Republicans as "straining every nerve of nigger worship" to defy the Supreme Court and the Constitution.[28]

The voters did not match the enthusiasm that party leaders showed for this election, discouraged in part no doubt by a heavy April snowstorm on election day.[29] Still, the Republican *Romeo Argus* could see on the side of freedom "Humanity herself, with outstretched arms— Justice, clothed in white robes—Religion, with all her holy offices—the spirits of her brothers, now lie unavenged on the plains of Kansas,—God and the right!" For the *Argus* humanity, like Justice's robes, was colored white. The "real question" was not slavery in the South, nor in the District, nor yet the interstate slave trade nor Fugitive Slave Law: ". . . the question . . . is—shall we have a free government, or a slave empire? Shall an aristocracy of 300,000 slave owners govern, or shall 25,000,000 of free men? It is not a *black* question at all but emphatically a *white* question."[30]

<hr />

[27] *Gazette*, Nov. 7, 1856; *Advertiser*, March 18, 1856; A.D.P. Van Buren, "Log Schoolhouse Era," *MHC*, 14: 388-89, on Chandler's speaking; George, "Zachariah Chandler," 28-29, 34, passim.

[28] *Free Press*, March 11, 1857, Wayne County Democratic convention, March 13, state convention; racism, April 5, 1857.

[29] *Free Press*, April 6, 7, 8, 9, 1857; *Advertiser*, April 8, 9, 10, 1857.

[30] *Argus*, May 21, June 4, 1857. Introducing the *Lansing Republican*, editor C. B. Stebbins said he would not talk of abolishing slavery in the South because "we have enough to do now in preventing its introduction upon new soil, and even into Northern States." Admitting slavery's *legal* rights in the South "the Republican party seeks to confine Slavery to the pound of flesh written into the bond," Oct. 27, 1857.

Even as Kansas slipped from view on the national scene it stoked Republican campaign fires through November 1858. Some Republicans continued to criticize slavery as an institution,[31] but most concentrated on "the ravaging influence of Southern power." The Democrats tried to talk of misappropriations, high taxes, a bankrupt state treasury, squandering of swamp and railroad lands, and of abolitionists and Know Nothings. Their state convention approved Buchanan and popular sovereignty and revealed much about their situation by their laborious definition of the latter.[32] The Democrats discussed state issues so much in part because the Republicans had conducted state affairs energetically for four years. In 1853, for example, the Democratic legislature appropriated approximately $125,000; the Republican in 1857 appropriated over $300,000. This state activism, of course, had been a trait of Republicanism's chief progenitor, Whiggery. But the Republican activity holding greatest salience for the electorate in the late 1850s consisted of their posture toward the South. As Moses Wisner accepted the 1858 Republican state convention's nomination for governor he called Republicanism "a party that has made the slave power of the South quail in its boots."[33] A defiant posture was necessary to regain the integrity of Northerners. Dred Scott, Lecompton, Southern attempts to revive the slave trade, all tied in, according to the *Advertiser*, with the growing Southern belief that Northern white laborers, mechanics, and all who follow any industrial pursuits, are as degraded and servile a class as their own slaves." As it was, Southerners assumed "that the slave oligarchy was 'born to rule' —that there is a higher degree of civilization and intellectual culture, and a more thorough knowledge of the science of government" at the South.[34]

Even as former abolitionists sat down in Republican conventions with former Whigs (and Democrats) to proclaim unyielding opposition "to all aggressions of the Slave Oligarchy upon the rights of free labor"[35] one gets the impression that Republicanism's 1860 campaign was not particularly antislavery as such. Republican leaders muted antislavery in spite of their abolition-liberty trappings. Even anti-Southernism became

[31] For a strong mixture of the old antislavery tone, see the debut editorial of Morgan Bates in the *Grand Traverse Herald*, Nov. 3, 1858.

[32] Democratic convention, *Free Press*, Sept. 3, 1858; also, *ibid.*, Oct. 13, 19, 23, 1857; the Republican course on Kansas was well represented by the *Romeo Argus*, 1857-58.

[33] Streeter, *Political Parties*, 262-63; *Advertiser*, Aug. 20, 1858; the Republican legislature also endorsed a railroad to the Pacific, *ibid.*, Jan. 30, 1858.

[34] *Advertiser*, Oct. 2, 23, 1858. Southern agitation to revive the slave trade provided Republicans with "proof" of Southern imperiousness: *Centreville Western Chronicle*, June 23, 1859; Republican Association of Washington, *The Slave Trade*, Tract No. II (1859), Jennison Collection, MSL.

[35] *Advertiser*, April 13, 1860. The Republicans capitalized on the late James Birney's name by nominating one of their hack legislators of the same name for Lieutenant Governor.

somewhat diffused. The more a political party anticipates victory the more it can afford to ride the waves bringing it to the winner's shore. There was, to be sure, the excitement of an intense militaristic campaign. But Republican leaders knew that the conditions making for a surge to them in 1856 had diminished little if at all. They could afford to moderate their image and let the actions of the national administration and Southern hotspurs speak for themselves. Western Michigan, according to traditional accounts, contained "radical antislavery" sentiment, at least more so than the rest of the state. It was appropriate, then, that the famed Kentucky abolitionist Cassius Clay should stump that area in 1860 for Lincoln. Yet one close study of the section concluded that "feeling was possibly not as extreme on the slavery issue as it was in other areas of the nation." Neither slavery nor even "bread and butter" issues such as the homestead, tariff, or railroads received particular stress, although "sectionalism" waxed strong.[36]

Of Lincoln most Michigan voters knew little or nothing. Seward had been well known for years, even before he came to Detroit in 1851 to defend the rebels of the "great Railroad Conspiracy" case—farmers and allies in Jackson County who had been conducting virtual guerrilla warfare against the Michigan Central Railroad because it refused to pay full value for livestock its trains killed, even as trains became faster and deadlier.[37] Thirty-eight "conspirators" were arrested and Seward's defense of them, despite the conviction of 12, must have made him popular as an "antimonopoly" defender of the small man. The New Yorker usually obeyed a pragmatic political ethic, but many believed him also a man of political courage. He could be trusted to confront the slave oligarchs. After Lincoln's nomination Seward came to Michigan as he had in 1856 to campaign for the Republican cause and once again dwelt on the power and arrogance of "the privileged class" of slaveholders before whom Northern representatives "must speak with bated breath and humble countenance." The Michigan delegation to the Republican convention in Chicago had favored Seward. Its chairman, Austin Blair, accepted his defeat with tears in his eyes but promised, nevertheless, a 25,000 majority for Lincoln.[38]

[36] Alan S. Brown, "Southwestern Michigan in the Campaign of 1860," *Michigan Heritage*, 2 (Winter 1960), 72, 67-69, 71. Reinhard Luthin, *The First Lincoln Campaign* (Cambridge, 1941), 148-50, emphasizes Republicans' conservatism on slavery in 1860.

[37] Charles Hirschfield, "The Great Railroad Conspiracy," *Michigan History*, 36 (1952), 97-219.

[38] Quote from T. Maxwell Collier, "William H. Seward in the Campaign of 1860, with Special Reference to Michigan," *Michigan History*, 19 (Winter 1935), 92, also 97-104; L. C. Nyman, "Michigan and the Republican Convention of 1860," unpublished paper, Detroit, 1960, BHC; Martin Deeming Lewis, *Lumberman from Flint: The Michigan Career of Henry H. Crapo, 1855-1869* (Detroit, 1958), 104-10.

Blair's nomination as governor in 1860 suggests a stronger anti-Southernism than that emitted by Michigan Republicanism's platform. Whig, Free Soiler, then Fusionist, Blair had been no friend of Know Nothings and closely identified with the Personal Liberty Law of 1855. The Republican wing of the party had obviously been given the top of the ticket, but the state platform offered no clues to the tribute rendered to the American or Democratic wings. Pragmatism rendered the platform brief and barren of issues, in marked contrast to the passion for the concrete of 1854 and 1856. The prospect of victory turns our politics of passion into a politics of pragmatism. Anti-Southern and sectional appeals, especially to "Independent Democrats," still laced Republican rhetoric at local levels. But even the superevangelical Republicans of Hillsdale, while hoping that their opponents would "repent" the "unwillful errors" of their ways, did not mention the word "slavery."[39]

But the passion was there. It would carry through the victory, hear the Southern alarums, and stiffen backs still more. Back in 1853 the Whig lawyer Jacob Howard had excited audiences with exposés of Jesuitism. On November 5, 1860, in Detroit's temporary "Wigwam," he bellowed out defiance against Southern fire-eaters. He asked his audience if they would be cowed by Southern threats of dissolving the Union if they elected Lincoln:

Will you receive in your faces such an insult as this? (No! No!) Will you go down on your knees and ask them who you shall vote for? (No! No!) We will have our own choice; we say we will not obey their demand; we will select the man of our choice, and if you will not permit it, we will stand ready—yes, 400,000 if need be—to fly to the field to maintain our rights. You may call this war; you may call it fratricidal war, if you like, but we shall do it. We will give you grape shot, if necessary, and put down treason and rebellion.[40]

Tradition since Streeter has it that factional disputes, personal jealousies, and even natural disasters plagued the Republican Party in the years between 1856 and 1860. Since the party was a coalition of men from at least three different old parties, jealousy over nominations and patronage inevitably broke out after the first blush of success. The Republican decline hit bottom in 1858 when the Democrats gained 1,982 votes over their 1856 Presidential total and the Republicans lost 6,200. Indeed, Bingham in 1856 had run ahead of his ticket so the total slippage comparing the gubernatorial figures was 9,135.[41]

[39] Republican state platform, *Advertiser*, June 8, 1860; *Hillsdale Standard*, Aug. 7, 1860; also, *Facts for the People*, Address of the Republican Central Committee of Ingham County, 1-4, *Advertiser*, Nov. 2, 1860.

[40] *Advertiser*, Nov. 6, 1860; also accounts of Jacob Howard's and William A. Howard's speeches at victory celebration, Nov. 14, 15.

[41] Streeter, *Political Parties*, 267-68; the impact of economic suffering on the 1858 election is discussed in Chapter XIV.

That decline is better gauged, however, by observing that the percentage decrease was from 57.2 in 1856 (president) to 53.7 (gubernatorial) in 1858—a loss of 3.5 points. But it is misleading to observe this out of context. Table XIII.2 showed that 1858 was a year of high turnout for a nonpresidential election. The Republicans in 1858 slipped from 1856 *but* did better than they had in 1854, when they received only 52.1 percent of the vote. It is worth recalling, too, that nonpresidential years since 1840 had been years of low turnout and habitual nonvoting especially by anti-Democratic elements. In *that* perspective one could view 1858 as a significant Republican achievement.[42]

Before examining Republican factions it is worth asking if the Democrats had factional problems. In Detroit in November 1857, they appeared harmonious and to be making a comeback. With the city election now held in that month the Democrats won an easy victory behind John Patton, a popular "mechanic." Kansas and the Know Nothings seemed "played out."[43] At a meeting of state leaders in Detroit on December 21, however, the Democratic comeback ended. The Lecompton Constitution split them into two warring factions, each leaving the meeting with their own version of what the Democrats stood for, much as Northern and Southern Democrats had come away from Cincinnati in 1856. Cornelius O'Flynn, Postmaster of Detroit, and Democratic editors from Grand Rapids and Battle Creek, led the Hunker-Buchanan faction.[44]

The spring 1858 elections boosted Democratic hopes with partial success, although the Douglasites interpreted Democratic victories as due to rejection of Lecompton and the national administration.[45] Fearing division, Democrats incanted ritual prayers of unity through the summer of 1858 and postponed their state convention hoping that Congress would settle the Kansas mess. The English compromise gave the Democrats a platform and a gubernatorial candidate who reflected the party's ambivalence. Charles E. Stuart of Kalamazoo had been a Provisoish Democrat in the 1840s, voted for the Fugitive Slave Law in 1850, defended Kansas Nebraska and the Cincinnati platform, but opposed Lecompton and supported the English bill compromise. His nomination was, according to Henry Ledyard, Lewis Cass's son-in-law, "an administration defeat, and a Douglas triumph." Stuart led the Douglas forces on

[42] On pp. 267-68 Streeter, *ibid.*, used the 1858 election to show Republican decline; in the next chapter, "Democratic Decline and Republican Advance," he used it to show Republican strength, 280-81.

[43] *Free Press*, Nov. 5, 1857; also Oct. 24, 28, Nov. 4; *Advertiser*, Nov. 4, 5, 7, 1857.

[44] A. Ten Eyck, Washington, to J. S. Bagg, Jan. 28, 1858, and Lyman D. ———, Ypsilanti, April 17, 1858, to John S. Bagg, Bagg MSS, Huntington Library.

[45] Ann Arbor, *Michigan Argus*, April 16, 1858; *Romeo Argus*, March 18, 1858; *Pontiac Jacksonian*, April 15, 1858.

the floor of the abortive national Democratic convention in Charleston in 1860. The defeat of this party war horse in 1858 predicted Douglas's defeat in Michigan in 1860.[46]

Perhaps the prospect of defeat permitted the Democrats to indulge themselves in an open break. This was one of the many ironies of 1860: the Republicans, with a strong antiparty tradition, subordinated all to party unity. The Democrats, who had made party regularity more binding on politicians than the Lord's commandments, now displayed a fever of "disorganization," especially among party leaders and officials. The vast Democratic majority supported Douglas. The regular county and district conventions of 1860 shook off Buchanan-Breckinridge loyalists and on June 26 the state convention backed Douglas and popular sovereignty. Douglas, it said, had the qualities "which enabled the immortal Jackson to face and destroy nullification"; he represented the true democratic party. For the gubernatorial race the Democrats again tapped John S. Barry and tried to convey its independence by criticizing the "violence of an abolition mob and the clamor of southern secessionists," both of whom preached the doctrine of Congressional "intervention" in the territories. This "despotic principle" distracted attention from Republican corruptions and gave "the national government a preponderance overshadowing local affairs." When a Kent County delegate asked the convention to approve the foreign and domestic policy of the Buchanan administration, the vote, with every delegate polled, was 140 to 6 against. As they had since 1854 the Democrats warmed to the subject of "local affairs" in their platform, dwelling especially on Republican financial waste and corrupt alliance with business interests.[47]

A month after the regular convention a group calling itself the "State Convention of the National Democracy" met in Detroit to ratify the Southern Democratic choices for 1860, Breckinridge and Lane. No more than a collection of chiefs and medicine men without Indians, these men in some ways truly represented the Democratic past. Their names and connections ran back to the days of the Territorial establishment of Lewis Cass. Prominent men associated with the clique were Henry Ledyard, A. S. Bagg, United States Marshal and member of the old Bagg clan, Cornelius O'Flynn, former postmaster, A. E. Gordon, former editor of the *Grand Rapids Enquirer and Herald*; Irish names seemed conspicuous. The President of the convention, surveying the group, saw before him the "old guard of the Democracy." More loyalist than the

---

[46] Henry Ledyard to J. S. Bagg, Sept. 24, 1858, Bagg MSS, Huntington Library. For Democratic preparations and conventions, Streeter, *Political Parties*, 277-80; Anne McCain, "Charles Edward Stuart of Kalamazoo," *Michigan History*, 44 (1960), 324-33; *Lansing Republican*, Nov. 9, 1858.

[47] *Free Press*, June 29, 1860; Streeter, *Political Parties*, 284-85.

king, they blamed the Democratic split on Douglas and vented their bitterness on his supporters whom they branded as bad as Lincoln and the abolitionists. Their bitterness toward Douglas blinded them to the incongruity of their actions and their declaration that "the greatest political calamity that could befall the country" was Lincoln's election. They adjourned, appropriately, to General Cass's home.[48]

The Cass-Breckinridge Democrats represented the past and federal patronage. Republican factions fought over issues and the wealth of state nominations and patronage available to the party since 1854. After 1856, when virtually the same group of leaders as in 1854 again triumphed, the restlessness of second-stringers who began to look to their place in the sun built to a crescendo in 1858. The discontented were primarily former Democrats and Free Soilers. Pressure also existed to give "*Young America* a fair proportion of the offices."[49]

The Republican "decline" of 1858 received intensive analysis from Republicans and Democrats. The *Advertiser* blamed bad weather, overconfidence, and nonvoting, but some Republicans joined the *Free Press* in pointing to "bolters and disorganizers." The Democratic paper wanted to believe that people had been sickened by "the continual humdrum" of Republicans campaigning on the "nigger question," saying that state institutions should be "managed on antislavery principles, going about the state playing on the abolition banjo."[50] Something else seems to have been present, too, at which Republican complaints about "bolters" barely hint. But local elections early in 1859 provide the clues with echoes of local elections in 1854, 1855, and 1856. "People's tickets" and other nonpartisan combinations took the field in 1859 to the accompaniment of zigzag ticket splitting by voters. In short, Know Nothingism, or some similar manifestation, still percolated through Michigan politics. Indeed, of all the possible causes of "disorganization" in Republican ranks in 1857-58 historians never considered the one that in many ways was the most likely: Know-Nothing restiveness under the shadow of sectionalism and their resentment of the party's increasing accommodation to segments of the "foreign vote." The surface evidence regarding the

[48] Streeter, *Political Parties*, 285-86; *Detroit Tribune*, Aug. 30, 1860; Lewis Cass to [John S. Bagg], July 9, 1860, Bagg MSS, Huntington Library.

[49] Henry Waldron to C. S. May, Jan. 11, 1857, May MSS, thought that "the Democratic wing of our party" should have had the Senator post "to allay possible discontent"; A. H. Morrison, St. Joseph, to May, May 20, 1858; same to same, July 15, 1858; same to same, Aug. 4, 1858, and Oct. 6, 1858; K. Bingham, Kensington to C. S. May, Dec. 6, 1858, May MSS; the last quotation referred to the state ticket, A. H. Morrison to C. S. May, June 17, 1858, May MSS, BHC.

[50] *Advertiser*, Nov. 4, 5, 1858; *Free Press*, Nov. 11, 14, 1858; *Pontiac Jacksonian*, Nov. 18, 1858; *Lansing Republican*, Nov. 9, 1858; *Hastings Republican Banner*, Nov. 9, 1858; also testifying that internal Republican splits cost votes, Z. Chandler to Henry W. Lord, May 11, 1860, Robert M. Zug MSS, BHC.

Know-Nothing presence in late 1858 is ambiguous and contradictory; of course *Free Press* accusations of the identity of Republicans and Know Nothings can easily be excavated.[51] But the inference to draw from the Republicans next major move as a party is unmistakably clear. Shortly after the 1858 election Republican papers began discussing the desirability of a registry bill to protect the purity of the ballot box from the "corruption" of illegal voting. From the top and grassroots of Republican ranks came calls for such a bill, and it became *the* party issue of 1859.

The *Lansing Republican* in December 1858, put a voter registration law on the agenda with a long argument in its favor. "Illegal voting, both by unnaturalized persons, and by actual residents of another country and subjects of another form of government has become an intolerable evil." The collector of Detroit wielded great power along 900 miles of lake coast. His minions imported "Kanuck voters" for elections; the rest of the year they received $60 ostensibly watching for smugglers. "Every line of railroad in . . . construction . . . becomes a nucleus and gathering point of men who having no real right to vote anywhere, for the most part, are induced by whiskey and bribery, to come up to the polls and swear that they are citizens."[52]

As the state legislature convened, a wave of renewed petition agitation greeted it, particularly from evangelicals. The Presbyterians and others had never accepted abolition of capital punishment and were now making that a special subject of pressure. Many petitions also came in on behalf of a "more stringent liquor law," and some also arrived for woman suffrage and "female education." But the greatest number of petitions, 40 to 50 or more, asked for a registry law.[53] They came, said the House committee to which they were referred, from all sections of the state, all classes of men: "lawyers, doctors, farmers, and mechanics; men of all professions, and of all creeds, and of all parties—Republicans, Democrats and Silver Greys." The committee believed the law would secure "civil and religious liberty" and was necessary to combat designing men or their servants who "inveigle, corrupt and induce the ignorant and unfortunate of our land" to break the law. The Democrat who led the fight against this proposal was, appropriately enough, E. H. Thompson of

---

[51] *Cass County Republican*, March 3, 1859; *Hastings Republican Banner*, Dec. 2, 1858; *Free Press*, Oct. 23, 1858, claimed that W. A. Howard said that "the Dutch, Irish, and French of our population were the scum of creation," and at the local election the "miserable s--s of b-----s came to the polls in a solid phalanx" against him; *Grand Rapids Daily Eagle*, Nov. 17, 1858; *Jackson American Citizen*, Oct. 28, 1858.

[52] *Lansing Republican*, Dec. 7, 1858.

[53] *Michigan House Journal, 1859*, 1018, for listing of petitions; one remonstrance against also arrived, 409. The Senate was not interested in restoring capital punishment, *Michigan Senate Journal, 1859*, 332-33.

Genesee whom Governor Ransom had appointed as first Commissioner of Immigration back in the 1840s. The Republican floor manager of the Registry Bill, McMahon, was foreign born: appropriately enough he was from Northern Ireland.[54]

After a tough fight the Republicans overcame internal opposition to pass the bill on February 12 by a party vote, 42 to 34. All 17 Democrats voting went against it joined by only 17 Republicans. All 42 votes for it were Republican. The bitterness of the fight appeared in the sarcastic amendments offered immediately after its passage. Thompson moved to title the law "A bill to consign the Republican party to Abraham's bosom, forever and forever." Alonzo Sessions, an Ionia Republican countered with "And the Democratic party to the other side of the ditch." A. W. Buel, former Democratic Congressman from Wayne offered this substitute title: "A bill to violate the constitution of this State, and deprive the people of their constitutional rights at all general, special and municipal elections." To which a Republican added: "And to prevent the manufacture of democrats on too short notice." None of these passed but they suggest the emotional intensity of the issue and the strong beliefs as to its practical political content. In the Senate a Democratic minority also had fought a bitter but hopeless battle against the Registry Bill. It passed on February 8, 17 to 14, with all 6 Democrats voting going against it. Republicans then closed ranks further in ordering the bill to take effect by a two-thirds, nonroll call vote.[55]

The furor over the Registry Bill had only begun. Election results thereafter were interpreted by both parties not only in relation to Dred Scott, Buchanan, etc., but also as tests of the Registry Bill. The Democratic legislators emerged from defeat to issue an Address denouncing this new "Alien Law in disguise" which would fall hardest on "American citizens by adoption." The *Pontiac Jacksonian* brought Michigan party warfare full circle by printing this Address side by side with the 1835 Address of the Democratic Territorial Convention on alien voting. The Republican Address of 1859, while discussing swamp lands, a homestead bill, appointment of an immigration agent, asylums, a normal school, and the agricultural college, devoted most of its attention to the Registry Law.[56]

[54] *Michigan House Journal, 1859,* 792-95; *Michigan Biographies,* 636-37, 452-53.

[55] *House Journal,* 851-54; on Feb. 11 the vote was 39 to 37, but the majority did not constitute a majority of members-elect; one Democrat voted for the bill and 16 against, 353; *Senate Journal,* 427-28, 459-60.

[56] *Advertiser,* April 5, 6, 1859; *Jackson American Citizen,* Feb. 24, 1859; *Grand Rapids Daily Eagle,* Feb. 19, 1859; *Pontiac Jacksonian,* March 24, also March 17, 1859; *Centreville Western Chronicle,* March 21, 31, April 21, 1859; *Free Press,* Feb. 25, March 25, April 2, 1859; Republican State Address, *Cass County Republican,* March 10, 1859.

In the 1859 local elections party lines dissolved before ticket splitting. John Brown's October raid on Harper's Ferry made little impact on Detroit's charter election the next month. Instead, the Registry Law commanded most attention. The Democrats' claim that it excluded laborers and poor men did not prevent the Republicans from winning the mayoralty and splitting other city offices with the Democrats. The symbolic character of the Registry Law at this point appeared in the Republicans moving on election eve, by fiat of the State Attorney General, to loosen voter registration requirements, allowing many voters to register as late as election day.[57]

The Law received only passing attention in 1860, but pressure for action against alien voting had not abated but only bided its time. In early 1861 the Republicans moved again to further preserve "the purity of elections" by passing a new and strengthened Registry Law.[58]

Thus, in both 1859 and 1861 Republicans moved to appease Know Nothing, nativist, and reformist sentiment in their party, to undercut illegal Democratic voting, and to make it difficult for aliens enfranchised under the 1850 Constitution to vote. They simultaneously rejected pleas from black and white citizens that black citizens be enfranchised. As reference groups manipulated by demagogues and party imagists, "Negroes" and "Aliens" had always been linked in political controversy over suffrage. Whenever Jeffersonian Republicans and later Democrats had sought to liberalize voting rights for the foreign born, opponents of alien voting (usually Federalists, then Whigs) and antislavery men had criticized them for inconsistency in denying the franchise to native born black citizens. In the 1840s mavericks in both major parties and abolitionists had supported "colored suffrage." Democrats generally maintained a massive hostility to the idea while Whigs had been neutral to passively sympathetic. Old abolition elements among the Republicans tried to promote colored suffrage in the 1850s but encountered a heightening wall of hostility from the white majority. The renewal of the slavery extension controversy activated and intensified white fear and prejudice toward free blacks. Democrats after 1854 escalated their frenzied exploitation of Negrophobia, sparing few devices and mincing few words in attempts to create a backlash against the "Black" Republicans. Republican responses, while not usually explicitly anti-Negro, endorsed or accepted white supremacy and a caste system for the free North. The anxiety of the fifties forced Republicans to be comparatively far more racist than the Whigs had ever been, even as they tried harder

[57] *Free Press*, Oct. 30, Nov. 11, 1859. For spring elections, *Cass County Republican*, April 7, 1859.
[58] *Facts for the People*, "Address" of the Republican Central Committee of Ingham County, 1860, 5; *Michigan Senate Journal, 1861*, 127, 495, 673, 729, 1136.

to help blacks. In 1859 substantial goodwill existed among Republican legislators towards enfranchising blacks with a property qualification. Even as Democrats raised cries of "amalgamation" a bill enfranchising blacks who owned freeholds of $200 (similar to New York state law) gained a simple majority of 40 to 37 in the House. Requiring a two-thirds majority, however, it failed, and the opposition of some one-fifth of the Republicans and all the Democrats killed it.[59]

Both in the legislature and in their newspaper propaganda Democrats labored to show that Republicans desired "to disfranchise and degrade adopted citizenry . . . and to elevate and enfranchise negroes." In the maneuvering on the colored suffrage bills a Democrat had proposed that all aliens with freeholds of $250 be allowed to vote: the defeat of this measure by all but two Republicans voting against it showed the Republicans "love for Sambo and Dinah, but their hatred of foreign born residents."[60]

In 1861 a small parade of petitions again asked the legislature for colored suffrage, including one from a convention of colored citizens protesting "Taxation with representation." The Republican House Judiciary Committee on Elections arrogantly lectured the petitioners on the proper form of writing petitions and predicted that the legislature would not soon pass such a measure, implying that popular sentiment was far from ready to approve blacks voting by the side of whites.[61] Thus did Republicans define the social borders of their crusade for freedom against Democratic party despotism and slave oligarchy.

[59] *House Journal, 1859*, 201, 204, 599, 650, 754, 787, 819, 930-32; *Pontiac Jacksonian*, Jan. 6, 1859; *Senate Journal, 1859*, 287-91; *Documents Accompanying the House Journal, 1859*, Doc. No. 25, favorable to colored suffrage.

[60] *Free Press*, Oct. 26, 1859; *Pontiac Jacksonian*, Feb. 3, 1859.

[61] *Michigan House Journal, 1861*, 1029, 259-60, 635, 1422; *Documents Accompanying the Senate Journal, 1861*, Doc. No. 28. Recent works on the antiblack impulses in Free Soil and Republicanism include: Eugene H. Berwanger, *The Frontier Against Slavery: Western Anti-Negro Prejudice and the Slavery Extension Controversy* (Urbana, 1967), and V. Jacque Voegeli, *Free But Not Equal: The Midwest and the Negro During the Civil War* (Chicago, 1967).

XIV

Republicans and Democrats: 1854–1860

The 1860 campaign rivaled 1856 in emotion and perhaps surpassed it in extravagance of display. Electoral armies trooped in endless parades, with bands and singing groups sending up a cacophony of enthusiasm. The quasi-military Republican Wide Awake Clubs, uniformed with caps, capes, and torches, drilled, watched polls, guarded Republican mobilization, and may be seen as an ominous portent of war mentality. The political temperature climbed early during 1860 in spring elections in which Republicans generally succeeded.[1] They rallied to cheer William H. Seward as Democrats whooped it up for Douglas when he whistle-stopped through the state. Yet the Democrats lacked the flair of the Republicans whose crusading energy was reminiscent of the political revivalism of 1840.

Almost 155,000 votes were cast for President. Lincoln captured the state with 88,480 votes or 57.1 percent of the total, while Douglas attracted 65,057 ballots—42 percent.[2] Although voter turnout slipped from 1856, there was an absolute increase of 23.2 percent in the total number of votes cast. The surge of 1856 continued to run against the Democrats in 1860. The Democrats lost even Wayne County in 1860. Though temporary, this defeat symbolized all the short-run influences working against the Democrats: anti-Southernism, antiparty, social tensions, high voter turnout, and more.

[1] *Michigan Christian Herald*, Sept. 27, 1860; the Preamble and Constitution of the "Zach Chandler Wide Awakes" is in the *Hillsdale Standard*, Sept. 4, 1860; a description of one of their marches, Sept. 18, 1860; on early political heat in 1860: *Advertiser*, April 4, 1860; *Centreville Western Chronicle*, April 12, 1860; George S. May, "Politics in Ann Arbor During the Civil War," *Michigan History*, 37 (March 1953), 53.

[2] Breckinridge polled 805 votes or .6 percent, and Bell and the Constitutional Unionists attracted 400 or .3 percent. The Constitutional Unionists nominated national but not state candidates, *Free Press*, Oct. 6, 1860. *Advertiser*, Aug. 31, 1860, for names of electors. As the vote indicated, this party received little attention.

The Democrats carried only Mackinac, Chippewa, Emmet, Cheboygan, Iosco, Bay, and Manitou counties: relatively undeveloped, agriculturally poor areas straddling the Straits of Mackinac and lining upper Saginaw Bay, where lumbering, mining, fishing, and a lingering fur trade provided the chief occupations. The far northern wilderness had always been Democratic. Like General Cass it symbolized the Democratic past, reaching back to the days when the American Fur Company, French Canadian voyageurs, and Federal frontier agents had been mainstays of the Democratic Republican establishment of the 1820s. The foreign born were common in most of these counties: Irish, English, Germans, and French Canadians were most numerous. Some were Catholics, many were hedonists. Since the 1840s it had been said that "there was no Sunday west of the Sault"—that is, west of Sault Ste. Marie at the eastern end of the Upper Peninsula. Some Cornish Methodists did work the copper and iron mines of the north and no doubt constituted part of the growing Republican minority. They were the most pietist of the mining frontier's groups and most receptive to the moral-evangelical appeal of Republicanism.[3]

PLACE, CONDITION, AND CLASS

In December 1854, Fusion editor Henry Barnes told Kinsley Bingham that their movement's strength was "in the country, not in the city. It will always be, from the settled character of its population."[4] Returns for Michigan's largest villages showed that Barnes had a point (Table XIV.1). In eight of the "cities" for which municipal returns were available separately from townships, the Republicans ran poorer than their statewide showing. In some areas the "city" or village returns can be compared to the rural townships adjacent to them. Here a somewhat mixed picture emerges. In 6 of 10 cases the Republicans ran better in the "cities" than in the townships. Given this finding and the size of the "cities," it is difficult to conclude that an "urban" environment made a great difference in voting behavior. Further, in Wayne County's 18 townships the correlation between rural occupations and Republican per-

---

[3] Mast, *Always the Priest*, is excellent on Cass's Republican establishment and the American Fur Co. in the 1820s, 313, 336-37. Arthur Cecil Todd, *The Cornish Miner in America* (Glendale, Calif., 1967), 114-50; Murdock, *Boom Copper*, 67, 68, 69, 199; Caroline M. McIlvaine, ed., *The Autobiography of Gurdon Saltonstall Hubbard* (Chicago, 1911), 15-17, 20; Robinson, *Cheboygan and Mackinac*, 17-22; Danford, "Lumbering," *Michigan History*, 26, 355-57; Robert James Hybels, "The Lake Superior Copper Fever, 1841-47," *Michigan History*, 34 (June 1950), 97-120.

[4] H. Barnes to K. S. Bingham, Detroit, Dec. 10, 1854, Executive Records, Elections, MHCom.

TABLE XIV.1

Republican Percentages in Michigan's Largest Towns, 1858–1860

	Republican Percentage	Total Vote	Population 1860
State Republican	57.1		
Detroit	51.9	8,463	45,619
Adrian	56.2	1,333	6,213
Ann Arbor	53.0	988	5,097
Grand Rapids (1859)	52.4	737	8,085
Jackson (1858)	57.7	939	4,799
Marshall	52.2	833	3,736
Battle Creek	68.9	791	
Monroe	49.0	758	3,892
Lansing	53.4	734	
Niles	47.1	613	
Combined City and Rural Township Returns			
Kalamazoo	57.4	1,347	
Coldwater	64.9	994	
Pontiac	50.4	834	

TABLE XIV.2

1860 Republican Percentages in Cities Compared to Adjacent Rural Townships

	City	Township
Detroit	51.9	49.5 (Wayne County aggregate)
Adrian	56.2	55.1
Ann Arbor	53.0	65.0
Jackson (1858)	57.7	54.2
Marshall	52.2	28.5
Monroe	49.0	36.0
Grand Rapids (1859)	52.4	74.7
Battle Creek	68.9	66.1
Niles	47.1	52.5
Lansing	53.4	72.4

centage strength was insignificant: —.122. Still, the Republicans did not run as well in large towns as statewide.

Comparison of the general economic condition of townships across the state shows that the more prosperous tended to be Republican. There was a particularly marked tendency for strong Republican towns to be more prosperous than strong Democratic townships. In 23 counties the top 1 or 2-banner Republican units were matched with banner Democratic units in 1860 as to mean value of farms. In 28 cases of 35 the Republican towns were more prosperous. Some of the Democratic units, however, were more prosperous than most Republican units, and the poorest towns in the entire group were all Republican. (See Appendix D)

Other tests of economic condition and party strength were less decisive, although pointing in the same direction. The correlation of mean
values per acre of farm land and Democratic percentage strength in 44
counties in 1860 yielded an insignificant negative finding: —.166. For
22 counties the mean value of farms in townships was correlated with
Republican percentage strength in 1860, and in 12 cases the correlations
were positive, although impressively high only in very few counties. In
only one country, however, was the negative correlation high (Table
XIV.3). Thus, while there may have been some relationship between

TABLE XIV.3

1860 Correlations of Mean Value of Farms with Republican Percentage
Strength in Townships in 22 Counties

Eastern		Central		Western	
Lenawee	.114	Calhoun	—.060	Barry	—.050
Macomb	.499	Clinton	.169	Berrien	.268
Monroe	—.200	Eaton	—.094	Branch	—.030
Oakland	—.030	Ingham	.204	Cass	—.193
St. Clair	.016	Kalamazoo	.252	Kent	.031
Washtenaw	.416	Lapeer	—.173	Ottawa	.538
Hillsdale	.401	Jackson	.253	St. Joseph	—.406
				Van Buren	—.024

prosperity and Republican strength in rural townships, the bottom layers
of rural classes contributed mightily to Republican voting strength. Nothing demonstrates this better than the case of the "Suffering Counties" of
1857-60.

One of the causes of Republican "decline" in 1858, according to
Streeter, was suffering caused by poor crops, a severe winter, rising
prices, food shortages, and a host of afflictions which beset the pioneers
of several north-central counties. The counties of Gratiot, Montcalm,
Tuscola, portions of Genesee, "probably" Saginaw, and parts of adjoining counties were particularly afflicted.[5] The Democrats, indeed, attacked
the Republican administration for sending money to Kansas while
farmers in Gratiot, Isabella, and Montcalm faced famine. Streeter said
that the northern counties carried by the Democrats in 1858 were "in a
frontier condition" and "suffered a great deal from the economic crises."
They were: Bay, Cass, Cheboygan, Emmet, Genesee, Grand Traverse,
Houghton, Iosco, Livingston, Mackinac, Manistee, Manitou, Oceana,
Ottawa, Saginaw, and Wayne.[6] The most striking thing about this list is
that Gratiot, Tuscola, Montcalm, and Isabella are not on it. Streeter used

[5] Streeter, *Political Parties*, 257-58.
[6] *Free Press*, Nov. 21, 1857; *Grand Rapids Daily Enquirer and Herald*, Sept.
13, 1857, quoted in Streeter, *Political Parties*, 265; also, *ibid.*, 268.

one group of counties to state his hypothesis and another group to support it.

Which counties suffered most in 1857? Gratiot, Tuscola, and Montcalm were indeed the most destitute and hard pressed, as were Sanilac and Lapeer, not only in 1857-58, but as early as 1854 and through 1859.[7] All 5 of these counties voted Republican in 1856, 1858, and 1860. Support for Streeter's claims comes only from the decline of Republican percentage strength in all 5 between 1856 and 1858, a mean aggregate decline of 5.4 points. Yet 4 of the 5 still exceeded the 1858 Republican statewide percentage. In 1860, 3 of the counties increased their Republican percentage.

TABLE XIV.4

Republican Percentages in 5 Poor Counties: 1856, 1858, 1860

	1856	1858	1860
Gratiot	74.0	65.2	61.0
Lapeer	59.9	55.6	57.7
Montcalm	60.3	59.5	57.7
Sanilac	79.9	69.9	68.9
Tuscola	64.2	58.7	68.1

In newly settled, poor areas generally in the late 1850s the Republicans did as well or better than Democrats. In 1856, 6 new counties gave election returns for the first time. Four voted comfortably Republican, 1 slightly so, and 1 voted Democratic. In 1860 in 9 new counties which officially recorded Presidential election returns for the first time 4 went decidedly Republican, 2 did so by a narrow margin, and 3 voted Democratic.[8] Thus, the frontier poor divided in their party preference but like the rest of the electorate showed a Republican tendency in 1860.

The rich also were predominantly anti-Democratic in 1860, although less so than they had been in 1844; at least that was the case with McCoy's Wayne County economic elite in 1860. Using wealth alone as an indicator McCoy assembled an elite of 135 men, whose partisan affiliations were as follows: Republicans 58 (43 percent), Democrats 48 (36 percent), Constitutional Union 3 (3 percent), and Unknown 25 (18 percent).[9] Two of the Democrats supported Breckinridge.

When McCoy subdivided the elite by party and economic role some

[7] See petitions from voters in those counties, Executive Records, Petitions, MHCom; Willard D. Tucker, *Gratiot County, Michigan* (Saginaw, 1913), 41, 46, 50, 62, 260-61.

[8] John S. Schenck, *History of Ionia and Montcalm Counties* (Philadelphia, 1881), 431-35, 446-60; *Portrait and Biographical Album of Sanilac County* (Chicago, 1884), 478-505.

[9] McCoy, "Wayne County Economic Elite, 1844, 1860," 115.

similarities with 1844 appeared. Landowners again displayed a strong Democratic tendency. Capitalist, entrepreneurial, and unspecialized business elements, with the exception of bankers, tended to favor Republicanism as they had earlier favored Whiggery. The association of "businessmen" with Republicanism, however, was not as strong as it had been with Whiggery. Ironically, Republicans worked harder than Whigs to convey a posture favorable to business and "enterprise."

Democratic manufacturers in Wayne present, as McCoy observed, a problem for anyone attempting to make a simple economic interpretation of the Republican Party. It cannot be assumed that the Republicans' tariff posture riveted to it the loyalty of all manufacturers. Six were Republican (38 percent); 6, Democratic; 3, Constitutional Union; and 1 had no identifiable party. Even when McCoy inspected those manufacturers who would be sensitive to tariff schedules she found that ironmasters, for example, split between the parties. Probably the only clear connection of economic interest and party support could be found in the shipping group. Two preferred Republicanism, 2 were of unknown party. The Republicans vigorously supported aid for river and harbor improvements and wove Democratic Presidential vetoes of improvements bills into their anti-Southern rhetoric. This may also have influenced McCoy's merchants. Twelve voted Republican (46 percent); 5, Democratic (19 percent); and 9 had no identifiable party (35 percent). In New York Philip Foner found that merchants took "conservative" positions in 1860, that is Democratic or Constitutional Union, but Michigan merchants, unlike those of New York, did not have important ties to Southern markets.[10]

Eber B. Ward, a Republican businessman with shipping and manufacturing interests, provides a classic example of the fusion of economic interest, sectional consciousness, and moral passion which the economic interpretation traditionally has seen as the driving force of Northwestern Republicanism. In 1860 Ward published a pamphlet boosting the Republican cause, arguing that a tariff would aid U.S. manufacturing and not Europe's, and would provide employment for men, women, and children. With the election over Ward rejoiced that "Satan is once more rebuked." Freedom, truth, and intelligence had triumphed, but so had "the laboring men and women of America over the countless wealth and cheaper labor of Europe." Poor whites North and South had won access to the "unoccupied West." The Christian could rejoice "because no pure Christianity can raise its voice where the conscience is crushed

---

[10] Thomas D. Odle, "The Commercial Interests of the Great Lakes and the Campaign of 1860," *Michigan History*, 40 (March 1956), 9-10, 18, 20-23. Philip S. Foner, *Business and Slavery: The New York Merchants and the Irrepressible Conflict* (Chapel Hill, 1941).

and freedom of thought abolished." Ward above all thanked "laborers and mechanics as well as farmers and miners . . . for their vote in favor of protection to American Industry."[11]

Ward typified those entrepreneurial elements who identified their interests with party, section, nation, and religion. Yet some businessmen supported Republican anti-Southernism even though they feared the economic consequences of alienating the South. Lumberman Henry H. Crapo, elected Fusion mayor of Flint in 1857,[12] believed that his business would suffer from Southern secession. But he said the crisis of 1860-61 resulted not from economic disorders but rather from the efforts of "Northern politicians and Southern slaveholders . . . to drive the North into making more concessions to the South . . . for the sake of peace." Although economic disorder probably would come "I say *no concessions*, no more compromises, nor toleration or forebearance towards secessionists and traitors. We have been harassed and annoyed by 'Northern doughfaces' and 'Southern fire-eaters' quite too long, and I am tired of it, as are the great mass of the Northern people."[13]

As in 1844 ethnic and religious factors influenced party choice among the economic elite far more impressively than economic role. Yankees, constituting 50 percent of the elite, had a Republican tendency: 58 percent of them were Republicans. Of the Republicans 70 percent were Yankees (compared to 54 percent of the Whigs). Yankees constituted a significant group in the Democracy and again were its largest single ethnic group: 34 percent. Religion seemed strongly related to party choice among Yankees. While 67 percent of the Presbyterians were Republicans only 14 percent were Democrats. (See Appendix E)[14]

Between 1844 and 1860 Episcopalians moved heavily into the Democratic camp. Among the entire elite the sect increased only slightly, but the Democratic elite contingent went from 36 percent to 50 percent, while the Whigs' 64 percent fell to 26 percent among Republicans. Of 15 former Whigs who joined the Democrats 43 percent were Episcopalians, and two of them were Yankees, the only two of that group to switch to Democracy. Among the Episcopalian Whigs of 1844 who be-

---

[11] Eber B. Ward, *Why the North-West Should Have a Protective Tariff and Why the Republican Party is the Safest Party to Trust with the Government* (Detroit, 1860), 121-22; *Detroit Advertiser*, Nov. 9, 1860. In 1859 one Republican businessman-entrepreneur sent Governor Wisner a series of articles from the *Detroit Advertiser* urging that Michigan pass "laws which will induce capitalists to establish manufactures among us." C. A. Trowbridge to Gov. Moses Wisner, Dec. 23, 1859, Executive Records, Legislative Correspondence, MHCom.

[12] Lewis, *Lumberman from Flint*, 107; Crapo had backed Fremont enthusiastically in 1856, 106.

[13] Crapo letters of Nov. 25 and Dec. 23, 1860, quoted in Lewis, *Lumberman from Flint*, 105, 106, 274.

[14] McCoy, "Wayne County Economic Elite, 1844, 1860," 175.

came Republicans McCoy found a very suggestive trait: all were probably of Presbyterian or Congregational origins and apt to be of a strong
pietist-moral reform bent.[15]

McCoy described the 1860 elite as a "New England establishment"
which could perhaps "be epitomized as a combination of reformist zeal
and capitalist energy. The typical member was a Yankee Presbyterian
Whig-Republican (61 percent of Yankee Whigs, 52 percent of Yankee
Republican Presbyterians) who was likely to be a merchant, manufac-
turer, or a capitalist." The core Democrat was by contrast likely to be
Yankee Episcopalian or no religion and a landowner. Religious, ethnocultural, and economic role differences proved stronger than class
solidarity and caused value conflicts among the elite deep enough to lead
to divergent party loyalties.

Among the masses of Wayne County and Detroit party cleavages also
cut across classes, although certain occupations leaned to particular
parties. From the 1860 manuscript schedules for Wayne County some
18,000 potential voters were classified by occupation, wealth, and nativity. Well over 7,100 of these potential voters lived in the county's 18
townships, some of which in 1850 had been in the frontier phase. By
1860, however, typical processes of socioeconomic differentiation had
taken place in all. (See Appendix B) Townships which had consisted
wholly of poor farmers in 1850 now possessed a distinct top layer of
prosperous farmers, as well as a bottom layer of farm laborers and
tenants. Just as striking was the encroachment by 1860 of urban occupations into the towns nearest Detroit, such as Springwells, Hamtramck,
Grosse Pointe, and Dearborn. But the proportion of urban or farm occupations did not seem to have any relation to party strength. Nor did the
proportion of rural lower classes have a significant effect on party
loyalty. "Ruralness" and Republican 1860 percentage strength correlated at −.122. The rural-lower-class correlation with Democratic
strength in 1860 was positive, +.228, and an increase over the +.158
correlation in 1850. As in 1850, however, the foreign born percentage
correlated far more highly with Democratic strength: +.469, although
it was lower than in 1850 (+.561).

Correlations for Detroit's almost 11,000 potential voters in 10 wards
in 1860 suggest the impact of ethnocultural influences on voting. Table
XIV.5 arranges the correlations of 9 variables with Republican percentage strength in 1860 in descending positive significance to dramatize the

---

[15] *Ibid.*, 176-77. The 1861 mayoral campaign pitted against one another elite
members who represented the opposing political strains isolated by McCoy. Henry
Baldwin, a benevolent Episcopalian of Presbyterian or Congregational descent,
ran on the Republican or Union ticket. Baldwin, strongly identified with temperance and other reform causes, lost to Democrat William C. Duncan, a non-
Yankee brewer of antireformist proclivities. *Ibid.*, 166-67.

polarities between ethnic groups but not between economic or occupational ones. (Correlations of *Democratic* percentage strength with foreign born and Irish were high, while Germans failed to correlate significantly with Democratic strength. The aggregate data on Detroit's Germans so far suggests only that they split between the parties. How the Germans divided, however, will be examined closely below.)

TABLE XIV.5

1860 Correlations of Republican Percentage Strength in 10 Detroit Wards with 8 Variables[a]

New British	.488[a]
White Collar	.132
Unskilled	—.053
Blue Collar (aggregate)	—.082
Germans	—.133
Skilled	—.174
Blue Collar Foreign	—.275
Irish	—.296

[a] Multiple regression analysis using 8 variables also indicated that the New British presence exercised the strongest positive influence on Republican percentage strength

Before examining voting in the 1850s by ethnic and religious groups, further examination of the party preferences of Detroit occupational groups has been made possible by a unique document. Some political leader in Detroit sometime during 1856 inscribed the names of 895 men in an account book, grouped alphabetically, followed by street address, and a checkmark in one of four columns headed: Fremont, Buchanan, Doubtful, and Fillmore. Using Detroit *Directories* for 1854, 1856, 1857, 1858, and 1859, the occupations of 651 of the men could be identified. The entire 895 lived mostly in the crowded wards close to the Detroit River, Wards 1, 2, and 3. The representativeness of this list is moot, but it seems reasonable to suppose that men appearing on such a list, especially those for Fremont and Buchanan, tended to be loyalists known for their party ties, and thus the lists probably were weighted toward men more intense than average in partisanship and political activity, the core voters.[16]

[16] Originally a "Scrapbook of Political Newspaper Clippings, 1850s-1870s," the lists of voters had to be uncovered by steaming off the clippings which had been pasted over them; the original is in BHC; a xerox copy is in my possession. If the same men appeared in different directories, and with a different occupation, the directories were arbitrarily given this order of priority after 1856: 1857, 1858, 1854, 1859. This involved very few cases.

The Fillmore supporters numbered 3 and thus tell nothing about that nativism which had been such a potent political force. However the "doubtful" group, 324 strong, may have been of uncertain party loyalty partly because of their vulnerability to nativism. No doubt such a large group of doubtfuls testified to the shaking loose of party loyalties by the events of 1853-56 and is of a piece with the heavy ticket splitting that went on in local elections during this period.

Detroit Voters in Poll Book, 1856

	Fremont		Buchanan		Doubtful	
Total	259		302		324	
Occupations identified	201	77.0%	213	70.0%	234	71.8%
Occupations unidentified	52	19.9%	65	21.3%	70	21.4%
No occupation	6	2.2%	24	7.8%	20	6.1%

Republicans (Fremonters) definitely tended to have higher status occupations than the Democrats (Table XIV.6). The doubtful group ranked slightly lower than the Democrats in status; the two were quite similar, with the doubtfuls having more unskilled and white-collar occupations and less of the skilled and professional groups. Overall differences in white-collar categories were not very impressive (except perhaps for the absence of Democratic managers). Within the blue-collar category, however, large gaps opened as the Democrats and doubtfuls had far more unskilled workers than the Republicans while the latter had far more skilled workers than the other two political groups. If each category is considered on a percentage basis in relation to the total group or the total identified (as in Table XIV.6) these tendencies still hold. The Republicans had the least percentages in both the no occupation and unidentified categories, which also fits with their higher status and stability. Further corroboration of this last point will come when similar but more detailed data relating to Lansing voters in 1858 is discussed.

ETHNICITY AND PARTY, 1854–1860

Any warning against generalizing about the foreign born as a group extends particularly to the Germans. Of all the immigrant groups voting in 1860 the Germans have received the most attention. Ethnocentric Germans and patronizing native scholars both established a tradition that the "German vote" of the Northwest "elected Lincoln." Recently such claims have been tested in controlled investigations determining how Germans in particular areas voted, and why some supported Lincoln

TABLE XIV.6

1856 Detroit Voters, 3 "Party" Groups by Occupation

	Percent of Identified			Percent of Total		
	Rep.	Dem.	Doubtful	Rep.	Dem.	Doubtful
Blue Collar Total	72	87	81	56	61	59
White Collar Total	27	14	19	21	9	14
Unskilled	14	43	45	11	30	33
Semiskilled	1	2	2	1	1	1
Service	4	2	3	3	2	2
Skilled	53	40	31	41	28	23
Sales	1	1	1	1	.6	1
Clerical	5	3	5	4	2	4
Managerial	6		3	5		2
Professional	3	1	1	2	.3	1
Proprietors	12	9	8	9	6	6
No Occupation				2	8	6
Unidentified				20	22	22

while others did not.[17] Taken together, old and new studies suggest a formidable number of variables influencing German political behavior: length of time in America; personal and family loyalties; class; economic role; education; urban or rural environment; degree of isolation; associational loyalties such as labor unions; place of origin in Germany; and religion.[18] Data that permit the systematic testing of all these variables in Michigan are not available, but enough evidence is at hand to determine some central tendencies among Germans.

In the 1850s Michigan Germans were, in the words of a Free Soil editor in 1854, "in the transition state." He claimed that "a great majority were now awakening" and moving away from the Democrats.[19] During 1856 Republicans called attention to German activities in their ranks as Whigs never had. In Detroit Republican campaigners regularly exhorted voters in both English and German; more German names appeared among lists of Republican ward officers; German bands and "lager beer-

[17] A recent and model study of this kind is Paul J. Kleppner, "Lincoln and the Immigrant Vote: A Case of Religious Polarization," *Mid-America*, 48 (July 1966), 176-95.

[18] William E. Dodd, "The Fight for the Northwest, 1860," *American Historical Review*, 16 (October 1910-July 1911), 774-88; Donald V. Smith, "The Influence of the Foreign-Born of the Northwest in the Election of 1860," *Mississippi Valley Historical Review*, 19 (September 1932), 192-204; Joseph Schafer, "Who Elected Lincoln?" *American Historical Review*, 47 (October 1941), 51-63; Andreas Dorpalen, "The German Element and the Issues of the Civil War," *Mississippi Valley Historical Review*, 29 (June 1942), 55-76; Jay Monaghan, "Did Abraham Lincoln Receive the Illinois German Vote?" *Journal of the Illinois State Historical Society*, 35 (June 1942), 133-39; George H. Daniels, "Immigrant Vote in the 1860 Election: The Case of Iowa," *Mid-America*, 44 (July 1962), 142-62. Of the earlier studies Schafer's was easily the best.

[19] *Detroit Daily Democrat*, Feb. 11, 1854.

hall" keepers also gained prominence in Detroit Republicanism.[20] In townships across the state German Republican clubs appeared. Republicans labored to create an impression of German movement to their side and after the election made large claims about the extent of German defection to their ranks. Indeed, a new German newspaper endorsed Fremont as had the previously Democratic *Volksblatt*, though the latter returned to the Democratic Party after 1856.[21]

Indications of German movement continued through the later 1850s. The Republican state administration encouraged it in 1859 by reviving the post of Immigration Commissioner and appointing two Germans successively as commissioners.[22] One of the motives behind such an action was indirectly expressed by an Ann Arbor Republican who in 1859 recommended to the State Treasurer "One of our German Republicans" for a job at the Sault Canal works: "The Republicans of Ann Arbor will be much obliged," he wrote, "we are so situated here that we need all the help we can get."[23] In 1860 the Wayne County Republicans, after a well-reported discussion of the matter, urged upon the Republican State Convention "the propriety and justice of selecting a German delegate to Chicago." The state convention not only chose the Wayne German candidate, but added another "tribute to the German members" by sending a second national delegate of German origin from Saginaw County. And on the list of electors for Lincoln in 1860 stood the name of Eduard Dorsch of Monroe, scholar-politician and German "48'er."[24]

What did all this activity add up to in votes? To a surprising extent the Germans remained far more loyal to the Democrats than has usually been supposed. Movement away from the Democrats occurred primarily among German Protestants and a smaller group of anticlerical rationalists. And not all German Protestants left the Democrats in 1860, perhaps not even a majority. The units in Table XIV.7 did not consist entirely of Germans, and not all of the Germans in them were Lutheran, although

[20] *Advertiser*, July 1-31, Aug. 1, 13, Sept. 1, 3, 20, 29, Oct. 3, 4, 9, 14, 15, 25, 1856.

[21] *Advertiser*, Aug. 26, Sept. 8, 1856; *Marshall Statesman*, Nov. 19, 1856; *Lansing Republican*, Oct. 21, Nov. 11, 1856. For similar claims in 1858, *Grand Rapids Daily Eagle*, Nov. 12, 1858; *Republican*, Nov. 2, 1858. Mark O. Kistler, "The German Language Press in Michigan: A Survey and Bibliography," *Michigan History*, 44 (September 1960), 306; *Advertiser*, July 8, 1856.

[22] Jenks, "Michigan Immigration," *Michigan History*, 28, 69-70, 78, 79-80; *Daily Eagle*, March 4, 16, 1859; also *Jackson American Citizen*, March 10, 1859.

[23] James McMahon, Ann Arbor, to John McKinney, May 6, 1859, Department of Treasury Papers, Letters Sent and Received, 1857-1882.

[24] *Advertiser*, April 13, 1860; J. Elaine Thompson, "The Formative Period of the Republican Party in Michigan, 1854-1860" (unpublished M.A. thesis, Wayne State University, 1949), 103-05; Harold G. Carlson, "A Distinguished 48'er: Eduard Dorsch," *Michigan History*, 19 (Autumn 1935), 429, 435; Thomas, *Nativism*, 240.

most were. The data there does not show a uniformly strong movement away from the Democrats and it cannot be presumed that German Lutherans were responsible for all that did occur. In Saginaw County,

TABLE XIV.7

Units with Concentrations of German Lutherans, Democratic Percentages, 1852 and 1860

	1852	1860
Saginaw County	61	45
Waterloo, Jackson County	67	64
Riga, Lenawee County	77	58
Freedom, Washtenaw County	67	81
Warren, Macomb County	67	50
Harrison, Macomb County	74	58
New Buffalo, Berrien County	62	40
Bainbridge, Berrien County	68	51
Bridgewater, Washtenaw County	58	60

for example, the Democrats still handily carried the homogenous German Lutheran town of Frankenmuth.[25] Rural German Lutherans did not move en masse away from the Democrats.

Rural German Catholics maintained their Democratic loyalty. Springwells and Hamtramck in Wayne County both had large German enclaves of Lutherans and Catholics in 1860, mostly the latter. Both units fell only slightly in Democratic percentage in 1860. The isolated German Catholic community of Westphalia, still a homogenous ethnoreligious enclave, voted 94 percent Democratic in 1860 as it had in 1852.[26]

In Detroit, Catholic and Protestant cleavages bore a close relation to party differences. In 1859 the Republicans encouraged the drift away from the Democrats by nominating Christian H. Buhl for mayor, a wealthy Protestant whose parents had come from Saxony.[27] Buhl ran well in wards of high German density, surpassing the previous Republican mayoral candidate as well as all aldermanic candidates on his ticket. His showing also bested Lincoln's in those wards in 1860. But party loyalties do indeed exert a relatively weak influence in city elections, and voters more easily split tickets to support individuals than they do in state or national elections.

In Detroit's 4 "German wards" from 1852 to 1864 (7, 10, 6, and 4),

[25] Streeter, *Political Parties*, 226.

[26] Nearby Dallas Township which received some German Catholic and Lutheran settlers in the 1850s went from 43 percent Democratic in 1852 to 66 percent in 1860, *History of Shiawasee and Clinton Counties*, 416, 420-21.

[27] Streeter, *Political Parties*, 282. The *Advertiser* commended the "independent Democrats and especially the Germans of the Fourth, Sixth, Seventh, and Tenth wards for supporting 'justice and humanity,'" Nov. 9, 1859. Buhl was not only a Protestant but also a member of the Whig-Republican Yankee Presbyterian elite.

the Democrats generally did well: 3 were Democratic in 1858, and all 4 were Democratic in 1862. Only in 1860 did wards 4 and 7 show sharp declines. Yet even in 1860 the Fourth Ward remained loyal to the Democrats (53 percent). Only in this ward, significantly, did Catholic Germans outnumber Protestant Germans. With the exception of 1860 most urban Germans seem largely to have retained their Democratic loyalty. The Republican party enlarged somewhat its minority strength among Germans, but this probably took place chiefly among German Protestants.

TABLE XIV.8

Democratic Percentages in German Wards, Detroit, Major Elections: 1852–1864

	Percentage German	1852	1854	1856	1858	1860	1862	1864
Ward 7	48	55	57	56	59	48	58	65
Ward 10	44				48	46	57	58
Ward 6	41	52	39	41	51	40	52	48
Ward 4	40	64	70	64	68	53	67	65

Why did the Republicans enjoy any success at all among Germans? How, as the *Niles Republican* wondered in 1856, could so many Germans vote "for the know nothing republican candidates"?[28] The answer lies in part in the exceptional treatment given to the Germans by the Republicans. More importantly, Independency's anti-Popery probably appealed to many Protestant Germans, while Germans may also have recognized that the Know Nothings had infiltrated the Democratic party in some areas.[29] Republican platform pledges of support for the rights of naturalized citizens were aimed squarely at the Germans. "English and Scotch and Protestant German citizens" occupied a very different place in Fusion-Republican feelings than did Irish Catholics. Republicans deliberately played off Germans and Irish against one another, frequently using the German Protestants as examples of the "good immigrants" who favored "American interests" while the Irish of course served always to define the bad foreigners. Republican rhetoric portrayed Germans as true to the principles of freedom for which they immigrated, while the Irish obeyed the slavery of "party."[30]

Despite Republican openness to a German alliance most Germans who sold or drank alcohol probably opposed Republicanism because of

[28] *Niles Republican*, Nov. 8, 1856; *Free Press*, Nov. 3, 1859.

[29] The *Saginaw Enterprise* published a letter from a German claiming this was true in Saginaw, *Advertiser*, July 22, 1856.

[30] *Advertiser*, March 13, 1855; Brown, "Southwestern Michigan in 1860 Campaign," *Michigan Heritage*, 2: 71; *Advertiser*, Oct. 22, 1858; *Daily Eagle*, March 30, 1859.

its identification with prohibition. Germans who cherished their traditional leisure pleasures were as repelled by the Republicans as by the Whigs. Christian Buhl perhaps represented the Americanized, upper-status Protestant German who could identify with moral reform, but Catholics and many non-Catholic hedonists would find this difficult. One Saginaw Valley German said he saw little choice in politics in 1855, with "slavery on the one side, the temperance humbug on the other."[31] Sectionalism and antislavery also joined the many pressures bearing on Germans in the 1850s but the relative weight of these issues is not clear. Certainly many Germans responded to the intense anti-Southernism of 1856 and 1860, but close examination of election data suggests that the impact of sectionalism and antislavery idealism have been exaggerated, both as to their preeminence among other influences in the 1850s and to their long-run effects.

Germans do not appear to have "hated slavery" more than other groups did. They disliked blacks of any kind as much or more than the natives did, though they did not display the Negrophobia found among Irish Catholics.[32] If the anti-Nebraska party exerted a special moral appeal for Germans because of attitudes to slavery it probably was combined with a moralism that stressed ascetic Yankee Protestant middle-class ethics of disciplined, moral, temperate conduct. This Protestant German rapport with Republicanism received no better expression than that given it in a public letter by Nicholas Greusel, Jr., Republican candidate for City Marshal of Detroit in 1856. His rival, a German saloon keeper in the Fourth Ward, had apparently attacked him for being rather straight-laced. Greusel answered that his opponent believed that to be fit for Marshal a man "must have the qualification of drunkenness; he must regularly attend a saloon, spend his money, lose his senses, and be called a good fellow." The city had had enough of such officers. "I do not wish you to think that I do not take a glass of lager beer when I feel like taking one; most of my German friends know this, and the better class of them will vote for him of whom they well know that he never disgraced them by being carried home on a dray." Greusel described his opponent further as "a man who despises religion, and sets all laws at defiance."[33]

The Republican party also attracted another group of Germans disrespectful of religion—political radicals. In 1856 at the "Black Repub-

---

[31] Saginaw German quoted in Streeter, *Michigan History*, 2: 297.

[32] This is substantiated in a paper in progress on white attitudes to "colored suffrage" in Michigan. In 1860 Republican speakers told Germans, as they told other voters, that Republicans knew the Germans had not left Germany so that "their children should labor side by side with the African slave," *Detroit Tribune*, Oct. 26, 1860.

[33] *Advertiser*, Feb. 25, 1856; also *ibid.*, Sept. 8, 1856; Thomas, *Nativism*, 211-12.

lican" display at the State Fair, the *Vindicator*'s editor noticed "some 200 German Red Republicans of the very worst stamp, comprising the association of young German turners . . . and the other secret German radical associations of this city." One Republican candidate for state legislator was in fact "a member of this priest-hating fraternity of dangerous infidels." The *Vindicator* advised German Catholics to vote against such men and after the election claimed that the "entire Infidel Red Republican German vote" was cast for Black Republicanism.[34] Unfortunately, there is little information otherwise available regarding the radicals. They probably voted Republican because of their antagonism to Catholic authoritarianism, their unusual political awareness which made them more vulnerable than the average German to appeals to Northern sectional pride and interests, and ideological opposition to slavery. Ironically, this kind of revulsion to slavery has usually been attributed to the radicals' very strange bedfellows in Republican ranks, the German Protestants.

Republican inroads on German Democratic voting strength were related to continued Irish Catholic support of the Democrats. Although the Irish found themselves uncomfortable in the factionalized party of 1853-55, Fusion-Republican actions drove them back to the Democrats: they really had nowhere else to go. If the Irish saw themselves as the special targets of anti-Popery they had considerable reason to do so. The Irish may have served the Republicans as a negative reference group far better than if they had given votes. In any case, Republicans tended to write off Irish Catholic votes.

Although a new Irish military company might march in Detroit's 1853 Fourth of July celebration, symbolically suggesting Irish participation in the community, yet the flourishing of Know Nothingism made Irish Catholics well aware that "the native American hate is more fiercely directed against the naturalized citizens of Irish descent than of any other foreign extraction."[35] Within the Democratic Party tension existed not only between them and native Protestants but also with French Canadians and Germans. The ethnic rivalries among different Catholic groups also pervaded, indeed to some extent originated in, the churches. The Irish, for example, complained all during the antebellum years of having non-English speaking priests of French, German, or Dutch origin.[36]

Thus, in the 1850s Irish Catholics felt increasingly isolated. An habitual Irish-baiter such as the *Detroit Advertiser* permitted itself unmitigated wrath when in 1858 it saw "miserable Irish rowdies, who had

[34] *Vindicator*, Oct. 11, Nov. 8, 1856.
[35] *Vindicator*, July 9, 1853, Jan. 27, 1855.
[36] *Advertiser*, March 3, 1855; Richard R. Elliott, MS Index to *Vindicator*, microfilm, University of Detroit Library; Mast, *Always the Priest*, 318-19; *Advertiser*, Aug. 3, 1858; O'Brien, "Le Pere Juste," *MHC*, 21: 263.

not the right to vote in their own country, and who were brought up like swine, at so much a head, bluffing and insulting all who dared to vote. . . . They are *owned* by the Locofoco demagogues of this city as much as Southern slaves are owned by their masters."[37] In 1859 a Grand Rapids editor expressed a prevailing Republican attitude when he observed the unqualified support given to the "Dimmicratic" ticket by the Irish and judged the Democrats welcome to it: "We want no slaves or cravens in our ranks." The great mass of Irish were unlike other foreign groups: "the Germans, Hollanders, Scotchmen, and people of all other nations, except the Irish, are divided in their political action, like the natives of our own country . . . this difference is respected by all." Though Germans and Hollanders had at first been strongly "prejudiced" for the Democrats they were now beginning to grow more "independent." Thus the Irish had no one's respect.[38]

Election returns and other data demonstrate massive Irish Catholic voting for the Democrats in the period 1854-60. It was easily 95 percent or more. Irish Catholics accounted for some 50 percent of the voters of Detroit's Eighth Ward in 1860. It remained strongly Democratic, going for Douglas by 60 percent. To the southeast the large village of Adrian, Lenawee County, had a concentration of Irish and other Catholics in its First Ward which bordered the railroad yard where many of the immigrants worked. Adrian's First was its only Democratic ward in 1860 (57 percent).[39] Far to the west Grand Rapids First Ward also contained a heavy "Irish vote." In 1854 a local politician promised Irish votes for the Fusion ticket, then applied to the new state administration for a reward. A local Republican, however, told Governor Bingham that while the applicant may have done what he could, "as the Irish Catholics generally gave their votes against us, I have supposed that he did not effect much." This continued to be the case as the First Ward voted 62 percent and 60 percent Democratic in 1858 and 1860.[40]

Irish Catholic farmers also maintained a strong Democratic loyalty. Erin, Macomb County, received some German Lutherans in the 1850s but was still voting over 80 percent Democratic in 1860 as in 1852. Nearby Emmet Township in St. Clair County, purely Irish and 98 percent Democratic in 1852, slipped to 81 percent Democratic in 1859 after its population became more heterogeneous. Washtenaw County's North-field continued to be a strong Democratic township of German and Irish

[37] *Advertiser*, Nov. 3, 1858; also *Cass County Republican*, Dec. 2, 1858.

[38] *Daily Eagle*, March 30, 1859; also, April 6; *Advertiser*, Feb. 7, Oct. 30, 1856, Nov. 11, 1858; *Vindicator*, April 4, 1857.

[39] Bonner, *Memoirs of Lenawee*, I, 503; Frank Krause, *City Map of Adrian* (Ann Arbor, 187?), BHC.

[40] Lovell Moore to Gov. Bingham, Jan. 10, 1855, Executive Records, Elections, MHCom; *Daily Eagle*, March 30, 1859.

Catholic voters. Irish Catholics probably helped give the Democrats majorities in 1860 in Bunker Hill and White Oak townships, Ingham County.[41] Thus, urban or rural, east or west, Irish Catholics voted as their friends and enemies said they did.

The Irish stood fast but like the Germans the new Dutch of western Michigan were in motion during the 1850s, primarily away from the Democrats. But the popular notion that antislavery caused a sudden huge Dutch switch is grossly inaccurate. In 1854 the Dutch voted strongly Democratic. *De Hollander* supported not only the Democrats but the Kansas-Nebraska Bill. The Dutch disliked abolitionists and blacks, and both these prejudices influenced their first reactions to Fusion-Republicanism.[42]

"Fusion" continued to represent the threat and arrogance of Whig evangelicalism with its potential threat to Dutch separatism. While prohibition must have appealed to many Dutch, enforcement of the liquor law in Ottawa County led to incidents that were offensive to the Dutch. The tendency of Republicans to stereotype the Dutch probably confirmed the impression that the *Nietweters*—Know Nothings—were allied with the Fusionists.[43] Yet even in 1854 some breakage from the nearly monolithic support of the Democrats could be discerned. In 1856 it became a beachhead. Ministers and "influentials" seem to have been disproportionately present among the early Republican boosters. Fremont clubs formed in Grand Rapids and in Holland, and Dutch defections in 1856 were visible enough to *De Hollander* and the *Kalamazoo Gazette* to denounce recusants as dupes of the Know Nothings.[44]

In the late 1850s Republicanism still left the mass of Dutch voters untouched. By 1857 Republicans at least had a newspaper in the Ottawa County area, Henry Chubb's *Clarion*. *De Hollander* stayed Democratic and two new Democratic papers appeared, the *Grand Haven News* (1858) and the *Ottawa County Register* (1859). In June 1860 a Republican paper, *De Grondwet*, appeared in Holland itself, published by

[41] Durant, *Ingham*, 228; Turner, *Ingham*, 87; letter from Grattan, Nov. 20, 1854, *Vindicator*, Nov. 25, 1854; Index to *Vindicator*. South of Kent in Berrien County the Democratic paper complimented the Irish of Niles for voting Democratic, *Niles Republican*, Nov. 8, 1856.

[42] Lucas, *Dutch Immigrant Memoirs*, I, 545, 536; in February 1855 *De Hollander* said that natural laws guided by God would eventually destroy slavery, meanwhile "political abolitionists" were having the opposite effect, quoted in Lucas, I, 547; *Centreville Western Chronicle*, Nov. 2, 1854; Ten Hoor remembered a book in his father's library defending slavery as "not contrary to the . . . Bible," "Dutch Colonists," *Michigan History*, 31: 357.

[43] Grand Haven, *Grand River Times*, March 15, 1854; *Marshall Statesman*, May 16, 1855; Lucas, *Dutch Immigrant Memoirs*, I, 547-48; Thomas, *Nativism*, 229-30.

[44] Lucas, *Dutch Immigrant Memoirs*, I, 545, 551-56; *Advertiser*, July 21, Oct. 30, 1856; *Grand River Times*, Oct. 29, 1856; *Kalamazoo Gazette*, April 11, 1856.

John Roost. Meanwhile, in the 1859 legislature Henry Barns, one of the editor-architects of Fusion, delivered a eulogistic report on the Holland Colony and asked the state to grant swamp lands to the colony to help construct internal improvements.[45] Yet in 1859, the election returns for Justice of the Supreme Court from Holland and Zeeland clearly showed that "the colony still sustains the Sham Democracy." The "Republican cause is steadily gaining ground" but the Democrats still won a majority. Holland elected John Roost supervisor and the rest of the Republican town ticket in April 1860, but then gave a solid majority for Douglas in the fall.[46] Unfortunately only returns for Holland Township are avail-

TABLE XIV.9

Michigan Dutch Townships Party Voting: 1852–1860

	Holland		Zeeland		Fillmore		Olive	
	Dem.	Rep.	Dem.	Rep.	Dem.	Rep.	Dem.	Rep.
1852	123–96%	5–4%	128–91%	11–9%	47–78%	13–22%		
1854	105–63%	61–37%	24–28%	62–72%	16–50%	16–50%		
1856	129–63%	74–37%	55–60%	36–40%				
1857	154–72%	59–28%	139–94%	9–6%	24–47%	27–53%	48–100%	
1859	182–53%	159–47%	112–64%	64–36%				
1860	208–66%	105–34%						

able for 1860. Yet Democratic strength there, Democratic emphasis on Republican contempt for the Dutch, and the energetic campaigning of the "Holland Invincibles" suggest that Dutch voting in 1860 closely resembled that in the town of Holland.[47] A leading historian of the Dutch pioneers, Professor Henry Lucas, has observed that although some Dutch areas in the Midwest voted Republican in 1860, "The Hollanders were generally unwilling to forsake the Democratic party."[48]

Dutch loyalty to the Democrats is sometimes explained in terms of

[45] *Daily Eagle*, April 6, 1859; letter to *Advertiser*, April 7, 1859. *Michigan Senate Journal, 1859*, 245-58.

[46] A. S. Kenzie, "Newspapers in Ottawa County," *MHC*, 9: 295-300; *Advertiser*, April 5, 7, 1860; Pieters, *Dutch Settlement*, 158.

[47] *Western Chronicle*, Sept. 27, 1860; *Kalamazoo Gazette*, Oct. 5, 19, 1860.

[48] Lucas, *Dutch Immigrant Memoirs*, I, 560-61, 562. Lucas claimed, however, that a majority of Dutch in Grand Rapids and Kalamazoo voted Republican in 1860. Unfortunately, the data to test that claim are not available. For example, Lucas said that Grand Rapids Third Ward was "heavily Dutch" and voted Republican by 285 to 190 with 80 votes going to minor candidates. But scrutiny of census population schedules (on microfilm) for Grand Rapids in 1860 shows that no more than 15 percent of the adult males in that ward were actually born in Holland, though the Third did contain a proportionately large number of Holland born compared to other wards. On the other hand, the Republican majority in the Third was probably related to the fact that almost 60 percent of its adult males were from New York or New England and were probably Yankee Protestants; there were 4 clergymen living in the ward: 1 Presbyterian, 1 Baptist, and 2 Methodists, all from New York or New England.

Dutch revulsion to Republican prohibitionism: thus the Democratic Party was "the party of license . . . more liberal with other people's rights and with strong drink."[49] But this view overlooks the religious asceticism of the great majority of western Michigan rural Dutch in 1860. Among the rural pietists, party divisions probably reflected not cleavages between pietists and secularists—consensus existed on piety—but rather cleavages along status, class, occupational, geographic, cultural, or other lines. The question of assimilation, for example, was such a basis of disagreement, coinciding, apparently, with party divisions. Religious Dutch leaders who were willing to assimilate into American society understood that they had to adopt the dominant values as well. These assimilationists also tended to embrace Republicanism. Other equally pietist Dutch, including probably the mass of the rank and file as well as older leaders, desired rather to preserve their ethnic heritage, resisted assimilation, and were far more reluctant to move away from the Democrats.[50]

One influence working on both assimilationists and conservatives to erode their Democratic loyalties was anti-Popery. Signs of Dutch attitudes to Catholicism in the 1850s were few but unmistakably hostile. In the 1880s a local politician, explaining why Zeeland was then heavily Republican, said that the "great change" in politics began "in the trying period of the war." Promoting Republicanism were "first, the Democratic party's record on secession and rebellion, finance and tariff; second, the intense jealousy with which the Zeelanders regard their civil and religious right and our public schools system, all of which they regard in constant danger from the Catholic hierarchy which, together with the liquor interest of the country, is a standing menace to free institutions." The importance of free "public schools" in this Republican's mind, in fact, overshadowed any other issue.[51] This explicit and articulate version of postwar Republican ideology did not necessarily exist in the 1850s, but its foundations were laid then.

Although they have attracted far less attention than other immigrant groups, the New British actually moved into the Republican camp in formidable numbers in the 1850s. The New British had earlier favored the Whigs, and as Catholic complaints regarding the identity of "Irish Orangeism" and Fusion indicated, many British Protestants became

[49] Adrian Van Koevering, "The Dutch Colonial Pioneers of Western Michigan," 3 vols, MS, MHCol., 490-91.

[50] The appeal of the laissez faire ethic because of an alleged hedonist strain cannot be taken seriously in regard to the rural Dutch pietists. This notion may have some validity for Dutch in some of the large towns. On different attitudes toward assimilation, Ten Hoor, *Michigan History*, 31: 363-64; Paul Honigsheim, "Religion and Assimilation of Dutch," *Michigan History*, 26: 54-55, 59-61; Lucas, *Dutch Immigrant Memoirs*, I, 224, shows a Zeeland settler remembering the assimilation issue arising as early as 1850.

[51] Lucas, *Dutch Immigrant Memoirs*, I, 251, 248, 250; also 548 and 512; Pieters, *Dutch Settlement*, 109.

zealous Republicans. In the 1850s E. B. Ward and other Republican capitalists located the Eureka Iron Company and Wyandotte Rolling Mills in Ecorse Township. The village of Wyandotte mushroomed as English, German, and Irish workers poured in. Nearby Monguagon's percentage of New British rose from 12 percent in 1850 to 44 percent in 1860. The simultaneous influx of Irish and German Catholics probably balanced the political impact of the increase of British Methodists and no great decline of Democratic strength occurred in these towns. The Republicans, however, underlined their New British connection in 1856 by nominating Duncan Stewart, a "sound gallant Scotchman," to run for state senator in the district which included Wyandotte and Monguagon. Moreover, the leaders of the new Republican Association of Ecorse in 1856 were predominantly English.[52] Even the New British of Sanilac County, who voted Democratic through 1854, switched to Republicanism later in the decade. So rapid was the change that whereas 70 percent of 358 voters were Democrats in 1852, 80 percent of 1,005 voters were Republicans in 1856, as were 70 percent of 1,304 voters in 1860. The core of New British settlement in Sanilac had been Lexington Township: 72 percent Democratic in 1852, it was 70 percent Republican in 1860. In nearby Lapeer County a mixed group of Scots, English, and New Yorkers settled Burlington Township in the 1850s. Methodist in religion, this town of British stock gave the Republicans 80 percent of its vote in 1860.[53]

The New British were one of the two largest groups among the 149,000 foreign born in Michigan in 1860. Less noticeable than the Germans or Irish because of their English language and Protestant religion, the 26,000 English and 6,000 Scots together exceeded the Irish total of about 30,000 persons but were slightly less than the German group of nearly 39,000. However, part of the Irish group were Northern Irelanders, allied to the New British Protestants in religion and sentiment, and in 1860 many of the 36,000 Canadian born immigrants were also thus allied—a group that contained many English, Welsh, and Scot Protestants.[54] Immigrants of British Protestant ethnic strains may very well have been the largest of the "foreign" groups in Michigan in 1860. Thus,

---

[52] Farmer, *Detroit*, I, 100; *Advertiser*, Nov. 3, July 11, 1856; Mrs. Joseph DeWindt, *Proudly We Record: The Story of Wyandotte, Michigan* (1955), 21, 27, 29, 49, 229-30; "Lake Superior Iron," *Michigan Pamphlets*, 5 (1860); E. P. Christian, "Historical Associations Connected with Wyandotte and Vicinity," *MHC*, 12: 323-24; *The Village of Wyandotte: Its Present and Prospective Advantages* (1856), 1-3; Farmer, *Detroit*, I, 1328; Thomas H. Christian, "History of St. Stephen's Parish, Wyandotte," BHC.

[53] *Portrait and Biographical Album of Sanilac County*, 560, 478; H. R. Page, *Lapeer County*, 196-202.

[54] For a convenient summary of United States Census data for 1860, United States Civil War Centennial Commission, *The United States on the Eve of the Civil War* (Washington, 1963), 63.

while the dramatic activities of some German and Dutch voters received considerable fussing over, the most numerous group in the Republican coalition was the New British.

RELIGION AND PARTIES, 1854–1860

In the 1850s Republicans evangelicalism was less dominated by Yankee Presbyterianism and the greater political unity among Protestants reflected the search for harmony of revivalism, enjoying a flush of success in the 1850s. Paramount in producing greater Protestant unity on the political front, however, was the wider recognition of Popery as a threat to Americanism. Republican success among Protestants depended to no small degree on the identifying in native minds of Catholicism with "party," Democracy, and slavocracy.

In 1854 and 1856 many Protestant clergymen openly backed Fusionism. If the volume of Democratic complaints against the "black-coated rascals who preached politics" be a measure, then the cadre work of Republican clergy declined after 1856.[55] In the mid-fifties, in fact, political evangelicalism seemed to peak on several fronts, particularly those of nativism and anti-Popery. As a quasi-partisan issue temperance, too, never gained more prominence at any time before the Civil War than in the years 1853-56. Temperance revivals blossomed in spots in the later 1850s but temperance as a political issue became subdued. Republicans, as Democrats charged, grew less willing to fight elections on the basis of "Whiskey or No Whiskey." Rather, they tended to capitalize on their temperance-morality image and the Democrats' wet image whenever they could.[56] In the mid-fifties, too, came the high tide of Republican anti-Mormonism, part and parcel of the evangelical countersubversive impulse. The Mormons constituted another all-Christian (Protestant) enemy who naturally gave all their votes to "the *party*."[57] The fall of Strang's Mormon kingdom followed shortly thereafter, but while it lasted it added to the fires of political evangelicalism forging the emerging Republican Party.

Although the Detroit Presbytery warned in 1856 against "political sermons" as a source of dissension, and the Synod of Michigan remained relatively conservative on slavery, Presbyterians as of old marched in the

[55] *Kalamazoo Gazette*, Nov. 17, 1854; *Jackson Patriot*, Oct. 22, 1856; *Niles Republican*, Nov. 8, 1856; *Advertiser*, July 11, 2, 8, 1856; the *Gazette* criticized the Republican legislator, Rev. A. St. Clair, as a "universal bore and eternal busybody," Nov. 8, 1856, also Nov. 29.

[56] *Advertiser*, April 9, 1857; Tucker, *Gratiot*, 53-54; *Daily Eagle*, Nov. 18, 1858; Baxter, *History of Grand Rapids*, 200; *Niles Republican*, Nov. 27, 1858; *Advertiser*, April 4, Nov. 3, 4, 1860; Farmer, *Detroit*, I, 841.

[57] *Pontiac Gazette*, Nov. 25, 1854, also June 23, 1855; *Lansing Republican* March 25, 1856; *Romeo Argus*, June 18, 1857.

vanguard of evangelicalism. The Synod campaigned for restoration of capital punishment, stiffer prohibition laws, and against "the growing desecration of the Sabbath produced by the introduction of customs brought of late years into our country by a portion of our foreign population."[58] Cultural questions within Michigan society absorbed the attention of the Presbyterian leadership. On October 13, 1860, Reverend Duffield's 25th Anniversary Address dealt with the history and progress of temperance reform at length. The Synod, he said, brooked no compromise with intemperance or Sabbath desecration. On "the sin and shame of American slavery" it took a middle road, avoiding "ultraism" and "fanaticism," and keeping "wars and fighting" except in a few instances out of its congregations.[59] Thus, while many individual Presbyterians occupied conspicuous places in the anti-Southern and antislavery causes, officially the denomination took a position on slavery far more conservative than the Republicans. Congregationalists, however, trod as before where Presbyterians feared, extending their efforts for moral reform to include a stiff position on slavery, and defining for Presbyterians the near limits of "ultraism."[60]

Baptist leaders moved in the 1850s even further toward political evangelicalism than they had been in the 1840s. Their preoccupation with Maine Lawism, Sabbath desecration, and anti-Nebraska from 1853-54 made them virtual cheerleaders of the Fusion coalition. So too did their hatred of the Catholic priesthood and their flock of "drunken murdering Irish" who opposed everything moral and right.[61] In 1856 the state convention did not endorse the Republican ticket but it did urge voters "to act as becometh men who must give account to God in the day of judgment . . . and give their suffrage for such men only as they think will act in fear of God and defend the right." The *Free Press* judged that most Baptist pulpits "have been converted into political rostrums." The *Mich-*

[58] *Jackson Patriot*, July 11, 1855; *Niles Republican*, Sept. 20, 1856; Detroit Presbytery, "Minutes, 1855-1869," 81-85, MS, BHC; A.D.P. Van Buren, "Memoir of Hovey K. Clarke," *MHC*, 18: 326-38; *Free Press*, Oct. 20, 1859 contains the Synod of Michigan's "Report of Proceedings"; Detroit Presbytery, "Minutes, 1859," 17.
[59] *Free Press*, Oct. 14, 1860.
[60] Frederick Irving Kuhns, *The American Home Missionary Society In Relation to the Antislavery Controversy in the Northwest* (Billings, Montana, 1959), 22-23, 25; *Advertiser*, Oct. 31, Nov. 16, 1853; the Genesee Association of Congregationalists petitioned the state legislature to pass a personal liberty law in 1855, *Michigan House Journal, 1855*, 603; Van Buren, *MHC*, 14: 388; Farmer, *Detroit*, I, 841.
[61] *Herald*, Dec. 2, 1852; Feb. 3, 1853; Oct. 18, 20, for Proceedings of the Baptist State Convention. Irish: *Herald*, Sept. 7, March 23, 1854. The state convention commended the superintendent of the Michigan Central Railroad for prohibiting trains from running on the Sabbath, *Herald*, Nov. 2, 1854. Baptists and slavery: *Kalamazoo Gazette*, Feb. 24, 1854; *Herald*, June 5, Aug. 7, Oct. 2, 1856.

igan Christian Herald replied that it belonged to no party but would support that which "holds the same doctrine with us on the great moral questions."[62] The Republicans acknowledged their Baptist constituency by nominating Edmund B. Fairfield of Hillsdale for Lieutenant Governor in 1858. "Parson" Fairfield, President of Baptist Hillsdale College, was the most prominent evangelical Baptist in the state. In 1860 the *Herald* and state convention continued to back the party of morality.[63]

Election returns and census data show that "evangelical townships" across Michigan tended to vote strongly Republican in 1860. Table XIV.10 presents data for 29 such towns: other evangelical units undoubtedly existed but could not be identified. Only 3 of the 29 voted against Lincoln in 1860. In eastern Michigan 6 of 11 were 60 to 70 percent Republican, in the central section 6 of 11 voted 57 to 70 percent Republican, and in the west 3 of 7 had Republican percentages of 59, 61, and 72. The 3 Democratic and 9 weak Republican units included some prosperous townships, but there was a tendency for evangelicalism, prosperity, and anti-Democratic voting to be associated.

It has been argued that religious groups rising socioeconomically in the 1850s became middle-class moralists and voted Republican. Methodists and Baptists particularly rose in status, entered into "reform," and left the Democratic Party because of its connection with "irreligion," foreigners, Catholicism, and slavery.[64] One difficulty with this thesis in Michigan is that too many settled, prosperous Methodist units remained Democratic, while many frontier, poor Methodist units swung into the Republican camp. Far more intensive study needs to be made of those Methodists who became Republicans and those who remained Democrats before any such claims can be made.

Methodist leaders may have moved at a much different pace to Republicanism than did rank and file Methodists. From 1850 on Methodist leaders' engagement with social and political causes increased markedly. Earlier, for example, only a few clergymen had spoken out against slavery and the Wesleyan secession had carried off most of the church's evangelicals. In 1850 the Methodist Annual Conference denounced the Fugitive Slave Law but remained typically silent on slavery in general. The next few years saw rapid change: the Conference of 1855 declared

[62] *Herald*, Oct. 12, 1856; also on Kansas and the election, Oct. 30, Nov. 13, 1856. Replies of *Herald* to *Enquirer* and *Free Press*, Nov. 27, Dec. 18, 1856.

[63] *Advertiser*, Aug. 20, 1858; some Republicans may have thought Fairfield too identified with evangelicalism, *Hillsdale Standard*, Nov. 30, 1858; *Free Press*, Oct. 21, 1859; *Herald*, Oct. 27, Nov. 1, 10, 15, 1859.

[64] Seymour Martin Lipset, "Religion and Politics in American History," in Earl Raab, ed., *Religious Conflict in America: Studies of the Problems Beyond Bigotry* (New York, 1964), 66-67.

TABLE XIV.10

Evangelical Townships, 1860, Republican Percentage, Religiosity,
Evangelical Preference, Mean Value of Farms

Town, County	Republican Percentage	Religiosity	Evangelical Preference	Mean Value
	EASTERN MICHIGAN			
Plymouth, Wayne	66	112	63	(Prosperous)
Salem, Washtenaw	70	121	75	$3,332
Sylvan	62	59	75	3,367
Saline	64	53	67	3,473
York	52	58	66	3,077
Augusta	56	66	73	2,246
Highland, Oakland	48 (1859)	62	100	2,208
Milford	60 (1859)	63	62	2,743
Independence	51 (1859)	73	58	3,632
LaSalle, Monroe	40	53	71	2,061
Reading, Hillsdale	63	68	68	3,267
	CENTRAL MICHIGAN			
Stockbridge, Ingham	64	57	100	$2,235
Leslie	64	64	100	2,158
Eaton Rapids, Eaton	54	73	53	2,264
Brooklyn, Jackson	54 (1859)	53	79	3,584
Concord	69 (1859)	53	76	4,097
Allegan, Allegan	45 (1858)	136	NA	NA
Otsego	53	53	60	NA
Schoolcraft, Kalamazoo	69	66	69	7,476
Algona, Kent	57 (1859)	50	100	1,677
Alpine	57 (1859)	56	71	2,340
	WESTERN MICHIGAN			
Thornapple, Barry	72	120	58	$1,695
Rutland	61	76	60	1,558
Niles, Berrien	53	89	60	3,949
Ontwa, Cass	52	148	78	4,804
Pokagon	54[a]	68	64	4,060
White Pigeon, St. Joseph	49	110	71	3,449
Lawrence, Van Buren	59 (1859)	57	100	1,696

[a] Plus 3.3 percent native American

it to be the duty of Christian men "to vote right . . . as well as to pray right; and in view of the enormity of the National legislation embraced in the Fugitive Slave Act, and the repeal of the Missouri Compromise, we feel it incumbent on every Christian man to exert all possible influence against the extension of slavery by civil legislation."[65] The Detroit Conference was more conservative than the Michigan one on this question, but in eastern sections too a change was apparent. It no longer

[65] Macmillan, *Methodist Church in Michigan*, 182-83; one speaker at Jackson in 1854 was a Methodist minister, 181; Wesley Norton, "Methodist Church and Politics of Slavery: 1850-1860," *Michigan History*, 48: 200, 202-03, 206-07.

seemed that "nearly the entire clergy of the Methodist church" were arrayed behind the Democrats.[66] Methodism may have been "a major ally of the Republican party from its birth"[67] but some of the old Democratic cadres remained faithful. In 1858, after the Republicans nominated a prominent Baptist to run for Superintendent of Public Instruction, the Democrats picked as their candidate Daniel C. Jacokes, scientist, educator, and Methodist minister of "Yorker" (Dutch and German) descent. However, what can be inferred from this nomination about Methodist voting is not clear. A Grand Rapids minister later recalled that in 1859-60 his congregation were "red-hot Lincoln men. . . . My sermons were a strong mixture of gospel and politics."[68] On the whole this kind of evidence testifies to a Methodist trend away from the Democrats.

Yet it would be a mistake to discount the persistence of Democratic loyalty among many Methodists, including upwardly mobile prospering farmers. Too many biographies of local influentials in the county "histories" and "albums" of the 1880s testify otherwise. The available aggregate data nevertheless shows an anti-Democratic leaning among Methodists in 1860 unlike anything observed earlier. Table XIV.11 shows those units that were "pure" Methodist townships, that is, those which had both religiosity and Methodist preference of over 50 percent. Table XIV.12 displays towns pervaded by Methodism and some of the smaller sects that seemed to thrive in rural, frontier areas. Ethnic and party heritage still may have been strong influences in 1860.

Although it is difficult to estimate the extent of the shift of Methodists to Republican voting, the *direction* of the trend is unmistakable. Among Episcopalians, the traditional sectarian antagonists of Methodists, a shift in the opposite direction—*to* the Democrats is fairly obvious. Among McCoy's 1860 economic elite in Wayne County the Episcopalians, the second largest religious group among the elite, increased their numbers slightly over 1844 to become 26 percent of the 1860 elite. Of the 34 elite Episcopalians 9 were Republican (26 percent); 5, unknown (15 percent); and 17 were Democrats—or 50 percent, compared to 36 percent of the 1844 elite being Democrats. This exceeded by far any other change among the elite. McCoy found that Episcopalians who did not switch to the Democrats (those who were Whigs, then Republicans)

[66] *Lansing Republican*, May 22, 1855; *Advertiser*, July 8, Sept. 13, 16, 30, 1856; on Methodists in Jackson, *ibid.*, July 2, 1856.

[67] Norton, *Michigan History*, 48: 215.

[68] *Cass County Republican*, Sept. 16, 1858. Gregory: *Michigan Biographies*, 310; *Educators of Michigan* (Chicago, 1900), 16-18. Jacokes: *Representative Men of Michigan* (Cincinnati, 1878), Pt. 6, 42-43; Pilcher, *Protestantism*, 325-26; Grand Rapids quote: Macmillan, *Methodist Church*, 199-200, 207. President Lincoln gave special attention to "matters of the [Methodist] church" through patronage, Robert D. Clark, *Mathew Simpson*, 224-25, 226, 227, 230-35.

TABLE XIV.11

"Pure" Methodist Townships, 1860, Republican Percentage, Religiosity,
Methodist Preference, Mean Value of Farms

Town, County	Republican Percentage	Religiosity	Methodist Preference	Mean Value
Canton, Wayne	41	69	67	(Prosperous)
Blissfield, Lenawee	58	110	73	$2,673
Groveland, Oakland	54	75	100	2,327
Farmington	57	55	59	4,341
Sharon, Washtenaw	62	105	76	4,268
Lodi	48	70	57	3,817
Flushing, Genesee	53a (1856)	55	57	1,753
Napoleon, Jackson	70 (1859)	69	55	3,047
Milton, Cass	65	87	60	3,992
Barry, Barry	60	80	59	2,291
New Buffalo, Berrien	60	68	55	1,227

a Plus 10 percent native American, 1856

TABLE XIV.12

"Mixed" Methodist Townships, 1860, Republican Percentage, Religiosity,
Religious Preference, Mean Value of Farms

Town, County	Republican Percentage	Religiosity	Preference	Mean Value
Oakland, Oakland	40	56	50 Ma 50 OSP	$3,779
Hope, Barry	75	67	33 M 33 UB	913
Orangeville	62	80	43 M 21 UB	1,718
Baltimore	77	66	50 M 50 UB	1,255
Berrien, Berrien	49	74	22 M 22 UB 56 U	3,283
Buchanan	59	267	25 M 25 D 17 A 17 UB	2,319
Sturgis, St. Joseph	68b	89	28 M 39 S	4,777

a Key to letters
M   : Methodist
OSP : Old School Presbyterians
UB   : United Brethren
U   : Unionists
D   : Disciples of Christ
A   : Adventists
b Plus 3.5 percent Constitutional Union

were probably of Presbyterian or Congregational origins and apt to be of strong pietist or moral-reformist bent. In other words, the most evangelical Episcopalians stayed anti-Democratic.[69]

Census data for churches in 1860 is as useless as that for 1850 in studying Episcopalian voting. Except for a few scattered congregations, the denomination continued to be located in large towns or villages.[70] Relatively small among the major denominations, Episcopalians were vastly overrepresented among the elite. Because the denomination was a high-status group, McCoy's elite findings may be taken as fairly representative. The hierarchy's stolid nonevangelicalism through the 1850s fits very well with the thesis of a Democratic shift among the group at large. The numbers involved here are not very large: there were, for example, 45 Episcopalian churches in the state compared to 247 Methodist churches, not to mention uncounted Methodist classes and societies with no church buildings. But as in 1844, given the higher class and status of Episcopalians, they were an important Democratic group.

Episcopalians still held aloof from what the Democrats called "clerical interference."[71] The increased identification of Republicanism with evangelicalism no doubt repelled them, and evangelicals continued to identify Episcopacy with the forces of darkness. At least Reverend Duffield did this in 1860 in his 25th Anniversary Address, charging that the Episcopalian sect had "afforded a shelter for rum-sellers and grog-drinkers." Its ministers and members engaged in "zealous, persistent ridicule of the temperance reformation, and of the Presbyterian and other churches which have zealously embarked in it; and by the current exhibition and offering of intoxicating drinks on the part of the members and clergy generally of the Episcopal denomination . . . while odium was elicited against the alleged Puritanical strictness . . . [of] the Synod." This wayward sect had also "induced persons of wealth and fashion, and fond of a less rigorous morality" to withdraw from the Presbyterian fold to its own; many young men and ladies had been seduced to it and become drunkards.[72] Duffield typically associated the Episcopal "rich and fashionables" with a decadent life style. His derogation of "social position," "social estimation," and "pride of wealth" in this connection sounded strange coming from the leader of the denomination which disproportionately dominated Wayne's economic elite, a denomination whose sense of their own rigorous morality and whose class and group con-

[69] McCoy, "Wayne County Economic Elite, 1844, 1860," 176-77.

[70] Schedule of Social Statistics, Michigan, 1860, MHCom.

[71] *Free Press*, March 17, 1860; on Episcopal nonevangelicalism, Frank W. Hawthorne, *The Episcopal Church in Michigan During the Civil War* (Lansing, 1966), 1-3.

[72] Duffield's entire speech is printed on the front page of the *Free Press*, Oct. 14, 1860.

sciousness had long since earned them a reputation for exclusiveness, elitism, and bigotry. Duffield, of course, had no quarrel with riches or wealth per se, or with the manner in which they had been gained and how they were used. But he implied that those who had social position and riches had a greater responsibility to set the standard and tone of right moral conduct for the mass of society. God, as Mrs. Stuart put it, required more of the "*sober upper* class of society."[73]

Catholics, the majority of them very different from the high-status Episcopalians, also moved toward the Democrats in the 1850s. One might wonder how they could have become more Democratic, given their already overwhelming support of the Democratic Party. Yet there were differences among Catholics in the degree to which they voted Democrat: German Catholics, for example, had voted less Democratic than Irish. Upper-class Catholics had voted less Democratic than lower-class Catholics, at least according to McCoy's data for the 1844 Wayne elite. In that group 4 of 7 Catholics had been Whig. Here there was room for movement toward the Democrats and the evangelicalism and anti-Popery of the 1850s seems to have had this effect. Catholics in 1860 amounted to 7 percent of the Wayne elite, as they had in 1844 (though they amounted to far more than 7 percent of Wayne's population and thus were underrepresented in the elite). Of 10 elite Catholics only 2 were Republicans, 2 were unidentifiable, and 6 were Democrats.[74]

The mass of Catholics possessed less wealth and status than most Protestants—especially in rural areas. General socioeconomic differences acted both as a cause and reinforcement of religious and ethnic group antagonisms and different loyalties. But not all Catholics, urban or rural, were lower class or devoid of middle-class mores. Many prosperous Irish, German, French, and native Catholic farmers led their predominantly less prosperous townsmen in their Democratic organizations

[73] E. E. Stuart to Kate, June 22, 1850, *Stuart Letters*, I, 91. Duffield's attitude bears contrasting with the attitude toward classes of a Methodist minister at the Woodward Avenue Church in 1860-61: "I was not popular with the first families. I stood squarely up to my convictions in dealing with dancing and the theater, preaching against fashionable dissipation . . . and reached the conclusion that I must abandon all ambition and become a popular city preacher. I do not allude to an open compromise with the theater, and the dance, but to the disposition to attach so much importance to social life in general, as opposes an effectual barrier between the rich and the poor, allowing wealthy families to form a class as purely a caste as if it existed in India. I determined to ally myself with the 'lower strata.'" M. A. Brighton, ed., *Selections From the Autobiography of Rev. J. M. Arnold* (Ann Arbor, 1885), 26.

[74] Irish liquor dealers, while not in the elite, "occupied the best pews in the middle aisle" of Trinity Church, Index to *Vindicator*. These men were upper class in their ethnoreligious group and undoubtedly Democrats. Also holding pews in Trinity were "a certain cliquey group of old St. Anne's people [French] and some of the admirers of these, of celtic origin." It would be fascinating to know the politics of such cliques.

and in civil life generally. The Catholic solidarity that is suggested by the aggregate data (Table XIV.13) cut across rural class and occupational groups.

TABLE XIV.13

Catholic Townships and Counties,
Democratic Percentage, Mean Value of Farms, 1860

Town, County	Democrat Percentage	Religiosity	Catholic Preference	Mean Value
Grosse Pointe, Wayne	75	115	92	(Moderate/Lower)
Hamtramck	63	83	74	(Moderate/Lower)
Yankee Springs, Barry	46	114	71	$1,486
Exeter, Monroe	54	58	58	1,455
Westphalia, Clinton	94	high	100	1,753
Kenockee, St. Clair	57 (1859)	38	100	1,811
Salem, Allegan	57 (1858)	35	100	(low)
Dorr	63 (1858)	low	100	(low)
Silver Creek, Cass	27	27	100	2,857
Ash, Monroe	56	21	56	1,599
Frenchtown	73	low	high	1,699
Harrison, Macomb	58	low	high	2,110
Warren	50+	low	high	2,208
Erin	82	low	high	2,289
Monroe City, Monroe	50	moderate	60	
Houghton County	66 (1856)	15	45 Mining	
Cheboygan	79	89	100 Lumber	
Emmet	85	high	95	
Mackinac	69	89	78 Fish, lumber, trapping.	
Ontonogan	48	45	46 Mining	

ENSEMBLE: LANSING VOTERS IN 1858

In 1858 David Marion Bagley, a Republican politician in Lansing, recorded the party disposition of just about every voter in town. In rough alphabetical order he listed the names of 814 men in 5 groups: Republicans; Democrats; doubtful with Republican proclivities; doubtful with Democratic proclivities; doubtful with uncertain proclivities. In the state election of November 1858, 712 men voted and that number included the adjacent township of Lansing as well as the village center. Bagley's list contained only men from Lansing proper; the village was divided into wards the next year and in 1860, 734 men voted in the Presidential election. Thus the Bagley list was very complete. By checking the names through an indexed typescript of the 1860 federal census population schedule for Lansing it was possible to identify the following attributes of 425 of the men: age, occupation, personal property (in cash), real property, birthplace, ward of residence, and heads of household. Lansing sat in the midst of Ingham County's gentle farm land, but as the state capital it was not a typical central Michigan village. Although fairly isolated and small, and having no railroad connection with the outside world until after 1860, Lansing naturally contained an unusual number of clerical workers, printers, and officials, and other persons connected with the state administration.

The 425 identified men are not necessarily a representative sample of the Bagley list as they accounted for 53 percent of it. Therefore, caution must be taken in generalizing about groups within the population or electorate. One cannot, for example, take the total identified Germans or carpenters and then automatically assume that the party breakdown among them accurately reflected that group at large, since it may have been disproportionately represented among the identified. But as with the 1856 Detroit list it seems safe to assume that the sample does come close at least to representing party actives and loyalists who were a relatively stable part of the Lansing community. Further, 233 Republicans and 179 Democrats were identified, the Republican percentage of that total being 59.6. The Republicans in November 1858 actually received 56.5 percent of the Lansing vote.

It seems best then both to compare the composition of *party groups* and to observe the party loyalties of *social groups* as represented in the Bagley list. This immediately suggests the overall similarity of Republicans and Democrats in Lansing—similar to that found in Detroit in 1856 (Table XIV.14). Party, economic role, and ethnicity also, seemed related in Lansing as they were in Detroit and Wayne County.

More Republicans than Democrats, even among doubtfuls, could be identified (56 percent to 50 percent). This may have been due in part to Republicans being slightly more concentrated in higher status occupations. Unlike the Detroit 1856 scene, Democrats had a substantially higher percentage of skilled workers, giving them a preponderance among blue-collar workers. Republicans led in white-collar workers, hardly surprising in a state capital housing a Republican administration.

Democrats equaled the Republicans in the proprietor category, and despite their lower occupational ratings, Democrats were richer overall, having a mean total property holding of $3,718 compared to $3,477 for the Republicans. Significant differences emerged in real and personal property categories:

	Republicans	*Democrats*
Mean real property	$2,426	$2,840
Mean personal property	1,051	878

TABLE XIV.14

Composition of the Republican and Democratic Parties of Lansing in 1858

By Major Occupations—Percentages

	Unskilled	Semi-skilled	Service	Skilled	Sales	Clerical	Mgrs. Offs.	Prof.	Props.	Farms	Gent.
Republicans	9	0.4	1.0	40	1	6	2	12	15	11	(1)
Democrats	9	3.0	0.6	54	0	2	1	8	15	8	(1)

By Property Ownership—Percentages

Dollars	0	1–250	251–500	to 1,000	to 2,000	to 3,000	to 4,000	to 5,000	to 6,000	to 10,000	to 15,000	to 20,000+	30,000+	100,000+
Republicans	7	11	7	11	21	11	6	6	4	7	6	1	2	0.4
Democrats	8	9	8	13	25	10	5	4	3	7	4	2	1	2.0

By Major Native and Foreign Birthplaces—Numbers and Percentages

	New York	New England	New Jersey Penna.	Northwest	South	Ireland	Germany	England Wales	Belgium France	Canada
Republicans	129–55%	38–16%	14–6%	20–9%	—	6–3%	14–6%	7–3%	1–0.4%	5–2%
Democrats	83–48%	17–10%	8–5%	12–7%	2–5%	5–3%	28–16%	9–5%	2–1.0%	5–3%

By Age Group—Numbers and Percentages

Years	21–24	25–29	30–39	40–49	50+
Republicans	16–7%	34–15%	81–35%	66–28%	37–16%
Democrats	13–8%	25–15%	78–45%	30–17%	26–16%

Both groups owned far more real than personal property, but the Democratic lead in total property was based on their being richer in real property while they tended to be poorer in personal property. Yet when the parties are divided into 14 subgroups one is impressed again with their similarities.

The lowest occupational groups with the least money, on the other hand, were well represented in each party group. Democrats were underrepresented in white-collar occupations having $3,000 or less, and especially among small proprietors, while proprietors having $3,001 to $5,000 of property were heavily Republican. Democrats thus tended to be more of a lower-middle class party while the Republicans were more of a middle and upper-middle class party. Most of the very richest men in Lansing were Democrats.

The Democrats had twice as many foreign born in their ranks:

	Native		*Foreign*	
Republicans	201	86%	33	14%
Democrats	122	71%	50	29%

New Yorkers and New Englanders led the native predominance in Republican ranks while Germans concentrated heavily in Democratic.

In mean age the parties were close together, with Democrats slightly younger, 37.4 years of age, than Republicans, 38.5. These data offer no support for the traditional contention that Republicans were younger than Democrats. The 30 to 39 age group constituted 45 percent of the Democrats and only 35 percent of the Republicans, while the 40 to 49 age group accounted for 28 percent of the Republicans and only 17 percent of the Democrats. The 30 to 39 age group of Republicans and Democrats resembled the rest of their groups. Other differences noted above between party groups simply seemed to be accentuated in this category: a greater portion of Democrats were German, blue-collar, skilled workers, and richer in real and total property. The 40 to 49 groups of both parties were richer than the 30 to 39 group, except in the category of real property. Whatever the reasons, the generation that grew to maturity during Andrew Jackson's presidency listed toward the Republicans, while a younger generation, socialized into politics during the 1840s, had a Democratic tendency.

When the various social groups are compared by party division, one is again overwhelmingly impressed with the similarities between the two groups, and the closeness of party competition among most social groups. (See Appendix F) The following groups (of 10 or more voters) were disproportionately (60 percent or more) Republican: clerks (78.9 percent); professionals (67.5 percent); owners of $4,001-$5,000 (68.2 percent); $5,001-$6,000 (60.0 percent); $10,000-

$15,000 (65.0 percent); natives (62.2 percent); New Jersey-Pennsylvania born (60.8 percent); New England born (67.8 percent), Northwest born (60.6 percent); and 40 to 49 year olds (66.6 percent).

The following groups were disproportionately Democratic: foreign born (60.3 percent); German born (62.2 percent); and blue-collar workers owning no property (61.9 percent).

If the 16 men owning $20,000 or more of property are taken as a whole, they are split evenly between the parties. The Republicans, however, constituted 80 percent of the $30,000 to $100,000 group, while the Democrats constituted 80 percent of the $100,000-plus group. While the top wealth holders had a substantial number of Republicans, then, the big money was Democratic, and it was in real estate. This is understandable in a town which had been chosen as the site of the state capital in 1847, when it was trackless wilderness, because of the manipulations of a shrewd pressure group of legislators and land speculators who were predominantly Democrats.[75]

The attributes of the 19 "doubtfuls" of all categories who could be identified suggest a strong correlation between low class and status and weakness of party identification. The doubtfuls overall were slightly younger (mean age 35 years) and much poorer than the party loyalists, having an average total property of $1,181, real $691, personal $490. The doubtful data also corroborates the thesis that Germans, being more intensely subjected to crosspressures than most other groups in the population, were in motion in the 1850s. The percentage of Germans in the total sample of 425 was 12, while the percentage of Germans among the total doubtful category was higher than among Republicans or Democrats, 31 percent. The foreign born in general constituted about 22 percent of the total sample, but 47 percent of the total doubtful. Thus lack of wealth and social standing, foreign birth and recent arrival, made for uncertainty of political loyalty in Lansing in 1858.

The data also lent strong support to an assumption central to this entire work, namely that families were generally socialized into the same politics, usually that of the father. In 19 cases where couples of fathers and sons or brothers or uncles or nephews were identified, only two pairs had conflicting party loyalties.

Finally, but of great significance, fragmentary evidence relating to religion confirms the central tendencies sketched above. Six clergymen turned up among all those identified. Only 1 of these, a German Lutheran, was a Democrat. On the Republican side were 3 Methodist Episcopal churchmen, born in New Hampshire, New York, and Ireland, an Old School Presbyterian from New York, and a Free Will Baptist

[75] Frank E. Robson, "How Lansing Became the Capital," *MHC*, 11: 237-43.

from New York. Among the unidentified Republicans, too, was a "Rev.," probably another native Protestant clergyman of some kind.

A check of Inghan County history yielded similar results.[76] This printed source contained the names of 75 persons connected with Lansing's early religious history, involving 9 Protestant denominations. Checking these against Bagley's list, the religion of only 21 men could be identified with any certainty.

	Demo- crats	Republi- cans
Methodists	1	8 (including 3 probables)
Presbyterian		3
Congregational		4
Baptist	1	
Episcopal	3	
German Methodist	1	

This data is hardly as reliable or extensive as one would desire, but, except for the one Baptist who was a Democrat, it strongly supports, or at least, does not contradict, the generalizations above.

SUMMARY

Democrats retained voting strength in the northern reaches of the lower peninsula and the remote mining, lumbering, and fishing lands of the upper peninsula. This relatively undeveloped, sparsely populated area had large numbers of foreigners, Catholics, and hedonists. "Urban" and "rural" differences, to the limited extent that they existed, do not seem to have made a difference in voting behavior. Among the frontier poor both Democratic and Republican loyalists could be found, perhaps more of the latter.

Religion, ethnicity, and economic role seem to have been the most salient influences on voting behavior, both among economic and political elites and rank and file voters. Shifts to the Republican ranks from the Democratic took place among probably all social groups in the 1850s, but some of the more publicized of these movements have been exaggerated. German Protestants and rationalists moved toward the Republicans, but a majority still may have remained Democratic. Urban and rural German Catholics did remain staunchly Democratic. Irish Catholics, wherever they were to be found, became more Democratic than before—assuming that it was possible. The Dutch Reformed Christians of western Michigan did not, contrary to legend, somersault to the Republicans by 1860. They voted largely Democratic through 1860; but the

[76] Durant, *Ingham,* passim.

Republicans did establish a beachhead that later would be enlarged. The New British, although already a strongly anti-Democratic group in most areas, established a more uniformly Republican stance.

Evangelical Protestant groups grew in size and prestige in the 1850s, added new allies—especially among Methodists—and led the movement into the Republican coalition. Indeed, the Republican party, though perhaps less explicitly, was far more the *Protestant party* than the Whig had ever been. Unity in politics gave many Protestants the sense of Christian (Protestant) *oneness* which they pursued in the hope of one "Great Revival" which would dissolve sectarianism. In the 1850s the Republican Party probably gave this hope much more encouragement than it ever achieved through the churches and their direct mechanisms.

Catholics had been strongly Democratic, probably less so at upper-class levels. Republican evangelicalism produced greater Catholic Democratic solidarity at all class levels.

XV

*Party, the Antiaristocratic Impulse
and the Evangelical Revival*

The 1850s, not the Civil War, inaugurated a new party hegemony in Michigan. The Fusion-Independent victory of 1854 established a new coalition that would dominate the state into the 1860s and beyond.[1] Analysts who focus on national or sectional elites making decisions central to the process of Civil War causation should be aided by the description of social forces creating the Republican coalition and Democratic defeat in a Northern state. Elements of the local social and political context, long taken for granted, have been cast in new perspectives, at times radically different from traditional interpretations.

In the 1850s social group conflict within Michigan intensified, even as sectional antagonism toward the South grew more widespread and, in some quarters, fierce. But to describe the atmosphere as pervaded by "fanaticism" is misleading. Since 1860-61 the "deplorable" influence wielded by "extremists on both sides" has been much discussed, especially in connection with the abolitionists, as have "events" (presumably meaning chance), or too many Presidential elections, or an excess of democracy or individualism, or the wellsprings of irrationality having their source in financial dislocations, mobility, religious revivals, or some mystical deep. The problem with all these *eventually* relevant aspects of the later 1850s is to determine precisely to whom they pertained. With "extremists" one wants to know which decisions they made or shaped. John Brown, to be sure, contributed mightily to the paranoia of Southerners and to the schemes of those fostering paranoia, just as Preston Brooks did more to sectionalize the North than 20 abolitionists. But to understand Northern attitudes as represented by the Republican Party

[1] Walter Dean Burnham, "Party Systems and the Political Process," in Chambers and Burnham, eds., *The American Party Systems*, 294-95. Samuel P. Hays, "A Systematic Social History," 29-30, University of Pittsburgh, 1969. Professor Hays delivered a shorter version of this paper at a conference in October 1969, and was kind enough to send me copies of both.

one must discover and analyze the use made by the leaders of Brown and Brooks. Into what symbolic patterns did they fit tariffs, homesteads, internal improvements, Dred Scot, border ruffianism, Topeka, Lawrence, Lecompton, transcontinental railroads, William Yancey, R. B. Rhett, and others? Michigan Republicans wove these things into anti-Southernism. While capitalizing on antislavery and abolitionist traditions, they protested often that they were neither "nigger worshipers" nor abolitionists. They wanted primarily, they insisted, to contain the slave oligarchy and by 1860 they demanded only the barest specifics of its containment, but by then that brought Southern secession.[2]

Michigan Republican leaders exuded *intransigence* in 1860-61, a will to "face down" any Southern threats or bullying. At stake for them were very basic matters: "We have asserted our manhood at the north in electing the man of our choice for President," said Henry Crapo. "I hope really we shall not disgrace ourselves by being frightened out of our senses and manhood, and like whipped curs instead of independent and enlightened Freemen, yield up our own success."[3] Republicans displayed this spirit privately, and publicly—in celebrations of their election victory, in showing contempt for Buchanan's January 1861 request for a day of fasting, in sending a tough-minded delegation to a "Peace Conference" in February, in scoffing at Southern blustering, and in general stiffening their backs. In his inaugural address as governor Austin Blair declared secession to be revolution and "an overt act of treason" which the federal government must treat as such: "It is a question of war that the seceding States have to look in the face."[4]

Although the triumphant coalition had explicitly emerged as a political

[2] In an abrupt change from its partisan hysteria of the 1850s, Wilbur Storey's *Free Press* on Nov. 11, 1860, candidly blamed Lincoln's election on Buchanan, "the Lecompton infamy," and the proscription of Douglas by Buchanan and the "seceders" at the Charleston and Baltimore Democratic conventions. Lincoln could not have been elected, he said, without the help of Southern politicians.

[3] Letter of Dec. 14, 1860, quoted in Lewis, *Lumberman from Flint*, 108. Crapo further advocated firmness and no concessions "to men in open rebellion and in an attitude of treason. We have in fact nothing to concede. . . . the verdict of the people has been recorded that slavery should be confined to its present limits," Letter of Dec. 23, 1860, 108-09.

[4] Fuller, ed., *Messages of the Governors*, II, 441-42. A Republican victory celebration in Lansing warned that "they that take the sword, shall perish by the sword," *Lansing Republican*, Nov. 14, 1860. The attitude toward the peace congress of the Republican State Committee is displayed by A. Sheley, E. C. Walker, *et al.*, to Austin Blair, Feb. 5, 1861, Executive Records, Petitions, MHCom. Also showing Republican intransigence: C. R. Patteson, Ypsilanti, to Gov. Blair, Jan. 4, 1861, Executive Records, Elections, and Benjamin C. Cox, St. Clair, to Austin Blair, Dec. 10, 1860 and E. C. Walker to Austin Blair, Jan. 7, 1861, Executive Records, Legislative Correspondence, MHCom; Frederick D. Williams, "Robert McClelland and the Secession Crisis," *Michigan History*, 43 (June 1959), 158; George S. May, "Ann Arbor and the Coming of the Civil War," *Michigan History*, 36 (September 1952), 241-43.

party, antipartyism lingered on in the later 1850s, both as rock-bottom sentiment and as a convenient rallying cry for dissident political factions. Republicans, of course, still denounced Democrats for their slavish attachment to party and connected "the despotism of party" with the Southerners' rule over the Northern Democrats and their domestic slaves. Thus, anti-Southernism and antiparty continued to merge as they had in the initial Fusion-Independent response to Kansas-Nebraska. In 1860, for example, Hillsdale County Republicans declared themselves "actuated by principle alone, and that party zeal with us is not a blind impulse," while William Seward told Detroiters that all old parties were passé because they were dependent on "mere discipline for their cohesion."[5]

How enduring was Republican antipartyism? Did it serve as a distinctive attribute continuing to set Republicans apart from Democrats, regardless of changing political circumstances and the passage of time? Its significance is suggested by Professor Samuel J. Eldersveld's highly regarded analysis of political parties in the 1950s, based on intensive research in Wayne County, Michigan, i.e., metropolitan Detroit, its suburbs, and countryside. Eldersveld found that to Democratic and Republican leaders the words "loyal" and "strong" in relation to partisanship had quite different meanings, and Republicans were considerably less committed to their party than Democrats. Rank and file Democrats exposed to party activity placed much greater emphasis on leaders' opinions than Republicans similarly exposed, and Republicans were generally more cynical. Eldersveld also found that Democratic voters showed a high subgroup identity as well as high party loyalty, and he suspected that these two attributes were related.[6] The discussion above of antebellum antipartyism, ethnocultural groups, and "cultural politics" strongly suggests that the roots of these dispositions were so located orig-

[5] Antipartyism and anti-Southernism came together in several editorials of the *Romeo Argus*, esp. June 25 and Dec. 31, 1857; a factional People's Ticket in Kalamazoo appealed to antipartyism, *Kalamazoo Gazette*, Oct. 22, 1858; *Hillsdale Standard*, Aug. 7, 1860; on Seward, T. Maxwell Collier, "William H. Seward in the Campaign of 1860, with Special Reference to Michigan," *Michigan History*, 19 (Winter 1935), 101-02. Republican state platform of 1856, *Advertiser*, July 10, 1856; also, *Advertiser* Aug. 20, 1858. Joseph R. Williams expressed his disgust with party politicking in 1858: "this patching, tickling, bargaining policy is certainly nauseous to the Republican Stomach," letter to C. R. May, Nov. 12, 1858, May MSS, MHCol. *Jackson American Citizen*, March 10, 1859. A young anti-slavery Republican said "I am not *overmuch* attached to any party or party man and I believe we are almost totally wanting in real *Statesmen* while *politicians* abound," entry Dec. 3, 1859, "William Woodruff Diary," MHCol. In 1860 the *Christian Herald* noted its disinclination to recognize any party "as a permanent institution"; citizens should act independently "yet many seem to unite with a party as they do with an ecclesiastical sect, with . . . unflattering subjection to its discipline," Aug. 9.

[6] Samuel J. Eldersveld, *Political Parties*, 468-73, and 95-97.

inally in the dynamics of the political culture as it took shape in the 1830s and 1840s.

Yet Republican skepticism toward party loyalty was relatively weak in the superheated 1850s. Republican leaders, including evangelicals, defended their organization as a special kind of no-party movement which had broken with traditional usages and allowed free play to individual conscience and judgment. The mystique of Fusion-Independency must have given sustenance and color to these claims long after they lost substantial validity.) Once these premises were established, Republicans developed a corollary tenet regarding the morality of voting. Surely it was a significant change for anti-Democrats to be told within a party context in 1856 that voting "is a power for good or evil, for which I am personally responsible, to humanity and God." Votes were recorded in heaven "as for or against the cause of Virtue, Freedom and Truth." The *Christian Herald* in 1860 objected to any subjection to party regularity but recognized a Christian's duty to be involved in politics. Many had advised Christians to keep out of political life, said the *Herald*, but politics and religion were not irreconcilable as long as the Christian made "his politics, as everything else, subservient to God. Political action, voting even, should be performed with [a] conscientious regard to the Divine will."[7] Thus, the evangelical plunge into politics in the 1850s brought with it a set of arguments implicitly justifying *the moral party*, which was temporary and noncoercive of individual conscience. Evangelical antipartyism had changed in some respects, though it continued to insist as before on the unity of politics and religion.

The moral party was the Protestant party. The realignment of the 1850s harnessed anti-Popery to the cause of the Northern party—greater Protestant unity preceded greater Northern unity. War with the South made more explicit the party's claims to being the American party. During the nineteenth century books in public schools taught children that the United States was a Protestant nation. The usual New England authors of these books, like evangelicals, easily equated American nationalism with Protestantism. The latter was the true source of American liberties.[8] Party, religion, and national character all intertwined.

In the 1830s the Democrats had ensconced themselves in the self-conscious popular heart as champions of egalitarianism and defenders against evangelical attempts to Christianize society. There had been considerable, though not at all complete, overlap of the egalitarian and anti-evangelical impulses. The Democrats' persuasive rapport with these

<hr />

[7] *Advertiser*, Sept. 16, 1856; *Herald*, Aug. 9, 1860; also, *New York Evangelist* quoted in *Advertiser*, Sept. 8, 1856.

[8] Elson, *Guardians of Tradition*, 7, 58, 62, 173, 185.

political strains had helped create heterogeneous coalitions that formed political majorities. The 1850s brought a radical break in the Democrats' near monopoly of the egalitarian thrust. This upheaval allowed Republicans to convey their own egalitarian appeal more convincingly than the Whigs ever had. Anti-Southernism more than any other Republican appeal permitted the accession of egalitarianism to the evangelical tradition. Specifically, the portrayal of the Democratic party as the preserve of "slave power aristocrats" gave the Republicans a viable antiaristocratic appeal never generated by the Whigs.

For years the Democrats, from the time of Jackson, had successfully capitalized on the antiaristocratic or egalitarian impulses rampant in American society amidst the apparent breakdown of deferential social and political patterns.[9] The most sincere tribute to their success probably came from the many Whig complaints over the years that the Democrats had the far superior name—by which they usually meant also that the Democrats had captured a popular and antiaristocratic image.[10] In the 1850s the masses who turned against the Democrats had not become abolitionists. But after 1854 the Republicans assiduously worked on the "slave-power" theme. At the heart of this orchestration lay the charge that slavery was an aristocratic institution, and that its extension implied the extension of political, social, and economic privileges enjoyed by a small class of white slaveholders who ruled the South, and who sought to keep the North at heel through its pliant politicians. Many examples of Republican antiaristocratic rhetoric relating to sectional issues might be produced easily. One of the best came in the announcement of a meeting by Detroit's Seventh Ward Republicans in 1856: "Let every lover of freedom and hater of slavery and its *aristocratic privileges* be on hand.—The free men of the United States want no privileged class to lord it over them with a cowhide in one hand and a slave coffle in the other." (Italics in original)[11] In 1856, especially, Republicans worked diligently to establish this image. Early in the year, in Detroit's city election, they even complained of the Democratic candidate for mayor as an upper-class snob of aristocratic pretensions.[12] And in the fall William Seward swept through Michigan, describing in detail the ramifications

[9] For an impressionistic discussion of antiaristocracy in the 1830s, Miller, *Jacksonian Aristocracy*, 3-25.

[10] One Whig proposed that although Whigs could not "break this charm" of the Democracy's name, they could neutralize it by assuming the name of "Democratick Whig," Oliver Johnson to William Woodbridge, Nov. 19, 1839. In 1839 one in fact finds anti-Democrats calling themselves "Democratic Whig" or "Republican Whig," Marshall *Western Statesman*, Sept. 12, 1839.

[11] *Advertiser*, Oct. 25, 1856; also *Advertiser* editorials Oct. 6, 7, 29, 1856. Luthin, *First Lincoln Campaign*, discusses Republican use of the slaveholder as a "symbol of the overbearing aristocrat," 187-88.

[12] *Advertiser*, Jan. 30, Feb. 1, 1856.

of privilege for the pampered class which sought the extension of slavery. On election day the *Detroit Advertiser* blared to the world in banner headlines that "The issue of today's Contest is between ARISTOCRATS AND SLAVEHOLDERS! and the Free Working Men of the Union!"[13]

Thus, in the 1850s a political evangelicalism became revived, politicized, and broadened by anti-Popery, nativism, temperance zeal, and other Protestant moralisms. Then it married itself, through anti-Southernism, to an egalitarian tradition with which it had earlier been a natural political enemy. Earlier, the secularism of egalitarianism had created incompatibility between the two. The Pope and the slaveholder gave them common ground on which to fuse.

Whiggery had been a mass party, mostly unsuccessful. The defection of the abolitionists helped keep it a minority party after 1840. Native Americanism, meanwhile, did not develop an independent political life. But in 1852-53 nativist anti-Catholicism began to disrupt both parties and proved fatal to Whiggery in such a way that the fires consuming the old party created a phoenix which was a victorious new political coalition. This transformation began at local levels and the most significant changes took place within local sociopolitical contexts. Parties and traditional loyalties were uprooted and in flux within communities well before dramatic national events spurred on realignment and contributed mightily to the final shape of political parties. Anti-Democratic coalitions, usually called "Fusion" or "Independent," formally replaced town, county, and state Whig parties, but the continuity of anti-Democratic leaderships and constituencies was strong, especially the latter. Fusion-Independent hierarchies adapted quickly in Michigan, in contrast to other states or localities where anti-Democratic factions sometimes fought it out for the next six years. The absence of factionalism among the Fusionists in Michigan primarily reflects cooperation between Know Nothing and anti-Nebraska elements. A rapport had long existed between nativist anti-Popery and anti-Southernism in Michigan, and Whig leaders had often been identified with native American tendencies. Such traditions made the passage to Fusion and then Republicanism easier. Many older leaders kept their positions in politics after 1853. Elsewhere the native American party sometimes existed as a separate force with entirely new leaders, and formidably changed the composition of anti-Democratic leadership by 1860.[14] Though no systematic study has been

[13] *Advertiser*, Nov. 4, 1856; Seward quoted *Advertiser*, Oct. 4, 1856; also Martha M. Bigelow, "The Political Services of William Alanson Howard," *Michigan History*, 42 (March 1958), 4-5.

[14] In Pittsburgh in the 1850s the old patrician elite formerly associated with the Whig party withdrew from both parties while new men, on the vehicle of Know Nothingism, rose to power in the Republican party, Holt, *Republican Party in Pittsburgh*, 184-218, 263-313. The interpretation here agrees with Holt's highly signifi-

made of party elites for Michigan in the 1850s, the mechanics of Fusion there suggest that changes in party leadership were not as impressive.

In some important ways Michigan politics differed from those of other states in the period from 1835 to 1860. But a case study of this kind does more than insist that particular states must be understood according to local and idiosyncratic conditions. While respecting the unique, it goes beyond providing "the Michigan exception" to the big generalization which professional historians love to quote or quarrel with but few trouble to examine in detail. Only close analysis of manageable political communities can provide insight into the shaping of mass party loyalties, but this does not mean that the process of social causation was purely local. Rather, the kinds of value conflicts and social cleavages moving voters in the 1830s and 1850s in Michigan were characteristic phenomena of American society and politics. The kinds of social conflicts underlying Michigan politics cut across this highly mobile society and, in a sense, traveled with footloose Americans.

---

cant study at many points regarding the kinds of processes affecting politics in the 1850s. See also the superb study of the political realignment of the 1890s, Paul Kleppner, *The Cross of Culture: A Social Analysis of Midwestern Politics, 1850-1900* (New York, 1970), esp. 69-91.

Appendices

Index

A

Sources of Election Returns by Minor Civil Divisions

Sources for territorial election returns are given in the text or notes at the appropriate places. The primary source of election returns for counties by township or ward units, 1837 to 1860, was the Statements in from County Canvassers, Executive Records, Elections, Michigan Historical Commission, Lansing. These valuable records are incomplete, however, and were supplemented wherever possible by checking newspapers or the records of county clerks. In the case of some counties, the county clerk's office contained records with data giving nearly complete profiles of election returns for all units in the period from 1837 to 1860. For most counties, however, voting profiles for townships were compiled as a patchwork of returns from the Executive Records, county clerk's files, newspapers, or other sources. At the end of this process, those counties for which none or one or two gaps for major elections existed were: Barry, Berrien, Branch, Calhoun, Cass, Clinton, Hillsdale, Ingham, Kalamazoo, Kent, Lapeer, Lenawee, Macomb, Monroe, Oakland, St. Joseph, Van Buren, Washtenaw, and Wayne.

Following is an alphabetical list of counties indicating where newspapers or county clerks' offices were able to fill gaps (or in a few cases duplicate the Executive Records).

Allegan
  Allegan County Clerk. Election Returns. 1854, 1858
Barry
  Coldwater Sentinel, Nov. 22, 1850
  Hastings Republican Banner, Nov. 25, 1858, Nov. 22, 1860
Berrien
  Niles Republican, Nov. 26, 1842, Nov. 25, 1843, Nov. 15, 1845, Nov. 11, 1860
Branch
  Detroit Morning Post, Nov. 13, 1837
  Coldwater Sentinel, Nov. 22, 1850
Calhoun
  Marshall Western Statesman, Nov. 21, 1839, Nov. 19, 1840, Nov. 11,

1841, Nov. 17, 1852, Nov. 29, 1854, Nov. 26, 1856, Nov. 17, 1858, Nov. 21, 1860

Marshall Democratic Expounder, Nov. 19, 1847

Clinton

Clinton County Clerk. Election Returns. 1848, 1850 Referendum, 1851

Eaton

Eaton County Clerk. Election Record. 1852, 1856, 1858, 1860

Marshall Western Statesman, Dec. 19, 1839

Detroit Advertiser, April 8, 1859

Genesee

Detroit Free Press, Nov. 21, 1839

Grand Traverse

Traverse City, *Grand Traverse Herald*, Nov. 26, 1858, April 15, 1859, Nov. 23, 1860

Hillsdale

Jonesville Expositor, Nov. 19, 1840, Nov. 21, 1841, Oct. 23, 1842

Hillsdale Gazette, Nov. 21, 1850

Hillsdale Standard, Dec. 2, 1856, Nov. 23, 1858, Nov. 27, 1860

Ingham

Jackson Sentinel, Dec. 18, 1839

Lansing Republican, Nov. 23, 1858

Jackson

Jackson Sentinel, Nov. 20, 1839

Jackson Patriot, Dec. 7, 1847, Nov. 28, 1848

Jackson American Citizen, Nov. 21, 1849, Nov. 27, 1850, Nov. 19, 1851, Nov. 24, 1852, Nov. 20, 1856, Nov. 25, 1858, April 14, 1859, Nov. 19, 1862

Kalamazoo

Kalamazoo Gazette, Nov. 11, 1837, Nov. 17, 1838, Nov. 12, 1841, Nov. 18, 1842, Nov. 19, 1847, Nov. 19, 1858

Kent

Grand Rapids, *Grand River Eagle*, Nov. 22, 1850, Nov. 11, 1858, April 13, 1859

Lapeer

Lapeer County Clerk, County Canvass. 1856, 1858

Lenawee

Adrian, *Michigan Whig*, Nov. 21, 1838

Adrian Expositor, Dec. 3, 1850

Adrian, *Michigan Expositor*, Dec. 2, 1851, Nov. 23, 1852, Dec. 6, 1856, Oct. 13, 1859

Adrian Evening Expositor, Nov. 15, 1858

Adrian Weekly Watchtower, Nov. 14, 1860

Livingston

Howell, *Livingston Courier*, Dec. 6, 1843

Brighton, *Livingston Courier*, 1844

Livingston County Clerk, Miscellaneous Records. [Election Returns.] 1845-60

Macomb

Macomb County Clerk. County Canvass. 1850, 1860

Monroe

Detroit Free Press, Nov. 17, 1837

Oakland

Detroit Advertiser, Nov. 21, 1837, Nov. 22, 1839

Pontiac Jacksonian, Dec. 2, 1858, April 28, 1859

Ottawa

Ottawa County Clerk, County Canvass, 1851, 1852

Grand Haven, *Grand River Times*, Nov. 22, 1854, Dec. 10, 1856, April 22, 1857

St. Clair

Detroit Free Press, Nov. 18, 1839

St. Joseph

Detroit Advertiser, Dec. 4, 1837

Centreville Western Chronicle, Nov. 17, 1849, Nov. 16, 1850, Nov. 15, 1851, Nov. 18, 1852, Nov. 23, 1854, April 14, 1859

Constantine Weekly Mercury, Nov. 14, 1858, Nov. 15, 1860

Washtenaw

Washtenaw County Clerk. Election Records, 1829-69

Wayne County

Wayne County Clerk. Election Returns, 1838-1904

Books 1 (1838-57) and 2 (1858-83)

Detroit City Election Returns

Journal of the Common Council, City of Detroit, from Sept. 21, 1824-1843, Vol. I, pp. 18-19, 28-29, 56-57, 66-67, 106, 133-34, 143-44, 169-71, 198, 234, 264, 316-17, 369, 416, 489-491 (1838), 543-545, 600-602, 667-673, 753, 810, 812; Vol. II, *1844-1852*, and the next volume tend to give only the names of the candidates and those elected.

The two most helpful sources of city election returns were the two major newspapers:

Detroit Advertiser, April 16, 24, 1839, March 7, 1840, March 2, 1841, March 10, 1843, March 12, 1844, March 8, 1845, March 7, 1846, March 8, 1847, March 8, 1848, March 8, 1849, March 9, 1850, Nov. 8, 9, 10, 11, 12, 1860

Detroit Free Press, March 6, 1851, March 6, 1852, March 9, 1853, Nov. 2, 1853, March 10, 1854, March 11, 1855, Nov. 10, 1857, Nov. 7, 1858, Nov. 10, 1859

B

Small Farmers in Three Wayne County Towns

The assertions that many of the small farmers in the towns in Table III.6 were upwardly mobile and that the towns generally were emerging from the frontier stage rests primarily on comparison of Wayne County's three small farmer towns, Romulus, Sumpter, and Taylor, in 1850 and 1860. The comparison of farm status-occupation groups for both years makes clear the general economic thrust of the towns. In 1850 none of the towns had farmers who owned farms worth over $3,000; all had very few farm laborers or tenants. By 1860 the middling group had flattened and groups at the bottom and top in 1850 had increased. In Romulus and Sumpter the upper levels increased somewhat more than the lower while in Taylor the reverse was true.

	Romulus					*Sumpter*			
1850	No.	Per-cent-age[a]	1860 No.	Per-cent-age	1850 No.	Per-cent-age	1860 No.	Per-cent-age
Farm laborers	7	5	38	11	4	4	16	9
Tenants	0	0	12	4	2	2	25	14
$0—500	60	44	37	11	47	48	27	16
501—1,000	31	23	47	14	27	28	50	29
1,001—3,000	17	13	94	28	8	8	41	24
3,001—5,000			16	5			6	3
5,001—9,999			1	.3			2	1

	Taylor			
Farm laborers	1	2	21	15
Tenants	2	3	13	10
$ 0—500	24	41	23	17
501—1,000	17	29	33	24
1,001—3,000	7	12	31	23
3,001—5,000			4	3
5,001—9,999			1	.7
10,000 +			1	.7

[a] Percentages are according to total potential voters, farm and urban, not just farm.

In 1860 the percentage of farmers with farms worth under $1,000 or less in 1850 dropped from 67 to 25 in Romulus, from 71 to 41 in Taylor, and from 75 to 45 in Sumpter. Not all of the movement was upward; in each town the number and proportion of farm laborers and tenants increased also. But the thrust both upwards and downwards indicated the growing complexity of the towns and passage from a simpler state of development closer to the "frontier."

C

Towns with Evangelical Preferences over 50 Percent
but Religiosity under 50 Percent

EASTERN MICHIGAN	Evangelical Preference	Religiosity	1850 Party Percentage
Ray, Macomb	100	16	53D
Richmond, Macomb	100	30	64W
Armada, Macomb	100	35	59W
Lyon, Oakland	100	35	64W
Troy, "	56	32	67W
Avon, "	100	31	59D
Southfield, "	60	30	52D
Novi, "	100	28	67W
Bloomfield, "	52	19	66D
Highland, "	100	18	54D[a]
Oakland, "	100	10	51D[b]
Lodi, Washtenaw	100	41	51WFS[b] (54)
Rollin, Lenawee	100[c]	42	72W
Raisin, "	100[d]	45	65W
Macon, "	100	20	58W
Woodstock, "	100	22	58D
Franklin, "	60	41	77W
Madison, "	71	29	74W
Fairfield, "	100	23	54W

[a] Unrepresentative, usually strong Democratic vote
[b] Mean percentage elections 1848-52
[c] Includes Quaker preference of 33 percent
[d] Includes Quaker preference of 53 percent

CENTRAL MICHIGAN			
Concord, Jackson	71	43	60W
Columbia, "	100	26	63D
Leoni, "	100[a]	31	60D
Albion, Columbia	55	33	53W
Union, Branch	50	39	64WFS[b]

[a] Includes Free Will Baptist preference of 50 percent
[b] 1850 election return

WESTERN MICHIGAN	Evangelical Preference	Religiosity	1850 Party Percentage
Comstock, Kalamazoo	100	33	64W
Kalamazoo, "	68	43	54D
Oshtemo, "	100	27	82W
Schoolcraft "	100	37	64W
Climax, "	100	40	68W
Richland, "	100	25	61W
Colon, St. Joseph	100	47	59W
Walker, Kent	100	24	52W
Allegan, Allegan	100	33	60D (1852)
Gunplain, "	100	34	65WFS (1852)
Jefferson, Cass	100	45	57D

The eastern group of towns with evangelical preferences but low religiosities (under 50 percent) list heavily to the anti-Democratic side. Beyond census indicators, searching of county histories supplied more evidence to support this pattern. Such towns as Palmyra, Lenawee County; Wheatland, Hillsdale County; and Armada, Richmond, Bruce, and Washington, Macomb County displayed the hallmarks of piety or were liberally sprinkled with evangelical associations and voted heavily Whig-Free Soil.[1] In the middle of Michigan's "thumb" the edge of the frontier could be found in "Pious Hadley," which voted 70 percent Whig in 1850. Hadley, old by Lapeer County standards, had been settled by western New Yorkers of New England stock and Methodist and Baptist beliefs. A temperance society formed early (1836) in the town's life and "exerted a great power . . . both morally and socially." Revivals of the emotive-action sort often rocked the Hadley folk.[2] Nearby the township of Almont voted 64 percent Whig in 1850. Settled by New Yorkers, New Englanders, and Scots, temperance societies swept the town clear of whiskey in the early 1840s. Methodists, Congregationalists, Baptists, and United Presbyterians all organized societies in Almont.[3] Westward in Genesee County the two 1850 banner Whig towns of Atlas and Grand Blanc both contained ex-western New Yorkers, antislavery tendencies, and a total of 8 religious societies by 1854. The Democratic towns of Genesee enjoyed comparatively little "religion." Indeed, the dominant ethos of the entire county was that of the burned-over district from which its early settlers had come.[4]

The data above for central Michigan give a misleading picture. Additional evidence suggests a very strong tie between evangelicalism and anti-Democratic politics in the central counties. One cannot read the history of famous Jackson County (birthplace of the Republican Party) without being im-

[1] Whitney and Bonner, *History of Lenawee County*, II, 61-64; *History of Hillsdale County, Michigan* (Philadelphia, 1879), 190-96; *History of Macomb County, Michigan* (Chicago, 1882), 359, 360, 361, 366-67.

[2] *History of Lapeer County, Michigan* (Chicago, 1884), 87-88. In 1858-59 an itinerant evangelist, "Crazy Allen," set the Baptists to singing and dancing and "one unfortunate young man became demented."

[3] *History of Lapeer County*, 33, 38, 41-50.

[4] *History of Genesee County, Michigan* (Philadelphia, 1880), 251-59; 237-47; 334-41, 355-63. Wood, *History of Genesee*, I, 230-33, 206, 729.

pressed with the intense political moralism of many of its inhabitants.[5] Similarly, in Calhoun County the village and town of Battle Creek as well as rural and pious towns delivered few votes to the Democrats and many for morality.[6] The outstanding evangelical town in Calhoun was Leroy, of which it was said that while in it "you could not get out of sight of an abolitionist home, or a tamarack swamp, they both appeared to be indigenous," and that "Education, religion, and especially antislavery had a coeval existence."[7] South of Calhoun western New Yorkers and a Presbyterian minister had settled Algansee township on the Indiana border. Baptists were thickest in this 64 percent Whig town in 1850. Nearby Union Township harbored fugitive slaves, voted Whig and antislavery, and included Congregationalists and Methodists. Girard had a similar political hue, with Baptists and Free Will Baptists present. Rural Gilead had no churches but emitted an "advanced moral and religious feeling," as well as public spirit, thrift, and a "bold stand for temperance."[8]

Western Michigan did present a more genuinely mixed situation. Comstock, Kalamazoo County, sustained as early as 1832 the "spirit of the Pilgrims," and Baptists, Congregationalists, Presbyterians, revivals, and Sunday schools blossomed in this anti-Democratic town. In Schoolcraft, of the same politics, several religious groups transmitted the New England ethos. Early settlers had been heterogeneous but included some Vermonters who always fraternized "partly, perhaps, because they were all Henry Clay Whigs." In all of Kalamazoo the Democrats fared poorly; only 2 towns, Wakesha and Brady, could be called Democratic. Religion lacked roots in both.[9]

LaGrange and Ontwa, Cass County, deviated from towns with high evangelical preferences and high religiosity by not voting anti-Democratic (Table VIII.2). Ethnic and sectional origins may have been factors. LaGrange's New School Presbyterians and Ontwa's Presbyterians and Baptists probably came from the South. Cass County early received a heavy emigration of ex-Virginians and Carolinians, by way of Indiana, Kentucky, and Tennessee. In Howard township, settled by Northerners and Southerners, the early settlers divided into "two parties," one called Yankees, which indiscriminately included all Easterners whether from New England or not, and "Hoosiers," who probably included ex-Indianans and ex-Southerners.[10] Cass balanced

[5] *History of Jackson County, Michigan* (Chicago, 1881), 908-36, 1032-33, 1116-18; also 214, 512, 515. *Michigan Freeman*, Sept. 23, 1840. Jackson, *American Citizen*, March 23, 1853, film, Jackson Public Library. McGee, "Early Days of Concord," *MHC*, 21: 427, 430-31.

[6] *History of Calhoun County, Michigan* (Philadelphia, 1877), 82-85, 95-96; E. G. Rust, ed., *Calhoun County Business Directory*, 1869-70 (Battle Creek, 1869), 200-01, 218. O. C. Comstock, "Calhoun County," *MHC*, 2: 414; *ibid.*, 3: 352-57.

[7] Van Buren, "Log Schoolhouse Era," *MHC*, 14: 363-65. Comstock, *MHC*, 2: 233. Rust, ed., *Calhoun County Directory*, 1869-70, 221-25.

[8] Crisfield Johnson, *History of Branch County, Michigan* (Philadelphia, 1879), 213, 207, 230-33, 239, 240, 244, 252, 258.

[9] *History of Kalamazoo County, Michigan* (Philadelphia, 1880), 309, 351-91, 509, 529-31, 549; Oshtemo, the top Whig town, also lacked visible religion, 412.

[10] Fuller, *Economic and Social Beginnings*, 274, 301-02; Rogers, *History of*

these Democratic outposts with Whig-Free Soil units such as Pokagon, Silver Creek, and Newburg, in which one must search hard for traces of piety.[11] Finally, on the western shore, Waverly, Van Buren County, voted anti-Democratic and carried on lively revivals and politics. In this timbered, poor rural town, Methodists and Free Will Baptists had organizations.[12]

Cass County, 219-20, 341. While the MS census lists a New School Presbyterian Church, the county history mentions a Baptist Church and some Methodists.

[11] Rogers, *Cass County*, 195, 173.

[12] *History of Berrien and Van Buren Counties, Michigan* (Philadelphia, 1880), 546, 548. *Van Buren County Gazeteer*, 1869 (Decatur, Mich., 1869), 185.

D

1860 Mean Cash Value of Farms in Banner Republican and Democratic Townships, by Section

EASTERN

Democrat		County	Republican	
Frenchtown	$1,699	Monroe	Dundee	$1,828
Erie	2,627		Milan	1,772
Riga	2,176	Lenawee	Ogden	2,099
Woodstock	1,956		Franklin	2,582
Dexter	3,801	Washtenaw	Pittsfield	5,555
Erin	2,289	Macomb	Armada	3,264
Harrison	2,110			
Emmet	1,694	St. Clair	Brockway	2,348
Lynn	1,214		East China	5,656
Goodland	1,199	Lapeer	Burlington	1,265
Rich	1,188		Hadley	2,069
Handy	2,222	Livingston	Cohoctah	2,344
Genoa	3,117		Green Oak	2,923
White Lake	2,213	Oakland	Troy	2,768
Delhi	2,446	Ingham	Onondaga	2,739

CENTRAL

Democrat		County	Republican	
Waterloo	$2,021	Jackson	Tompkins	$2,519
Pulaski	2,915		Leoni	2,715
Wakesha	419	Kalamazoo	Prairie Ronde	7,136
			Richland	4,189
Eaton	1,724	Eaton	Oneida	2,066
			Sunfield	1,546
			Vermontville	2,218
Clarence	1,507	Calhoun	Leroy	2,619
			Penfield	3,564
			Bedford	2,922
Dallas	1,329	Clinton	Lebanon	1,877
Westphalia	1,733		Duplain	1,507
Ovid	1,459		Bengal	1,969
Fulton	970	Gratiot	Elba	760
			Sumner	1,230

WESTERN

Democrat		County	Republican	
Noble	$1,924	Branch	Gilead	$2,663
Howard	2,643	Cass	Silver Creek	2,857
LaGrange	4,397		Volina	3,499
Oronoko	3,386	Berrien	Watervliet	1,653
Lake	1,696			
Overseil	1,078	Allegan	Cheshire	893
Pine Plains	1,540		Ganges	2,310
Dorr	960		Martin	2,748
Olive	913	Ottawa	Crockery	2,243
Zeeland	1,106		Chester	1,420
Holland	972		Allandale	2,015
Byron	1,740	Kent	Lowell	2,154
			Cannon	2,014
Arlington	1,578	Van Buren	Waverly	1,601
			Deerfield	674
Carlton	2,070	Barry	Johnston	2,301
			Baltimore	1,255
			Hope	913

Note on Measuring Relative Wealth (Aggregate) of Detroit Wards in 1860

The percentage of blue-collar workers in various occupations was found by hand counts of the 1860 manuscript schedule of population for Detroit wards. These percentages were used in several computations in the text. Their reliability as an indicator of relative socioeconomic status was checked against other aggregate data from tax assessors' records. Although the order varied, with 1 or 2 exceptions, using 4 different measures, the same group of "poor" wards appeared in each case.

Wards with Greatest Percentages of Blue-Collar Workers		*Household Furniture: Lowest Mean Values ($)*		*Real Estate: Lowest Mean Values ($)*	
Ward	Percent	Ward	Percent	Ward	Percent
10	91	9	1.7	4	143.9
9	86	10	2.4	8	144.6
8	83	8	2.9	7	147.1
7	82	7	7.9	9	249.9
4	75	6	10.7	6	255.8
6	71	5	11.6	5	276.3

Carriages: Lowest Mean Values ($)		*Personal Valuation: Lowest Mean Values ($)*	
Ward	Percent	Ward	Percent
9	1.1	7	38.3
8	1.3	9	41.9
10	2.5	6	51.1
5	2.9	5	60.9
7	3.2	10	61.0
6	3.6	8	94.2

Party Affiliations of Elite in Wayne County in 1860

1860 Economic Elite, Wayne County: Party Affiliations of Four Major Religious Groups

	Presbyterians		Episcopalians		Catholics		No Religion	
	Number	Percentage	Number	Percentage	Number	Percentage	Number	Percentage
Republican	25	67	9	26	2	20	8	29
Democrat	6	14	17	50	6	60	12	43
Unknown	8	19	5	15	2	20	7	25
Constitutional Union			3	9			1	3
		100		100		100		100

1860 Economic Elite, Wayne County: Party Groups by Religion

	Republican		Democratic		Constitutional Union		Unknown	
	Number	Percentage	Number	Percentage	Number	Percentage	Number	Percentage
Presbyterian	28	48	6	12			8	32
Episcopalian	9	14	17	38	3	75	5	20
Catholic	2	4	6	10			2	8
No Religion	8	15	12	25	1	25	7	28
Congregational	4	7						
Baptist			2	4				
Methodist	3	5						
Unitarian	4	7	4	8			2	8
Church of Christ			1	3			1	4

F

Party Affiliations in Lansing in 1858

Ethnic Groups by Party, Lansing 1858

	Republican		Democrat		DD		DR		U	
	No.	Per-cent	No.	Per-cent-	No.	Per-cent	No.	Per-cent	No.	Per-cent
Native	201	62.2	122	37.8						
Foreign	33	39.7	50	60.3						
New York	129	59.7	83	38.4			3	1.4	1	0.5
New Jersey-Pennsylvania	14	60.8	8	34.8	1	4.3				
New England	38	67.8	17	30.3			1	1.7		
Northwest	20	60.6	12	36.4					1	3.0
South	—		2							
Ireland	6	50.0	5	42.0	1	8				
Germany	14	31.1	28	62.2	2	4.4			1	2.2
England-Wales	7	36.8	9	47.3					3	15.8
Belgium-France	1	33.3	2	66.7						
Canada	5	45.4	5	45.4	1	9.0				

Property Groups by Party, Lansing 1858

Dollars	Republican		Democrat		DD		DR		U	
	No.	Per-cent	No.	Per-cent-	No.	Per-cent	No.	Per-cent	No.	Per-cent
0	16	53.3	14	46.7						
1-250	26	55.3	15	31.9	2	4.2	1	2.1	3	6.3
251-500	16	51.6	13	41.9			2	6.4		
500-1,000	25	47.2	23	43.4			3	5.6	2	3.7
1,001-2,000	49	51.6	43	45.2	1	1.0	1		1	
2,001-3,000	25	56.8	18	40.9	1	2.3				
3,001-4,000	15	57.7	9	42.3						
4,001-5,000	15	68.2	6	27.3			1	4.5		
5,001-6,000	9	60.0	5	33.3	1	6.6				
6,001-10,000	17	58.6	12	41.4						
10,001-15,000	13	65.0	7	35.0						
20,000+	3	50.0	3	50.0						
30,000+	4	80.0	1	20.0						
100,000+	1	20.0	4	80.0						

Major Occupations by Party, Lansing 1858

	Republican		Democrat		DD[a]		DR[b]		U[c]	
	No.	Per-cent	No.	Per-cent-	No.	Per-cent	No.	Per-cent-	No.	Per-cent
Unskilled	21	51.2	16	39.0	1	2.4	1	2.4	2	4.8
Semiskilled	1	14.2	5	71.4					1	14.2
Service	2	66.6	1	33.4						
Skilled	94	48.7	93	48.1	1		4		1	
Sales	3	100.0								
Clerk	15	78.9	3	15.7			1	5.2		
Manager	5	71.4	2	28.6						
Professional	27	67.5	13	32.5						
Proprietor	35	52.2	26	38.8	3	4.5	2	2.9	1	1.5
Gent.	1	50.0	1	50.0						
Farmer							1			

[a] Doubtful with Democratic proclivities
[b] Doubtful with Republican proclivities
[c] Doubtful with uncertain proclivities

Age Groups by Party, Lansing 1858

	Republican		Democrat		DD		DR		U	
Age	No.	Per-cent	No.	Per-cent-	No.	Per-cent	No.	Per-cent-	No.	Per-cent
21-24	16	53.3	13	43.3					1	3.3
25-29	34	53.1	25	39.1	1	1.5	4	6.2		
30-39	81	48.5	78	46.7	3	1.8	1	.6	4	2.4
40-49	66	66.6	30	30.3	1	1.0	1		1	
50+	37	56.9	26	40.0			2	3.0		

Poorest Blue-Collar Groups by Party, Lansing 1858

	Republican		Democrat		DD		DR		U	
Dollars	No.	Per-cent	No.	Per-cent-	No.	Per-cent	No.	Per-cent-	No.	Per-cent
0	8	38.1	13	61.9						
250 or less	24	57.1	11	26.2	2	4.8	2	4.8	3	7.1
500 or less	12	48.0	10	40.0			2	8.0	1	4.0
1,000 or less	31	56.3	21	38.2			2	3.6	1	1.8

Index